DESIGNING PERSONALIZED USER EXPERIENCES IN eCOMMERCE

T0135107

Designing Personalized User Experiences in eCommerce

Edited by

Clare-Marie Karat
IBM TJ Watson Research Center

Jan O. Blom
Nokia Research Center

and

John Karat
IBM TJ Watson Research Center

KLUWER ACADEMIC PUBLISHERS

DORDRECHT / BOSTON / LONDON

HUMAN-COMPUTER INTERACTION SERIES

VOLUME 5

A C.I.P. Catalogue record for this book is available from the Library of Congress

ISBN 978-90-481-6599-5 (PB)
e-ISBN 978-1-4020-2148-0 (e-book)

Published by Kluwer Academic Publishers,
P.O. Box 17, 3300 AA Dordrecht, The Netherlands.

Sold and distributed in North, Central and South America
by Kluwer Academic Publishers,
101 Philip Drive, Norwell, MA 02061, U.S.A.

In all other countries, sold and distributed
by Kluwer Academic Publishers,
P.O. Box 322, 3300 AH Dordrecht, The Netherlands.

Printed on acid-free paper

Printed in the Netherlands.

TABLE OF CONTENTS

ABOUT THE AUTHORS

Jan Blom
Concept Design Group
Nokia Research Center
Itämerenkatu 11-13
00180 Helsinki, Finland
jan.blom@nokia.com

Professor Pamela Briggs
School of Psychology and Sport Sciences
Northumbria University
Newcastle upon Tyne
NE1 8ST, U.K.
p.briggs@unn.ac.uk

Carolyn Brodie
IBM TJ Watson Research Center
19 Skyline Drive
Hawthorne, NY 10532 USA
brodiec@us.ibm.com

Lorrie Faith Cranor
School of Computer Science
Carnegie Mellon University
5000 Forbes Ave.
Pittsburgh, PA 15213
lorrie@cs.cmu.edu
http://lorrie.cranor.org/

Maria Francesca Costabile
Dipartimento di Informatica
Università di Bari
Via E. Orabona, 4

70125 Bari, Italy
costabile@di.uniba.it

Dr. Antonella De Angeli
Self-Service Strategic Solutions
NCR Financial Solutions Group Ltd.
Kingsway West
Dundee DD2 3XX Scotland
antonella.de_angeli@nrc.com

Marco Degemmis
Dipartimento di Informatica
Università di Bari
Via E. Orabona, 4
70125 Bari, Italy
degemmis@di.uniba.it

Benedict G. C. Dellaert
Faculty of Economics and Business Administration
Maastricht University
PO Box 616
6200 MD Maastricht
The Netherlands
B.Dellaert@MW.unimaas.nl

Fabio del Missier
ITC-irst, Electronic Commerce and Tourism Research Laboratory,
Via Solteri n. 38
Polo Tecnologico, I
38100 Trento (TN), ITALY
delmissier@itc.it

Horst Dietrich,
7d Software GmbH & Co. KG,
Oberstr. 14b
20144 Hamburg, Germany
horst.dietrich@7d.net

Stefano Paolo Guida
Dipartimento di Informatica
Università di Bari
Via E. Orabona, 4
70125 Bari, Italy
guida@di.uniba.it

Richard Halstead-Nussloch
Southern Polytechnic State University
1100 South Marietta Parkway
Marietta, GA 30060 USA
rhalstea@spsu.edu

Gerald Häubl
School of Business
University of Alberta
Edmonton, Alberta T6G 2R6
Canada
Gerald.Haeubl@ualberta.ca

Linda J Helgesen
Electronic Banking, Nordea
P.O. Box 1166, Sentrum
NO-0107 Oslo Norway
linda.helgesen@nordea.no

Leo Heng
Nordea IT
Nihtisillantie 3
FIN-00020 Nordea, Finland
leo.heng@nordea.com

Mika Hiltunen
Nordea,Internet- and Mobile Banking
Kutojantie 3
FIN-00020 Nordea, Finland
mika.hiltunen@nordea.com

Christoph Hoelscher,
Centre for Cognitive Science,
University of Freiburg,
Friedrichstr. 50
79098 Freiburg, Germany
hoelsch@cognition.uni-freiburg.de

Keith Instone,
ibm.com,
1605 Indian Wood Circle
Maumee, OH 43537 USA
instone@us.ibm.com

Clare-Marie Karat
IBM TJ Watson Research Center
19 Skyline Drive,
Hawthorne, NY 10532 USA
ckarat@us.ibm.com

John Karat
IBM TJ Watson Research Center,
19 Skyline Drive
Hawthorne, NY 10532 USA
jkarat@us.ibm.com

Alfred Kobsa
School of Information and Computer Science
University of California, Irvine
Irvine, CA 92697-3425 USA
kobsa@uci.edu

Oriana Licchelli
Dipartimento di Informatica
Università di Bari
Via E. Orabona, 4
70125 Bari, Italy
licchelli@di.uniba.it

Henry Lieberman
MIT Media Laboratory
20 Ames St
Cambridge MA 02139 USA
lieber@media.mit.edu

Pasquale Lops
Dipartimento di Informatica
Università di Bari
Via E. Orabona, 4
70125 Bari, Italy
lops@di.uniba.it

Kyle B. Murray
School of Business
University of Alberta
Edmonton, Alberta T6G 2R6
Canada
kbmurray@ualberta.ca

Francesco Ricci
ITC-irst, Electronic Commerce and Tourism Research Laboratory
Via Solteri n. 38
Polo Tecnologico, I
38100 Trento (TN), ITALY
ricci@itc.it

Timo Saari
M.I.N.D. Lab / Center for Knowledge and Innovation Research
Helsinki School of Economics; and
User Experience Research Group
Helsinki Institute for Information Technology
Tammasaarenkatu 3
00180 Helsinki, Finland
saari@hkkk.fi

Giovanni Semeraro
Dipartimento di Informatica
Università di Bari
Via E. Orabona, 4
70125 Bari, Italy
semeraro@di.uniba.it

Markus Stolze
IBM Research Zurich Laboratory
Säumerstrasse 4
CH-8803 Rüschlikon, Switzerland
mrs@zurich.ibm.com

Michael Ströbel (Stroebel)
BMW Group, Germany
80788 München (Muenchen), Germany
mis@researchworkx.de

Maximilian Teltzrow
Institute of Information Systems
Humboldt University Berlin
10178 Berlin, Germany
teltzrow@wiwi.hu-berlin.de

Valerie Trifts
School of Business Administration
Dalhousie University

6152 Coburg Road
Halifax, Nova Scotia B3H 3J5
Canada
Valerie.Trifts@dal.ca

Marko Turpeinen
Helsinki Insitute for Information Technology
Tammasaarenkatu 3
00180 Helsinki, Finland
marko.turpeinen@almamedia.fi

Earl Wagner
MIT Media Laboratory
20 Ames St
Cambridge MA 02139 USA
ewagner@media.mit.edu

Dadong Wan
Accenture Technology Labs
161 North Clark Street
Chicago, IL 60601 USA
Dadong.wan@accenture.com

CLARE-MARIE KARAT, JAN BLOM AND JOHN KARAT

INTRODUCTION AND OVERVIEW

A Guide for the Reader

1. INTRODUCTION

In the Spring of 2003, the three of us facilitated a workshop at the ACM SIGCHI CHI 2003 conference on Human Factors in Computer Systems. The two-day workshop focused on designing personalized user experiences in eCommerce and was attended by a community of about 20 people from around the world who represented academia, industry and government perspectives on the topic. All of the participants share a professional interest in human computer interaction (HCI), and the group represents different skills and experience in the behavioural and computer sciences. The group works in research, development and consulting areas involving the design and evaluation of user interfaces and tools, as well as information architecture and computer programming related to commercial web sites.

During the last half on the second day, the team worked together to develop the structure for this book. We decided that research and practical experience that we wanted to document fit into four areas:

1. Theoretical, Conceptual, and Architectural Frameworks of Personalization
2. Research on The Design and Evaluation of Personalized User Experiences in Different Domains
3. Approaches to Personalization Through Recommender Systems
4. Lessons Learned and Future Research Questions

In this introductory chapter, we will provide an overview of the ideas and research provided in each of the major sections of the book and highlight some of the interrelationships between the chapters.The contact information for all of the chapter authors is provided in the front of the book if you would like to contact people to follow up on ideas or questions you might have regarding their work.

1

Clare-Marie Karat et al. (eds.), Designing Personalized User Experiences in eCommerce, 1—6.

2. THEORETICAL, CONCEPTUAL AND ARCHITECTURAL FRAMEWORKS OF PERSONALIZATION

In this section, the authors present a variety of inter-related conceptual and architectural frameworks of personalization. For example, the Karat, Karat and Brodie chapter on *Personalizing Interaction* describes a conceptual framework for personalization, the variables involved, a research agenda and a methodology for conducting research and building towards predictive capability in this area.

Toward Psychological Customization of Information for Individuals by Saari and Turpeinen complements the Karat et al framework with other theoretical perspectives and research areas including perception and emotion. They address the question: "What is good and desirable personalization?" sketching a possible answer to this issue informed by psychological theory and empiric evidence from the point of view of user experience and discuss some conceptual implications for system design. Their work describes "psychological customization" and make connections to behavioural theory to build a framework for producing desired cognitive and emotional effects in system users..

Briggs, Simpson, and De Angeli present a framework for trust in *Personalization and Trust: A Reciprocal Relationship?* and discuss empirical data related to it. In their developmental model trust evolves in three stages of interacting with the service: (1) first impressions and initial trust building activities, (2) further involvement with the site and the first transactions, and (3) subsequent relationship development. The authors discuss the link between the model and personalization, and go on to describe an online experiment in which this association was investigated.

Lorrie Faith Cranor identifies the relationship between privacy and personalization in *I Didn't Buy It for Myself.* She brings the personalization context into the privacy principles that are guiding professionals in the development of standards, tools, products and services to protect the privacy of individual's personal information. She discusses the attributes of different types of personalization systems, the risks in the different types of privacy violations, the state of privacy laws around the world, and how organizations might make tradeoffs in privacy risks in the different possible approaches to personalization systems.

Keith Instone's chapter on *An Information Architecture Perspective on Personalization, Navigation, and Changing the Direction of Hypertext*, he provides the reader an understanding of the basic building blocks in information architecture (IA) and how personalization works from an IA point of view. He describes how to bring together the conceptual framework of personalization with its implementation in development. He then takes an IA view of personalization research, and challenges the HCI community in terms of the future research needed to advance the field.

Hoelscher and Dietrich examine how website providers can provide value to users through real-time site monitoring in *eCommerce Personalization and Real-Time Site Monitoring.* The authors describe 7d, a comprehensive personalization server system, which combines several data sources and personalization strategies to generate the recommendations. Two real life usage scenarios are presented in order to highlight the deployment of the personalization strategies as well as challenges and benefits of the 7d system. This chapter augments the information architecture perspective provided by Keith Instone in the previous chapter.

3. RESEARCH ON THE DESIGN AND EVALUATION OF PERSONALIZED USER EXPERIENCES IN DIFFERENT DOMAINS

In this section, the authors of the chapters provide a variety of perspectives on personalization research and case study experience in designing and evaluating the effectiveness of personalization in different domains. Leading the way in this section, Hiltunen, Heng and Helgesen discuss the case study of the implementation of personalization functionality in the case study of eBanking in *Personalized Electronic Banking Services: Case Nordea.* They describe the context of the user scenario of Internet banking, human-computer interaction issues and opportunities in Internet banking, and the particulars of the case study of Nordea. Personalization is defined in the context of Internet banking, with a discussion of the customer and a bank's reasons for and against personalization. Design ideas about how to provide the value to customers in the design of personalized eBanking are illustrated.

In *Personalized Ubiquitous Commerce: An Application Perspective,* Wan introduces the concept of ubiquitous commerce or uCommerce and illustrates how personalization can support self-service in home improvement tasks over the Internet. Wan addresses the use of technology and personalization well beyond the "desktop" by considering household items such as medicine cabinets and closets. The chapter offers descriptions of several very interesting prototype systems, and in combination they certainly offer an interesting perspective on the direction of pervasive technology. Across the very different home-oriented domains covered in the prototypes described here (the Magic Medicine Cabinet, the Online Wardrobe and the Virtual Handyman), Wan describes the roles personalization can play.

Another domain for personalization on the Internet is in the area of electronic government. In *Self-Service, Personalization and Electronic Governement,* Halstead-Nussloch introduces his topic through a story about self-service in grocery stores emerged in the United States from the 1930's to the 1950's. He examines the motivation for this innovation in commerce in brick and mortar stores and eCommerce, and then compares and contrasts eGovernment and eCommerce. He examines the major personalization issues in eGovernment and considers what eGovernment can learn from eCommerce.

Brodie, Karat, and Karat explore the role of trust in personalizing the user experience of IT decision makers making purchasing decisions and getting support for IT products on an eCommerce site in the chapter entitled *How Personalization of An eCommerce Website Affects Consumer Trust.* The authors make a distinction between personalization features and policies and, through a number of user studies, show how these facets of personalization have an impact on an individual's willingness to share personal information with the site.

The Haeuble, Dellaert, Murray, and Trifts chapter on *Buyer Behavior in Personalized Shopping Environments* reviews a series of research studies their team has conducted on buyer behavior and the various factors that influence shopping online. In particular, they discuss personalized product recommendations, personalized product-comparison tools, and the role of interface personalization on customer loyalty.

4. APPROACHES TO PERSONALIZATION THROUGH RECOMMENDER SYSTEMS

This section of the book includes four chapters on the topic of recommender systems. Ricci and Del Missier use the scenario of travel agents on the Web to explore *Supporting Travel Decision Making Through Personalized Recommendation*. A hybrid recommender system is introduced, which integrates content-based methods, collaborative filtering, and case-based reasoning to support information search and choice processes concerned with travel decision making. Ricci and Del Missier also present the results of a study in which a prototype system utilizing this technology was user tested.

A complementary chapter that focuses on the tools that can be used to provide personalization on eCommerce sites is the Degemmis, Lops, Semeraro, Costabile, Guida, and Licchelli chapter on *Improving Collaborative Recommender Systems by Means of User Profiles*. This chapter describes how knowledge of customers stored in behavioural profiles may be integrated into the personalization algorithm in order to increase its computational efficiency, and hence scalability. The system is evaluated empirically by using statistical accuracy metrics.

Wagner and Lieberman use the scenario of a user transaction in eCommerce to illustrate the value that personalization can bring to the experience in *Personalization for Debugging eCommerce*. Their chapter focuses on the role that personalization can play in providing "self-service" assistance after transactions have been completed (e.g., by keeping track of purchases and providing assistance in the context of information saved about specific transactions). They suggest that there are many instances where someone wants to contact a company with a variety of questions about previous transactions, and that keeping track of the context of a previous transaction (e.g., not just that someone purchased an airline ticket, but what exchange policy was in place when they did it) can be valuable. Wagner and Lieberman point out that the organization's policies themselves can be explained in reference to the customer's transaction context. More importantly, the customer can benefit from personalized explanations of processes of the organizations with which he interacts.

Stolze and Strobel investigate the role of personalized recommendations as a teaching tool through the scenario of purchasing electronic equipment in Recommending as *Personalized Teaching: Towards Credible Needs-based eCommerce Recommender Systems*. The authors point out that recommender systems need to provide more than just a result (recommendation) in order to be trusted by users. In their chapter they argue that an essential ingredient for enhancing consumer confidence in recommender systems will be to enable consumer learning by providing a guided transition from a needs- to a feature-oriented interaction. Instead of giving the user "expert advice", Stoltze and Strobel aim to provide users with a personalized learning experience that supplies them with the information they need to decide and to trust that the recommended product best matches their current needs.

5. LESSONS LEARNED AND FUTURE RESEARCH QUESTIONS

Teltzrow and Kobsa's chapter on *Impacts of User Privacy Preferences on Personalized Systems* provides a meta-analysis across a series of survey research studies conducted by a variety of authors around the world. They examine research, methods, and technology questions to highlight the advances in the field. They also relate these results to the findings of various authors of chapters in this book.

Jan Blom looks to the future in his chapter and discusses *Challenges for User-Centric Personalization Research*. He describes psychological implications of personalized user interfaces, design drivers for personalization, ecological validity, and the benefits of personalization. He challenges the field to address personalized user interfaces through integration of marketing, computer science, and user experience perspectives.

6. EDITORS' FINAL REMARKS

We would like to provide some perspective about how you the reader may be able to best use this book. As is true in almost any aspect of interaction design, if the project team does not develop a usable and useful design, the user is unlikely to value the resulting system or take pleasure in using it. This is true with personalization as well. Personalization is not a silver bullet in itself; a personalized user experience has the best chance of success if it is developed using a set of best practices in HCI including understanding who the target users of a system are and working with them to understand their goals and tasks related to the system, their context of use, and incorporating this perspective in the design of the system. With this as a basic starting point, please consider the information that is provided in this book as a means of helping you to understand the scope of items you need to take into consideration in designing and building a personalized user experience. The experience and knowledge that the authors of each of the chapters provides may be very valuable to you in identifying possibilities that you had not considered and alerting you to issues that you can resolve by being aware of them in the beginning of a project and taking a "big picture" view of the topic of designing personalized user interfaces.

A final point to guide the readers is that you will see variation across the chapters in terms of the granularity of the approach that each of the authors addresses personalization. You may think of this as a dimension. For example, some chapters tackle personalization from the point of view of a specific technology. This is illustrated in some of the chapters on recommender systems including the Ricci and

Del Missier chapter on developing personalization technologies for travel decision making. At the other end of the dimension are the "big picture" approaches illustrated in the Saari and Turpeinen or Instone chapters where the work could be taken to apply to a general set of technologies. This perspective may serve to remind us of the multifaceted nature of the HCI domain and the opportunities and challenges for all of us in the field.

JOHN KARAT, CLARE-MARIE KARAT AND
CAROLYN BRODIE

PERSONALIZING INTERACTION

Directions for HCI Research

1. INTRODUCTION

We believe that the user experience in human-computer interaction (HCI) will be different as the systems with which we interact become more aware of the context of the interaction. We consider context broadly here: referring to information about who is involved in the interaction and what they are trying to accomplish. By capturing and acting on information about the situation in which an interaction takes place – e.g., who is providing input, where they are, what time of day it is and so on, systems will be able to make broad use of personal information to guide the interaction in the particular user-task context. Just as in human-human interaction, knowledge of who someone is interacting with is a key part of the context the interaction, and understanding the context shapes the interaction and contributes to the determination of appropriate responses. A phrase like "it's time" can trigger responses ranging from a dash to the hospital with one's spouse to a slow march up the stairs to bed for a young child to a reply of "time for what?" to a stranger. But understanding all of what goes into the context of an interaction between two people (or between a person and a machine), is a daunting task. We simply do not know how to capture all the information in a context that is relevant to an interaction. Furthermore, we feel that context is not static but is quite dynamic even over short periods of interaction. This is even more the case as we think about addressing thechnology which we carry with us (like cell phones) or that we encounter outside of traditional office settings such as the home. However, it does seem possible, if challenging, to think about systematically developing systems which develop and utilize information about people – both as individuals and as representatives of a group with common characteristics. This will be our focus here.

   We believe that making our systems more intelligent will largely mean making them better able to respond intelligently to specific people and situations based on information contained in a wide variety of context elements (e.g., who, where, and

7

Clare-Marie Karat et al. (eds.), Designing Personalized User Experiences in eCommerce, 7—17.

when in an interaction), and think that building on the "who" in the simple conversational context is central to success.

Obviously there are many possible approaches to collecting information about context, and then using it in the interaction. For example, information about a user can be either explicitly gathered or implicitly obtained. Broadly speaking, we can call the use of any information about the user to alter the content presented **Personalizing Interaction**. Remembering what I did the last time I used an application or identifying where I am and providing information specific to that location present possibilities for personalizing interaction through use of the context information of previous use and physical location. The difficulty is not in seeing that context can be useful in interactive system design, but in deciding what elements of context might be important, and how to respond to them appropriately. While there has been a fair amount of research aimed at enabling systems to tailor interaction based on some understanding of the user, prior work has only examined narrow contexts. Examples are click-stream analysis to infer user goals (e.g. Barrett, Maglio and Kellem, 1997) or collaborative filtering (Burke, 1999) to guess user interests. We seek to advance previous research thinking by developing a contextual model of personalization that incorporates a number of different personalization features, all of which are aimed at using personal data to deliver value to a user.

We believe an important research focus should be the development of a model of the value that can be realized through the sharing of personal information for different user and provider contexts. This model should cover costs (e.g., how difficult is it to collect and analyze the context information) and benefits (e.g., what kind of change in value does the user gain from the use of the information) associated with personalization features. The primary objective would be to create a model of value for different personalization technologies in different use contexts and an associated tool for use by designers and developers. What would be unique and valuable about the work would be that it could systematically explore the entire personalization space, not just one point in it. We think this shift in focus is necessary to understand how to use personalization effectively. Building a tool for developers that allowed them to incorporate the right personalization features with appropriate user interfaces would be a follow-on to this work. We believe that radically improved interaction will happen when users understand the value they can receive and system builders have the tools to appropriately utilize user data in guiding human-computer interactions.

2. RESEARCH VISION AND FOCUS

Currently, most interactions with computers take place between a system that understands little of the particular user (i.e., the system has a very limited **user model** or none at all) and individuals who have limited understanding of the system or application (i.e., they have a limited **conceptual model of the system**). Over the last few decades, the general population has developed more sophisticated conceptual models of the systems they interact with, while the technology has made relatively small advances in advancing its understanding of the human. We view a future in which human-computer interaction is greatly enhanced through advances in the ability of technology to utilize personal information about users to realize better, more valuable interactions. While there are many technological approaches to personalization underway, they do not look at value and the goals of personalization in a systematic way. That is, there is no general model of the costs and benefits users consider when deciding if they might want to disclose information to a system or another party, and no general model to guide developers in making decision concerning how to personalize interaction with a particular system.

We believe there are several key issues to be addressed in moving toward a world in which systems can make use of personal information to develop more responsive interactions with users. These include (1) identifying the dimensions necessary to model the anticipated benefits of personalization in different contexts, (2) characterizing value propositions for users and system owners for personalization costs and benefits, (3) developing a model of user and system context dimensions relevant to different personalization techniques, and (4) providing information in a way that can guide middleware and application developers in the appropriate use of personalization techniques, and creating reference user interfaces for the acquisition of personal information and the display of the status of personalization of the application or system with which the user is interacting. These are described in detail in the sections below.

While personalizing interaction can apply to any system, our discussion will be focused on issues in eCommerce system design. In general, these are systems in which someone is providing service to a customer. The service provider generally seeks to make a profit, and the customer generally seeks to fulfill a need. The interaction can be viewed as one in which both parties are trying to obtain some value. While we consider our work as research in personalization, the terms context aware, adaptive interface, and tailored experience are also appropriate descriptions of the elements we are addressing.

2.1 Identify the Dimensions of Personalization

Personalizing interaction does not consist of a single method or technique. Context is very broad and dynamic, and it is not clear what aspects of it are relevant in most situations. This makes the decision of what information to use in personalizing a system difficult. Beyond what to collect and use, there are questions of how to gather information. Systems can obtain information about the context of an interaction in a variety of ways (e.g., explicitly or implicitly), and can use this information to influence an interaction in a variety of ways. Faced with these challenges, we believe a worthwhile research goal would be to develop models of personalization which build on an understanding of the variety in personalization techniques possible to predict the value of various approaches for given contexts. While there are approaches which attempt to build models based on psychological theory (e.g., Karat, Karat, and Ukelson, 2000; Saari and Turpeinen, this volume), our approach is more empirical in nature. We assume that the value of personalization varies over individuals, use context, and personalization approach or techniques, and seek to understand the nature of this variation at a high level. At a high level, our proposal would be to collect information on the value of personalization for a range of contexts and to develop a model to capture our understanding of the relationships. Figure 1 illustrates this approach for one (hypothetical) personalization technique whose value is measured at four values for eBusiness context and individual characteristics. A key to developing such a predictive model will be the use of statistical analysis (Duda, Hart, and Stork, 2001) that allow us to generalize from a tractable number of data points collected. One of the key research challenges to applying the statistical analysis successfully will be identification of key context and user characteristics for each personalization feature.

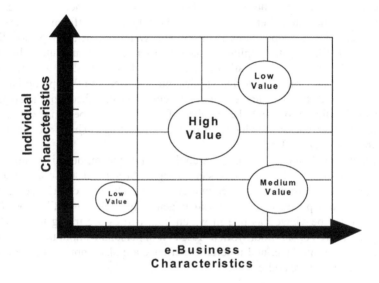

Figure 1. *Hypothetical value of personalization for one technique measured at several context characteristics.*

We consider personal information as including a very broad range of elements - from relatively stable identifying information such as age and income to more dynamic state information such as where I am or what goal I am trying to accomplish to information which might be less observable such as attitudes or emotional state. At this point in our understanding of personalizing interaction, we do not assume that any particular characteristic of a user is most important. Similarly, we do not assume that personalizing interaction based on some particular technique will be uniformly successful in all eCommerce environments. Thus, we see gathering data in a form that can be compared across a range of user and task contexts is important.

Our research work in developing a personalization strategy for ibm.com (Alpert, Karat, Karat, Brodie and Vergo, 2003; Karat, Vergo, Brodie, Karat, and Alpert, 2003) helped us formulate an approach to evaluating personalization features. Our focus in that work was to develop an understanding of how personalization might be most effectively implemented on the ibm.com site. For this research we collected and explored a range of personalization features (75 in all were considered - Karat et al., 2003 describes the categories in more detail). Our initial work aimed to identify a wide range of techniques that researchers and developers considered relevant to personalizing interaction. The techniques were gathered through a mixture of literature search, broadcast messages to computer science research communities, and development contacts within and outside of IBM. Once we were satisfied that the collection offered fairly broad coverage of techniques that might be relevant to the topic, we carried out a classification exercise in which resulted in 12 categories for the 75 features. For the next stage of our work, we decided to include at least one technique from each of the 12 categories in planning our studies. We will not go into great detail on the specifics of the techniques or categories here. Our intention is to describe a general framework rather than to argue for the value of particular techniques.

We carried out a number of scenario-based studies to look at user-perceived value in a number of contexts. In each study, we would provide participants with a description of an interaction or with a prototype system, in which various personalization features were illustrated. For example, on signing on to a system the participant might be provided with a list of previous (fictional) purchases and recent product information about those items. We gathered user value data (in this series of studies we used questionnaires and asked for perceived value of various features to the task at hand). Table 1 below summarizes some of this data for a target user category (experienced technology purchasers) for PC, Server and Option purchases across 28 personalization features. While we recognize that there might be limitations to the methodology employed in our initial studies (since we were studying participants who were not actually making purchases or providing real personal information), we do believe that this work highlights some issues in personalization research. Our research convinced us that personalizing interaction should not be thought of as optimized through use of a single feature, but rather should be considered as selecting from a space in which **different features can have different values depending on the user and business contexts**. We came to consider the space of possible personalization techniques as the Personalization Feature Space (PFS), and believe that developing a characterization of this space is an important research goal.

We suggest that future research should explore the PFS through a systematic examination three relevant dimensions. These include the **personalization feature category** (e.g., the characteristics of the various personalization techniques), **user characteristics,** (e.g., predisposition to trust, interaction goal), and **business context** (e.g., product offering, business goals). We believe that the effectiveness of personalization efforts are a function of these three components (i.e., Effectiveness = f (feature, user characteristics, business context)). Determining the critical components of these three dimensions requires work which is part empirical and part analytic. The empirical work involves collection of user data in a variety of personalization contexts through methods similar to those we used in our previous work. The analytic work requires organizing the dimensions through the use of learning algorithms so that they represent more than categorical data. Without some way of understanding the relationships between points on the customer, provider and personalization dimensions, progress in understanding the space reverts to an intractable (at least for a small team) data collection task. Our belief is that we can reduce the data collection task by reducing the factors relevant to personalization to a few quantifiable elements, but we also believe that there is considerable work needed to bring about such a vision.

Table 1. Mean ratings for top 17 personalization policies and features in Study 2 and 3.

User Control of Personal Data	6.4*	6.4*
Automatic Support Alerts	5.9	6.2*
Order History Provided	6.1*	6.1*
Help me find what I need	5.6	6.1*
Suggest Alternate Products	5.6	6.0*
List of Products You Own	5.5	5.8
Login Feedback	5.6	5.8
Wish List	5.1	5.8
Personal Book	5.4	5.6
Saved Shopping Carts	5.6	5.6
Transaction Tracking	6.2*	5.6
Only info Needed is Asked For	6.0*	5.5
Constrained Search	5.6	5.5
Adapt Presentation, Transient Data	5.5	5.5
Adaptive Navigation	5.6	5.2
Information Valid Across the Site	5.6	5.0
Contact Company in Context	5.5	5.0

* = Top-rated items in Study 2 and Study 3

2.2 Characterizing Value Propositions

An important component in our proposed research is to model personalization for e-business as involving an exchange between two or more parties. In general there are two roles in the interaction - that of **customer** and that of **provider** of product or service. Further, we view the essential goal of personalization as providing **increased value to both parties** through the use of personal information. Most research to date has focused primarily on personalization as providing value to the user (customer) of a system without considering costs which might be perceived by the user. We suggest that a more complete model would view a person as providing information about themselves at a cost in return for some promised benefit. This exchange can be viewed as involving a value proposition (or model) in which the value to the customer is a function of the costs of divulging information and the perceived benefits of doing so. The cost can be more than just the effort required to let the system know who the user is. For example, it might include costs associated with risks from "misuse of information." We extend the notion of a value proposition for personalization to include consideration of the provider's value proposition - that is, the value of any personalization feature to the organization responsible for developing the system is a function of the cost of implementation and the benefits obtained for doing so. Thus, for the Customer, value of personalization = f (cost of divulging, perceived benefits) and for the Provider, value of personalization = f (cost of gathering information, perceived value). For the Provider's Value Proposition (PVP), costs and benefits can generally be reduced to a monetary expression. For the Customer's Value Proposition (CVP), costs and benefits are more complex, and can involve other factors. Specifically, we suggest that the costs must be viewed within a framework that includes Security, Privacy, and Trust, and that the benefits must be viewed within a framework of human values that extends beyond simple economic benefit. To go one level deeper in our system of relationships, we view Customer Cost for a personalization feature to be a function of the information requirements of the feature (e.g., explicit or implicit information), the context of the interaction (e.g., for one-time visit or long-term relationship), customer trust of the provider (e.g., well known or new contact), and personal predispositions to divulge information (e.g., no fear or generally wary). As a part of the research we expect to fully develop the system of relationships (functions) that make up the personalization context by adding components (e.g., the Provider Cost function), and adding detail to the entire framework.

2.3 Developing the Models

We believe a research goal should be to develop predictive models of value. Determining the relationship between personalization features and customer and provider value requires work which is part empirical and part analytic. The empirical work would extend work mentioned above aimed at identifying personalization dimensions. We see collecting additional data on user characteristics as a part of the overall activity, so that these can be related to systematic differences in perceived value of personalization technology. We also believe that the overall research should include a study of provider values associated with technologies. In this we include investigation of the effectiveness (in terms of value gained by the provider) of various techniques along with the costs of implementation. Our experience to date suggests that eCommerce sites that can be viewed as personalizing interaction, have not been excited about sharing such data with the research community, but we hope that this can change over time.

The class of models that we propose here includes analytic work which employs regression and factor analysis of data collected and categorized (or other related analysis techniques). Our belief is that through statistical analysis of the data, we can identify key value factors and relate those to possible personalization technologies. For example, we found that the Privacy Policy employed by a provider is of highest concern to customers in deciding how willing they were to divulge information. In some contexts we expect privacy to be a major component of the value model for customers (i.e., that users view the cost of divulging some information as high).

We see a value for predictive models which can predict both Customer and Provider value for Personalization Technologies in a Customer and Business Context. Work in the various chapters of this book provides examples of the work needed to identify the necessary components of this model.

The complexity at the heart of the proposed research focus arises because the value of a personalization feature depends on the context in which it is used, both from a customer and business perspective. For this reason, we view this research work as driven by cycles of user-based explorations in some well selected space followed by attempts to build and evaluate prototypes for exploration in different user and business contexts. Research in this phase should include empirical validation of the Value Models for customers and providers (with representative users) and validation of the model with a broader range of technologies than used in the initial work. Thus we see a process of tuning the model and attempt to test it with a broad class of existing and anticipated technologies.

2.4 Developing a Decision Support Tool for Personalization Technology

Once model have been constructed, we believe an effort should be made to use them to inform design of eCommerce systems. One way to do this would be through the design and development of a decision support system (DSS). The purpose of a DSS would be to allow designers and developers to make use of personalization models to identify the types of personalization features that would provide the most value to their customers and best help them achieve their business goals. If the DSS user could describe the customer and provider context, our vision is that the system would provide guidance on how to personalize the application. The tool could also give illustrations of reference user interfaces for recommended personalization features.

Decision support systems that only provide recommendations are, at times, of limited value to the developer because they do not give the developer any basis for determining the value of the recommendations generated. To overcome this limitation we suggest that the results of the feature selection algorithms be used to provide an explanation of the choice of features. The explanation provided by a DSS could show the degree to which the characteristics of an eCommerce site and customer set are correlated to the value of each feature recommended. Additionally, the DSS could provide designers and developers with the ability to do "what-if" analyses to predict the impact on the value propositions of changes in site or customer characteristics. For instance, if a site has targeted web-savvy business customers, the developers might be interested in seeing what features would also be of value to non-business, home shoppers – thus giving them a tool to estimate the magnitude of changes in personalization features needed to expand the target of their business and marketing campaigns.

3. RELATED RESEARCH

Building such a model of personalizing interaction would be a daunting task, and it is important to note that this conception of personalization does not stand alone. We view personalization as closely tied to Privacy and Security research (e.g., the P3P standard and the efforts of OECD), as well as to issues in Trust. While Privacy deals essentially with a user's control over information about them, personalization is concerned with the value that might be realized by a party from sharing information. In general, Security research has to do with the confidence that data cannot be compromised or taken by unauthorized sources. We believe that both Customers and Providers view security as essential to proceeding with any interaction between them. Extending this, we view trust as an important element of the value propositions for both customers and providers in any interaction.

When we talk about personalization we are addressing a whole range of information types and possible values to customers and businesses. For example, various activities within IBM (both in Research and in the Divisions) are aimed at "knowing the user" on an individual level and as a member of some category of users (e.g., self-reliant web savvy). These efforts include everything from attempting to identify emotional state (though facial expression), current goal intention (though gaze or click stream), to product preferences (through explicit questions). Technologies vary in computational complexity - including various rules engines or user model based calculations. This proposed research is not aimed specifically at identifying a single "best technique". We do not believe this is a reasonable objective, because our previous work suggests that (1) the value of techniques to any customer will vary with the role of the customer at any given time, (2) the value of a technique to a business will depend on the kind of business objectives they have, and (3) there are likely to be interactions between techniques resulting in a package of techniques that would be optimally effective. Schonberg et al (2000) make the point that combining user data from multiple sources is likely to yield benefits for both the customer and the business. Exploring and modeling the space, rather than exploring a point in the space is needed for significant advance in the value of personalization to all parties. All work in this area has been point oriented. The emergence of ideas like Virtual Identities and Hailstorm-like architectures make work with a broader view increasingly important.

Currently, little is known about the concept of personalization or how to successfully apply it across a variety of domains that involve different types of interactions between people and computers. Peppers and Rogers (1997) introduced the concept of one-to-one marketing as a basis for competitive advantage for enterprises in the interactive age. The notion of personalization is central to this approach and yet the authors have no theoretical framework for personalization: they do not know how personalization works and what the limits of its use are. Godin (1999) introduced the compelling concept of permission marketing without a framework of how to address the concept in the networked world. Amazon has determined through very expensive trial and error attempts how to provide some personalization for customers of books and music. It is not at all clear that their approach can be successfully generalized to other domains such as information technology, health care, or finance/insurance. Our research on personalization, for example, has demonstrated that in the domain of information technology, customers do not value collaborative filtering that tells a customer what other customers like them have purchased (Karat, Brodie, Karat, Vergo, and Alpert, 2003). The personalization research by others that is currently underway focuses on the use of implicit data collection and dynamic processing that attempts to "guess" what the customer wants. We have research evidence from customers that focus on dynamic processing of implicit data to alter navigation is the wrong focus.

Our Research team has conducted a series of research activities in the personalization area that show that personalization is a breakthrough concept in the networked world of human-computer interaction. One result from our previous wark was that in an eCommerce settting, customers viewed personalization as more important than usability. It was seen as a way for customers to quickly accomplish their goals and avoid a whole host of problems in a particular web application (Karat, Brodie, Karat, Vergo, and Alpert, 2003). Customers in our studies were excited about the ability of personalization to save them time and for personalized applications to do some of their work for them. The value exchange is that customers will disclose information to a trusted party in return for immediate value in the goal they are pursuing. These same customers told us they would be strongly opposed to personalization of certain areas and goals. We do not know the bounds of personalization, or if there is a particular cluster of features that are key to personalization across domains.

The research suggests that for networked business-to-business and business-to-consumer interactions, systems have the opportunity to provide an entirely new type of customer service. The information will enable a type of relationship with the customer through the Internet that has all but vanished in the real world - a type of relationship where the provider knows the customer and can deliver value through the knowledge of the history of past interactions, customer requirements, and where the provider can even anticipate and fulfill needs that the customer has not yet recognized. A critical basis for this relationship is trust. Our research has suggested that brand name of the provider is a critical component in whether the customer will trust the provider and disclose information in the first place. An initial opt-in to a personalized application should be very minimal, provide value immediately, and slowly build a profile of customer data that the customer owns.

4. CURRENT USES

There are numerous commercial vendors in the personalization domain. Generally, their software products incorporate some or all of the following personalization features: filtering content or targeting marketing offers based on business rules; collaborative filtering or "recommender" technologies which use the past buying behavior of an individual customer along with that of *other* consumers to recommend products to that particular customer that he or she may be interested in purchasing; some form of analysis tools for adjusting offers and determining the effectiveness of personalization rules and marketing campaigns; data and application adapters for integrating data from multiple sources and customer touch points. A few examples of these products include WebSphere Personalization, LikeMinds, and Vignette. Additionally, many companies who produce Customer Relationship Management (CRM) products, such as Axiom and Siebel, have implemented a number of personalization features as part of their CRM functionality. Another type of personalization technology supports single, centralized user profiles that allow users to define what information each web site that they visit can have access to. Examples of this technology include Microsoft's Hailstorm and the IBM research's myPrivacy project. Although there has been a tremendous amount of development in the area of personalization technologies and companies are spending a great deal of money on these products (some of the software applications cost in the mid-six figure range), it is not clear how and when each of these technologies is of real value to customers.

5. REFERENCES

Alpert, S.R., Karat, J., Karat, C-M., Brodie, C., Vergo, J.G. (2003). User Attitudes Regarding a User-Adaptive eCommerce Web Site. *User Modeling and User Adapted Interaction, 13* (4), 373-396.

Barrett, R., Maglio, P., & Kellem, D. (1997). How to personalize the Web. SIGCHI Conference proceedings on Human Factors in Computing Systems. New York: ACM.

Burke, R. (1999). Integrating Knowledge-Based and Collaborative-Filtering. In *Proceedings of AAAI 1999 Workshop on AI and Electronic Commerce* (pp. 14-20).

Duda, R. O., Hart P., and Stork, D. G. (2001). Pattern Classification, New York: John Wiley and Sons, Inc.

Godin, S. (1999). *Permission marketing: turning strangers into friends, and friends into customers,* Simon and Schuster.

Karat, J., Karat, C-M., & Ukelson, J. (2000). Affordances, motivation, and the design of user interfaces. Communications of the ACM Special Issue on Personalization. *43* (8), 49-53.

Karat, C-M., Brodie, C., Karat, J., Vergo, J., & Alpert, S. (2003). Personalizing the user experience on ibm.com. IBM Systems Journal, *42* (4), 686-701.

Peppers, D., and Rogers, M. (1997). *Enterprise One to One: Tools for Competing in the Interactive Age,* New York: Doubleday.

Schonberg, E., Cofino, T., Hoch, R., Podlaseck, M., & Spraragen, S. (2000). Measuring success. Communications of the ACM Special Issue on Personalization. *43* (8), 54-58.

TIMO SAARI AND MARKO TURPEINEN

TOWARDS PSYCHOLOGICAL CUSTOMIZATION OF INFORMATION FOR INDIVIDUALS AND SOCIAL GROUPS

1. INTRODUCTION

1.1 Mind-Based Technologies

Personalization may turn out to be an important value driver for future commercial applications and services in a one-to-one world in which automatic and intelligent systems tailor the interactions of users and systems in real-time. In addition to practical case-studies of personalization systems it may be important to take a broader top-down view on the phenomenon. The critical success factor of personalization systems may be to successfully answer the question: "What is good and desirable personalization?" This chapter will sketch one possible answer to this issue informed by psychological theory and empiric evidence from the point of view of user experience and discuss some conceptual implications for system design.

When a user perceives information via media and communications technologies, she is psychologically transported into a quasi-natural experience of the events described. This is called presence. In presence, information becomes the focused object of perception, while the immediate, external context, including the technological device, fades into the background (Biocca and Levy, 1995; Lombard and Ditton, 1997; Lombard et al, 2000).

Various empirical studies show that information experienced in presence has real psychological effects on perceivers, such as emotion based on the events described or cognition of making sense of the events and learning about them (Reeves and Nass, 1996). When using collaborative technology for computer-mediated social interaction, the users experience a state called social presence during which users may, for instance, experience intimacy of interaction or feeling of togetherness in virtual space (Lombard and Ditton, 1997; Lombard et al, 2000). During social presence users also experience various other types of emotional and cognitive

19

Clare-Marie Karat et al. (eds.), Designing Personalized User Experiences in eCommerce,, 19—37.

effects, such as interpersonal emotion, emotion based on being successful at the task at hand and learning from shared activities or shared information. However, in the context of user experience-studies and human factors-studies in HCI the psychological effects occurring in both human-computer interaction and computer mediated social interaction have not been thoroughly researched and conceptualised at a more general level. Moreover, there is a need to integrate and implement the individual-centric and social interaction-centric approaches to emotional and cognitive effects at the level of system design.

To better define the approach of the authors to information technology, we first discuss six basic ways of seeing technology. First, technology may be seen as instrumentation that extends human activity and capability (Olson, 1974). Second, technology may be seen as a device and method for generating, processing and delivering information. This involves the fact that there are authors of information (both human and machine) and receivers of information and the information describes imaginary or factual states of the world (Saari, 2001). Third aspect of technology is that by generating and delivering information, technologies become a way to know of the events of the world (Rogers, 1986). Fourth, communication technology also creates a 'way of being' as it penetrates everyday life. When people use communication technologies they become a part of everyday life (Sobchack, 1994). Fifth, technology may be thought of as tools. This is the most common way of thinking of technology, as a hammer or a saw to accomplish a task with (Miller, 1978). Sixth, technology may be thought of as something capable of emerging beyond its original purpose. People may use technologies creatively and invent surprising uses for them (Chesebro and Bertelsen, 1996).

Media- and communication technologies as special cases of information technology may be considered as consisting of three layers (Benkler, 2000). At the bottom is a *physical* layer that includes the physical technological device and the connection channel that is used to transmit communication signals. In the middle is a *code* layer that consists of the protocols and software that make the physical layer run. At the top is a *content* layer that consists of multimodal information. The content layer includes both the substance and the form of multimedia content (Billmann, 1998; Saari, 2001). Substance refers to the core message of the information. Form implies aesthetic and expressive ways of organizing the substance, such as using different modalities and structures of information (Saari, 2001).

Further, media- and communication technologies may be called Mind-Based if they simultaneously take into account the interaction of three different key components: i) the individual differences and social similarities of perceptual processing and sense making of different segments of users, ii) the elements and factors inherent in information and technology that may produce psychological effects (physical, code and content layers), iii) and the consequent transient psychological effects emerging based on perception and processing of information at the level of each individual.

For instance, with Mind-Based Technologies one may vary the form of information per user profile, which may systematically produce, amplify, or shade different psychological effects (Saari, 2001; Saari, 2002; Saari, 2003a, Saari,

2003b). In a way, Mind-Based Technologies are more sensitive to the information they deliver, to the user of technology and especially to the psychological states of the user when processing the information. In this way, such technologies share much in common with the six basic ways of seeing technology presented above; but at the same time they involve a meta-understanding of an interactive and fluid relationship between technology, information, the user and the effects of using technology at the psychological level per each individual. This type of system design approach may be of practical use, as it is known that individual differences in processing information may produce sometimes quite large variance in the intensity or type of psychological effects, such as depth of learning, positive emotion, persuasion, presence and other types of psychological states and effects (Saari, 2001; Saari, 2002; Saari, 2003a; Saari, 2003b).

1.2 Basics of Psychological Customization

Information presented to individual users or a group of users may be personalized and customized on the basis of the types of immediate psychological effects it is likely to enable or create in certain individuals or groups. Psychological Customization may be used for controlling social interaction-centric and individual-centric influence of the substance and form of information on emotional and cognitive effects during and shortly after presence and social presence (Saari, 2003a; Saari, 2003b; Saari and Turpeinen, 2003; Turpeinen and Saari, 2004). Psychological Customization may be considered an operationalization and technique of implementing the concept of Mind-based Media and Communications Technologies (Saari, 2001; Saari, 2002; Saari, 2003) in system design.

Initially, Psychological Customization includes modeling of individuals, groups, and communities to create psychological profiles based on which customization may be conducted. In addition, a database of design rules is needed to define the desired cognitive and emotional effects for different types of profiles. Once these components are in place, content management technologies can be extended to cover variations of form and substance of information based on psychological profiles and design rules to create the desired psychological effects.

One basic example is a recommendation system. The system knows the user's profile, such as type of personality, and the desired psychological effect is set to positive emotion in as many page-views of the recommendations as possible. The user starts using the system and finds an interesting product that the system recommends to her. The form of the recommendation information is tailored to the user's profile and desired psychological effect in real-time when the page uploads to make the realization of positive emotion as probable as possible. The system may select the modality of recommendation from text to audio, or from audio to animation; the system may change the background colours of the page and modify the shape and colour of the navigation buttons, for instance. In this case, the system will try to do everything possible to facilitate positive emotion but change the substance of the recommendation itself. Naturally in some cases depending on type of user and the type of recommendation, the available databases of recommendation information and the available means of Psychological Customization of form of recommendation information, the effect to be achieved is more or less likely to occur. However, even effects that provide some percentages or tens of percents of more targeted positive emotion may make a difference in attitudes towards the product and buying behaviour. This is especially true if the recommendation system website has masses of users and hence even a slight increase in sales effectiveness may add up to significant amounts of income.

It should be noted that to build a smoothly functioning Psychological Customization system one should do much more research and gain more evidence of the systematic relationships of user profiles, information forms and psychological effects than what is currently reported in scientific experiments with available methods of acquiring such complex information. Hence, the full description of the detailed design guidelines for Psychological Customization is well beyond the scope of this single chapter.

2. MODEL OF EMOTIONAL AND COGNITIVE EFFECTS

2.1 Modeling and Measuring Transient Psychological Effects

When a user is interpreting information, a complex set of interrelated "gateway variables" may influence the "outcome variables" like his psychological states, such as presence, and experience of the information, including learning and emotion (Saari, 1998; Saari, 2001). These gateway variables may be clustered as *Mind* (individual differences and social similarities of perceivers), *Content* (information substance and form embedded in technology with certain ways of interaction) and *Context* (social and physical context of reception) (Saari, 1998; Saari, 2001). Being able to systematically and reliably predict the relationships of the gateway variables is the key to Mind-Based Media and Communications Technologies and Psychological Customization. This is complex and it may be sensible to concentrate only on the most robust psychological effects with certain tasks.

With the possibility of real-time customization and adaptation of information for different perceivers it is hypothesized that one may vary the form of information within some limits per the same substance of information. For instance, the same substance can be expressed in different modalities, or with different ways of interaction with the user and technology. This may produce a certain psychological effect in some perceivers; or shade or amplify a certain effect. This approach may also be suitable for creating psychological effects during computer mediated social interaction.

Mind-Based Technologies can serve as a framework for producing personalized, rule-based psychological effects. In Figure 1 the interaction of media and communications technology and the user in context with certain types of tasks is seen as producing transient psychological effects. Media and communication technology is divided into the physical, code and content layers. The user is seen as consisting of various different psychological profiles, such as individual differences related to cognitive style, personality, mental models and other differences. Certain contexts and tasks may be more or less open to some types of psychological effects to emerge than others.

It is of essence to be able to model and capture the systematic relationships of technology, user and psychological effects. If this can be done, one may claim that it is possible to build various types of technologies that are based on the probable and systematic control of various psychological effects.

One may discuss transient psychological effects. These may range from immediate millisecond-level reactions to tens of minutes of effects. One key focus is that Psychological Customization takes place within one particular session of using a particular technology and content. This is because long-term psychological effects may be beyond the horizon of prediction. Even in transient psychological effects it may be difficult to capture the real-time psychological states of a user.

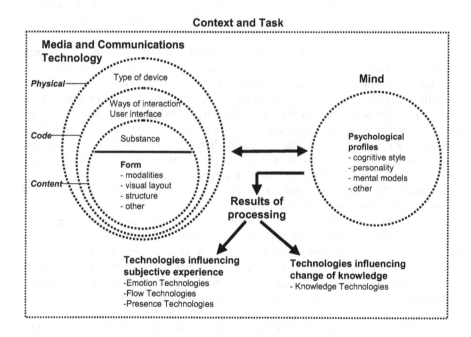

Figure 1. *Mind-Based Technologies as a framework for producing psychological effects. Adapted from Saari (2001).*

Mind-Content-Context- gateway variables are also fluid; they form new types of relationships and acquire new values as the different layers of technology change. Here one may focus on the reasonable temporal resolution of capturing user's psychological states and adapting content to the user within a single session of using an information system. From the point of view of user's psychological states, it may be reasonable not to concentrate on creating too many simultaneous effects, but concentrating on some key effect area, such as intensity and valence of emotions or efficiency of cognition. Also, one may wish to keep an emotional effect stable for some time as the user is using a system, rather than trying to change it constantly. Hence, the system will not try to create chaotic and over-complex psychological states, rather it should concentrate on providing and guiding desired types of "simple streams" of user experiences and psychological effects.

Obviously it is a highly complex task to model and capture user's psychological states and effects, such as efficiency of cognition, emotional states and moods or depth of presence or involvement and even more difficult to do so in real-time. However, using psychophysiological signals, such as heart rate and its indexes, EMG, EEG, GSR and also micro events of the visual system, such as eye-movement, may be of help here. For instance, psychophysiological signals may be considered as revealing the conscious and non-conscious emotional states of the user as well as the amount of workload on cognitive processing and level of attention. Similarly, patterns of eye-movements and other eye-related measures may be used for detecting changes in cognitive processing.

For example, some research has been conducted to measure and model presence in real-time. Presence is a mental construct that is, at least in part, related to the distribution of attention during the performance of tasks in virtual environments. Attention may be studied with eye-tracking. The simplest way is to measure with eye tracking the degree to which user's attention is distracted away from the media stimuli. Another possibility is to analyze which aspects of the mediated information the user looks at and the order in which different areas of media stimuli are processed. For instance, if the user feels present in the mediated environment, her attention is presumably directed most of the time to the relevant information. The third possibility is to classify attentional states to focused attention and distributed attention on the basis of eye fixation duration. (Laarni et al, 2003)

In psychophysiology, one may suggest that (a) phasic heart rate (HR) deceleration (i.e., orienting response) provides a quantitative measure of automatic attention and (b) respiratory sinus arrhythmia (RSA) provides a continuous quantitative measure of controlled attention. When the eye movement data is synchronized with the cardiac data, one can perform a fine-grained analysis of the relationship between the visual elements of the mediated stimulus and physiological responses. While eye movements provide a measure of the direction of attention, cardiac data (phasic heart rate deceleration, respiratory sinus arrhythmia) provide a quantitative measure of controlled attention. (Laarni et al, 2003)

Consequently, one possible realization for capturing user's psychological states and effects is to have the user linked to a sufficient number of measurement channels and sensors of various bodily signals. Naturally the extraction of biosignals should be done in a non-intrusive manner if possible. In consumer applications, one may use cameras integrated into computers or mouses with the ability to track heart rate, for instance. In more mission-critical situations such as military command and control-systems and aviation, the signals may be collected with more robust groups of sensors. However, also with some consumer applications such as gaming it may be that users would feel motivated to actually use advanced sensors to connect to the game better as people are already using force feedback wheels in driving games or advanced joysticks for flight games, for instance.

These signals then would verify to the system whether a desired psychological effect has been realized. Another approach would be to conduct a large number of user studies on certain tasks and contexts with certain user groups, psychological profiles and content-form variations and measure various psychological effects as objectively as possible. Here, psychophysiological signals or eye-tracking methods may be used as well as questionnaires and interviews. This would constitute a database of design-rules for automatic adaptations of information per user profile to create similar effects in highly similar situations with real applications. Naturally, a hybrid approach would combine both of these methods for capturing and facilitating the user's likely psychological state.

However, even though with specific focus areas one may achieve results concerning for instance positive emotion and individual differences in in-depth processing of information, to build a more comprehensive database of results covering more types of psychological states and effects remains a laborious and also expensive task requiring a lot of research resources. It may be also that with current scientific methods it is possible to achieve quite satisfactory results predicting the phenomenon, but there is a challenge of integrating the various methods of experimental psychology together to cover psychological effects in a more multisided manner. Another challenge is to test the feasibility of achieved laboratory results in real-life tasks and field conditions. To do this one may need tools such as ambulatory psychophysiology and mobile eye-tracking devices.

2.2   Customizing for Psychological Effects

Traditional mass media channels have not been amenable to efficient personalization and customization. At best, these media have been able to tailor content to reflect perspectives of a local community within the parameters used in market segmentation strategies. Internet-based technologies for content management and personalization introduce a new set of tools for serving individuals and communities of much wider variation sizes and types (Erickson, 1995; Riecken, 2000). Based on the principle of variability, many potential versions of the same media product or a particular collection of information may be available for different users (Manovich, 2001).

Layer of technology	Key factors
Physical	**Hardware** - large or small - mobile or immobile - close or far from body (intimate personal-social distance)
Code	**Interaction** - degree of user vs. system control and proactivity through user interface
	Visual-functional aspects - way of presenting controls in an interface visually and functionally
Content	**Substance** - the essence of the event described - type of substance (factual/imaginary; genre, other) - narrative techniques used by authors

	Form
	1. Modalities
	   - text, video, audio, graphics, animation, etc.
	2. Visual layout
	   - ways of presenting various shapes, colours, font types, groupings and other relationships or expressive properties of visual representations
	   - ways of integrating modalities into the user interface
	3. Structure
	   - ways of presenting modalities, visual layout and other elements of form and their relationships over time
	   - linear and/or nonlinear structure (sequential vs. parallel; narrative techniques, hypertextuality)

Table 1. *Key factors influencing individual-centric emotional and cognitive effects of technology, adapted from (Saari, 2001).*

One may discuss the "packaging" of information, which means how the different dimensions of information are put together into a certain type of package, including form and substance. The content can be selected and organized in different ways and the presentation of content can be tailored to suit the needs and preferences of the individual. This may include personal preferences for layouts or colour schemes.

This tailoring may result in different looking products based on the display device or publication style (Weitzman and Wittenburg, 1994).

Table 1 addresses the key factors that may influence psychological effects of information. For instance, a user may wish to have certain substance of information with as much video material as possible and have the system completely take over the control and present a personalized tv-newscast-type of information flow. Another example would be that the user has a profile that indicates it is beneficial for him to receive information in textual modality and the system may try to alter the information flows presented to him accordingly.

The view of the authors is that psychological effects especially occurring during social presence when in social computer mediated interaction have not been sufficiently researched. It can be hypothesized, however, that at least roughly similar psychological influences can be created via personalizing substance and form of information during social interaction as with individual-centric human-computer interaction. Thus the idea of gateway variables could be extended to tasks involving social interaction in the light of the factors presented in Table 1.

In sum, Mind-Based Media and Communications Technologies and Psychological Customization are created via real-time variations of i) substance, ii) form and iii) code layer (interaction and controls) within a certain technological device per certain user profiles. These elements interact in complex ways when producing psychological effects. The role of hardware should not be neglected. A device with a large screen or a portable device with smaller screen with user-changeable covers may also influence the emerging effects. The relevance of this framework to personalization research and HCI is evident as it may provide an approach to gaining access to and partly controlling the psychological states of the users of information systems.

2.3 Validating the Need for Psychological Customization

Even though no actual system has been implemented yet for Psychological Customization, empirical evidence supports the feasibility and validity of the idea of Psychological Customization. The key idea is that there seem to be several cognitive and emotional effects that are moderated by individual differences, for instance. This suggests the need for Psychological Customization Systems that optimize the presentation of information to different target groups having different psychological profiles. Further, there is considerable evidence in literature that varying the form of information creates for instance emotional and cognitive effects. The design rules for Psychological Customization may be roughly divided into i) social rules and ii) perceptual and information processing related rules.

For example, in the area of social rules Reeves and Nass (1996) have conducted research revealing that people respond to information technology in ways behaviourally similar to human-human interaction in the areas of flattery, team-building, credibility, persuasion, frustration and a range of other areas. In the area of perceptual and information-processing- level rules there are also various other sources for effects that have to do with how the form of information may influence psychological effects in conjunction with key individual differences. Specifically there is some recent experimental research supporting the idea, concept and need for Mind-Based Technologies and Psychological Customization.

For instance, Ravaja (2002) examined the moderating influence of dispositional Behavioral Inhibition System (BIS) and Behavioral Activation System (BAS) sensitivities, Negative Affect, and Positive Affect on the relationship between a small moving vs. static facial image and autonomic responses when viewing/listening to news messages read by a newscaster with 36 subjects displayed on a PDA. Autonomic parameters measured were respiratory sinus arrhythmia (RSA), low-frequency component of heart rate variability, electrodermal activity (EDA), and pulse transit time (PTT). The results showed that dispositional BAS sensitivity, particularly BAS Fun Seeking, and Negative Affect interacted with facial image motion in predicting autonomic nervous system activity. A moving facial image was related to lower RSA and EDA and shorter PTTs as compared to a static facial image among high fun seekers, while there was no, or an inverse, relationship between these variables among low fun seekers. Facial image motion may contribute to sustained attention particularly among high fun seekers, given that it may increase the so-called sense of presence and act as a positive incentive for high fun seekers, partly because of their higher need for stimulation.

Ravaja et al (2003) indicated the influence of subliminally presented emotional facial pictures on news presented on a PDA consisting of video material on emotion, attention and memory performance. Kallinen (2001) found that the use of headphones vs. speaker listening of audio news presented on a PDA influences evaluation and emotional responses to news. Kallinen and Ravaja (2002) found that playing raising and falling chromatic background melodies when reading and listening to news presented on a PDA influences emotional responses to news.

In media studies it has been found that different modalities, such as visual and auditory, may lead to different kinds of psychological influences and the valence of a preceding subliminal stimulus influences the subsequent evaluation of a person evaluated (Cuperfrain and Clarke, 1985; Krosnick et al, 1992). In educational studies it has been shown that different ways of processing information influence learning and emotion of stimuli with certain modality (Riding and Rayner, 1998). Research concerning emotional influences on the cognitive processing of information has often concentrated on how different emotions related to information change the way users pay attention to, evaluate and remember the mediated message. This research has results on the influence of emotional information as increasing the user's self-reported emotion (Lang et al, 1996); attention (physiological and self-reported) (Lang et al, 1995) and memory for mediated messages, particularly arousing messages (Lang, 1990; Lang et al 1995; Lang et al, 1996). Studies in experimental psychology have shown that recognition and memory can be influenced or even enhanced by previous exposure to subliminal visual or auditory images of which the subjects are not consciously aware (Kihlström et al, 1992). Some of these effects are produced in interaction with individual differences, such as cognitive style, personality, age and gender.

There is little research conducted in the area of psychological effects in the context of customized computer mediated social interaction. However, one may apply the approach of gateway variables to social interaction also. The interaction of two users may be seen as based on the mutual interaction of two sets of Mind, Content and Context- variable clusters (Saari, 1998). The content is the substance and form of social interaction, for instance a text used in a real-time messaging system. The other user within his Context sends information that is Content for the other user to receive. The other user makes sense of the Content sent to him and experiences various psychological effects during social presence with the other user. He may construct a reply to the message and send it to the other person. The interaction continues as the participants construct and make sense of the messages exchanged.

3. MODELING INDIVIDUALS, GROUPS AND COMMUNITIES

To be able to conduct Psychological Customization the system needs a model of the user or users. In fact, customization is always based on some type of model of an individual, a group or a community. These three can be considered separately:
- *user modeling*, which includes a profile of an individual user,
- *group modeling*, which is based on similarities between user profiles and forming a user cluster using some form of automated technique, and
- *community modeling*, which includes a profile about the community as a whole, not as the sum or the average of its individual member's profiles.

A user model is computer-accessible presentation of information about an individual regarding specified domains of use. This user model can consist of data explicitly given by the user for the purposes of modeling, implicit observations of user's behavior. The personalization can also be based on inferred data about the user that is stored in the user model. For example, based on user behaviour, the user can be assigned with some probability to belong to an identified segment. One may also classify users baseds on their personality, cognitive style and other psychologically relevant factors. The actual personalization is then done on a segment-by-segment basis.

Recommendation systems using *collaborative filtering* techniques categorize users automatically into groups or 'neighborhoods' based on similarities between user profiles. The tools use these neighborhoods to recommend new items to similar users, or to recommend users to each other (Shardanand and Maes, 1995).

Community modeling can be used to model the collective group, especially in a case of joint activity. Although communities have been profiled from several perspectives - for example psychological sense of a community (Chavis et al., 1986) or socio-economic profiles of local communities - there is not much literature on methods regarding community modeling from the point of view of their joint practice.

Community is not static – new members can arrive and existing members can leave at any time, but there is a sense of belonging to a group of individuals, and the group is relatively stable (Wenger, 1998). Instead of communities defined solely by geographic region or by joint interest, the web-enabled communities are often communities of practice that engage in a joint enterprise via mutual engagement

(Wenger, 1998). Most communities engage in some degree of collective cognition – the interactions through which they learn from one another's experiences, set common strategies, develop a shared vocabulary, evolve common norms and means, and evolve a distinctive and shared way of thinking (Agre, 1998).

User modeling, group modeling and community modeling may be used simultaneously in customization (Turpeinen, 2000). Our approach is to promote this hybrid usage of individual and social modeling in the context of psychological customization.

4. PSYCHOLOGICAL CUSTOMIZATION FOR INDIVIDUALS AND SOCIAL GROUPS

Basic principles of Mind-Based Media and Communications Technologies in producing psychological effects for individuals and groups may be utilized with Psychological Customization. For instance, if one wishes to produce more or less emotion with certain form of information embedded in a particular device with a certain user interface, one would have to know which types of variations of form may cause which types of qualities of emotion for the different perceivers. The same principle may apply to other psychological effects, such as presence, learning, persuasion or so. One may then hypothesize of individualized information products, such as Knowledge Media (Saari, 1998; Saari , 2001) that would enhance in-depth learning, or Emotion Media (Saari, 2001), which would produce certain types of emotions. One may also think of Presence Media (Saari, 2002) that may produce desired types of presence or Flow Media that may facilitate flow-states (Saari, 2001). These concepts may be extended to include also social interaction in producing group- or community-based emotion, cognition and presence.

Emotional and cognitive effects of information are related to communication within social networks as follows: one may manipulate manually or with automated systems the substance and the form of information. It is obvious that in social interaction the users may construct the substance and form of for instance MMS-messages exchanged manually. However, the form of the message may also be varied with automated systems. The information needed to conduct these automated manipulations can be accessed via individual and social modeling and profiling of the users. For instance, a user with an intention to create positive emotion in the other user with the way of presenting his textual message may utilize a background colour predicted to induce a mild positive emotional state in the receiving user based on his profile.

In a more detailed account, Psychological Customization involves i) a given pool of information to be presented to different users within a certain task, ii) a database of desired psychological effects per each user or user segment, such as positive emotion, set by the users themselves or the service provider, iii) a database of user profiles, iv) a database of meta-descriptions of the substance and form of the information to be delivered to users, v) a database of design rules of how the elements of information, such as form, will probably influence the transient psychological states of the different users, vi) sensors and sources of information that assess the psychological state of the user in real-time, such as psychophysiology, eye-tracking, video camera shots, sound, browsing behaviour monitoring and other possible sources and vii) an AI-component that monitors the realization of psychological effects and provides the necessary intelligence for the system to function.

This approach differs from present content management systems that are often based on filtering substance of information for individuals. It also differs from computer supported collaborative work (CSCW) approach in that it does not concentrate on enabling work on shared objects and tasks. It also actively involves the detection and modeling of user's psychological state in real-time.

In essence, Psychological Customization goes beyond the mere technical or task-based approach to content management technologies. It poses the question: how to utilize these technologies to create desired optimal psychological effects, such as positive emotion and efficiency of cognition with certain substance or within certain collaborative tasks?

It should be noted that privacy is one of the main social and technical challenges underlying any system that customizes media content for individual users. Considering the intimacy of psychological effects and user profiles the role of privacy protection is essential. The privacy issues in personalization are dependent on the physical storage location and modes of access to personal information. Also, there are technical mechanisms for providing pseudonymous service in which the user has persistent and verified digital identity and profile, but the actual identity of the individual is not known (Brands, 2000).

5. APPLICATION AREAS FOR PSYCHOLOGICAL CUSTOMIZATION

Psychological Customization can be applied to various areas of HCI, such as Augmentation Systems, Notification Systems, Affective Computing, Collaborative Filtering, Persuasive Technology and Messaging Systems.

It is hypothesized that the selection and manipulation of substance of information takes place through the technologies of the various application areas of Psychological Customization. Underlying the application areas is a basic technology layer for customizing design. This implies that within some limits one may automatically vary the form of information per a certain category of substance of information. The design space for Psychological Customization is formed in the interaction of a particular application area and the possibilities of the technical implementation of automated design variation.

For instance, Augmentation System refers to a system, which may enhance cognitive processing and understanding of a particular substance of information (Elo, 1996; Turpeinen, 2000). In news services, a particular article may be surrounded by other articles and additional information windows as well as graphs related to the base-article selected on the basis of a user profile. Displaying related articles or other additional information to the user may enhance the understanding of the basic story (Turpeinen, 2000). Augmentation may be varied for instance for experts and novices. Adding the possibilities of real-time variation of design may produce applications in the both the substance and form of information is varied for maximum cognitive efficiency. This means that the augmentations may be altered by modality or some other means per user profile.

Information Filtering refers to a system in which a software program filters the substance of information according to the user profile. Also here one may automatically vary the design within some limits per user. Notification System implies a way for the computer to alert the user of some noteworthy events, such as arrival of new email. It may be that also here one may vary the design of the substance of such a notification to create an effect of urgency or pleasantness, or to maximize attention to the notification, for instance.

Affective Computing refers to systems in which the computer is receiving real-time feedback of the emotional state of the user and may use this information to adapt its actions, such as when displaying certain substance of entertainment information, like a movie. With automated design variation, one may vary some emotional components of the substance to create desired emotional effects. A feedback system may then pick up the efficiency of the variations made to make sure an effect has been realized in a particular user.

Collaborative Filtering is a technique to offer personalized substance of information or recommendations based on clustering individual users into groups by buying behavior or some other dimension. Collaborative Filtering as a technique may be altered by automated variation of design to present the substance, for instance a book recommendation as substance may be altered in design to create a desired effect, such as maximum credibility of the recommendation for a particular user.

Persuasive Technology refers to human-computer interaction in which there is an underlying goal to change the attitudes and behavior of the user (Fogg, 2002). For instance, one may motivate users to quit smoking via motivating games. Also socially intelligent agents may be classified as persuasive technology. Often with agents an illusion of being in interaction with another human being is created in the user via using for example animated agents in e-Commerce. It is known that both the substance of the interaction (what is being sold and what the agent says) and the form of interaction (how information is presented, what is the appearance and personality of the agent) influence for instance trust, persuasiveness, emotion and liking of the transaction (Reeves and Nass, 1996). What Psychological Customization may add here may be more personalization of the way of presenting information in an eCommerce site as well as it may vary the appearance or other features of the agent without changing the substance, i.e. what the agent says.

A Messaging System entails computer mediated social interaction, like, MMS, chat or CSCW-software usage. By varying the design of MMS messages for instance one may be able to create emotional effects in the receivers of the message. Similarly, cognitive processes may be optimized for each individual user with the personalization of different aspects of the form of information embedded in a CSCW-software suite.

A more detailed example of an application for Psychological Customization includes facilitating desired emotions with eCommerce systems to make the systems more persuasive. The goal of persuasion may be to enhance brand awareness of the products sold or to sell more products if the information related to the products on an eCommerce site is presented in a way to facilitate positive emotion, for instance. Affective Computing may be used to create desired emotional states to enhance persuasiveness.

In accordance with particular emotional reactions or moods attention may be increased, memory may be influenced, performance in problem solving may be enhanced and judgment and decision-making may be influenced (Clore and Gasper, 2000; Reeves and Nass, 1996; Isen, 2000). One may focus on "primitive" emotional responses or emotions requiring more extensive cognitive appraisal and processing. Both of these types of emotions can be linked to various psychological consequences. Consequently, with Emotion Media-type of personalized information products one may focus on i) creating immediate and primitive emotional responses, ii) creating mood and iii) indirectly influencing secondary effects of emotion and mood, such as attention, memory, performance and judgment.

With eCommerce systems one may facilitate positive emotional responses for instance by selecting the modalities of the information to be displayed according to the processing styles and alter visual layouts of the interface according to the personalities of the users. The ease of processing information and the similarity-attraction between visual layouts and personalities may create positive emotional states. As for brand awareness one may indirectly influence memory with the facilitation of positive emotion and increase memory-based performance on the task such as brand recognition and recall. By increasing attention one may increase the likelihood of the user of an eCommerce system to learn product information more efficiently. Positive emotion and mood also has the effect of making the user adapt a less risk-prone approach to making decisions (Isen, 2000). This may be used to present product information in a familiar manner creating a safe atmosphere around to product to make it more desirable when the user is making purchasing decisions in a positive mood.

As regards to presence, one may discuss a military command and control-system in which an officer at a distant locale is trying to grasp a rapidly advancing battle situation and respond to it by giving correct and efficient commands to the field troops. The officer is linked with psychophysiological sensors and eye-tracking capability to the computer he uses. This means the computer can assess the state of presence of the user in real-time. Should the officer's state of presence be below set minimum for the task at hand, the system may react by giving warnings to the user of "fatigue" of then present some additional stimuli that may enhance presence with the given task. Also, in tele-surgery based applications a system may warn the doctor of the decrease of sense of presence which may be harmful to the task at hand and suggest a small break or some other measures to be taken.

6. CONCLUSION

Mind-Based Technologies and Psychological Customization as a research area has some overlap with usability studies and design studies. For instance, in usability studies the pleasantness and the aspect of having fun with interfaces have been addressed (Monk and Frochlich, 1999). Affective computing has been developed in the area of computers and emotion (Picard, 1997). Accordingly, in design-related research there has been for some time discussion about emotion and design (Hirsch et al, 2000).

However, according to the authors´ knowledge no other comprehensive framework of varying form of information to systematically create emotional and cognitive effects has been presented. Differences to other approaches to influencing user experience are various. Usability studies traditionally address the question of how to make difficult technology easy to use. Usability is at least partly founded on the idea of optimal human-machine performance, i.e. how well a user can manipulate and control a machine.

While this is certainly important, in consumer applications, like games, online news, e-Commerce and peer-to-peer computer mediated social interaction the emphasis of the use of the computer may well be in the arena of psychological effects rather than on usability as such. Games may be used to experience emotional arousal and excitement, online news may be used to learn of the events of the world and e-Commerce vendors present their wares in a persuasive manner to users. Consequently, Psychological Customization is founded on the idea of creating a desired psychological effect with the available means of automatic variation of substance and form of information. It may be seen as partly based on or adding to usability studies. Naturally, if an interface is not usable, it may not be possible to systematically create psychological effects.

Design-based approaches to interface design have adopted the perspective of creating desired experiences, such as positive emotion for a user. However, what is lacking is the systematic and explicit, communicable, knowledge of what exactly in the elements of design may produce such effects. Also, the influence of individual differences of the users in the variation of the effects remains unknown. Moreover, it may be difficult to alter hand-made designs rapidly, and almost impossible to do it in real-time. Psychological Customization does not claim to replace design as such, it may rather be a tool for designers to systematically vary some elements of an interface in real-time within a hand-designed template. For example, one may create psychologically validated basic interface templates for designers as tool sets to facilitate desired emotions

From the point of view of contribution to HCI community, Psychological Customization poses a possible change in the perspective to technology. One may view technology as a source for creating added value for a user, such as enabling desired emotional and cognitive effects. However, it is beyond the scope and aim of this single chapter to provide detailed and ready-to-use, low-level practical advice on how exactly to design for desired psychological effects. There are case-studies in which various effects have been studied in the area of mediapsychology, educational psychology and experimental psychology but only a few examples in the HCI area.

This may also be partly due to the fact that HCI research does not very often conceptualise the users as possessing individual differences related to perceiving and processing information presented via user interface and the consequential differences in user experiences. It is evident, that designing for the "average user experience" is economical and may cover many of the usage-cases, but in some more "mission critical" application areas it may be sensible to closely match the information form and user interface to the type of user. Naturally, if one wishes to design for different types of user experiences for different segments of users, this may require new types of methods for capturing the user experience as well as systems for automatic variation of the form of information and user interface discussed in this chapter to inform design.

As for having clear hypothesis on how different technologies may be used to facilitate for instance positive emotion, it may be said that the most obviously fruitful focus area of manipulation in different application areas may differ. An example of a persuasive e-Commerce system was given. Further, for example, in Messaging Systems it may be sensible to concentrate on MMS-message templates (colours, shapes, animations, other) that can be used to facilitate a desired emotion. In Augmentation Systems, such as augmented online news services, it may be sensible to find out the most efficient ways of supporting in-depth information processing with types of additional information elements and their modalities. In Affective Computing, one interesting area is the personalized generation of background textures, colours, shapes and sounds in games based on navigation in 3D space to facilitate desired emotions. In military command and control-type systems one may concentrate on situation awareness-type of issues as related to presence.

In sum, to be able to realize Psychological Customization one may have to conduct a number of experimental studies in which certain applications with certain tasks are tested in laboratory and field conditions. Laboratory methods, such as psychophysiology, may be used for indicating emotional effects in addition to qualitative methods. However, the real challenge comes from conducting research with more ecological validity than laboratory studies. It may be fruitful to see how the most intense and probable psychological effects in laboratory simulations hold together in everyday contexts. This may be studied with contextual inquiry- type of methods and with ambulatory psychophysiological tools as well as with mobile eye-tracking systems. To do this professionally would mean to integrate relevant aspects of the methods together in a parallel manner to form the basis of a new field-based method for studying user experience.

Also, one should develop content management technologies to utilize the design rules acquired from user studies. Further, prototypes are needed in selected application areas of Psychological Customization to investigate and explore the technological challenges underlying user experience-based adaptive system design and most of all to realize the first system designs.

In the light of the considerable amount of experiments and development work needed to realize Psychological Customization it is evident that the effort and collaboration of various multidisciplinary research groups will be much needed on this emerging area of HCI.

7. REFERENCES

Agre, P. E. (1998). Designing Genres for New Media: Social, Economic, and Political Contexts, In Jones, S.G. (ed.) Cybersociety 2.0: Revisiting Computer-Mediated Communication and Community, Thousand Oaks: Sage Publications

Benkler, Y. (2000) From Consumers to Users: Shifting the Deeper Structures of Regulation. Federal Communications Law Journal 52, 561-63.

Billmann, D. (1998) Representations. In Bechtel, W. and Graham, G. (1998) A companion to cognitive science, 649-659. Blackwell publishers, Malden, MA.

Biocca, F. and Levy, M. (1995) Communication in the age of virtual reality. Lawrence Erlbaum, Hillsdale, NJ.

Brands, S. (2000). Rethinking Public Key Infrastructures and Digital Certificates; Building in Privacy. MIT Press, Cambridge, MA.

Chavis, D.M., Hogge, J.H., McMillan, D.W. (1986). Sense of community through Brunswick's lens: a first look. Journal of Community Psychology, No. 14.

Chesebro, J. W. and Bertelsen, D. A. (1996) Analyzing media. Communication technologies as symbolic and cognitive systems. The Guilford Press, New York and London.Cuperfain, R. and Clarke, T. K. (1985) A new perspective on subliminal perception. Journal of Advertising, 14, 36-41.

Clore, G. C. and Gasper, K. (2000). Feeling is believing. Some affective influences on belief. In Frijda, N.H., Manstead, A. S. R. and Bem, S. (Ed.), Emotions and beliefs: How feelings influence thoughts (pp. 10-44). Paris/Cambridge: Editions de la Maison des Sciences de l'Homme and Cambridge University Press.

Elo, S. K. (1996) PLUM: Contextualizing news for communities through augmentation. Master's thesis, MIT MediaLab, Cambridge, MA.

Erickson, T. (1995) Designing agents as if people mattered. In Bradshaw, J. M. (eds.) Software agents, 79-96. AAAI Press/The MIT Press, Menlo Park, CA, Cambridge, MA, London, England.

Fogg, B. J. (2002) Persuasive technology. Using computers to change what we think and do. Morgan Kaufmann Publishers, New York.

Hirsch, T., Forlizzi, J., Hyder, E., Goetz, J., Stroback, J., and Kurtz, C. (2000) The ELDeR Project: Social and Emotional Factors in the Design of Eldercare Technologies. Conference on Universal Usability, 2000, pp. 72-80.

Isen, A. M. (2000). Positive affect and decision making. In Lewis, M. and Haviland-Jones, J. M. (Ed.), Handbook of emotions (2nd ed.) (pp. 417-435). New York: Guilford Press. Kallinen, K. (2001) Speakers versus headphones: preference, valence, arousal and experience of presence in audio PDA news. In Michitaka Hirose (Ed.) Human Computer Interaction INTERACT ' 01, Amsterdam: IOS Press, 805-806.

Kallinen, K. and Ravaja, N. (2002) Creating tension from chromaticism: self-reported judgments of and physiological responses to audio news with raising versus falling chromatic background melody [CD-ROM]. In M. Britta & M. Melén (eds.), Proceedings of the 10th anniversary conference of the European Society for the Cognitive Sciences of Music: Musical Creativity. Liège, Berlgium: University of Liège.

Kihlström, J. F., Barnhardt, T. M. and Tataryn, D. J. (1992) Implicit perception. In Bornstein, R. F. and Pittmann, T. S. (eds.) Perception without awareness. Cognitive, clinical and social perspectives, 17-54. Guilford, New York.

Krosnick, J. A. , Betz, A. L., Jussim, J. L. and Lynn, A. R. (1992) Subliminal conditioning of attitudes. Personality and Social Psychology Bulletin, 18, 152-162.

Laarni, J., Ravaja, N. & Saari, T. (2003). Using eye tracking and psychophysiological methods to study spatial presence. In The Online Proceedings of PRESENCE 2003. http://www.presence-research.org/

Lang, A. (1990) Involuntary attention and physiological arousal evoked by structural features and mild emotion in TV commercials. Communication Research, 17 (3), 275-299.

Lang, A., Dhillon, P. and Dong, Q. (1995) Arousal, emotion and memory for television messages. Journal of Broadcasting and Electronic Media, 38, 1-15.

Lang, A., Newhagen, J. and Reeves. B. (1996) Negative video as structure: Emotion, attention, capacity and memory. Journal of Broadcasting and Electronic Media, 40, 460-477.

Lombard, M. and Ditton, T. (1997) At the heart of it all: The concept of presence. Journal of Computer Mediated Communication, 3 (2).

Lombard, M., Reich, R., Grabe, M. E., Bracken, C. and Ditton, T. (2000) Presence and television: The role of screen size. Human Communication Research, 26(1), 75-98.

Manovich, L. (2001) The language of new media. The MIT Press, Cambridge, MA, London, England.

Marcel, A. J. (1983) Conscious and unconscious perception: An approach to the relations between phenomenal experience and perceptual awareness. Cognitive psychology, 15, 283-300.

Miller, C. R. (1978) Technology as a form of consciousness: A study of contemporary ethos. Central States Speech Journal, 29, 228-236.

Monk, A.F. and Frohlich, D. (1999) Computers and Fun, Personal Technology, 3, 91.

Olson, D. R. (1974) Introduction. In Olson, D. R. (eds.) Media and symbols: The forms of expression, communication and education, 1-24. University of Chicago Press, Chicago.

Picard, R. (1997) Affective Computing. MIT Press, Cambridge, 1997.

Ravaja, N. (2002) Presence-related influences of a small talking facial image on psychophysiological measures of emotion and attention. Proceedings of the 5th Annual International Workshop Presence 2002. Porto, Portugal: University Fernando Pessoa

Ravaja, N., Kallinen, K., Saari, T. and Keltikangas-Järvinen, L. (2003) Effects of Suboptimally Presented Facial Expressions on Emotion, Attention, and Memory when Viewing Video Messages from a Small Screen. Submitted to Journal of Experimental Psychology: Applied

Reeves, B. and Nass, C. (1996) The media equation. How people treat computers, television and new media like real people and places. Cambridge University Press, CSLI, Stanford.

Riding, R. J. and Rayner, S. (1998) Cognitive styles and learning strategies. Understanding style differences in learning and behavior. David Fulton Publishers, London.

Riecken, D. (2000) Personalized views on personalization. Communications of the ACM, V. 43, 8, 27-28.

Roediger, H. L. (1990) Implicit memory: Retention without remembering. American Psychologist, 45, 1043-1056.

Rogers, E. M. (1986) Communication technology: The new media in society. Free Press, New York.

Saari, T. (1998) Knowledge creation and the production of individual autonomy. How news influences subjective reality. Reports from the department of teacher education in Tampere university. A15/1998. Licenciate thesis.

Saari, T. (2001) Mind-Based Media and Communications Technologies. How the Form of Information Influences Felt Meaning. Acta Universitatis Tamperensis 834. Tampere University Press, Tampere 2001. Doctoral thesis.

Saari, T. (2002) Designing Mind-Based Media and Communications Technologies. Proceedings of Presence 2002 Conference, Porto, Portugal, pp. 79-87.

Saari, T. (2003a) Designing for Psychological Effects. Towards Mind-Based Media and Communications Technologies. In Harris, D., Duffy, V., Smith, M. and Stephanidis, C. (eds.) Human-Centred Computing: Cognitive, Social and Ergonomic Aspects. Volume 3 of the Proceedings of HCI International 2003, pp. 557-561

Saari, T. (2003b) Mind-Based Media and Communications Technologies. A Framework for producing personalized psychological effects. Proceedings of HFES′03 -conference. 13.-17.10.2003 Denver, Colorado.

Saari, T. and Turpeinen, M. (2003) Psychological Customization of Information for Individuals and Social Groups. Proceedings of MCPC′03- conference, Munich, Germany 6.-8.10. 2003

Shardanand, U., Maes, P. (1995). Social Information Filtering: Algorithms for Automating "Word of Mouth". Proceedings of CHI'95 Conference on Human Factors in Computing Systems, ACM Press.

Turpeinen, M. (2000) Customizing news content for individuals and communities. Acta Polytechnica Scandinavica. Mathematics and computing series no. 103. Helsinki University of Technology, Espoo.

Turpeinen, M. and Saari, T. (2004) System Architechture for Psychological Customization of Information. Accepted for publication in proceedings of HICSS-37- conference, 5.-8.1. 2004, Hawaii.

Wenger, E. (1998). Communities of Practice: Learning, Meaning, and Identity. Cambridge University Press, Cambridge, UK.

Weitzman, L., Wittenburg, K. (1994) Automatic presentation of multimedia documents using relational grammars. In proceedings of Second ACM International Conference on Multimedia. 15-20 Oct. San Francisco, 443-451.

PAMELA BRIGGS, BRAD SIMPSON AND ANTONELLA DE
ANGELI

PERSONALISATION AND TRUST:

A RECIPROCAL RELATIONSHIP?

1. INTRODUCTION

Trust and personalisation are related constructs. Trust is generally accepted as a pre-requisite for good personalisation practice. Customers are not likely to reveal confidential information about themselves to an untrustworthy party, and they may be suspicious of data harvesting practices if they feel the information may be misused in some way.

But the converse relationship might also hold: good personalisation practice may be a pre-requisite for trust building online. At present, relatively few studies of trust suggest an important role for personalisation in the formation of trust, but we argue below that personalisation may play a larger role than that suggested by the current trust literature. Following a critical review of online trust studies, we suggest that personalisation is important for the development of trust in long-term relationships between consumer and online vendor, but argue that its role in short-term interactions is unclear. We then present a study that explores the extent to which people may be influenced by the promise of a personalised transaction, in order to clarify the influence of personalised practices on initial trust judgments.

Most researchers agree that trust is a vital construct for e-commerce. It has been argued that in order to develop a successful e-commerce business:

> "The factors that produce a sense of trustworthiness need to be identified, in their entirety. Their interactions need to be understood, and their relative importance determined." (Cheskin/Sapient, 1999)

Unfortunately researchers also agree that trust is an extremely difficult construct to work with, since it takes its meaning, chameleon-like from the context in which it operates. Thus trust is defined differently within the different fields of philosophy, sociology, psychology, management, political science and – most recently – human-computer interaction. Furthermore, different manifestations of trust have been observed within any one field – each with antecedents and consequences particular to a specific context. Within the psychology literature, for example, a distinction is made between the kinds of trust that support transient interactions and those that support longer-term relationships (e.g. Meyerson et al., 1996) but even within the

39

Clare-Marie Karat et al. (eds.), Designing Personalized User Experiences in eCommerce, 39—55.

latter, it is argued that people can experience both cognitive trust, based on rational decision-making and emotional trust, based on strong feelings towards another individual (e.g. McAllister, 1995). Such various manifestations of trust have led researchers such as Corritore et al. (2003) to conclude that there is not one unitary trust concept, but:

> "a multi-dimensional family of trust concepts, each with a unique focus."

The picture is further complicated, within an e-commerce context, by the fact that customers must be prepared to place their trust not only in an online vendor but also in the technology that underpins an interaction. Understanding the context for trust, therefore involves understanding issues of encryption and data security as well as understanding the development of a psychological bond. Bollier (1996), for example, argued that:

> "It may be conceptually useful to distinguish between issues of "hard trust," which involve authenticity, encryption, and security in transactions, and issues of "soft trust", which involve human psychology, brand loyalty, and user-friendliness.....it is important to see that the problems of engendering trust are not simply technical in nature.....Trust is also a matter of making psychological, sociological, and institutional adjustments." (Bollier, 1996)

Researchers do agree, however, that trust is only really understood in terms of some associated, underlying risk (Brien, 1988; Mayer et al., 1995). The act of trust is thus the act of making oneself vulnerable to one or more threats but the nature of trust critically depends upon the nature of those threats. Grabner-Krauter et al. (2003) have explored the risks inherent in e-commerce transactions and point out that online consumers are faced with both:

– *System-dependent uncertainties* including technological errors and security gaps located at the desktop or the marketplace server; and
– *Transaction-specific uncertainties* which relate more closely to the behaviours of the Internet merchant – the quality of the products on sale and the professionalism of the transaction.

Both types of uncertainty hold significant threats for the consumer. Thus in an e-commerce context, trust in an online vendor invokes *inter alia* the threat of financial loss, of privacy violation, identity theft and a threat to personal reputation. Other threats include exposure to spam and various telemarketing initiatives[1] and while these may seem less serious threats, the fact that they occur so commonly has led some authors to argue that these nuisance threats are likely to have a devastating effect on the fabric of the Internet (Weinstein, 2003).

In other Internet contexts – for example those involving personal discourse or advice-seeking online, then the threats may be even more diverse, yet very few researchers have explicitly looked at the way in which these different threats affect trust development, although elsewhere in this book there are detailed discussions of the threats inherent in revealing personal information.

---

[1] IBM Multi-National Consumer Privacy Survey. Available at: http://www-1.ibm.com/services/files/privacy_survey_oct991.pdf

Despite a general lack of information about the specific vulnerabilities underpinning an act of trust, a number of researchers have tried to model trust in online exchange by focussing on those attributes of an online organisation or web site which facilitate trust. Some of these models have a purely theoretical basis (e.g. Corritore et al., 2003), whereas others are grounded in empirical research (e.g. Bhattacherjee, 2002; Briggs et al., 2002; Egger, 2001; Lee and Turban, 2001; McKnight and Chervany, 2001; see also Grabner-Krauter et al., 2003, for a recent overview). At first the picture of trust emerging from these studies is confusing and contradictory. Some researchers argue that trust (or a related construct, credibility) is primarily influenced by the extent to which a site is attractively and professionally designed (e.g. Fogg et al., 2002) while others argue that trust is a function of the competence, integrity predictability and/or benevolence of the site (e.g. Bhattacherjee, 2002). Some, but not many authors highlight the importance of personalisation in the formation of trust judgments.

The confusion clears, somewhat, however, when a staged or developmental model of trust is adopted, since it is likely that different factors are influential at different times. An example may illustrate this point. Imagine a potential customer searching the Internet for a bargain flight. He or she may well be put off a site which has poor usability or unprofessional design, while being drawn to a site which exemplifies good design and professional values. In other words their first impression will be highly influential in the early stages of the process of buying online. Once they have actually found a site which offers a good price, however, they are then likely to engage in a more detailed analysis of the company itself before committing themselves to a transaction. These two stages have been highlighted by a number of authors. Thus, for example, Briggs et al., 2002 borrowed from the persuasion literature in social psychology to identify (i) a *heuristic stage* where an initial trust impression is formed, and (ii) *an analytic stage* where a decision to engage properly with the site is made. In contrast, McKnight and Chervany (2001) identified a preliminary stage of (i) *intention to trust* from a later stage of (ii) *trusting activity*.

The process does not stop there however, and a more realistic assessment of the development of trust should include a third stage in which a (iii) *trusting relationship* develops between the customer and the vendor. This then generates a three-stage model of the process of trust development – as originally proposed in the Cheskin/Sapient report (1999). They described the stage of building trust and accompanying activities such as browsing, searching and comparing; the stage of confirming trust and associated acts of registering with a site and checking transactions, and finally the stage of maintaining trust, which they see in terms of a more informal habit-like relationship with the vendor.

This third stage is an important one for e-commerce, since any company worth their salt would wish to secure loyal custom. Revisiting the example above, our customer may wish to purchase a second, third or fourth flight. If their experience with a particular online vendor has been positive, in other words if their details were handled securely and competently and they received their tickets and/or booking notifications promptly and were able to communicate appropriately with the company, then they are likely to go back to that same firm. In this way a trusting relationship can develop over time.

The surprising thing about the literature on trust in e-commerce is that so little of it addresses this third relationship component. Indeed it is a great weakness of the trust literature that most of the empirical studies reported explore only the first stage of initial trust or intention to trust. Only two of the studies reviewed by Grabner-Krauter et al. (2003) investigated real transactions and these were limited to short-term interactions. Participants in almost all of the other studies were not required or even not allowed to perform a shopping transaction. Yet when the trust literature is interpreted in terms of the three stages outlined above (the first impressions involved in building trust, further involvement with a particular site leading the first transactions and subsequent relationship development) it starts to make a good deal of sense.

Stage 1: First Impressions and initial trust building activities

To begin with, let us explore those investigations that ask participants to briefly visit a site or sites and then tender some evaluation of trustworthiness. Such participants have very low involvement in this process and would expect (following the logic of Chaiken, 1980) that their trust judgments will be based on first impressions and will be highly influenced by the attractiveness and ease of use of the site. A number of studies support this.

Consider, for example, an investigation of credibility online from the Stanford Persuasion Laboratory (Fogg et al., 2002). Note that credibility is a concept closely related to trust, and the Stanford Lab has conducted some of the largest studies of those factors, which influence consumer judgments of credibility. In their 2002 study, consumers were asked to compare two sites drawn from one of ten different domains and to make a judgment about which of the sites was more credible. They were asked to supplement this judgment with comments and notably 46.1% of those comments reflected design qualities - as indicated by the following sample of comments drawn from four participants:

> "More pleasing graphics, higher-quality look and feel."

> "Actually, despite the subject of the Web site, it looks very credible. This may be due to the subdued color scheme and the font used on the left-hand side of the page."

> "Not very professional looking. Don't like the cheesy graphics. Looks childish and like it was put together in 5 minutes."

Such comments are remarkably similar to those elicited in a recent qualitative investigation of trust in sites offering advice and information to potential house-buyers (Briggs et al., 2002, Study 1). In that investigation people were asked to search the Internet for relevant information and then discuss which sites they would return to and which they would reject. A positive first impression was linked to good design and an absence of amateur mistakes as well as to indications of expertise, while a negative first impression was more explicitly tied to poor design.

Other studies have focussed on the impact of specific design features. Thus, for example, the presence or absence of trust markers such as VeriSign or other seals of approval can have an immediate effect in promoting trust (as in Cheskin/Sapient, 1999), while photographs have also been found to influence trust judgments – although the extent to which they have a positive or a negative effect is related to a number of other aspects of site design (e.g. Riegelsberger et al., 2003; Steinbruck et al., 2002).

Stage 2: Further involvement with the site and the first transactions

Those investigations that involved real customers, or that required some protracted engagement with a site or those that have asked customers about the general principles underpinning e-commerce transactions have generated a family of trust models with reasonable agreement. In general the models suggest that trust which supports online engagement is influenced by perceived integrity and expertise, predictability or familiarity of content and reputation (e.g. Bhattacherjee, 2002; Briggs et al., 2002, study 2; Fogg et al., 2001; McKnight and Chervany, 2001). A number of studies also highlighted the importance of interface factors (ease of use and functionality) which help to reduce the transaction costs of an exchange (e.g. Egger, 2000, 2001; Lee, Kim and Moon, 2000).

For example, Bhattacherjee (2002) developed a psychometric scale for trust in online transactions which was tested in two field trials and modified accordingly. The resultant seven item scale tapped into three trust elements:

Ability – both in terms of expertise and information access.
- Example: 'Amazon has the skills and expertise to perform transactions in an expected manner'.

Integrity - encompassing issues of fairness of conduct in transactions, customer service and data usage.
- Example: 'Amazon is fair in its use of private user data collected during a transaction'.

Benevolence – in terms of keeping the customers interests in mind and in terms of showing empathy and responsiveness to customer concerns.
- Example: 'Amazon is open and receptive to customers needs'.

The last two constructs also underpin Lee and Turban's (2001) model of trust, (accompanied by constructs related to general trust in Internet shopping and in an individual's propensity to trust) and there are remarkable similarities too with the trusting beliefs identified by McKnight and Chervany (2001), namely benevolence (defined by them as the belief that the other will act in one's own interest), integrity (the belief that the other makes good faith agreements, tells the truth and fulfils promises), competence (the belief that the other has the ability or power to do what needs to be done) and predictability (the belief that the other's actions will be consistent).

Stage 3: Subsequent relationship development

What happens after an initial transaction has been completed remains unclear since very few studies of trust in e-commerce have explored the longer-term *relationships* between consumer and vendor that may obtain.   In other words most of the investigations recently reported explore the kinds of trust judgments that might underpin one-shot purchase decisions, hardly any look at changes in trust over time. This omission is particularly surprising when we consider that all of the early models of trust between individuals focussed explicitly on the build up of a relationship over time.

Yet it is clear that trust is a *consequence* as well as an expectation of action which means that initial trust judgements will be modified by experience. This common-sense interpretation of trust was evident in Rotter's original view of interpersonal trust, where trust in a generalised other could develop from successful and consistent exchanges with parents and siblings. The point was made more clearly by Gambetta (1988) who argued that the point where we shift from saying, "I don't trust X" to "I trust X", is a threshold on this continuum which will vary with individual tendencies (e.g. a predisposition to trust) and experience: "trust is not a resource that is depleted through use; on the contrary, the more there is the more there is likely to be" (Gambetta, 1988, p. 234). The catastrophic impact of negative experience on trust is also highlighted by Lee and Moray (1992, 1994).

Perhaps the clearest work on the offline development of trust comes from Lewicki and Bunker (1995) who explored the development of trust in work situations. There they found a clear developmental trend from an initial *deterrence-based* trust which was all about penalties imposed on violation of contracts, to a *knowledge-based* trust which was characterised by judgments of expertise and predictability of the interaction (see models above). Finally workers reached a *shared-identification-based* trust where workers were confident that they shared a common set of values.

Not surprisingly, those online studies taking a longer-term perspective on trust also emphasise the importance of shared values between customer and vendor. In these studies, trust in a longer-term e-commerce relationship is a function not only of competence and predictability, but is highly influenced by the extent to which e-vendors are good communicators and show sensitivity to the personal values and circumstances of the consumer. In this way good personalisation practices are shown to be important for the development of a trusting relationship.

For example, in a study which explored the extent to which Internet users would revisit an online store (i.e. exhibit customer loyalty), Lee, Kim and Moon (2000) found that trust was a function of three factors: (i) the comprehensiveness of the information given out to customers; (ii) the perception of shared values between the customer and the store and (iii) the quality of communication between the store and the customer.

Similarly, in Egger's (2000, 2001) studies of online customers, good personalised communication between customer and vendor was shown to be vital to the development of trust. Egger developed MoTEC (A Model of Trust for Electronic Commerce) where Trust is initially determined by three factors: (a) the users knowledge of the domain and reputation of the vendor, (b) the impression made by the interface, and (c) the quality of the informational content as assessed by the consumer, but where a fourth factor – relationship management - becomes influential over time:

> "Relationship management reflects the facilitating effect of timely, relevant and personalised vendor-buyer interactions on trust development (pre-purchase) and maintenance (post-purchase)." (Egger, 2001)

The importance of this fourth factor was highlighted in a subsequent study exploring trust judgments of users of an online casino (Shelat and Egger, 2002). In that study relationship management issues were found to be crucial – gamblers were only prepared to trust an online casino if they could communicate promptly and swiftly with the organisation and verify prompt payment of winnings.

The influential role of good personalised transactions was also highlighted in a large-scale study of credibility conducted at the Stanford persuasion laboratory (Fogg et al., 2001). Over 1400 participants completed a questionnaire concerned with those factors they felt made web sites more or less credible. One of the scales in the questionnaire measured 'tailoring' of content and included the following four items:

– The site sends emails confirming the transactions you make
– The site selects news stories according to your preferences
– The site recognizes that you have been there before
– The site requires you to register or log in

Tailoring was found to increase credibility, although the effect was more profound for the older users. In other words, older respondents reported higher credibility evaluations for sites that used some type of tailoring.

Perhaps the clearest demonstration of a role for personalisation in online trust comes from a study in which people were asked about advice on the Internet (Briggs et al., 2002). This was an online questionnaire based study in which a total of 2,893 respondents said that they had actually sought advice online. These individuals were asked to give information about the site they had used in terms of issues related to trust as identified in an extensive review of trust literature. These include aspects of site usability and interactivity, peer commentary, personalisation, host reputation, perceived expertise, independence, familiarity and predictability of process. In a regression analysis a clear three-factor model of trust emerged with factors as follows:

1. *Source credibility* – the extent to which information and advice came from a knowledgeable source, was prepared by an expert, seemed impartial and was readily available. This factor was highly predictive of participants' decisions to follow the advice (see below) and ties in very strongly to models of information credibility in the literature (e.g. Fogg et al., 2001).

2. *Personalisation* - did the respondent feel involved in the process? Was the site interactive? Was the information tailored to the participant? Were different courses of action suggested, and was a peer commentary available?

3. *Predictability* – Did the site meet the respondents' expectations. Had they used the site before and did they already know something about this domain? Did the site operate in a predictable way? Was it branded with a familiar name and/or logo?

Personalisation, then, can be seen as an important enabling factor for trust in online advice, and indeed in other studies of trust in e-commerce that have explored full engagement with web sites.   Effective personalisation tools and a good communication strategy seem important pre-requisites for the maintenance of a loyal long-term customer-vendor relationship

However this leaves us with something of a conundrum, since trust has been identified as both a pre-requisite and a consequence of good personalisation practice. In other words, an individual is more likely to disclose personal information in an atmosphere of trust, but that same individual is more likely to trust an organisation which shows sensitivity to his or her personal circumstances. It begs the question of just what happens the first time people are asked to give up personal details to a relatively unknown e-commerce site.

In some of the studies reviewed above there is an implicit suggestion that a site which promises an interactive, personal service may be regarded as more trustworthy than one which is somehow less interactive. Thus, for example, several studies of e-commerce sites argue that in order to promote trust the online site must somehow give a richer impression of the kinds of off-line experiences users are familiar with.   Some authors describe this as a process of *virtual re-embedding* (e.g. Riegelsberger et al., 2003) arguing that a variety of surface cues may be used to engage users both emotionally and cognitively in the interaction. Photographs may help with this process, as we have already seen, but the promise of interactivity can also make a difference. A study by Basso et al. (2001), for example, found that the first impressions of an online store were affected by the presence of an Instant Messaging (IM) facility. In other words, those participants who could interact with a sales agent via IM found the store to be trustworthier.

Thus the promise of a personalised relationship may well affect trust judgments made during early interactions with a site. In order to explore this issue further, we conducted a study in which we explicitly explored issues of trust and self-disclosure during a first transaction. Before describing this study in detail it is worth noting that this study was one of three investigations in a project concerned with identifying those online factors capable of influencing trust in online advice. The project utilised the principle of triangulation – i.e. it sought evidence from three different sources, in this case three different methodologies: a qualitative investigation, a large-scale questionnaire and finally an experimental manipulation of those factors emerging as important for trust. Details of the first two studies can be found in Briggs et al. (2002).

2.   AN EMPIRICAL INVESTIGATION OF PERSONALISATION AND TRUST

2.1 *Method*

Four versions of a travel insurance website were created by UK-Premier.com Ltd. (see table 1, below), in which personalisation was manipulated by the inclusion of key questions which asked for personal details, which were then (i) incorporated or

(ii) ignored in later screens. For both the personalised and non-personalised sites two false travel insurance companies were constructed. One was designed to reflect a relatively young start-up company, whereas the other was accompanied with text, font and graphics meant to suggest a more established organisation – with details about the companies' histories included. Both sites were professionally designed and were modelled on existing travel insurance companies. In addition, the personal data questionnaires built into the sites were modelled on those insurance companies who aim to provide a low-charge policy cover in exchange for enhanced disclosure of relevant information.

Participants were 107 students at the University of Northumbria, all of whom were intending to spend some time travelling and who therefore had an interest in travel insurance. Participants were told that the University of Northumbria had been commissioned by a travel insurance company to conduct research on their website. They were led to believe that the website was authentic, and were told that they should visit the site, filling in details of their travel insurance needs, where appropriate, and then fill in some questions about the site. They were also told that they could genuinely purchase the travel insurance on offer, if they felt it was worthwhile. It is worth pointing out at this stage that the students were thus led to believe that they were interacting with a live corporate site where they could genuinely purchase travel insurance.

Participants were then given a unique identity code and were logged on to one of the four travel insurance websites. They worked through the various fields on the site, and were then directed to a follow-up questionnaire – based on the offline questionnaire described by Briggs et al. (2002).

Individuals were unaware that four different versions of the site existed. After completing the final questionnaire, participants were thanked and debriefed. They were assured that any data capable of personally identifying them would be automatically stripped from the log kept for each individual. Table 1 gives a breakdown of the design and procedure.

Table 1. *Phases of the investigation*

	Personalised 'established' (P-E)	Personalised 'new' (P-N)	Impersonal 'established' (I-E)	Impersonal 'new' (I-N)
Type of site	Suggests that company is well established	Includes bland text about the company	Suggests that company is well established	Includes bland text about the company
	Site offers a personalised quote based on participants' circumstances	Site offers a personalised quote based on participants' circumstances	No personalisation	No personalisation
Consumer input phase	All four sites request information, both personal (e.g. questions about health problems), and less personal (e.g. questions about requirements for car insurance) . A few key questions are compulsory, including three 'key' questions concerning (i) use of a money belt (ii) a pre-planned itinerary and (iii) use of travellers' cheques, which then branch to different pages.			
Company response phase	Answers to three 'key' questions branch onto one of eight personalised responses.		Bland responses are provided which are impersonal with respect to 'key questions'	
Consumer decision phase	All participants are free to browse three suggested policies: 'highly recommended'; 'recommended' and 'alternative'. Participants exit the site by choosing one of three options: 'buy', 'reserve without commitment' and 'exit'.			
Site evaluation phase	All participants go on to answer a questionnaire about the site they've just visited. This is a slightly modified version of the internet questionnaire described by Briggs et al. (2002).			

2.2 Results and Discussion

There were several dependent measures, as follows:
1. A measure of disclosure in terms of the number of voluntary information fields omitted. Measures were also taken of preparedness to respond 'yes' to risky behaviours, although naturally this last measure was somewhat dependent upon individual differences.

2. A measure of 'preparedness to take advice'. This was derived from the participants' willingness to consult the 'highly recommended' site above the others.
3. A measure of commitment to the product. This measure simply reflected participants' selection of one of the three final options: 'buy' 'reserve without commitment' or 'exit'.
4. A measure of participants' attitudes to the site in the form of a 32 item questionnaire, which included manipulation checks as well as questions about trust.

All personal identity data was automatically deleted, but participants' responses to all other fields were automatically logged, along with a record of their browsing behaviour prior to making their final selection of buy, reserve without commitment, or exit. Data from the follow-up questionnaires were also logged automatically.

The first point to note was there were no significant behavioural differences across sites in terms of self-disclosure, preparedness to take advice and commitment to the product. All of the measures suggested very high compliance. Thus, for information disclosure, only 2 people who viewed a personalised site and only 3 who viewed an impersonal site withheld any information at all. Participants were also very willing to reveal problems. Table 2 below gives the percentage of 'yes' responses to the three most sensitive questions asked of participants. It is not possible to draw any conclusions about the extent to which these revelations are a function of site manipulation or simply a function of the participant population allocated to a particular site – but it is interesting to note the number of individuals prepared to admit to problems.

It is certainly possible that these high disclosure reflect a general society trend towards an increasingly relaxed attitude to the disclosure of personal information. Recently, for example, a Harris Poll report of 1,010 U.S. adults (Taylor, 2003) noted a marked drop in the number of people who were unconcerned about privacy issues. Some 74% of people were willing to allow people to have access to, and to use, their personal information with the proviso that they should understand the reasons for its use, see tangible benefits for sharing the information and believe that care is taken to prevent the misuse of the information. With these figures as a baseline, the disclosure behaviours observed in the present study seem less extreme.

Table 2. *Percentage of 'yes' responses given to key personal questions.*

Question	P-E	P-N	I-E	I-N
Has the person to be insured any physical or mental defect or infirmity?	7%	10%	0%	4%
Have you ever been refused holiday insurance?	15%	17%	7%	4%
Has any insurer … ever terminated an insurance policy?	0%	0%	11%	0%

With regard to subsequent behaviours 85% of participants in the 'personalised', and 82.5% of those in the 'impersonal' condition viewed the 'highly recommended' options first. Once again it is difficult to know whether this degree of compliance is tied to the experimental nature of this study (where participants are completing the online form in a laboratory setting) or whether it reflects a wider compliance in the real world. In any case, while the degree of compliance observed here is interesting the data did not provide any useful evidence concerning differences between groups.

The follow-up questionnaire, however, generated some interesting differences in the subjective evaluation of the four sites. For 22 (of the original 32) questions, scores were given on a seven point Likert scale. Means for these questions are given in Table 3, along with any significant effects derived from 2x2 analyses of variance (ANOVA) conducted on the data for each of the questions.

Table 3. *Mean responses to twenty-two scale items on the follow up questionnaire*

Question (1=disagree totally 7=agree totally)	P-E	P-N	I-E	I-N	ANOVA
The advice appeared to be prepared by an expert	5.21	4.65	4.87	5.00	n.s.
The advice came from a knowledgeable source	5.29	4.83	4.82	4.82	n.s.
There were comments from other users on the site	2.29	2.48	2.86	2.65	n.s.
The site was owned by a known and respected company	4.00	3.50	3.91	3.71	n.s.
I had to wait a long time for the advice	1.83	2.17	2.41	2.53	n.s.
Different travel insurance options or courses of action were suggested	6.04	5.17	3.86	5.29	Pers ** E x P **
The site was hard to use	1.82	2.09	2.59	2.71	Pers *
I didn't feel involved in the way the site tried to find appropriate advice.	2.92	3.17	3.82	3.88	Pers *
The site was interactive	4.75	4.78	4.82	4.35	n.s.
The advice was tailored to me	4.65	4.09	4.09	4.41	n.s.
The reasoning was explained to me	3.68	3.57	4.18	3.0	Est **
The site offered the opportunity to contact a person	3.17	3.35	2.91	2.65	n.s.
The advice appeared to be impartial and independent	4.21	4.48	4.00	3.82	n.s.
I was offered good advice	4.71	4.70	4.45	4.29	n.s.
The way the site went through the process of giving advice was predictable	4.83	5.05	4.32	4.29	Pers *
The site wasn't really useful in helping me make the right decision	3.33	3.61	3.50	4.18	n.s.
I trusted the advice	4.21	3.83	3.82	3.24	n.s.
The company isn't very well established	4.37	4.78	4.45	5.06	Est **

Responses to the questionnaire indicated relatively positive feelings about the site. Thus for example, people tended to agree with statements such as 'the advice appeared to be prepared by an expert'; 'the advice came from a knowledgeable source'; 'I was offered good advice' and disagree with statements such as 'I had to wait a long time for the insurance advice' and 'the site was hard to use'. It was also the case that the most positive responses were given by participants in the 'established-personalised' site as one might predict.

With specific regard to the with the personalisation manipulation, participants in the 'personalised' conditions were significantly less likely to disagree with the statement 'I didn't feel involved in the way the site tried to find appropriate advice'. This makes sense given the nature of the manipulation – and shows that they took account of the fact that personal questions were asked of them. However they didn't feel that the resulting advice was tailored to them any more than individuals in the impersonal conditions, and so here we see that the promise of personalisation has a relatively small impact.

It may be an important impact, however, since those in the personalised condition did generally feel more positive about the site. They felt, for example, that they had been offered more choice, that the site was more predictable and that it was easier to use. These are important issues that we know feed into trust judgments, and yet there were no real differences between the sites. So what is it about the promise of personalisation that gives people a more positive impression? Regarding the option choices, it may simply be that phrasing the various options in terms that reflected participants' inputs somehow made them more salient. In effect this was a cheat – but it is an interesting cheat and one with significant effects on users' judgements of the quality of the site. The idea that participants pay more attention to choices when they seem to incorporate information that they themselves have provided is one that is worth exploring in more detail.

Finally, it is worth mentioning that the model of trust which was generated from over 2,500 participants in our online study was supported by this offline sample of 107 participants and so this data can also be taken as part-validation of the Briggs et al. (2002) three-component model of trust incorporating *source credibility, predictability* and *personalisation*. Why do we consider these components (and the associated questionnaire) more appropriate than, say, Bhattacherjee's (2002) trust scale based on the concepts of ability, integrity and benevolence? In part because our interest has been explicitly on the judgements people make of a web-site rather than the beliefs they bring to an interaction. In addition we sought to demystify trust by breaking it down into judgments based on observable qualities. Benevolence defies this – indeed it is a construct as elusive as trust, which means that there is some danger of circularity.

We should also question whether the methodology described above is the most appropriate one with which to address questions of trust. As stated earlier, this investigation was designed to compliment two other studies – one a qualitative investigation and the other a large-scale questionnaire-based survey (reported in Briggs et al., 2002). All three studies addressed actual examples of trusting behaviour, rather than simply exploring trusting intentions, but the current study was the only one to follow a simulated e-commerce transaction. The question remains as to whether the simulation developed here was sufficiently convincing. Other studies have asked similar research questions but using scenario-based methods in which users try to imagine the extent to which they would disclose information in a particular setting. In a study by Olivero (2001) for example, participants were presented with a description of an online drug store and asked whether they would be prepared to disclose certain types of personal information. Such methods are useful, but have their own limitations with regard to the extent to which planned and actual behaviours converge. The simulations described here overcome such difficulties, but future studies should probably include post-hoc interviews, which assess the extent to which users believe the sites to be real.

3. FUTURE DEVELOPMENTS

A staged model of the development of trust in e-commerce has been proposed, wherein personalisation practices are seen as important for the development of a longer-term relationship between the customer and the online vendor. It has also been suggested (on the basis of work by Basso et al. and our study above) that the promise of personalised communication might exert some limited influence on trust judgments made during the early stages of e-commerce interaction. There remains one other issue to discuss, relevant to question posed at the start of the chapter – i.e. the question of whether or not a personalised e-commerce service can generate trust. This remaining issue concerns reputation.

A number of studies have acknowledged that reputation can play a role early on in the process of trust development. In other words, a recommendation from a friend, or a well-known reputation or brand can influence a new customer and can lead to that all-important first purchase. Briggs et al. (2002) found that peer commentary on a site was linked to trust in online advice. Yet very few studies of trust in e-commerce have explored trust development in the kinds of e-commerce, which are supported by online reputation systems.

Reputation systems are very effectively utilised in online marketplaces and electronic auction sites like eBay. These provide a form of e-commerce in which transactions are made, not between a customer and a business, but between individual members of the collective (both buyers and sellers). eBay is the Internet's most successful online auction house, and is ranked as one of the most successful online businesses to date, but in eBay neither the vendor nor the customer know each other, and customers are given only brief descriptions of items submitted by unknown parties. Boyd (2002) attributes the remarkable success of eBay to the build up of a kind of community trust based in part upon the fact that individuals are not anonymous, but have unique identities and can therefore be given feedback ratings from other users. The resulting reputation system works effectively and new users visiting the site are able to take the comparatively 'low risk' first step of trusting a vendor with a known reputation.

It makes sense to think about the ways in which reputation can be tapped more explicitly in e-commerce environments, and yet with the exception of the Boyd study, we know of no explicit investigations of consumer trust development as a function of reputation or recommender systems (note however there is a large literature on trust in agent exchanges). There is a huge research agenda here. For example, are the systems themselves trusted? Some expects have shown that they are relatively easily manipulated and not entirely safe (e.g. Xiong and Liu, 2003; Zacharia et al., 2000) but the attitudes of users are less clear. There are also huge questions about the role of social identity in reputation and recommender systems. For example, it is likely that the algorithms supporting collaborative filtering could draw like-minded people together to build trust rapidly in the early stages of an e-commerce relationship. Certainly we know that such methods can help to build sales, but their explicit role in trust development is uncertain.

The literature on trust in e-commerce is young and probably raises more questions than answers at the moment. It is also a literature based on relatively thin empirical evidence (since, as we've argued, so few studies have explored the development of real customer relationships). It is likely that we will learn much more about the relationship between trust and personalisation over the next few years and there are certainly a number of interesting issues to explore.

What about recommendations regarding future e-commerce systems? As far as we can judge – from our own studies and the state of the research literature at the moment – a trusted website clearly requires the following: Firstly, some assurance of competence on the part of the company and an indication that those providing information have the requisite expertise and professional standing. This can be signalled both by design and content. Secondly, predictability. It should be consistent with other sites in the same domain or should borrow from off-line practices – to the extent that the user feels he or she is in familiar territory and feels that the steps in a transaction are relatively predictable. Essentially there should be no major surprises. Thirdly, a non-threatening invitation to the user to offer-up personal information. This should be accompanied by an explanation of why the information is required and of how it is to be used. It should not necessarily take the form of a privacy policy – since not all users will understand the importance of this (although such a policy should be available). These assurances should rather be incorporated naturally into the transaction, and crucially – they must be worthwhile for the user – i.e. they must have some utility. This last statement might seem surprising in the light of our findings with regard to 'cheats' – but trust is not solely about one transaction, the key issue for trust in the longer-term is that organisations deliver on their promises.

4. ACKNOWLEDGEMENTS

The original research described in this chapter was funded by the former NCR KnowledgeLab, London.

5. REFERENCES

Basso, A., Goldberg, D., Greenspan, S. and Weimer, D. (2001). First impressions: emotional and cognitive factors underlying judgments of trust in e-commerce. *Proceedings of the 3rd ACM conference on Electronic Commerce.* New York: ACM Press.

Bhattacherjee, A. (2002). Individual Trust in Online Firms: Scale Development and Initial Test. *Journal of management Information Systems, 19* (1), 211-241.

Bollier, D. (1996). *The Future of E-Commerce.* The Brookings Institution.

Boyd, J. (2002). In community we trust: Online security communication at eBay. Journal of Computer-Mediated Communication, 7 (3). Retrieved January 15, 2004, from: http://www.ascusc.org/jcmc/vol7/issue3/boyd.html.

Brien, A (1998) Professional ethics and the culture of trust *Journal of Business Ethics,* 17, 391-409

Briggs, P., Burford, B., De Angeli, A. & Lynch, P. (2002). Trust in Online Advice, *Social Science Computer Review, 20,* 3, 321-332.

Chaiken, S. (1980) Heuristic versus systematic information processing and the use of source versus message cues in persuasion. *Journal of Personality And Social Psychology,* 39, 752-766.

Cheskin Research and Studio Archetype/Sapient (1999). Ecommerce trust study. Retrieved July 16, 2003, from: http://www.cheskin.com/p/ar.asp?mlid=7&arid=40&art=0&isu=1

Corritore, C.L., Kracher, B. and Wiedenbeck, S. (2003). On-line trust: concepts, evolving themes, a model. *International Journal of Human-Computer Studies, 58,* 737-758.

Egger, F.N. (2000). "Trust Me, I'm an Online Vendor": Towards a Model of Trust for E-Commerce System Design. in: G. Szwillus & T. Turner (Eds.): CHI2000 *Extended Abstracts: Conference on Human Factors in Computing Systems,* The Hague (NL), April 1-6, 2000: 101-102, ACM Press.

Egger, F.N. (2001). Affective Design of E-Commerce User Interfaces: How to Maximise Perceived Trustworthiness. In: Helander, M., Khalid, H.M. & Tham (Eds.), *Proceedings of CAHD2001: Conference on Affective Human Factors Design,* Singapore, June 27-29, 2001: 317-324.

Fogg, B. J., Marshall, J., Laraki, O., Osipovish, A., Varma, C.,Fang, N., Paul, J., Rangnekar, A., Shon, J., Swani, P. & Treinen, M. (2001). What Makes Web Sites Credible? A Report on a Large Quantitative Study, *Proceedings of CHI 2001, March 31- April 4, Seattle* New York: ACM Press.

Fogg, B. J., Kameda, T., Boyd, J., Marchall, J., Sethi, R., Sockol, M. and Trowbridge, T. (2002). *Stanford-Makovsky Web Credibiltiy Study 2002: Investigating what makes Web sites credible today,* A Research Report by the Stanford Persuasive Technology Lab & Makovsky & Company, Stanford. University. Retrieved July 15, 2003, from: http://www.webcredibility.org

Gambetta, D. (1988) Can we trust trust? In I.D. Gambetta (Ed.) *Trust: Making And Breaking Cooperative Relations.* Oxford: Basil Blackwell.

Grabner-Krauter, S. and Kaluscha, E.A. (2003). Empirical research in online-trust: a review and critical assessment. *International Journal of Human-Computer Studies,* 58, 783-812.

Lee, M.K.O., and Turban, E. (2001). A trust model for consumer Internet shopping. *International Journal of Electronic Commerce,* 6 (1), 75-91.

Lee, J., Kim, J. & Moon, J.Y. (2000). What makes Internet users visit cyber stores again? Key design factors for customer loyalty. *Proceedings of the Conference on Human Factors in Computing Systems* CHI 2000 (pp. 305-312). New York ACM.

Lee, J. & Moray, N (1992) Trust, control strategies and allocation of function in human-machine systems, *Ergonomics, 35* (10), 1243-1270.

Lee, J. & Moray, N (1994) Trust, self-confidence, and operators' adaptation to automation *International Journal of Human-Computer Studies, 40,* 153-184.

Lewicki, R.J. and Bunker, B. (1995). Trust in relationships: A model of trust development and decline. In B. Bunker and J. Rubin, (Eds.) *Conflict, Cooperation and Justice.* San Francisco: Jossey-Bass.

Mayer, R.C., Davis, J.H., Schoorman, F.D. (1995). An integrative model of organizational trust. *Academy of Management Review, 20* (3), 709-734.

Meyerson, D., Weick, K.E., Kramer, R.M. (1996). Swift trust and temporary groups. In R.M. Kramer and T.R. Tyler (Eds) *Trust in Organizations: Frontiers of Theory and Research.* Thousand Oaks, CA: Sage Publications, 166-195.

McAllister, D.J. (1995) Affect-Based And Cognition-Based Trust As Foundations For Interpersonal Cooperation In Organizations *Academy Of Management Journal 38* (1); 24-59.

McKnight, D. H. and Chervany, N.L. (2001). Trust and Distrust Definitions: One Bite at a Time. In R. Falcone, M. Singh and Y.-H. Tan (Eds.) *Trust in Cyber-societies.* Berlin: Springer-Verlag.

Olivero, N. (2001). *Privacy negotiation and self-disclosure in e-commerce exchanges*. Paper presented at the conference *Psychology and the Internet: A European Perspective*, Farnborough, UK.

Riegelsberger, J., Sasse, M. A., & McCarthy, J. (2003). Shiny happy people building trust? Photos on e-commerce websites and consumer trust. *Proceedings of CHI2003*, April 5-10, Ft. Lauderdale, Fl., USA. New York: ACM Press.

Rotter, J. (1967). A new scale for the measurement of interpersonal trust. *Journal of Personality, 35* (4), 651-665.

Shelat, B. and Egger, F.N. (2002). What makes people trust online gambling sites? An empirical study to identify on- and offline factors that influence gamblers' perception of an online casino's trustworthiness. *Proceedings of CHI 2002*. New York: ACM Press.

Steinbrück,U., Schaumburg, H., Duda, S. & Krüger, T. (2002). A picture says more than a thousand words - photographs as trust builders in e-commerce websites. In *Proceedings of Conference on Human Factors in Computing Systems CHI 2002*, Extended Abstracts (pp. 748-749). New York ACM Press.

Taylor, H. (2003). Most People Are "Privacy Pragmatists" Who, While Concerned about Privacy, Will Sometimes Trade It Off for Other Benefits. The Harris Poll #17, March 19, 2003. Retrieved January 15, 2004, from: http://www.harrisinteractive.com/harris_poll/index.asp?PID=365

Weinstein, L. (2003). Inside risks: Spam wars. *Communications of the ACM 46* (8), pg 136.

Xiong, L. and Liu, L. (2003). A reputation-based trust model for peer-to-peer ecommerce communities. Proceedings of the conference on Electronic Commerce. New York: ACM Press.

Zacharia, G, Moukas, A. and Maes, P. (2000). Collaborative reputation mechanisms for electronic marketplaces. Decision Support Systems, 29, 371-388.

LORRIE FAITH CRANOR

'I DIDN'T BUY IT FOR MYSELF'

Privacy and Ecommerce Personalization[*]

1. INTRODUCTION

Ecommerce web sites are increasingly introducing personalized features in order to build and retain relationships with customers and increase the number of purchases made by each customer. While survey data, (Personalization Consortium, 2000; Personalization Consortium, 2001), user studies (Karat, *et al*, 2003), and experience (Manber, 2000) indicate that many individuals appreciate personalization and find it useful, personalization also raises a number of privacy concerns ranging from user discomfort with a computer inferring information about them based on their purchases to concerns about co-workers, identity thieves, or the government gaining access to personalization profiles. In some cases users will provide personal data to web sites in order to receive a personalized service, despite their privacy concerns; in other cases users may turn away from a site because of privacy concerns (Ackerman, *et al.,* 1999; Culnan and Milne, 2001; Cyber Dialogue, 2001, Berk, 2003). As recent studies have suggested that the benefits to a web site of offering personalized services often do not outweigh the costs (Berk, 2003), it is important to consider ways of designing personalization systems that will maximize the return on the investment. Improving the privacy associated with these systems so that web site visitors are more willing to trust and use them is a step in that direction.

This chapter begins with a discussion of the privacy risks associated with personalization. It then provides an overview of the fair information practice principles and discusses how they may be applied to the design of personalization systems, and introduces privacy laws and self-regulatory guidelines relevant to personalization. Finally, the chapter describes a number of approaches to personalization system design that can reduce privacy risks.

2. PRIVACY RISKS

Ecommerce personalization poses a variety of risks to user privacy. Most of these risks stem from the fact that personalization systems often require that more

---

[*] This chapter is a revised version of a paper presented at the 2003 ACM Workshop on Privacy in the Electronic Society (WPES).

Clare-Marie Karat et al. (eds.), Designing Personalized User Experiences in eCommerce, 57—73.

personal data be collected, processed, and stored than would otherwise be necessary. This section provides an overview of several privacy risks that may be caused or exacerbated by ecommerce personalization systems. These risks are summarized in Table 1.

Table *1. Privacy risks from ecommerce personalization*

Risk	Examples of possible consequences	Examples of parties to whom personal information might be exposed
Unsolicited marketing	Unwanted email, postal mail, and telephone calls; time wasted deleting email, throwing away mail, answering calls	Employees of personalized web site; employees of companies to whom marketing lists are sold; employees of companies that perform marketing services
Computer "figuring things out" about me	Individuals feel uncomfortable or embarrassed; characteristics inferred by computer become available to people who would otherwise not know this information; inaccurate information inferred by computer becomes available to people who believe it to be accurate	Employees of personalized web site; any other parties that gain access to profile
Price discrimination	Individuals are treated differently based on profile; higher prices	Employees of personalized web site
Information revealed to other users of same computer	Other users of computer may learn confidential information; other users of computer may be able to gain access to accounts	Other users of computer such as family members or co-workers
Unauthorized access to accounts	Identity theft, fraud, stalking	People that run personalized web site, someone who steals password
Subpoena	Information used against individual in court case	Law enforcement officers or participants in legal dispute; public (if information obtained becomes part of public record)
Government surveillance	Individual could be detained by law enforcement for questioning or arrested	Law enforcement officers

One of the first privacy risks that Internet users mention is unsolicited marketing (Cranor, *et al.*, 2003). Arguably, the consequences of unsolicited marketing are less severe than the potential consequences of some of the other privacy risks discussed here. Nonetheless, this risk is of great concern to users, and a strong desire not to receive unwanted marketing communications may be a factor in some users' decisions not to engage in ecommerce (Culnan and Milne, 2001; Cyber Dialogue, 2001). Users have concerns that information they provide for use in personalized ecommerce may be used to send them targeted advertising, or may be sold to other companies that may advertise to them. They often fear that the more a company knows about them, the greater the interest that company will have in marketing to them.

Many users are also concerned about a computer "figuring things out" about them. They are not comfortable with the idea that a computer might be able to make predictions about their habits and interests. In some cases, individuals are frustrated because the computer's predictions appear to be off base and they are afraid that someone might find out and draw incorrect conclusions as a result. In other cases, individuals are concerned because the computer's predictions are uncannily accurate, and perhaps reveal information that they thought other people didn't know about them. Some users of the TiVo digital video recorder have been surprised at the television selections their TiVo makes for them based on their TV viewing history, and some even believe their TiVo has made inferences about such personal characteristics as their sexual preference (Zaslow, 2002). Regardless of the accuracy of a computer's inferences and prediction, many individuals are simply uncomfortable with the idea that their activities are being "watched." Additional concerns arise when there is a mismatch between users' perceptions about privacy and the types of data collection and use that actually occur (Adams, 1999).

Individuals are also concerned that companies will profile them in order to facilitate price discrimination. While economists point out that price discrimination can often benefit both businesses and consumers, consumer reaction to price discrimination is usually quite negative. In addition, effective price discrimination often leads to increases in the amount of personal information associated with a transaction (Odlyzko, 2003). Individuals may be concerned not only about the possibility of being charged higher prices because of information in their profile, but also about the fact that they are being treated differently than other people (Turow, 2003).

Another privacy risk associated with personalization is that users may inadvertently reveal personal information to other users of their computer. When cookies are used for authentication or access to a user's profile, anyone who uses a particular computer may have access to the information in a user's profile. This leads to concerns such as family members learning about gifts that may have been ordered for them and co-workers learning about an individual's health or personal issues. In addition, when profiles contain passwords or "secret" information that is used for authentication at other sites, someone who gains access to a user's profile on one site may be able to subsequently gain unauthorized access to a user's other accounts, both online and offline.

The possibility that someone who does not share the user's computer may gain unauthorized access to a user's account on a personalized web site (by guessing or stealing a password, or because they work for an ecommerce company, for example) raises similar concerns. However, while family members and co-workers may gain access inadvertently or due to curiosity, other people may have motives that are far more sinister. Stalkers and identity thieves, for example, may find profile information immensely useful. Ramakrishnan *et al.* (2001) have also suggested ways that users may be able to probe recommender systems to learn profile information associated with other users.

A risk that most people don't consider is that the information in their profile may be subpoenaed in a criminal case or in civil litigation. For example, increasingly Internet records are subpoenaed in patent disputes, child custody cases, and a wide variety of lawsuits. Information about what someone has purchased, eaten, read, or posted is proving important to many cases. In addition, other types of profile information that may reveal interests, habits, or personal preferences may be important, especially in cases where the character of the plaintiff or defendant is important. Much of this information may be logged by ecommerce systems that store transaction records, even if they offer no personalization. However, a personalized system will typically store information that goes beyond transaction records, and may potentially store the information for a longer period of time than would be necessary if it were used only to support a transaction.

Finally, as the United States and other governments have been initiating increasing numbers of surveillance programs in the name of fighting terrorism, the possibility that information stored for use in ecommerce personalization may find its way into a government surveillance application is becoming increasingly real. This places users of these services at increased risk of being subject to government investigation, even if they have done nothing wrong.

As new personalization applications are developed that take advantage of a wider range of information (such as information in a user's calendar or address book), or are designed to run on mobile devices and take advantage of information about a user's precise physical location (Gandon and Sadeh, 2003; Warrior, *et al.*, 2003), additional privacy concerns are likely to emerge. The privacy risks discussed here are all likely to become magnified in these new environments.

3. APPLYING FAIR INFORMATION PRACTICE PRINCIPLES

Several sets of principles have been developed over the past three decades for protecting privacy when using personal information. The Organization for Economic Co-operation and Development (OECD) Guidelines on the Protection of Privacy and Transborder Data Flows of Personal Data (1980) are one of the best-known sets of fair information practice principles. Many other sets of guidelines and some privacy laws are based on these principles.

The eight OECD principles provide a useful framework for analyzing privacy issues related to ecommerce personalization. The principles are paraphrased here and discussed in the context of ecommerce personalization. In these principles, the term *data subject* refers to the person about whom data has been collected, and the term *data controller* refers to the entity that controls the collection, storage, and use of personal data.

Collection Limitation. Data collection and usage should be limited. In the context of ecommerce personalization, this suggests that personalization systems should collect only the data that they need, and not every possible piece of data that they might find a need for in the future. The approaches described in Sections 5.2 and 5.3 can also serve to limit data collection.

Data Quality. Data should be used only for purposes for which it is relevant, and it should be accurate, complete, and kept up-to-date. In the context of ecommerce personalization, this suggests both that care be taken to make sure data is used for relevant purposes (that is, don't use data to make inferences that are irrelevant to the data), and personalization systems should provide the ability for individuals to update and correct the information in their profiles.

Purpose Specification. Data controllers should specify up front how they are going to use data, and then they should use that data only for the specified purposes. In the context of ecommerce personalization, this suggests that users be notified up front when a system is collecting data to be used for personalization (or any other purpose). Privacy policies are often used to explain how web sites will use the data they collect. However, by also providing notice about data use at the time the data is collected, sites can more effectively bring this information to the attention of users at the time when it is most relevant. Software tools such as P3P-enabled web browsers may also assist in conveying meaningful privacy notices to users (Cranor, 2002).

Use Limitation. Data should not be used or disclosed for purposes other than those disclosed under the purpose specification principle, except with the consent of the data subject or as required by law. In the context of ecommerce personalization, this suggests that data collected by personalization systems should not be used for other purposes without user consent. This also suggests that sites that want to make other uses of this data develop interfaces for requesting user consent.

Security Safeguards. Data should be protected with reasonable security safeguards. In the context of ecommerce personalization, this suggests that security safeguards be applied to stored personalization profiles and that personalization information should be transmitted through secure channels.

Openness. Data collection and usage practices should not be a secret. In the context of ecommerce personalization, this suggests, as with the Purpose Specification Principle, that users be notified up front when a system is collecting data to be used for personalization. Users should be given information about the type of data being collected, how it will be used, and who is collecting it. It is especially important that users be made aware of implicit data collection.

Individual Participation. Individuals should have the right to obtain their data from a data controller and to have incorrect data erased or amended. In the context of ecommerce personalization, this suggests, as with the Data Quality principle, that users be given access to their profiles and the ability to correct them and remove information from them.

Accountability. Data controllers are responsible for complying with these principles. In the context of ecommerce personalization this suggests that personalization system implementers and site operators should be proactive about developing policies, procedures, and software that will support compliance with these principles.

Table 2 provides a summary of the OECD principles and how they can be applied to ecommerce personalization. The lessons for ecommerce personalization derived from each principle can be expanded further in the context of a specific application. For example, Patrick and Kenny (2003) have performed a similar analysis and made detailed user interface design recommendations for an Internet job search tool.

Table *2. OECD privacy principles and their lessons for ecommerce personalization*

Principle	Lessons for ecommerce personalization
Collection limitation	Collect only the data you need
Data quality	Don't use data to make inferences irrelevant to the data; provide mechanisms for individuals to update and correct information in their profiles
Purpose specification	Tell users when data is used for personalization
Use limitation	Don't use personalization data for other purposes without user consent
Security safeguards	Take reasonable security precautions with stored personalization profiles and transmit personalization information through secure channels
Openness	Tell users when data is being collected for personalization and make sure they are aware of implicit data collection
Individual participation	Provide mechanisms for individuals to update and correct information in their profiles
Accountability	Be proactive about developing policies, procedures, and software that will support compliance with these principles

4. PRIVACY LAWS AND SELF-REGULATORY GUIDELINES

Privacy laws and self-regulatory guidelines can influence the types of personalization systems that can be deployed in practice. Here is an overview of some of the ways laws and guidelines may impact ecommerce personalization systems. It is by no means a comprehensive review of privacy laws or guidelines.

In the United States, most privacy laws are sector-specific. In many sectors, no privacy laws restrict personalization systems on ecommerce web sites. However, financial sites, children's sites, and health-related sites may need to design their personalization systems carefully to comply with legal requirements. For the most part this involves providing adequate notice about the personalization system. In some sectors, there are restrictions on third party sharing of data that may be relevant. Children's web sites are prohibited from collecting personally identifiable information from children under age 13 without consent of a parent. In addition, US sites need to be aware of any state laws that may impact them as well as the privacy laws in other countries where some of their customers may reside.

US companies that provide targeted advertising services to multiple web sites and are members of the Network Advertising Initiative (NAI) must comply with the NAI Principles (2000), which are enforceable by the US Federal Trade Commission. These principles prohibit use of sensitive data in targeted marketing and require that merger of personally identifiable information with previously collected non-personally-identifiable information occur on an opt-in basis only. They also require companies to provide adequate notice, allow individuals to access their information, and offer opt-out opportunities.

A number of other industry organizations such as the Online Privacy Alliance, the Direct Marketing Association, and the Personalization Consortium have adopted self-regulatory guidelines that may be applicable to their members' ecommerce personalization efforts.

In Europe, comprehensive privacy laws impact the design of ecommerce personalization systems across every sector. These laws, which are based on the OECD principles, require privacy notices and access provisions and restrict secondary uses and third-party data sharing. Kobsa (2002) analyzed the European Data Protection Directive and the German Teleservices Data Protection Act and found a number of restrictions that would affect ecommerce personalization on sites under the jurisdiction of German law. For example, raw data from usage logs must be deleted after each session and usage logs from different services must not be combined, except for accounting purposes. In addition, anonymous and pseudonymous services must be provided when possible, and user profiles must always be pseudonymous. These laws also restrict the ability of sites to fully automate decisions that would have significant impacts on individuals (for example, related to employment, credit, etc.).

5.   REDUCING PRIVACY RISKS IN ECOMMERCE PERSONALIZATION

The previous sections have identified privacy risks and outlined privacy-related legal requirements, guidelines, and principles that are relevant to ecommerce personalization. This section discusses several approaches to system designs that reduce privacy risks and make privacy compliance easier. No single approach to ecommerce personalization will always provide the desired functionality while protecting privacy. There are tradeoffs associated with each of these approaches.

The degree of privacy risk posed by an ecommerce personalization system is often directly related to the type of personalization the system performs. Section 5.1 describes four axes of personalization and discusses where on each axes the more privacy-friendly personalization systems tend to fall.   Sometimes other system requirements prohibit a design that falls on the privacy-friendly end of each of these axes, however.   In this case designers may need to take steps to add privacy enhancements to a system design, using the fair information practice principles as a guide. For example, the collection limitation principle suggests system designs that minimize the amount of personally identifiable data stored by the ecommerce web site. This in turn reduces the risk that data may be misused by the company or its employees, limits exposure in the event of a security breach, and minimizes the amount of data that might be subject to subpoena. Section 5.2 and 5.3 discuss two approaches to data minimization that may be useful for designers of ecommerce web sites: pseudonymous profiles and client-side profiles. Section 5.4 discusses the importance of designing systems that put users in control, addressing the data quality and individual participation principles and supporting the ability to request consent from users in compliance with the use limitation principle. Of course, to be effective, all of these approaches need to be augmented by appropriate security safe guards and well-articulated privacy policies that are enforced throughout an enterprise.

5.1 Types of personalization systems

Several general types of personalization systems are considered here that differ on four axes, as illustrated by Figure 1. In this chapter the two extreme ends of each axis are discussed. However, many personalization systems include components representative of both ends and thus fall somewhere in the middle of the spectrum. The ends of each axis are labelled in the table according to whether they tend to be more or less privacy invasive. I have used the word "tend" here because there are exceptions. In general it is relatively easy to design a privacy-friendly personalization system if it is placed on the end of each of the four axes where systems tend to be less privacy invasive. Designing a privacy-friendly personalization system that sits on the other end of these axes is possible, but requires that mechanisms be put in place to reduce privacy risks and concerns.

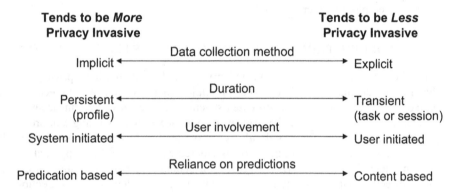

Figure *1. Four axes of personalization systems and their impacts on privacy*

5.1.1 Data collection method
- *Explicit data collection.* Personalization is based on demographics, preferences, ratings, or other information explicitly provided by a user. Typically, *recommender* personalization systems require users to rate a number of items in order to receive recommendations about other items that may interest them. Other systems allow users to create personal pages or customize their view of a site based on their personal preferences or demographics.
- *Implicit data collection.* Personalization is based on information inferred about a user. For example, a user's search queries, purchase history, or browsing history may be used to infer interests or preferences (Claypool, *et al.,* 2001).

Systems that use explicit data collection methods tend to be more privacy-friendly than systems that use implicit data collection methods because users are more aware that data collection is taking place and may be able to make a conscious decision about whether or not to provide their data. When data is collected implicitly, systems can be made more privacy-friendly through the use of easy-to-understand notices and opportunities to control what information about themselves gets collected and stored. This is discussed further in Section 5.4.

5.1.2 Duration

− *Task- or session-focused personalization.* A simplistic way of providing task-focused personalization is to place advertisements on pages where they are most obviously relevant—for example, advertising pay-per-view boxing matches in the sports section of a news site and cookware in the home and garden section. A more sophisticated way of providing task-focused personalization is to make suggestions based on actions a user has taken while performing a task (Herlocker and Konstan, 2001). For example, if a user places a pair of women's running shoes in her shopping basket, a web site might suggest that she also purchase athletic socks, running shorts, or a sports bra. Such personalization is based on information provided by or inferred from the user during the current session or while completing the current task.

− *Persistent profile-based personalization.* Many personalization systems develop profiles of users and add explicitly provided or inferred information about users each time they return to the site. Cookies may be used to recognize returning visitors automatically and retrieve their stored profiles, or users may be asked to login to the site.

A focus on task- or session-based personalization reduces privacy concerns and facilitates compliance with privacy laws because little or no user profile data need be stored in order to facilitate personalization (Herlocker and Konstan, 2001). A session cookie might be used to store some information temporarily, but that information can be deleted at the end of the user's session.

Depending on the goals of personalization, task-based personalization may be able to provide many of the benefits of profile-based personalization. It may be sufficient to know only the kind of task in which the user is currently engaged rather than information about her preferences or past activities. Focusing on a user's current task may allow for a simpler system architecture that need not facilitate the storage and retrieval of user profile data. In addition, it eliminates the problems that may occur when a system offers recommendations to a user that are consistent with her overall profile but not relevant to her current task. For example, when a user is shopping for a gift for someone else, recommendations based on her personal preferences may not be relevant. Likewise, once a user completes a particular task, she may no longer be interested in receiving recommendations related to that task. For example, while a user may be interested in advertisements from car dealers while she is shopping for a new car, once she has completed the purchase these advertisements will no longer be relevant to her.

Personalization derived directly from a user's request rather than from predictions based on that request allows for less data to be stored and fewer privacy concerns. A system that simply reports the availability of other products in the same category of products a user has expressed interest in, for example, is unlikely to raise the kinds of concerns about a computer knowing a user too well that are often raised by recommender systems.

The simplest kind of task-based personalization—simply promoting like products together—does not require the development of a personalization "system" and may not even be considered personalization. For some applications, this approach is often more cost effective than developing a system that attempts to infer user preferences (Berk, 2003).

5.1.3 User involvement

- *User-initiated personalization.* Some sites offer users the option of selecting customizations such as stock tickers that display stocks of interest, weather forecasts for the user's region, or news related to topics the user has selected. Users might also select their preferred page layout or the number of items they want to see displayed, or they might provide information about their display and bandwidth constraints and ask to have a site optimized accordingly.
- *System-initiated* personalization. Some sites attempt to personalize content for every user, even if users do not request customized features and take no explicit actions to request personalization. In some cases, sites provide a way for users to opt-out of personalization.

User-initiated personalization tends to be more privacy-friendly than system-initiated personalization because users are more aware that personalization is taking place and can make a conscious decision about whether or not to activate it. System-initiated personalization can be made more privacy friendly through the use of notices and opportunities to disable the personalization.

5.1.4 Reliance on predictions

- *Prediction-based personalization.* Some sites use user's explicit or inferred ratings to build user profiles that can be compared with the profiles of other users. When users with similar profiles are discovered, the system predicts that they will have similar preferences and offers recommendations to one user based on the stated preferences of the others. Such systems are often referred to as *recommender* systems or *collaborative filtering* systems. Thus, for example, if Jane and Sue provide similar ratings for 10 books, a recommender system might suggest to Jane two other books that she didn't rate at all but had been rated highly by Sue. The suggested books may not necessarily be on the same topics as any of the books Jane rated herself.
- *Content-based personalization.* Some sites use the specific requests or other actions of a user to trigger automatic personalization. For example, if a user buys a book on Internet privacy, the site may suggest other books on Internet privacy. In this case the site is not using ratings to predict other types of books the user might like to buy, but simply offering the user additional books on the same topics as the book she already bought.

Content-based personalization tends to be more privacy-friendly than prediction-based personalization because it does not require that user profiles be stored. Prediction based personalization can be made more privacy friendly through the use of techniques to improve the privacy associated with user profiles.

5.1.5 Real world examples

Examples of personalization are readily apparent at many ecommerce web sites. For example, Riedl (2001) found 23 independent applications of personalization on the Amazon.com web site. As of December 2003, the Amazon.com[1] web site appears to use all of the types of personalization mentioned in this chapter, including features that fall on both ends of each of the four axes of personalization.

- *Data collection method.* Amazon allows users to provide explicit ratings for books and other products, which it uses to recommend other items to a user. It also uses information about past purchases and what items a user has looked at as implicit data with which to make recommendations. Users are directly in control of the explicit ratings they provide. In order to reduce privacy concerns and improve the usefulness of their recommendations, Amazon allows users to specify that some of the implicit data in their profiles should not be used when making recommendations. However, users cannot have this data removed from their profiles altogether.
- *Duration.* Amazon provides task-based personalization by creating a link to a page of items recently viewed by the user with suggestions for related items that might be of interest. Amazon also provides profile-based personalization by offering recommendations to the user based on her entire purchase and recommendation history.
- *User involvement.* Most of the Amazon personalization is done by the system automatically. However, users can edit their personalization settings and turn off some types of personalization or ask that certain items not be considered as part of their profile. A user can proactively rate items in order to have them considered as part of her profile. She can also request that payment information be stored to enable more convenient ordering.
- *Reliance on predictions.* Amazon makes predictive recommendations to users based on an analysis of a user's ratings and purchases compared with other users – including a "customers who bought this book also bought" feature. Amazon also provides users with lists of items in the same category as the item they requested.

---

[1] Throughout this chapter Amazon.com is cited as an example because it is a well-known web site on which ecommerce personalization can be observed in a variety of forms. The author has no affiliation with Amazon.com and no knowledge of the Amazon.com personalization systems beyond what can be inferred from reading material posted on the Amazon.com web site as of June 2003.

5.2 Pseudonymous Profiles

Often an individual's name and other personally identifiable information are not needed in order to provide personalized services. For example, recommender systems typically don't require any personal information in order to make recommendations. If personal information is not needed, personalization systems can be designed so that users are identified by pseudonyms rather than their real names. This reduces the chance that someone who gains unauthorized access to a user's profile will be able to link that profile with a particular individual, although it does not eliminate this risk. Someone who gains access to a user's account by using her computer or by learning her user name and password may be able to gain access to a pseudonymous profile. Furthermore, some combination of non-identifiable information contained in a pseudonymous profile may prove identifiable in practice, especially when combined with information stored in web usage logs (Malin, *et al.,* 2003). Nonetheless, pseudonymous profiles are a good way to address some privacy concerns. In addition, companies may find it significantly easier to comply with some privacy laws when they store only pseudonymous profiles rather than personally identifiable information.

For increased privacy protection, sites that employ pseudonymous profiles should make sure that this profile information is stored separately from web usage logs that contain IP addresses and any transaction records that might contain personally identifiable information. Web usage logs should be scrubbed so that they do not contain information that would allow pseudonymous profiles to be linked with other data.

Arlein *et al.* (2000) propose an architecture for pseudonymous personalization using information collected by multiple web sites. This system allows users to specify multiple personae that are stored on persona servers residing in the network. Users can grant web sites privileges to read or write to a specific persona. In addition, web sites can further restrict access to data they have written to a persona.

Kobsa and Schreck (2003) propose a more complex architecture for personalization services that use pseudonymous profiles. They envision the existence of user modeling servers that can communicate with users and personalization services via anonymous channels. While this architecture may prove too heavy for adoption by a single ecommerce web site, it is an interesting model that might be considered by a group of sites or as part of a single-sign-on/electronic wallet protocol.

5.3 Client-Side Profiles

Another option for reducing the privacy concerns associated with user profiles and satisfying some legal requirements is to store these profiles on the user's client (computer) rather than on a web server. This will ensure that the profiles are accessible only by the user and those who have access to her computer.

Client-side profiles may be stored in cookies that are replayed to a web site that uses them to provide a personalized service and immediately discards them. The information stored in these profiles should be encoded or encrypted so that it is not revealed in transit and it is inaccessible to other people who have access to a user's computer or to viruses or other malicious programs that may look for personal information stored in cookies.

A personalization interface that uses client-side scripting may be able to provide personal services by examining user profile information on the client without ever having to transmit it to the web site.

Canny (2002) proposes an architecture for a recommendation system in which participants compute a public "aggregate" of their data to share with members of their community. Individuals can then compute their own personal recommendations without revealing their individual data. He suggests that such an approach might be particularly useful in a ubiquitous computing setting where users may desire recommendations about everyday activities but are concerned that detailed information about their own activities not be revealed.

5.4 Putting Users in Control

Regardless of the approach taken to personalization, implementers who want to be sensitive about privacy concerns and comply with the fair information practice principles need to develop systems that give users the ability to control the collection and use of their information. Users should be able to control what information is stored in their profile, the purposes for which it will be used, and the conditions (if any) under which it might be disclosed. They should also be able to control when and if personalization takes place. In some cases, such controls may be required by law.

Developing a user interface that allows users to control the information in their profiles is a complicated problem, especially if the interface provides controls that go beyond a very course level of granularity. Lau et al. (1999) explored interfaces for a software tool that allows a user to create privacy rules for sharing web browsing histories. They found interfaces that require users to set privacy rules individually for every object in the system were too tedious for users, and they recommended that interfaces be developed that allow users to specify privacy policies that apply automatically to objects as they are encountered. However, formulating a privacy rule is a complicated task, which may require a deeper understanding of privacy issues than many users have as well as the ability to anticipate future activities that hold particular privacy concerns for a user. Some of the lessons learned by developers of Platform for Privacy Preferences (P3P) user agents may prove useful in developing privacy interfaces for personalized ecommerce services (Cranor, 2002; Cranor et al., 2003).

A number of ecommerce web sites give users access to their profiles; however, it is not clear that many users are aware of this, and reports from operators of some personalization systems indicate that users rarely take actions to proactively customize their online experiences (Manber and Robison, 2000). To update personalization profile information on Amazon.com, for example, requires users to proactively go to their personalized "Your Account Page" and select from several items in a "Recommendations" section near the bottom of the page. Here users can edit previous explicit ratings they have given, as well as review their transaction and rating history and request that certain items be excluded from consideration when Amazon makes recommendations to them in the future. This interface essentially requires users to make individual privacy decisions for every object in the system, which can be quite time consuming. In addition, as users make new purchases, they have to remember to update their settings.

An interface might be developed that could allow Amazon shoppers to specify general privacy policies that would apply automatically. Such policies might allow users to specify, for example, that certain categories of purchases never be used to make recommendations, or that purchases be excluded from their profiles after six months. Or perhaps a user might want to specify that purchases made using her business credit card should be considered in her recommendations but purchases made using her personal credit card should be excluded. These types of rules would be useful to a user who can anticipate in advance the types of purchases that she would not want to have influence her recommendations. However, it might prove difficult for most users to formulate these kinds of rules.

An alternative approach that would require less foresight on the part of users would be to allow them to specify privacy preferences as part of the transaction process. Thus, when a user enters her credit card number and shipping address, she would also be prompted to decide whether this transaction should be excluded from her profile. She might establish a default setting that would apply to all her purchases unless she indicated otherwise, or even specify general policies like the ones described above that could be overridden easily for a specific purchase. A system-wide default might be that items that users have indicated have been purchased as gifts are excluded from a user's recommendation profile (indeed, Amazon appears to exclude gift purchases from recommendation profiles already). A user interface might even include a box that allows a user to claim a purchase is a gift ("I didn't buy it for myself") as a way of disassociating herself from that particular purchase—similar to the habit some people have of requesting advice "for a friend" in an attempt to protect their own privacy.

A more sophisticated approach might allow users to establish multiple personae that would each have their own personalization profile. Thus, a user could have a separate profile for personal and business purchases, and could have a profile for each individual for whom she buys gifts. Besides addressing some privacy concerns, such an approach would likely lead to better personalization because it could offer recommendations within the appropriate context. Of course, designers of such a system should consider potential privacy concerns of gift recipients.

The Amazon interface allows users to exclude purchases from their recommendations, but not to remove them from their profile altogether. Excluding purchases from recommendations addresses some privacy concerns, but leaves others unaddressed. While legal and liability issues may require that Amazon retain transaction histories for some amount of time, there should be some retention period after which these histories need not be retained if a user prefers. Furthermore, even within the retention period, Amazon might allow users to request that all or part of their transaction histories not be made available through the web.

When user interfaces are developed that allow users to control the use of their information, it is also essential that back end systems be put in place that can properly carry out each user's instructions. This is easiest when personalization profiles are used only for web site personalization; however, some companies also make use of this data for postal mail marketing or other purposes. When these companies have databases spread across many different computer systems, as users change their personal settings these changes must be propagated across multiple systems that may store data in different formats. Furthermore, policies and procedures need to be put in place to limit access to these databases and ensure that those who have access to this data respect each user's privacy settings.

6. CONCLUSIONS

This chapter has reviewed several privacy risks related to ecommerce personalization and discussed privacy principles, laws, and guidelines that may impact the design of personalization systems. While no simple universal formula exists for designing a privacy-protective ecommerce personalization system, there are a number of approaches that may be helpful depending on the functionality and design requirements of a particular system. In general personalization systems tend to be most privacy friendly when they are explicitly activated by users, make use of data explicitly provided by users, use data obtained only during the current session, and perform personalization based directly on the content of information the user provides. When data must be stored in profiles and retained beyond a single session, pseudonymous profiles and client-side profiles may enhance the privacy of a system. Pseudonymous profiles are a good approach when personalization information need not be tied to personally identifiable information. Client-side profiles are useful when personalization services can be performed on the client. Interfaces that put users in control of the collection and use of their data as well as the types of personalization provided can make most personalization systems more privacy friendly, although further work is needed to develop privacy interfaces that are both usable and provide flexible control.

I see two major challenges for the human computer interaction community in the area of ecommerce personalization and privacy. The first challenge is to develop usable interfaces that allow users to control the use of their personal data and make privacy-related choices in a meaningful way that does not interfere with their use of a web site. The second challenge is to design interfaces that allow users to find what they are looking for with minimal need for user profiles, especially profiles tied to personally identifiable information.

Web site designers should also keep in mind that in some cases the goals of ecommerce personalization can be achieved at a lower cost and with fewer privacy risks through good web site design that makes it easy for users to find what they want. Many personalization interfaces build user profiles so that they can try to infer or anticipate user needs and offer relevant suggestions; however, users often already know what they are looking for, and good navigation design can help them find it (Berk, 2003). Where personalization adds value to a site, careful attention to design can reduce the amount of personally identifiable information necessary to make personalization successful, minimizing privacy risks and increasing user acceptance and trust.

7. REFERENCES

Ackerman M.S., Cranor, L.F., and Reagle, J. (1999) *Privacy in E-Commerce: Examining User Scenarios and Privacy Preferences.* In *Proceedings of EC'99* (Denver, CO), ACM Press, 1-8. http://doi.acm.org/10.1145/336992.336995

Adams, A. (1999) *The Implications of Users' Multimedia Privacy Perceptions on Communication and Information Privacy Policies.* In *Proceedings of Telecommunications Policy Research Conference,* (Washington, DC). http://www.cs.mdx.ac.uk/RIDL/aadams/TPRC%20final.PDF

Arlein, R.M., Jai, B., Jakobsson, M., Monrose, F., and Reiter, M.K. (2000) *Privacy-Preserving Global Customization.* In *Proceedings of EC'00,* (Minneapolis, MN, October 17-20), ACM Press, 176-184. http://doi.acm.org/10.1145/352871.352891

Berk, M. (2003) *Beyond the Personalization Myth: Cost-effective Alternatives to Influence Intent.* Jupiter Research Site Technologies and Operations, Volume 2.

Canny, J. (2002) *Collaborative Filtering with Privacy.* In *IEEE Symposium on Security and Privacy,* (Oakland, CA), 45-57. http://citeseer.nj.nec.com/canny02collaborative.html

Claypool, M., Brown, D., Le, P., and Waseda, M. (2001) *Inferring User Interest.* IEEE Internet Computing, (November/December): 32-39.

Cranor, L. (2002) *Web Privacy with P3P.* O'Reilly & Associates.

Cranor, L., Guduru, P., and Arjula, M. (2003) *User Interfaces for Privacy Agents.* Under review.

Culnan, M. J. and Milne, G. R. (2001) *The Culnan-Milne Survey on Consumers & Online Privacy Notices: Summary of Responses.* http://www.ftc.gov/bcp/workshops/glb/supporting/culnan-milne.pdf.

Cyber Dialogue. (2001) *Cyber Dialogue Survey Data Reveals Lost Revenue for Retailers Due to Widespread Consumer Privacy Concerns.* http://www.cyberdialogue.com/news/releases/2001/11-07-uco-retail.html.

Gandon, F.L. and Sadeh, N.M. (2003) *A Semantic e-Wallet to Reconcile Privacy and Context-awareness.* In *Proceedings of the Second International Semantic Web Conference (ISWC03).*

Herlocker, J.L. and Konstan, J.A. (2001) *Content-Independent Task-Focused Recommendation.* IEEE Internet Computing, (November/December): 40-47.

Karat, C. M., Brodie, C., Karat, J., Vergo, J., and Alpert, S.R. (2003) *Personalizing the user experience on ibm.com.* IBM Systems Journal 42(4): 686-701.

Kobsa, A. (2002) *Personalized Hypermedia and International Privacy.* Communications of the ACM, 45(5): 64-67.

Kobsa, A. and Schreck, J. (2003) *Privacy Through Pseudonymity in User-Adaptive Systems.* ACM Transactions on Internet Technology, 3(2):149-183.

Lau, T., Etzioni, O., and Weld, D. S. (1999) *Privacy Interfaces for Information Management.* Communications of the ACM, 42(10): 89-94.

Malin, B., Sweeney, L., and Newton, E. (2003) *Trail Re-identification: Learning Who You are From Where You Have Been.* Carnegie Mellong University, School of Computer Science, Data Privacy Laboratory Technical Report, LIDAP-WP12. Under review. http://privacy.cs.cmu.edu/people/sweeney/trails1.html

Manber, U., Patel, A., and Robison, J. (2000) *Experience with Personalization on Yahoo!* Communications of the ACM, 43(8): 35-39.

Network Advertising Initiative Principles. (2000) http://www.networkadvertising.org/aboutnai_principles.asp

Odlyzko, A. (2003) *Privacy, Economics, and Price Discrimination on the Internet.* In *Proceedings of the Fifth International Conference on Electronic Commerce* (ICEC'03), Pittsburgh, PA.

Organization for Economic Co-operation and Development. (1980) *Recommendation Of The Council Concerning Guide-Lines Governing The Protection Of Privacy And Transborder Flows Of Personal Data.* Adopted by the Council 23 September 1980. http://www.datenschutz-berlin.de/gesetze/internat/ben.htm

Patrick, A.S. and Kenny, S. (2003) *From Privacy Legislation to Interface Design: Implementing Information Privacy in Human-Computer Interaction.* In *Proceedings of Privacy Enhancing Technologies Workshop (PET2003),* Dresden, Germany. http://132.246.128.219/legint/pet-workshop-patrick-kenny.pdf

Personalization Consortium. (2000) *Survey Finds Few Consumers Unwilling to Provide Personal Information to Web Marketers in Exchange for Better Services.* http://www.personalization.org/surveypress.html

Personalization Consortium. (2001) *New Survey Shows Consumers Are More Likely to Purchase At Web Sites That Offer Personalization.* http://www.personalization.org/pr050901.html

Ramakrishnan, N., Keller, B.J., Grama, A.Y., and Karypis, G. (2001) *Privacy Risks in Recommender Systems.* IEEE Internet Computing, (November/December): 54-62.

Riedl, J. (2001) *Personalization and Privacy.* IEEE Internet Computing (November/December): 29-31.

Turow, J. (2003) *Americans & Online Privacy: The system is Broken.* A Report from the Annenberg Public Policy Center of the University of Pennsylvania. http://www.asc.upenn.edu/usr/jturow/internet-privacy-report/36-page-turow-version-9.pdf

Warrior, J., McHenry, E., and McGee, K. (2003) *They Know Where You Are.* IEEE Spectrum, (July) 20-25.

Zaslow, J. (2003) *If TiVo Thinks You Are Gay, Here's How to Set It Straight: What You Buy Affects Recommendations On Amazon.com, Too; Why the Cartoons?* The Wallstreet Journal, (26 November). http://online.wsj.com/article_email/0,,SB103826193687235690800.html

KEITH INSTONE

AN INFORMATION ARCHITECTURE PERSPECTIVE ON PERSONALIZATION

1. WHAT IS INFORMATION ARCHITECTURE AND WHY IT MATTERS

Information architecture is the structural design of shared information environments (AIfIA, 2003). In terms of e-commerce web sites, the information architecture encompasses the organization of the content and functionality, the labelling system and the navigational scheme (Rosenfeld & Morville, 2002). Users interact directly with the user interface of a web site: scanning a list of links and selecting one, clicking on an icon to add an item to their shopping cart, and filling out a form. Users also interact with the content directly: reading introductory text to determine what each category is about, studying product details descriptions and pictures to see if this is what they want to buy, and comparing specific product features. The information architecture is the "invisible" layer between the user interface and the content.

In typical e-commerce sites, the information architecture specifies:

- The major organizational scheme of the site, such as by topic, by audience type, by task. Amazon.com is organized into stores ("electronics" and "baby"), many airline sites are organized around tasks ("search for fares" and "check in for your flight") and several computer companies use audience groupings ("home office", "small business", "government").
- The product organizational system, such as by price, by brand, by use, by category. The product categorization scheme is the most important aspect of helping users find what they want.
- The labels used for the product categories and functionality. For example, does "Bonus bonanza" convey the proper brand for the site while also letting users know this is the section of sale items?
- The global navigation: the links that are persistent across the pages of the site. The most important items, such as the shopping cart and search, as well as the major organizational schemes (stores or tasks) are usually the ones worthy of such prominence within the information architecture.

75

Clare-Marie Karat et al. (eds.), Designing Personalized User Experiences in eCommerce, 75—93.

–   The local navigation: how users navigate within a product category, for example.
    The music section of a store will have different local navigation than the
    clothing section.
–   The contextual navigation: how users navigate across the major sections to get to
    "related items" and how the business enables "cross-selling". This often includes
    linking from the book section to music and videos products. For example, a Star
    Trek book would have related links to Star Trek videos, DVDs, toys and
    clothing.

As this "middle layer" between the user interface and content, the information
architecture is often hard-coded directly into the web site. For example, the global
navigation is pasted directly into the top of the site's pages, making it difficult to add
or remove links across the site. Or, product sub-categories are added directly to
pages and as products evolve over time, the sub-categories could become empty –
yet they remain on the page. More sophisticated sites create a separate layer for the
information architecture – a meta-data layer. The information architecture
components are specified as meta-data on objects and the site is generated
dynamically from the meta-data. For example, labels for categories are not
embedded in a page or the product descriptions but instead come from a database.
Thus, changing a product category label from "Bikes, scooters and more" to
"Wheeled vehicles" is a simple change because products are tagged to the category
and the label is generated separately.

This dynamic, middle layer for the information architecture is a crucial
requirement for personalization systems. This level of abstraction provides the
ability to generate different experiences based on attributes of the user – it enables
personalization. The chapter next goes into detail on this information architecture
framework for personalization. The framework connects user profiles with content
profiles and uses personalization rules to determine the user experience.

The framework acknowledges the centrality of the information architecture to the
personalized user experience, but it does not provide answers: it only us a means to
structure our questions. In this, there are still many unanswered questions for
personalized user experiences. The remainder of the chapter presents the changing
landscape and what research issues need to be addressed. Personalization is
changing the basic hypertext model – bringing content to users instead of forcing
users to concentrate on navigation. The resulting shift in the information architecture
of e-commerce leads to many design questions of how we convey to users where
they are and who they are.

2. AN INFORMATION ARCHITECTURE FRAMEWORK FOR
PERSONALIZATION

The information architecture framework (Instone, 2000) is a model that shows how
IA impacts the various aspects of the personalized experience. The meta-data

connects the user and content profiles while the personalization rules bring the system components to the user interface.

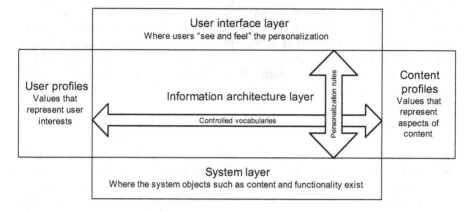

Figure 1. The information architecture layer defines the meta-information that connects the user profiles with the content profiles. The IA layer also includes personalization rules that use controlled vocabularies to build the personalized user interface from system components.

2.1   User and content profiles

Users will have certain characteristics that will need to be tracked for personalization. These attributes may describe:
−   where they are located (geographically),
−   what their role is (buyer, manager, assistant), and
−   what their interests are (science fiction books, Frank Sinatra music, mainframes, animal print clothing).

Similarly, the content will have characteristics that will need to be leveraged for effective personalization. These could be:
−   price,
−   creator of the product: author (of the book), singer or composer (of the music), artist (of the artwork),
−   brand of the product, and
−   location where the service is offered.

These sets of attributes and their possible values are governed by a controlled vocabulary. For each attribute, there needs to be a consistent set of values used throughout the entire system. For example, many products have variations on their names. If users can specify they are interested in "PlayStation 2" but the information about the product is tagged "PS2" there will be gaps in the personalization. In addition to standardizing on a product vocabulary, the other profile values must be synchronized. Values could include geography (are profile values based on country, state, city of postal code?), topic (what subject category scheme is used?) and person (how do you resolve the common occurrence of misspelled author names in book classification?). This part of the information architecture forms the foundation of the personalized user experience. The strategic IA decisions, such as the taxonomies chosen and the granularity of the tagging, will affect the quality of the personalization as much as the tactical execution (the accuracy of the tagging).

2.2 Personalization rules

The controlled vocabulary provides the foundation for a quality user experience. A very good "static" (non-personalized) e-commerce site can be built based on a controlled vocabulary, but to get personalization, you need specific business rules that govern how user and content profiles are matched up. The personalization rules will be a combination of business requirements (selling more higher margin products, for example) and user requirements (such as finding products that match their interests).

Personalization rules bridge the gap between the system objects of content and functionality and the user interface. A personalization rule will determine when certain users see certain pieces of content and how specific functionality is presented. Some rules can be content-focused, such as showing the featured sale items for all users on the site home page. To support a personalized user experience, however, the rules need to be based on user profile values. "Show sale items from categories the user has purchased from before" would be a more personalized rule: for example, users who have purchased Jazz music would see sale items tagged "Jazz music" and not sale items tagged "Mystery novels".

2.3 Profile layer

To understand the information architecture layer in more detail, we can break it down into sub-layers for profiles and vocabularies. The top sublayer is the profile layer, where specific values for the attributes are used to determine what content to present to which user under what conditions. A user's profile exists here and can be changed explicitly by user actions (such as filling out a form that requests particular profile information), or implicitly by certain actions (such as buying certain products). Likewise, a profile of the content exists and is matched with user profiles through a set of rules.

Meta-information for a piece of content can be changed explicitly by users, such as by reviewing a movie with a "thumbs up" rating. Users can also implicitly modify the content profile. For example, purchases of a product can be tracked and enough purchases could change the value for popularity of that product from "average" to "hot," thereby affecting other users' experiences.

Table 1. *Users can be explicitly or implicitly involved in setting user and content profiles.*

User Involvement	User Profile	Content Profile
Explicit	Fill in a form of where they are located, what they want to subscribe to, etc.	Pick a favorite brand for different types of products.
Implicit	Viewing several pages on a single product.	Products purchased, which products were purchased at the same time.

The level of user involvement is an important aspect of personalization because:
- Too much explicit user involvement up front usually turns users away.
- A mix of explicit and implicit over time supports lifecycle personalization and allows users to build up a sense of trust before they commit more sensitive profile information.
- Users can set content profiles to affect *other users'* personalization results (often called collaborative filtering).

In addition to having users set attribute values, they can be set manually (by system managers) or automatically by some software process. Combining manual and automatic profile setting provides the most economical way to leverage the information architecture and implement personalization features.

Table 2. *Profiles can be set by humans (managers, users) or by software*

Profile Setting	User Profile	Content Profile
Manual	– Managers assign profile values for users (such as after a sales call) – User assigns own profile (see table 1)	– Humans tag content by assigning values to attributes – Humans validate automatic classification recommendations – User assigns content profile (see table 1)
Automatic	– The system detects certain values, such as browser version or language.	– Auto-classification software assigns attribute values based on rules and concept extraction, such as assigning brand name values based on text in product descriptions.

2.4 Vocabulary layer

Beneath the profile layer are the vocabularies which regulate the assignment of attribute values. At the vocabulary layer, the attributes themselves are defined and the set of acceptable values (preferred terms) are specified. The relationships between attributes are defined, such as child and parent attributes. For example, if we know that a user owns a "German Shepherd," then a thesaurus can take us to a broader term "Large Dogs," which we can match with products for "Large Dogs," and in the end display transportation cages that are the right size for this German Shepherd owner.

Both users and content have their own attributes, but they are likewise coordinated to make sure that the higher-level profile information is in sync. Or, defined in the reverse, the vocabulary is the set of all attributes and values, while a profile is merely one specific instance of the vocabulary (for a specific user or for a specific piece of content).

2.5 Personalization rules across the profile and vocabulary layers

The personalization rules operate at the profile and vocabulary sub-layers. The most powerful rules operate on the set of attributes as a whole, at the profile sub-layer. When user and content profiles share the same attributes, then we can make rules that work for all values of those attributes. For example, we can make a profile rule that states: *show CD's sung by this user's favorite artist*. If the user profile has a "favorite artist" attribute that shares the same values as the content profile's "sung by" attribute, we can make a general-purpose rule that works for all values.

If profile-layer rules are not possible, we would have to make a series of lower-level rules based on each value in the vocabulary:

– If the `favorite_artist` is "Elvis," show CDs `sung_by` "Elvis Presley."
– If the `favorite_artist` is "The Beatles," show CDs `sung_by` "Paul McCartney" and "John Lennon" and "Ringo Starr" and "George Harrison."

In these examples, we are using personalization rules to make up for gaps in the information architecture: "Elvis" tagging is not consistent and bands like "The Beatles" have to be hard-coded as a rule instead of designed into the IA.

Vocabulary layer rules based on specific values of the user and content profiles often point out a weakness in the IA layer. They are useful in isolated cases, however, to cover rapidly-changing business needs. For example, we might want to offer the sale price for all users whose `breed_ownership` is "Daschund" because they are turning out to be some of the most loyal customers. Or we may want to feature video games whose brand is "Nintendo" (because we make more money on them at the current time) but not whose brand is "PlayStation." Since the business context changes rapidly, it is usually best to use the personalization rules as the means of implementing them in the short term and eventually embedding them into the controlled vocabularies and tagging over time, as needed.

2.6 Implications of the framework

The information architecture-centered framework for personalization defines a middle layer that includes controlled vocabularies and personalization rules. It shows how user attributes and content are mapped together and how the rules leverage them to build a personalized user experience. The framework helps explain what happens beyond the technology: what is involved in making personalization effective. As such, it is a useful for asking additional research questions (beyond what personalization features users want and what algorithms to use to offer recommendations).

The next section introduces some of the research questions raised by the information architecture framework and even more fundamental research issues driven by an IA perspective, such as the hypertext metaphor change that personalization demands.

3. IA RESEARCH ISSUES FOR PERSONALIZATION

3.1 Current practices

The first place to apply the information architecture perspective on personalization is to document current e-commerce best practices within the IA framework. Understanding things like how current e-commerce sites gather user profile values implicitly and explicitly, what controlled vocabularies are used, and how personalization rules are used to address user and business needs will help us identify gaps in the best practices and recommend areas for further research.

Wu, etal, 2002, used this IA framework to categorize the personalization on current sites. Twenty-seven popular websites were evaluated based on various types of implicit and explicit personalization. E-commerce sites scored high on personalization in support of differentiating products and recommending purchases. Research questions that arose from the study include understanding the differences between physical product e-commerce (such as buying a book and having it shipped) and information product e-commerce (such as buying access to information online).

The Wu study is merely a first step in the process of systemically analyzing personalization practices in order to help us understand the larger issues. Studies involving more comprehensive sets of site, more refined coding schemes for personalization, and tying the analysis to business factors (such as sales effectiveness and repeat business) are needed.

3.2 Changing the direction of hypertext

An information architecture perspective on personalization must go beyond documenting best practices, however: it must address the fundamental way that personalization changes the way users think about e-commerce. Personalization as a whole takes us a step closer to Ted Nelson's vision of Xanadu (Nelson, 1993). Most of the web today is "ordinary hypertext", where users go from page to page via links. Pages are grouped into sites. This navigation metaphor uses language like "visit my site", "go to this page" and "you are here". On the web, the site is the basic unit of place, with conventions such as the site logo going in the upper left of the page and taking users to the site home page (Adkisson, 2002). Search engines group resulting pages into sites. Billboards, TV ads and t-shirts point users to sites in order to get them to do their e-commerce there.

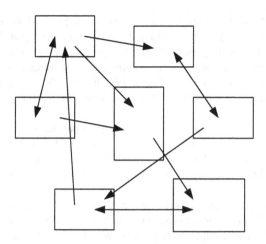

Figure 2. *In ordinary hypertext, users navigate from place to place – users go to the information. Each rectangle is a "place" and users evaluate where they are to determine where to go next. (Adapted from Nelson, 1993)*

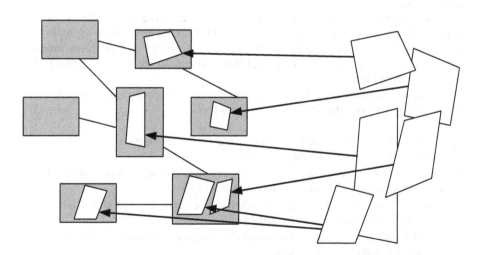

Figure 3. *In compound hypertext, the key flow is reversed – the content comes to users in different contexts. Each rectangle is a "context" and content is adapted to each context. When the adaption is based on user profiles, this is called "personalization". (Adapted from Nelson, 1993)*

Pages almost always include indications of where a user is within the site. The most common user interface element to convey where you are has turned out to be the breadcrumb (Instone, 2002). Other conventions are used less often but include hiliting the current section the user is in and the "site map on a page".

Whether the "lost in hyperspace" problem is real or not, there are very good reasons to tell users where they are for e-commerce. Customers need to know who they are doing business with: buying a PC directly from the manufacturer is different from going thru a reseller, which is different than buying from a student in Edmonton.

Finding the right product is the key first step to purchasing it, and letting users know where they are helps them figure out where to try next in their quest for whatever they want to buy. Also, knowing where you are helps you return there at a later date – complex purchases evolve over time so being able to find something a second time.

The navigation metaphor is therefore a crucial part of the user experience for e-commerce sites. This is merely "ordinary hypertext" however – personalization is a step closer to Nelson's "compound hypertext" where the basic metaphor is reversed. Instead of users going from place to place, the content comes to the user in a personalized user experience. Instead of visiting a site, you can personalize your portal to go get the local weather, sports scores and best car prices from your favorite sites and bring them to you. Instead of being obsessed about where you are, you need to worry about where things are coming from, why they are here, and what else are you missing.

Even without personalization, e-commerce sites have found the value of compound hypertext and have implemented in various ways. One example are product category pages – pages where a user has chosen a high level product category but there are subcategories that they can choose from before getting to a specific product list page.

There are commonly 4 different types of product category pages, depending on how products are "bubbled up" to the category level:

- Level 1 – No products are listed on the category pages, users must select a subcategory before seeing any products
- Level 2 – A few "featured products" are presented by the main purpose of the category page is to drill down into a subcategory
- Level 3 – The focus of the page is shifted to a selected set of products, but selecting a subcategory is still available
- Level 4 – All products are presented at the category level and subcategories become optional filters for users

Level 1
No products are listed on the category pages; users must select a subcategory before seeing any products

Level 2
A few "featured products" are presented (on the right) but the main purpose of the category page is to drill down into a subcategory

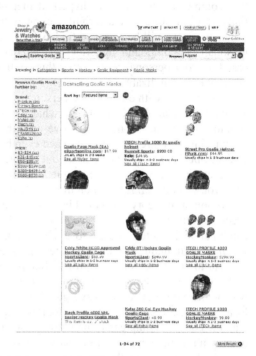

Level 4
All products are presented at the category level (1-24 of 72 here) and subcategories become optional filters for users (brand and price in this case)

Level 3
The focus of the page is shifted to a selected set of products, but selecting a subcategory (on the left) is still the key navigation

Figure 4. *Each level of product category page shows more and more products, gradually shifting the model from ordinary hypertext to compound hypertext.*

Aspects of compound hypertext are finding their ways into current e-commerce implementations, even without personalization. Compound hypertext in combination with personalization provides that most significant changes in the conceptual model for e-commerce.

3.3 Compound hypertext and personalization

In e-commerce, the ordinary hypertext metaphor is about not getting lost as you find the right store and the right section within that store. Compound hypertext means products will be easier to find as they are not buried in the back of the store. Personalized compound hypertext means that products will be brought forward based on your personal profile. It is this control over how content is presented that drives the personalization experience.

One concern with e-commerce personalization is the possibility that you may not always be in complete control over what you get. You will be able to subscribe to certain services that work and remove ones that do not, but there are also forces at work trying to figure out what you need even before you realize it. That is part of the world of business – you are a buyer but people are also allowed to try to sell to you. The grey line between selling people what they want and convincing them to buy what you want to sell is based on the quality of the personalization.

Although in theory you could have a pure navigation metaphor at one end of the spectrum and a pure personalization metaphor at the other, the real world is a combination of both. You go to a site, log in, and get a personalized experience within that domain. Within that site's personalized experience, some content is brought to you based on your profile, but you are also free to "wander around" and go to other pages. Even if you start at a personalized portal, it only takes a click or two before you realize you have gone to a new place: you might have gotten the local sports scores brought to your portal, but when you indicate that you want to read the corresponding game summaries, you are whisked away to espn.com – and it quickly turns into yet another ordinary hypertext experience.

It is this mixing of the navigation and personalization metaphors in compound hypertext that raises the most fundamental questions about how to design personalized user experiences. As new as the web is, many conventions have formed for the navigation metaphor – how to tell users where they are and where they can go next. Most conventions for the personalization metaphor are not as well set. And the relationship between the two metaphors will be the main user experience challenge for e-commerce sites over the next few years.

4. NAVIGATION AND PERSONALIZATION EXAMPLES

The classic "lost in hyperspace" problem has been translated to the web (Instone, 1997) as: Where am I? What is here? and Where can I go next? This had lead to a set of design patterns (Van Duyne, 2003) that help users understand where they are on the web: what site they are at, what section of the site they are in, and what the page they are on is all about.

Personalization is changing this. Instead of concentrating on where you are, the more important questions are becoming Why is this here? and What am I missing? "Why is this here" addresses the logic that is used to personalize the experience. For example, why is a certain set of books recommended: is it based on my past purchases, or because of some other aspect of my profile such as gender, interests or even by some inferred behaviour (such as spending a lot of time browsing a specific category). "What am I missing" addresses the concern that any personalization can be limiting and users often want to "step out of it" to get a generic and comprehensive experience. For example, if a list of products is personalized, then how do users get to the full list that is not personalized?

4.1   Where am I design

A key design point for the navigation metaphor is indicating where a person is so that they can evaluate where to go next. For example, Figure 5 shows an examples where the global navigation area at the top of the page is used to indicate the brand (Eddie Bauer logo) and store (Clothing & Gear tab). The local navigation area on the left tells us where are in the Men's department and the section devoted to Shirts. The design is supposed to help users figure out where to go next, such as drilling down to select a shirt by its name or filtering by selecting a type of shirt on the left. The design is also supposed to convey other aspects of the sites information architecture, such as there being a totally different women's store. When users do not pick up on these design cues, they often get confused. For example, a user might select the WOMEN link and expect to be taken to a page about Shirts for women since this is a page about shirts for men. Helping users understand differences like this, between global and contextual navigation, are one of the main purposes of Where-am-I design.

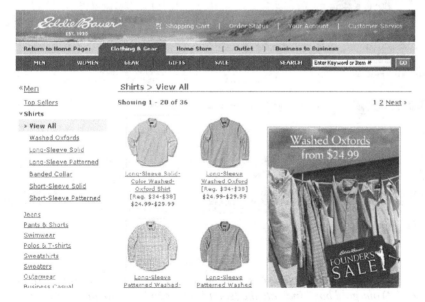

Figure 5. *At eddiebauer.com, users are told they are at Eddie Bauer, in the Clothing & Gear store, in the Men's department and finally, in the Shirts section.*

An open question is just how much Where-am-I design to present to users. Too much of it means the content itself is drowned out. A minimalist design would eliminate most of the global and local navigation, leaving only perhaps a breadcrumb to tell users where they are: none of the 75 major e-commerce sites studied by Adkisson, 2002, did this however. So there is definitely a perceived need for Where-am-I navigation for e-commerce.

4.2 Who am I design

Personalization adds a new layer to the user interface design questions. Instead of only having to answer Where am I, What is here, and Where do I go next, personalization requires us to address three more questions in order to create a compelling user experience:

- Who do you think I am? – The profile information that is the basis for the personalization
- Why is this here? – The rationale for the personalized experience, the rules that are determining what content is being presented, for example
- What am I missing? – The experience one would get without personalization and being able to turn off all or part of the personalization process

Figure 6. The top portion of the figure is amazon.com for an anonymous user: "Your store" and "Your gold box" indicate the features that can be personalized. Below: after logging in, my experience becomes "Keith's store" and "Keith's gold box" and I am greeted by name. These global navigation changes persist throughout the experience.

4.2.1 Who do you think I am

The first question users may ask in a personalized environment involves understanding who the system thinks they are. Are they logged in, and if so, what profile is being used to personalize their experience? A common follow-up would like be – "And how can I get you to forget something about me so that you no longer use it to personalize?" (The privacy implications are large, but we will focus on the user interface design only.)

Most personalized web sites say "Hello" to you by name on the home page as a way to let you know that you are logged in. As you navigate deeper, reminding people who they are becomes hit-or-miss. Amazon.com changes the global navigation to remind you but other sites, such as Wal-mart.com, do not.

Beyond just knowing it you are logged in or not, the key user question is about the details in their profile that are driving the personalization. Often this is a simple checklist that can be managed via "you account" functionality.

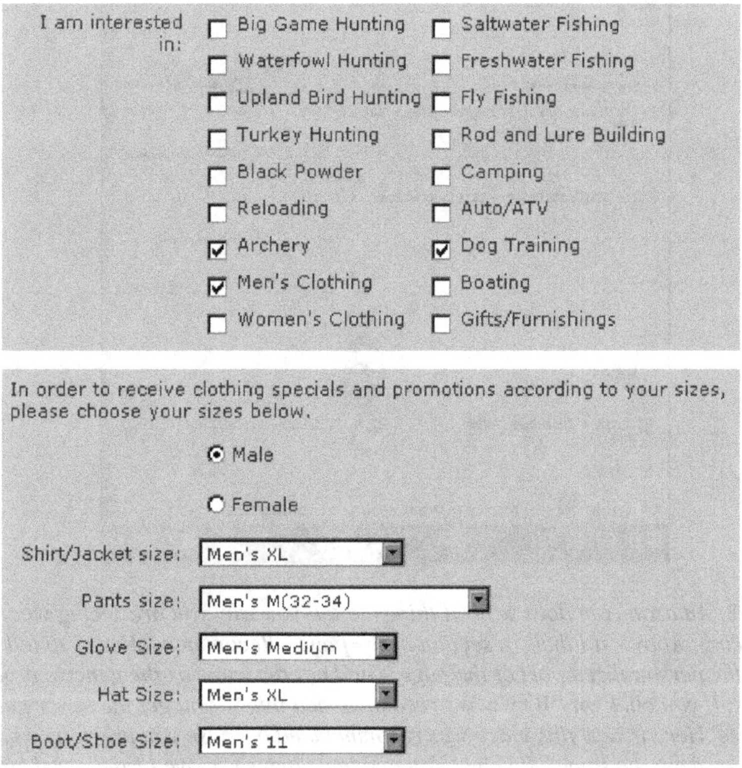

Figure 7. *An outfitter store lets you select your interests and clothing sizes within your profile.*

Figure 8. *Amazon.com does several things to tell you why you are seeing what you are seeing. Above, it labels a section of the page "Recommendations" to tell you this is the personalized part of the page – and not the same as the generic product listings. If you click on "Why was I recommended this?" you get the lower part of the figure. Here it says this video was recommended because you previously bought two videos from the same TV show. You can have items removed from consideration for recommendation and even rate the product poorly so that similar products will not be recommended again.*

More complicated editing of a profile is also necessary. For example, if a gift was purchased for someone else, users need to be able to mark it as a gift or have it deleted from their profile so that it does not improperly influence future personalization.

4.2.2   Why is this here

Once the level of trust is built and people feel that the system correctly knows who they are, the next questions arise about why users are seeing what they are seeing. Is a list of products the generic list that everyone sees, or has it been personalized in some way? If it has been personalized, then what rules were used to alter the experience?

The most common way to tell users why something is there is to separate the "recommendations" from the generic products – see Figure 8. Other possibilities include:

—   Telling users why a list of products was sorted a certain way – for example, "Toys are listed from least expensive to most expensive because you have indicated that price is more important than brand"
—   Explaining a business rule that is driving a special offer – for example, "Customers like you who have purchased vitamins from us in the past year can save 25% on the following health products"
—   When featuring products, list the profile value that is being used – for example, when listing hunting products, label the items listed because of an indicated interest in archery as "Featured archery items"

4.2.3   What am I missing

Once users know why the personalization is happening, they will also need to be able to "opt-out" of it any time. The immediate need for users is for them to temporarily turn of the effects of the personalization so that they can evaluate whether what they are missing is important or not. The most common way to do this is some of "see all" feature. For example, if a user profiled themselves as disliking Madonna and therefore her list of recent musical releases always omits her music, then there should be an easy way for her to see *all* recent releases, regardless of profile values – and thus including Madonna's music.

The design could make this an all-personalization-on or an all-personalization-off, moded design. Or it could offer various layers of de-personalization. For example, if I were at a video games store, I might be profiled as owning a "PlayStation 2" and preferring family video games, suitable for 4 players, and with a rating for "Everyone". But that could be a very limiting set of the all possible video games, so I could be offered ways to relax one of those profile values to gradually expand the range of possible video purchases. For example:

- PlayStation 2, Family, Everyone rating but for fewer than 4 players.
- PlayStation 2, 4 players, but not classified as family nor rated for everyone.
- Family, Everyone, 4 players, but for Xbox.

5. FUTURE RESEARCH

The framework described here for understanding the design implications of personalization does not answer any questions, however it raises awareness of how little we already know about users' expectations from personalization. In fact, the web and its early navigation metaphor are still young and we do not understand it well enough yet.

As personalization becomes are more important part of e-commerce, it will cause us to ask many of the following questions. These fundamental concerns about personalization should become key items on the human-computer interaction research agenda:

- How do we design the interface to convey to users "who you are"? How much detail about who-they-are do users want to know – is just acknowledging that they are logged in enough, or do they want ever aspect of personalization documented for them to review and change? How explicit should the personalization be?
- What user interface design conventions are needed to help users understand what the system knows about them (who they are), what effect it is having on their experience (why is this here) and how they can overcome the effects of personalization (what is missing)?
- How do the navigation and personalization metaphors co-exist? Is it better to discard the ordinary hypertext metaphor entirely and make the compound hypertext metaphor the primary model? When they co-exist, how to users "get in" to the personalization and how do they "get out" of it?
- How do users conceive of personalized e-commerce vs. other e-commerce? Do they "browse" a navigation-metaphor site but "subscribe to" a personalization metaphor site? Is a personalized page viewed as a different version of the "anonymous" page? When users log in, do they envision a whole new site experience, starting at the home page, or do they see their personalized experience as an adjunct to the default, non-personalized experience?
- Do users even care about what "magic" is happening behind the scenes in terms of personalization? Do they only care about the personalization rules if something unusual happens – but if the experience is good, then they would rather remain oblivious to what is happening? Is the personalization driven by privacy concerns and thus should always be explained in terms of what information is being shared and how it is being used?

For the human-computer interaction field to remain relevant to the evolving world of e-commerce, the HCI field must start addressing these personalization issues.

6. REFERENCES

Adkisson, H. (2002). Identifying De-facto Standards for E-commerce Web Sites. Thesis, University of Washington. http://hpadkisson.com/papers/

AIfIA (Asilomar Institute for Information Architecture), (2003). http://www.aifia.org/pg/about_aifia.php

Instone, K. (2002). Location, path and attribute breadcrumbs. ASIS&T 3rd Information Architecture Summit, March 16-17, 2002. http://user-experience.org/uefiles/breadcrumbs/

Instone, K. (1997). Stress test your site, September, 1997, Web Review. http://user-experience.org/uefiles/navstress/

Instone, K. (2000). Information architecture and personalization: An information architecture-based framework for personalization systems. Argus Center for Information Architecture. http://argus-acia.com/white_papers/personalization.html

Nelson, T. (1993). *Literary Machines*. Mindful Press.

Rosenfeld, L., and Morville, P. (2002*). Information Architecture for the World Wide Web*. Second edition. O'Reilly & Associates.

Van Duyne, D., Landay, J., and Hong, J. (2003). *The Design of Sites*. Addison-Wesley: Boston. http://designofsites.com/

Wu, D., Im, I., Tremaine, M., Instone, K., and Turoff, M. (2003). A framework for classifying personalization scheme used on e-commerce websites. *36th Annual Hawaii International Conference on System Sciences (HICSS'03)*, January 6 - 9, 2003, Hawaii. http://csdl.computer.org/comp/proceedings/hicss/2003/1874/07/187470222babs.htm

CHRISTOPH HOELSCHER AND HORST DIETRICH

E-COMMERCE PERSONALIZATION AND REAL-TIME SITE MONITORING

1. INTRODUCTION

A personalized eCommerce website promises benefits for both the customer and the owner of an online business. Ideally, a personalized website can present content and products that are more relevant to the individual customers' needs and interests, thus reducing the necessary navigation behavior and increasing customer satisfaction while facilitating product sales.

Personalization of a website has many facets to it, ranging from adaptive navigation support or personal preferences in page layout to personalized help or search interfaces. This wide range of adaptive features is illustrated in the Personalization feature clusters described in Karat et al. (2003, p. 690). In this paper we will concentrate on the features referred to in Karat et al. (2003) as recommendations and/or adaptive navigation.

Over the last years research in the User Modelling (UM) community has matured into the development of commercial personalization servers that deliver core components for personalizing complex websites (Fink & Kobsa, 2000; see also systematic overviews in Instone, 2000; Kobsa, 2001; and Burke, 2002).

It is important to realize that personalization servers are generally not intended for directly delivering the personalized web content, and especially its layout. A personalized user experience is based on the interplay of personalisation servers with the website's layout and interaction style. Nonetheless, personalization servers deliver the core functionality behind a personalized user experience.

The main challenge for any personalization server – or any user modelling system - is to correctly identify customer interests and characteristics without requiring undue efforts from the customer like extensive question-answering upfront. Delivering content or product recommendations that are considered irrelevant by the customer will have the most negative impact on the user experience and the customer's business relationship with the website.

Automatically identifying a customer's interests in the background is the basis for successful personalization and thus the indirect basis of the personalized user

95

Clare-Marie Karat et al. (eds.), Designing Personalized User Experiences in eCommerce, 95—117.
© 2004 *Kluwer Academic Publishers. Printed in the Netherlands.*

experience. In this paper we describe a comprehensive personalization server system that combines several data sources and personalization strategies to generate the most relevant recommendations possible. Most commercial personalization systems to date have been severely impaired by their reliance on only a single data source (see Fink & Kobsa, 2000; Schafer et al., 2000). Also, we will show that measuring customer behavior on a website is not only a vital data source for the automated personalization process, but also a tool for the website owner to identify user experience problems on a site (section 3).

The software and consulting company 7d has developed the 7d personalization system on the premise of identifying the customer's context of use, connecting recommendations to the customer's goals and interests while adapting to his current navigation on a website. The relevant context for eCommerce personalization consists of three areas: the customers, the content and the business needs. Customers have individual profiles representing their interests and behavior. Content can be classified and matched, based on various attributes. The business model has different rules for managing personalization. To reach successful personalization, we think it is necessary to focus on all three areas at the same time.

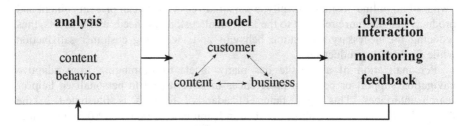

Figure 1.   *The personalization process model includes three steps of personalization: analysis of content and customer behavior, associations with business rules and interaction of customers with a personalization system including monitoring and feedback.*

The approach presented combines customer behavior with content analysis, associated with the underlying business model. The model in Figure 1 has been the high-level motivation for the architecture of the 7d personalization system described in the next section. Information about the customers and the website content is collected in the "analysis" phase and feeds into the "modeling" phase where customer profiles are compiled and related to content and business aspects. Recommendations are delivered in the third phase and initiate customer reactions that again inform the analysis phase in a feedback loop fashion.

To improve the quality of the resulting customer experience and to reduce the effort for companies in eCommerce, we use a complementary personalization model. The following section describes the approach of the 7d system. It joins three core techniques of personalization (behavior-based recommendation, content-based recommendation and rule-based recommendation).

These techniques are useful extensions for various e-business applications such as: managing customer relationships, targeting advertising and promotions, management of marketing campaigns. Further applications exist in areas outside eCommerce, especially corporate knowledge management efforts.

Although each application area may need specific tailoring, the core techniques used for personalization are quite similar. Therefore, different applications can be realized with the toolset of the 7d system according to the requirements of a website owner. The 7d system is integrated into the web system of a portal and provides personalized content such as articles, products or banners to the application and the front-end of the portal.

Section 3 explains a technology that visualizes the navigation behavior of the customers. It can be used both for success control and optimization in the 7d personalization system and the optimization of an eCommerce activity.

Finally two real-life usage scenarios are described to illustrate deployment strategies as well as challenges and benefits of a personalization system.

2. THE THREE-TIERED APPROACH

The 7d system's key characteristic is the integration of three complementary approaches, i.e. a combination of content-, behavior- and rule-based procedures.

7d software currently consists of several modules that may be combined in different ways to generate personalized recommendations. This makes it possible to realize scenarios for enterprise and customer portals that can be flexibly sized upon demand. These modules are used to technically implement three different basic approaches:

1. Behavior analysis: analyzes the paths customer take through a site, what content they are interested in when they use the site, and what customer segments they belong to.
2. Content analysis: based on linguistic methods that enable the classification of documents as well as the analysis of correspondence between documents.
3. Rules: logical links between customer characteristics (demographic data, interest profiles and customer clusters), used to trigger actions and steer processes.

The analysis results in a model of *customer characteristics* and *semantic relationships*. In the next step, the model is linked to the *business needs*. Relevant documents are then made available to the customer, whose response in turn affects the behavior analysis. This approach allows for automatic and continuous success monitoring of customer response to a given site in real time.

The recommendations of the various modules are united in **7d bot** and may be weighted by setting a variety of parameters, which makes it possible to adjust to a given portal's demands. The **7d bot** is also the general component that links the 7d system to the website. Note that the 7d system does not include the functions of a web server or a Content Management System (CMS). The 7d system is responsible for building and maintaining customer profiles and content profiles and for computing personalized recommendations as well as monitoring customer behavior.

The actual delivery of the content and the definition of webpage layout is not part of the 7d system and is instead delivered by the web server and the CMS.

The central aspect is the interaction with the customer in real time and the combination of these three procedures in a single application. The recommendation modules are joined in a feedback loop, so that modules can inform each other. Combining the approaches results in synergy effects – the rule-based and content-based procedures are particularly effective for new documents, while behavior analysis allows for longer-term optimization.

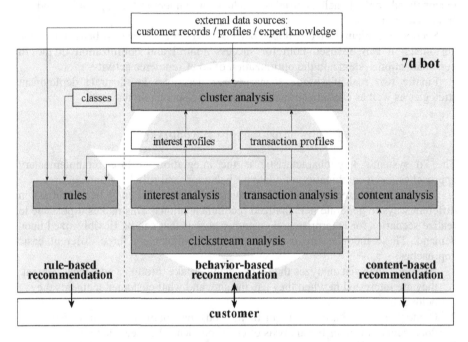

Figure 2.   *Diagram of the information flow between the various modules. The links between the individual modules allow the overall system to learn from current and long-term changes in customer behavior. The clickstream analysis uses current behavior both to recommend documents and to weight content analysis. Interest profiles and records of past transactions may be included in the calculation of customer segments. Interest profiles and customer clusters may be used to define rules.*

2.1 Behavior analysis

Behavior analysis techniques investigate the paths customers take through a site, what content they are interested in when they use the site, and what customer segments they belong to. Different methods of the behavior analysis can be favored or combined depending on the application or customer target group. The following table shows what methods can be used for which applications.

Table 1. *Behavior analysis techniques available in the 7d system*

	Clickstream analysis	Interest profiles	Cluster analysis
Anonymous customer	■	■	
Registered customer	■	■	■
Implicit personalization	■	■	■
Explicit personalization		■	■

2.1.1 Clickstream analysis

The 7d clickstream analysis models the behavior of customers by creating profiles based on their navigational patterns. This involves comparing the behavior of current customers to the site with similar behavior patterns shown by other (past) customers of the site. The resulting statistical model of interest profiles enables customers to take an optimized path through a website. Session IDs (the sequence of clicks while on a site) may be used as an indicator to record both anonymous and registered customers to the site. Individual modeling is carried out for registered customers to the site.

The technology is based on a graph model that shows the paths of customers to the site as self-optimizing graphs. This involves summarizing frequently recurring navigational sequences into a variety of different subsets defined by the length of the subsets. While a customer is navigating a site, his path is reviewed for similarity with all paths already aggregated in the system. Relevant recommendations are generated based on the longest shared subsets of visitors, thus becoming as specific as possible to the customers's navigation path.

Our system uses session IDs instead of standard server log data to analyze the paths in real time. Some other approaches use server log data for post-analysis (see Mobasher et al. 2002, 2003).

On the one hand, paths are aggregated as a directional graph. This makes sense as a document may be shown at various positions in the path, depending on the navigational behavior of visitors of the site. On the other hand, aggregation also occurs as a non-directional graph, showing global (overall) paths between the documents. In this way, **7d behavior** ensures that precise recommendations can be delivered even given a relatively limited data base (also referred to as "sparcity").

Temporary preferences of customers on the site are corrected by taking into account the age of the subsets generated. Subsets are subject to an aging process if they are no longer used by the customers of a site. For instance, if an area of a website is less appealing for seasonal reasons, the subsets generated in this area lose their significance. Parameters may be set to specify the rate at which they are corrected / eliminated.

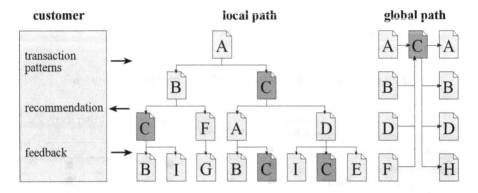

Figure 3. *The Picture shows customer behavior as graphs. This involves analyzing the paths taken in order to identify similarities in customer's use of the site. Then an optimized path through the site will be recommended.*

In comparison with other methods like collaborative filtering, this method also allows for an implicit personalization of anonymous customers. The customers do not need to provide explicit interest profiles. Furthermore, an ad hoc reaction on a change of interest is possible. If a customer moves in an online shop for purchasing literature for himself and his children, the navigation paths will be compared with paths of other customers, who searched for similar literature. The same process works for different customers with a common account. Since the method does not require a shopping basket, it is also suitable for other applications like advertisement, knowledge management or marketing campaigns.

2.1.2 Customer Interest profiles

The 7d system can create long-term interest profiles of anonymous or known customers. These profiles result from a customer's interaction with the relevant content of a portal (documents, articles, banners, products).

Analysis is based on a classification of the content and the current usage behavior. Also, individual profiles may be assigned to interest groups, which can be used for process control using rules, for additional statistical analyses, and to generate recommendations (see Fig. 2).

The creation of customer interest profiles requires three steps:

1. All of a site's documents are classified by content, using linguistic methods (see also section 2.2). This involves assigning them to a taxonomy in a weighted sequence. For each document, **7d profile** then identifies where it belongs in the document categories and how frequently the document was viewed. This results in an overview of document use by its affiliation with a given semantic category. Note that a document will usually be assigned to more than one class and that an association weight is calculated for each document to category relation.

2. Interest profiles may be created for each individual customer or for the total customer population as a whole. These profiles indicate the frequency with which documents in the various document categories were used. Since

documents are assigned with weighted values for their correspondence to taxonomy categories, the clicks on each document also lead to weighted counts of interest in the individual profile. Again a single click can identify a customer's interest in several taxonomy units.

3. There is also the option of defining prototypical interest profiles (peer groups). To do so, category nodes in the taxonomy are grouped into larger areas. These profiles may correspond to certain thematic areas in the site or to a specified target group. A customer's affinity for a given peer group can be used to trigger rules or carry out cluster-specific behavior analysis. Alternatively, peer groups can be defined by the automated clustering procedures described in section 2.1.3.

The validity of the profiles is monitored using confidence indicators, which indicate whether there is real interest in a document class or whether it was accessed more by coincidence. To arrive at such confidence indicators the interest of a customer is stored not in a single value but in a number of time slices, varying from the last e.g. half day to several weeks or months. The confidence indicator can be adjusted so that only customer interests that have been supported by a given number of clicks or have been observed over a defined period of time are considered for generating recommendations. This helps to keep artifacts of special events (news coverage of recent catastrophes, holiday shopping needs) from dominating a long-term view of customer interest. Nonetheless, short-term parts of the profile are available for personalization purposes as well, e.g., for special promotions during reoccurring events or marketing campaigns.

2.1.3 Cluster analysis

7d cluster analysis identifies and analyzes interest-based communities. Using a variety of data sources, it calculates flexible segments and makes them available to the other modules. The cluster analysis detects distinctive features and similarities in the way a site is used, or in the interaction between providers and customers.

The **7d cluster** analysis uses a k-means algorithm that allows for multiple-affiliation sorting. Depending on the degree of affiliation with a given trait, a customer may be assigned to several clusters. **7d cluster** is trained using representative traits, and new customers are then automatically added to the appropriate clusters. Cluster analysis involves the following steps:

1. Find representative traits: To arrive at relatively sharp clusters, traits are identified that are as statistically independent of each other as possible. Traits are weighted according to their importance.

2. Define clusters: The ideal number of clusters is specified to best differentiate between the segments. For each cluster, a typical representative is specified, which defines the center of the cluster.

3. Define the classifier: Pieces of information that are connected to the center of the cluster describe the classifier. This can be named and then may be used in the classification of new customers.

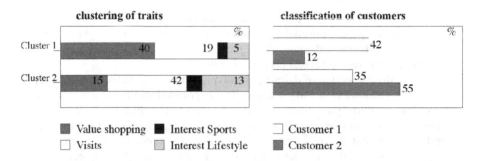

Figure 4.   *A cluster is defined using a combination of relevant traits and their predominance. This also represents the classifier. The classifier then determines how customers are assigned to a cluster. A typical rule based on segmentation of customers: "if customer 1 matches cluster 1 with > 40 % then the recommendation is product #432".*

Following the classification of customer information, a customer's cluster affiliation can be used to generate adaptive rules and used to trigger actions. For example, rules can be administered easier, if they do not have to be "manually" built across a number of customer features (age, gender, interests etc.) but on one class of customers (e.g. cluster #10). Such rules remain valid, even when individual customers float from cluster to cluster.

It also allows for monitoring customer movement between the segments. These movement trends are early indicators of a shift in interests or needs. Not only can behavior clustering be used to automate processes, it is also useful in success monitoring.

2.2 Content Analysis

Besides the observation of customer behavior, the analysis of the content of the website is the second building block of a successful personalization solution.

Very simply stated, the main goal of generating content-related recommendations is to identify documents that are similar to each other with respect to their content and potential customer interests. When a customer is accessing a document, it is assumed that he/she might be interested in further documents that cover the same or closely related topics. Good manual classification and, at the same time, extensive cross-linking by editors is available in only very few websites, since such manual labor is often not economically viable. Therefore, automated identification of content-related recommendations is an important strategy for improving the task of bringing the customer closer to relevant documents. The results of the content analysis described here are used not only for content recommendations, but also represent the content side of the customer profiling process.

The content analysis process combines two general strategies, a direct comparison of the words (or rather concepts and word combinations) in each text and the categorization of documents into categories. Note that *automatic* classification is not always a necessary part of generating content-based recommendations: Whenever systematic manual classification information for documents is available (e.g. Case 2 below), it is used to improve recommendation quality.

Unlike a purely statistical approach, in the 7d system, a series of linguistic analysis steps is performed before statistical techniques for determining document similarity and automatic classification are triggered.

The linguistic methods include a morphological analysis (stemming, composite noun analysis, synonym resolution, handling of specific vocabulary) and the use of an annotated lexicon. This lexicon contains about 300,000 entries with lexical and syntactic annotations, automated correction of spelling-errors and is available in several languages. A rule-based system is used for the morphological analysis and is also able to identify relevant collocations of words in text as well as high-frequency nominal phrases (word combinations). These play an important role in sharpening the process for classification and content recommendation analysis. With all these measures the raw text is transformed into a structure called the "conceptual index" which allows for a comparison of documents that is much closer to the semantic aspects relevant to humans. This is a key element of successful linking of documents on the basis of content similarity.

After these steps, statistical techniques are used to filter both irrelevant stop words (like "the") and insignificantly low-frequent words. The terms are also weighted according to normalized distributions which are either available for the general corpus of words or can be transformed into domain-specific word norms for individual projects in special domains. The classification process itself is based on well-established k-nearest neighbour (knn) methods. The specific advantages of the techniques used for content personalization in the **7d content** analysis are to be seen in the various steps of linguistic processing, especially the morphological methods and the sophisticated detection of relevant collocations.

2.3 Business Rules

Rules may be defined to present marketing measures in a customer-specific way or to guide the flow of information. Rules are defined using guidelines derived from a pool of customer or sales data, and allow for a meaningful steering of actions.

7d rule puts the rule into action by managing the linking between documents and groups of documents and enabling communication with external systems. Communication with CRM or shop systems is handled via Fast CGIs.

Users (site owner personnel) define rules using an administration tool. With a graphic interface, profile attributes of customers are logically linked (AND/OR) and assigned to documents. This involves combining customer characteristics (see Fig. 2) such as demographic data, clustered customer groups, interest profiles or past purchases with groups of documents using logical links. These groups of documents can then be published as positive or negative recommendations. It is also possible to define different lists of recommendations for the *true* and *false* variants of customer interest matches. Furthermore, a list of products bought in the past e.g., or recommendations accepted in the past, can be selectively included in or filtered out of the list of recommendations. A given rule is then combined with a document that triggers the rule's recommendations, so that the rules are triggered when the document is accessed.

3. REAL-TIME MONITORING OF CUSTOMER BEHAVIOR

As part of 7d's personalization technology we present a software for monitoring the behavior of website visitors.

With the **7d monitor** we have developed a tool that enables qualitative analysis of customers' behavior with a high degree of user comfort. In contrast to traditional web statistics the **7d monitor** offers the advantage of displaying the routes taken by visitors through a site in real time.

Possible usage scenarios for the **7d monitor** include:
- To screen the acceptance of current product offers and to determine an optimal positioning within an eCommerce site.
- To screen the acceptance of advertising and the paths which are taken from the ads to products and actual sales.
- To screen the order process including identification of navigation steps where order processes are terminated prematurely.

The various forms of visualization make it easier for the customer to identify connections between structural or substantive product criteria and visitor behavior. He thus has an efficient tool at his disposal with which to check on the success of his website and optimize it. It was not the objective of this development to offer multivariate data analyses as in a data mining system. Instead we focus on real-time visualization of customer navigation. The functionality of the **7d monitor** includes features such as shopping basket tracking and the analysis of marketing campaigns.

3.1 Checking success by means of behavioral analysis

The vast majority of website operators judge the success of their site merely by measuring the number of hits it obtains. Access numbers alone or shopping basket analyses say little about the quality of a website. For this reason qualitative analyses are gaining in significance alongside traditional quantitative methods.

Such qualitative methods not only show what decisions site visitors made but also how they reached their decision. In order to be able to generate this qualitative information we need to record visitors' points of entry and exit, the time spent at the site and their typical navigation patterns.

Besides a server log analysis, reporting and data mining techniques are often employed to carry out complex analyses of visitor behavior. These techniques enable connections and patterns to be uncovered allowing business opportunities to be spotted and existing ones to be improved. They are based on complex, multivariate, multidimensional, statistical methods which in most cases offer useful models for optimizing business strategies. However these procedures require powerful data acquisition resources. They also require a high degree of knowledge from the user in order to define relevant variables and interpret the results.

For many operators this leads to a conflict between on the one hand wanting to know their customers' behavior and on the other hand providing the necessary technical resources and meeting the know-how requirements. A further disadvantage of traditional data mining procedures is the time gap between the acquisition of data and the display of results. It is often not possible for a website operator to follow what is happening on his site on an ad-hoc basis. The ability to react quickly to the needs of customers is especially important in areas where constant updating of the site is required.

Thus, the **7d monitor** tool has been designed and developed as an alternative to existing data mining tools. **7d monitor** supplies users with qualitative information about the behavior of their customers with no time delay and without the training and computing needs of traditional data mining tools. Efficient algorithms for aggregating and visualizing behavior patterns are intended to make it easier for users to recognize their customers and their needs.

3.2 Data acquisition

In order to avoid laborious log file analyses, a procedure was developed to display the navigation patterns of site visitors in a tree map. Our data-collection engine records the paths taken by visitors through a website. In the process a document ID, session ID and a possible customer ID are stored in a database. The statistic engine identifies the paths taken by an individual visitor on the basis of a session ID and compares their paths with paths already taken by other visitors. The number of times a document is accessed is counted on the nodes of the tree, and how often a path is chosen in represented on the edges of the tree. In addition the system records from which document the visitor leaves the site.

In order to optimize the way in which the paths are displayed and in order to reduce the volume of information, parts of the tree structure which are chosen with particular frequency are divided into subsets of the whole tree. This method enables complex visitor behavior patterns to be displayed with relatively low volumes of data. Approaches for reducing the complexity of graphs have been described among others by Han et al. (1997) and Karypis et al. (1999).

As any one document can be found in different positions on the tree depending on the navigation behavior of the visitors, the **7d monitor** offers two ways of displaying the navigation tree. An individual document is shown in its position in local tree subsets, or a selected document is displayed in the context of the global paths which lead to or from this document.

3.2.1 Local path

This form of record shows an individual document in its various positions on the navigation tree. As the visitor can get to the site via different entry points, different trees are also shown. This means that the same document can occur in different trees in different positions.

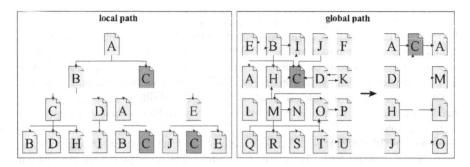

Figure 5.   *Local path: representation of a navigation tree with several sub-graphs for one entry point to the site. Global path: representation of a navigation tree globally recording all paths leading to and from the document.*

3.2.2 Global path

Irrespective the particular entry point, documents are also recorded in a global network structure. This structure consists of all paths linked to the document regardless of their direction. This also allows paths leading to and from the document to be shown as two directed graphs. This way all the paths leading to and from the document can be represented.

3.3 Architecture

The **7d monitor** has been developed as a multi-platform application. In order to make the visualization of paths and frequencies as fast as possible, all aggregates of behavioral data are calculated by a separate statistic engine. The 7d monitor then has the task of communicating with the statistic engine and visualizing its data. The advantage of this approach is that the 7d monitor has sufficient system resources available for complex visualization tasks.

3.4 GUI

In designing the **7d monitor** we set ourselves the goal of giving users diverse information in a clearly structured format. They should be able to conduct their own "visual data mining". Besides the ability of meeting data visualization requirements, the **7d monitor** also had to be easy to use for personnel from different departments like online editorial, marketing, shop management and site administration.

3.4.1 Path display

We decided to show visitors' paths as a graph as this is the clearest way to model navigation patterns. As hyper-complex graphs can be built up on large websites, we looked for a method for displaying them in a finite area. There was also the problem of displaying different entry points to one site. Clustering graphs was not an option because this would involve an unacceptable amount of computing power on the client machine. Other statistical methods were discarded due to the problems of interpreting the results.

In researching the visualization of large graphs we noticed that there were a huge number of theoretical papers as well as some experimental systems. Examples of experimental systems are: the „daVinci" project from the University of Bremen (Fröhlich et al., 1995) and „NicheWorks" from Wills (1997). An overview of experimental studies can be found in Dodge (1999) and Battista et al. (1999).

The disadvantage of all these approaches is that they have little relevance for practical applications. Their most prominent deficits are: long computing times, complicated navigation in the graphs, poor presentation and orientation, high demands made of presentation hardware and a lack of display flexibility.

We opted for an approach in which the user is presented at all times with no more than a section of the existing graph. In the process the user navigates through a tree or can jump to sub-sections of the tree. In selecting the visualization method we decided to use directed graphs.

The user interface (see Fig. 6 and 7) was designed to enable each graph to be displayed in fixed rows and columns. The first column shows the entry points into the site and each further column the next level of hierarchy down in the tree. The sequence of rows represents the order of page call-ups by frequency. The first row thus always contains the most frequently requested documents, etc.

The user can move interactively through this graph. With every mouse click the tree hierarchy behind each document is rebuilt. This has the advantage of allowing even very complex navigation patterns to be displayed in a limited area. The depth of the hierarchy is more or less infinite but depends on the recording depth of the particular graph. Fig. 7 shows the display of local paths and the display of global paths looks similar.

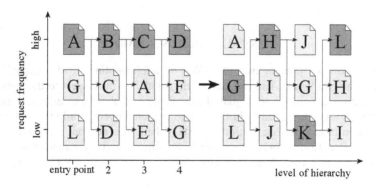

Figure 6.   *This figure gives a schematic representation of how a user navigates through a tree with several entry points. Each entry point represents a different tree.*

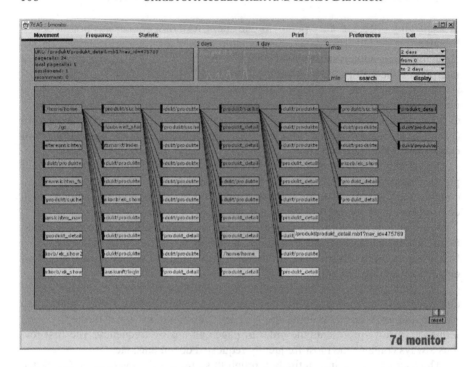

Figure 7.   *This figure shows the display of local paths. Besides the representation of a document in the hierarchy of a tree, the local page hits (in exactly this position in the graph) and global hits (over the entire navigation tree), the number of site exits in this position, the frequency with which the document was recommended and the complete path are all displayed. There is also a window for document hits (local and global) over the whole period selected.*

4. REAL WORLD SCENARIO

In this section we present two examples of implementing a 7d personalization system in the real world. The two cases differ widely with respect to the context of the application, the site owner's goal, the available data about the customers, privacy requirements and consequently in the technology employed: While in the first case only session-based personalization is established, the second case extends the personalization effort to longer-term profiling of individual – yet anonymous – users and more elaborate analysis and reporting for site planning and optimization.

4.1 Case 1: Session-based personalization at GEO.de

Since December 2002 www.geo.de has contained 7d personalization features in both its editorial content and shopping area. GEO offers high-quality content on topics from Culture, Geography and other sciences. These are comparable to the editorial spectrum of U.S. magazines like National Geographic and the web content is largely adapted from the GEO print titles. Additionally a web shop is available, presenting, alongside its print magazines, a selection of ca. 500 products which cater to a quality-oriented audience.

With the help of the 7d system, GEO.de can offer individualized content and shopping recommendations to its audience in an automated fashion and in real-time. Real time here means that recommendations are computed on the fly while the customer is traversing the site and that all user traffic can be directly monitored in the **7d monitor** application. The main goal of the project is to improve the customers' feeling of being catered relevant content and thus improve customer orientation of the site and ultimately foster customer satisfaction and loyalty, measured both in intensified usage of editorial content ("stickiness") and increased sales of shop products.

The two main parts of the GEO site, GEO content (editorial material and photo shows) and GEO shop, had mostly been separate entities for the customer in the past. Personalized recommendations are seen as a meaningful way to improve the interconnections between the editorial content and product offerings.

4.1.1 Technical approach

Limited data available about individual customers of the site was the key challenge of the project. The project members did not consider it feasible to implement measures to recognize individual customers across sessions, because a registration requirement for the site might drive away customers and the specific target audience of the site is seen as highly critical of e.g. cookie techniques. Therefore the project had to rely on those personalization modules that work properly with only single-session customer data. The customer of the GEO site is completely anonymous and no multi-session user profiles are compiled.

Figure 8.   *Graphical boxes with recommendations for shop products (top) and editorial content links (bottom) in the right side quadrant of the screen layout.*

The availability of content at GEO made a strong initial reliance of content-related personalization features a natural choice. These content-based recommendations are combined with the single-session user profiles collected in the **7d behavior** module (see above) and a grouping of customers based on the HTTP referrer.

There are different personalization schemes in place for the different parts of the website. In the editorial content part of GEO.de, customers are always given both content-based and behavior-based recommendations. These recommendations are clearly labelled as referring either to content-similarities or usage-overlap to give customers a better impression of why they have received these recommendations.

The customer grouping based on the HTTP referrer is grounded in the assumption that where a customer comes from typically implies a type of interest in the website. E.g, a customer who has entered the URL of GEO.de directly might be more interested in general overview of topics, while a customer who followed a deep-link from a search engine like Google is probably on a more focussed train of thought. The referrer-based customer groups are mainly used to parameterize how the content- and behavior-based recommendations are weighted, ranked and selected for display. This is controlled in a separate **7d bot** administration module that supplies the filters necessary to tweak the process depending on project necessities. Additionally, separate instances of the **7d behavior** module can be set up for each customer group to further target the precision of behavior-based (clickstream based) recommendations.

Ultimately, the combination of these techniques allows us to offer recommendations that are tightly linked to the current context of the site customer.

This means that both the content (terms and topic) of the current page and the way the customer has traversed are integrated into the best-fitting recommendation available.

Table 2. *Overview of personalization techniques at GEO.de (Case 1)*

GEO content site	GEO shop site
	rule-based recommendations
content-based recommendations	content-based recommendations
behavior-based recommendations	behavior-based recommendations
HTTP-referrer based user groups	HTTP-referrer based user groups
[no profiling across sessions]	*[no profiling across sessions]*

4.1.2 Issues in the GEO shopping project

In the shopping area of GEO, the GEO shop, some further considerations were necessary that take into account specific challenges of eCommerce scenarios.

Again, user groups are defined by analysis of HTTP referrers, but here they are interpreted with respect to more marketing-oriented criteria like involvement with the company brand or product types. These interpretations represent expert (marketing) knowledge of the site owners. The initial expert settings can be checked by comparing the expected behavior of the user groups with actual customer data, primarily with the help of the 7d real-time monitoring component (both success rates of the personalization components and customer click-paths). Thus, **7d monitor** plays equally important roles for site monitoring as well as for adjusting the parameters of the personalization modules to improve performance over time.

Unlike in the GEO content area, rule-based recommendations are seen as more relevant in the shopping world. Here sales managers have specific ideas and promotion campaigns that they test and reiterate with the **7d rule** engine. Once again, the **7d monitor** application can be used to collect vital feedback for the planning, testing and adjusting of rule-based recommendations and campaigns.

Since extensive product descriptions are available for the majority of products, direct content-based matches between products (and products categories) are used. But especially for the cross-linking of content and shop products, the **7d behavior** engine comes into play in the GEO shop as well. In combination with the other methods used it is an important tool for automatically identifying (and learning) which cross-connections most adequately correspond to customer interests, depending on their click-path through the shop and across the content-to-shop barrier.

4.1.3 Benefits & success of 7d personalization at GEO.de

The main benefit of the 7d system was that the time spent at the GEO content site, measured as session length, increased and the number of content pages accessed by the customer moved up correspondingly. At the same time, the automation introduced by the personalization system reduced the necessity for manual linking of pages.

The personalization project aims at further financial effects in the GEO shop by increasing sales in the shop. The combination of behavior-based recommendations with rule-based recommendations (representing marketing knowledge and goals) allow the site owner to target the current interests of the customer while also featuring those products that are most relevant or profitable from his own point of view. In addition to increased sales, the visibility of shop products in GEO content is improved by making targeted recommendations from content to commerce. At the same time, the data collected in the **7d behavior** engine not only automatically improves the selections made by the recommender system, but it also offers valuable performance and customer feedback to the shop owner.

The monitoring facilities employed at GEO.de have several benefits for the site owner. The site managers receive up-to-date, yet fully anonymous data sets about customer behavior that helps with the creation and testing of product bundles and campaigns and planning of future product portfolios. The data can be used to test the site owner's expectations about the popularity of articles and topics as well as how the customers traverse the site, often revealing usability limitations when discrepancies are observed. And finally, and maybe most importantly for the personalization project, the site managers and project members get feedback about the individual effects of the personalization components, allowing them to see which aspects to concentrate on for further improvement, e.g., the rule definitions.

4.2   Case 2: Personalizing a large-scale, high-traffic general interest Web portal

The personalization described in Case 1 did not include any individual profiling of customers that could be recognized over several visits (sessions). When personalizing a large-scale portal, new opportunities and challenges for profile-based personalization arise. The website of Case 2 can be characterized as a general-interest portal featuring news content, editorial material and services across a broad spectrum of topics. Hundreds of thousands of customers access the portal each week, either because it is set as their homepage or because they look for general-interest information. Information about communication services and to some extent eCommerce products also constitutes a large part of the portal's usage.

4.2.1   Profiles, privacy and personalization approach

Since the majority of the portal's customers are repeated and regular customers, building profiles of customer interests – both at the individual level but also at group levels – is a central aim of the personalization project.

To profile customers across session, they have to be tracked in a manner that is compatible with German and European privacy laws and that is also viewed as acceptable by the customers of the site. In the project, a multi-level approach to user tracking, including explicit consent of customers for more critical levels of profiling, is employed: Only customers who have given *explicit* consent to profiling and personalization receive personalized content. To do so, a customer must "register" for the site. If the customer wishes to receive automatic (implicit-profile based) recommendations he has to agree to a permanent cookie stored on his machine, that allows for his recognition across sessions (1st level profiling). The customer also has the opportunity to enter explicit preferences for personalization (a personal interest profile, possibly enriched with other personal data, 2nd level profiling). Here a registration with a customer name and password ensures that no other customers can access or change the customer's profile. Note, that even in this case no information is collected that could identify the individual customer. If personal information about the customer is to be included, it is pseudonymized (with MD5 coding etc.), so that no *personal* identification of the customer at the backend CRM systems occurs. At the same time, relevant group level analyses for marketing and web-planning purposes can be elegantly computed on such a data basis without compromising customer privacy rights and demands.

Customers who do not participate in the personalization but accept permanent cookies are included in *group-level* profiling. These profiles are compiled across sessions, but – in accordance with the law - are not used for any individualized actions or analysis. Instead, they are used for a general usage analysis of the site content and for identifying user groups with the help of clustering techniques (see **7d cluster** above). Also, such customer data, even if not used for recommendation due to privacy concerns, can be employed for the 7d behavior-based recommendation techniques as training material and thus seriously reduce possible cold-start or *sparsity* problems.

This multi-level approach to profile building – again combining content analysis with behavior tracking – can be used across all levels of the website for personalization and usage monitoring.

If the customer has entered explicit interests for his personal profile, this explicit information is collated with the observed behavior (implicit profile) to improve the recommendation quality.

Table 3. *Overview of personalization techniques in high-traffic portal (Case 2)*

Portal content area	Portal shop area
Multi-level user profiling	Multi-level user profiling
Content-based recommendations	Rule-based recommendations
[Behavior-based recommendations]	[Behavior-based recommendations]
Personal homepage (profile-to-content matching)	Product recommendations (profile-to-product-matching)

In the GEO case, the personalization was restricted to giving recommendations on content or product pages. In the portal case, personalization goes a few steps further on the output or presentation side. A personalized customer is presented with a fully personalized start page for each main topic area of the website (like sports, news, travel, etc.). When a customer accesses one of these start pages, his customer interest profile is matched to the content and classification of the latest articles in the respective area, creating a front page for the customer that contains those articles he is most likely to appreciate. In the shopping domain, this mechanism can also be used to automatically create individual product bundles and related offerings.

The rule based component of the 7d recommender system is also supplied with customer profile data, where applicable. Similar to Case 1, this is especially relevant and - as we see below - successful in the shopping domain.

4.2.2 *Monitoring of User Behavior and Personalization in Case 2*

Beyond the actual personalization, the profile data and the other usage data collected in this portal is further analyzed. The **7d cluster** algorithms and data cleaning techniques are specially suited to adapt the heterogeneous data levels available in the project and handle the considerable processing load of the extremely high numbers of user events (clicks) and profiles in this project.

One of the most interesting analyses regularly computed in this project is the segmentation of usage profiles into so-called peer groups. Peer groups consist of usually several tens to hundreds of thousands of (anonymous) customers, who access similar patterns of topics. This helps the portal management to better understand which topics go together and should be bundled, but also help match management expectations with actual usage.

Of course, in a large-scale personalization project success monitoring is becoming even more important. The techniques provided by the 7d monitoring and statistics tools are combined to continuously monitor the success of various aspects of the personalization system and its parameters. In such a performance critical environment with personal home pages, the monitoring of technical system performance is also increasingly relevant.

The analysis methods described here have first only been used for the core personalization of the portal's content area. Now the project is moving into personalizing the shopping area, the advertising component (banner tracking and personalized ad delivery) as well as a personalized search engine (like profile-based filtering of search results).

4.3 *Evaluation of Portal eCommerce Project:*

Our customer's portal (Case 2) features a diverse product catalogue of several thousand items. To test how well the customer profiles compiled earlier are applicable for eCommerce recommendations in the portal environment, a pilot project inside the larger personalization project was launched.

For this pilot project a subset of the product catalogue was selected and with the help of the **7d rule** component and a direct matching of profile features (customer interest in topics related to the product range in question) was implemented as the recommendation mechanism. Profile information was collected automatically over time by the **7d profile** module, while the sales experts modeled their sales rules in the **7d rule** GUI. The rules in this pilot project again referred to matching customer characteristics to individual products of product types.

A number of industry reports have reported between 10% and 30% increase in sales volumes or conversion rates for retail websites by personalized product recommendations (e.g. Kasanoff & Thompson, 1999; Forrester Research 1999; Robinson, 2002). The personalization efforts at Amazon.com are reported to have increased the conversions rate by about 20% (Gaffney, 1999).

For some of the eCommerce evaluations reported in the literature it is not clear whether the differences in sales volumes etc. are due to the quality of the recommendations per se or have to be attributed to group differences: When customers first have to *actively* visit a recommendation center on the website, they might have different levels of interest in the available products than the rest of the user population (self-selection effects). Therefore differences between personalized and non-personalized users have to be taken with a grain of salt (see especially: Kasanoff & Thompson, 1999, p. 27). The test scenario for the case described here is explicitly constructed to avoid this potential confounding by random assignment to treatments.

The tests were performed on the live website of Case 2 and participants were actual customers of the website and were unaware of test participation. Only customers for whom profiles had already been compiled in the past were included in the evaluation to avoid systematic differences between control and personalization groups.

Upon entering the shopping area of the portal, each customer was randomly assigned to one of two test groups and product recommendations were given on the following pages of their visit:

– 50% of the customers are provided with "static" recommendations, that do not rely on profile data and only correspond to the current page context.
– 50 % of the customers are provided with personalized recommendations that correspond to the customers' profile information. E.g., a customer who has – implicitly and/or explicitly – shown or stated an interest in LCD monitors or printers will receive matching product recommendations when browsing the computer hardware division of the eCommerce area.

A standard web server logfile does not provide the necessary statistics for examining the impact of the personalization implemented in the shopping area. The session-based logging features of the 7d system are used to generate reports of the click-through rates of individual products and product categories, both for customers with personalized eCommerce recommendations and for customers who only receive non-personalized recommendations.

For reasons of confidentiality, no specific figures can be released for our customer projects. But we can report that our tests in the shopping domain have been in line with results reported by industry sources (see above). The website owner in the specific case report here considered the positive impact (click-throughs and sales) of personalized recommendations as so successful that further eCommerce personalization projects were launched.

This leads us to conclude that product recommendations delivered by 7d technology have a significant positive impact on sales figures. This is especially the case when longer-term customer profiles are matched to corresponding product offerings. Note that we are not comparing personalized recommendations to non-targeted or even random recommendations. The control group in this test received recommendations that were manually selected to match the context of the page they appeared in. Therefore the increases found can clearly be attributed to the effect of further targeting the recommendation to the individual customer profile, thus a clear personalization benefit is established.

5. DISCUSSION

We have presented a personalization system that has been shown to succeed in real-life web projects both in the content media and the eCommerce domain.

The issue of fusing different recommendation techniques has been raised by Burke (2002) and in this sense the 7d system can be seen as a *hybrid* recommender system, combining both content- and behavior-based analyses as well as short-term and long term customer profiling. The integration of different methods is vital for our projects, since the context and available data about customers differs widely. This poses challenges on both the consulting and integration phase of the projects and makes several supporting components a necessity. On the one hand tools are needed to intelligently connect and precisely parameterize the recommender modules and data collection facilities. A number of graphical tools in the 7d system support this process. On the other hand high-quality real-time monitoring of site usage and personalization performance goes hand in hand with the before-mentioned needs. Although success monitoring tools often play only a minor role in discussions of personalization systems and strategies (but also see Schonberg et al, 2000), they do prove to be indispensable for successful real-life projects.

Another crucial factor for personalization success is customer acceptance which is closely connected to issues of privacy, data security and trust. For some projects, such as Case 1, privacy issues are addressed by strongly limiting the amount of data collected about the individual customer and resorting to alternative methods. Whenever more extensive data about the customer is to be included, like in Case 2, a careful balancing of customer and business owner perspectives is needed. We believe that the 7d system with its various technical approaches is well suited to be precisely adapted to project needs in this customer-to-site-owner balance. The multi-level personalization and privacy strategy in Case 2 allows the site owner to collect the data needed for optimized personalization success and business monitoring. At the same time it is not only fully compliant with the relevant judicial norms but is also transparent, i.e. gives the customer adequate feedback about what is collected about him and provides him with the opportunity to easily edit this profile data. The customer is in control of his data, as stressed for example by Karat et al. (2003).

The comprehensive personalization approach of the 7d system has proven successful for smaller, specialized sites as well as for extremely high-traffic general interest portals. This is especially the case for our efforts in eCommerce projects, which have been tested in controlled experiments like the one outlined in section 4.3. We are aware that the information we can release about specifics of the commercial success is limited. Therefore we hope that more case studies in this domain will be performed and reported in the future, both by ourselves and by other research groups.

6. REFERENCES

Battista, G. di, Eades, P., Tamassia, R. and Tollis, I.G. (1999). *Graph drawing; algorithms for the visualisation of graphs,* Prentice Hall.

Burke, R. (2002). Hybrid Recommender Systems: Survey and Experiments. *User Modeling and User-Adapted Interaction, 12,* 331-370.

Dodge M. (1999). Mapping the Net: Some ideas from cartography & geography. Presentation at the *ISMA: Network Visualization workshop,* 15-16th April 1999, San Diego.

Fink, J. and Kobsa, A. (2000). A Review and Analysis of Commercial User Modelling Servers for Personalization on the World Wide Web. *User Modeling and User-Adapted Interaction, 10,* 209-249.

Forrester Research (1999). *Smart Personalization.* Report published by Forrester Research Inc., Cambridge, MA.

Fröhlich, M. and Werner, M. (1995). Demonstration of the interactive graph visualization system daVinci. In *Proceedings of DIMACS Workshop on Graph Drawing,* 94, R. Tamassia, I. Tollis (eds.), Lecture Notes in Computer Science No.894, Springer Verlag.

Gaffney, J. (1999). *Personalization is no Longer a Luxury, it's "Critical", Report Says.* In ChannelSeven.Com. Available: http://www.channelseven.com/newsbeat/99features/news19991014.shtml [last checked: 2003-09-11]

Han, E.H., Karypis, G., Kumar, V. and Mobasher, B. (1997). Clustering in a highdimensional space using hypergraph models. In *Technical Report,* University of Minnesota, Department of Computer Science, 97-019.

Instone, K. (2000). *Information Architecture and Personalization. An Information Architecture-Based Framework for Personalization Systems.* Whitepaper. Available: http://argus-acia.com/white_papers/personalization.html [last checked: 2003-12-09]

Karat, C.-M., Vergl, J., Brodie, C., Karat, J., and Alpert, S. (2003). Personalizing the User Experience on ibm.com. *IBM Systems Journal, 42* (4), 686-701.

Karypis, G. and Kumar, V. (1999). A fast and high quality multilevel scheme for partitioning irregular graphs. *SIAM Journal on Scientific Computing, 20* (1), 359-392.

Kasanoff, B., & Thompson, T. (1999). *Advanced Strategies for Differentiating Customers and Partners: Software that Enables 1to1 Relationships.* Report published by Accelerating1to1 Inc. (Peppers+Rogers Group), Stamford, CT.

Kobsa, A. (2001). Generic User Modeling Systems. *User Modeling and User-Adapted Interaction, 11,* 49-63.

Mobasher, B., Berendt, B., Spiliopoulou, M. & Nakagawa, M. (2002). The Impact of Site Structure and User Environment on Session Reconstruction in Web Usage Analysis. In *Proceedings of the 4th WebKDD 2002 Workshop at the ACM-SIGKDD Conference on Knowledge Discovery in Databases (KDD'2002),* Edmonton, Alberta, Canada.

Mobasher, B., Berendt, B., Spiliopoulou, M., & Nakagawa, M. (2003). A Framework for the Evaluation of Session Reconstruction Heuristics in Web Usage Analysis. In *INFORMS Journal of Computing, Special Issue on Mining Web-Based Data for E-Business Applications,* 15 (2).

Robinson, Teri (2002). *Back to Basics: Personalization.* In CRMDaily.Com. Available: http://www.crmdaily.com/perl/story/17396.html [last checked: 2003-09-11]

Schafer, J.B., Konstan, J. and Riedl, J. (2000). Electronic Commerce Recommender Applications. *Journal of Data Mining and Knowledge Discovery, 5* (1/2), 115-152.

Schonberg, E., Cofino, T., Hoch, R., Podlaseck, M. and Spraragen, S. (2000). Measuring Success. *Communications of the ACM, 43* (8), 53-57.

Wills, G.J. (1997). Niche Works – interactive visualization of very large graphs. In *5th International Symposium, Graph Drawing '97,* Rome, Italy, Lecture Notes in Computer Science 1353, Springer Verlag.

MIKA HILTUNEN, LEO HENG AND LINDA HELGESEN

PERSONALIZED ELECTRONIC BANKING SERVICES

Case Nordea

1. INTRODUCTION

Internet banking has proven very successful both from the customers' and bank's points of view. Nevertheless, Internet banking has several HCI-related challenges. The role of HCI factors in research related to Internet banking is likely to increase over the years to come. Two of the most interesting challenges are how to serve a wide range of customers as well as possible, regardless of their differences, and, having a constantly growing variety of services in the Internet bank. Personalization may help us respond to some of these challenges, but exactly how this might be achieved is a complex question. The complex process of understanding the users' needs and translating these into targeted content and the issue of presenting the personalized content in a usable and compelling manner are major challenges. This chapter will discuss the unique characteristics of personal Internet banking from HCI and personalization viewpoints and describe the most important questions and some of the possible answers in the given context.

2. THE CONTEXT OF INTERNET BANKING

Internet banking (also referred to as online banking or cyber-banking) is one of the most important changes within the retail financial industry in the last hundred years or so. Internet banking, as generally understood, means using the Internet as an intermediary channel between the bank and its customers, allowing normal banking activities to be done with self-service, independently of time and place.

Different channels have different characteristics. One of these characteristics can be said to be the "freeness", the extent that particular channels are bound to or free from time and place (see figure 1). The traditional channel, the branch office, is at one end of this freeness scale. It requires the customer to travel to the physical branch office during business hours, stand in line and handle the banking issues face to face with the branch officers, in compliance with a common interaction pace. The other extreme is obviously Internet banking and especially its mobile variant. Mobile terminals can be used almost anywhere (not in planes of areas where are no

Clare-Marie Karat et al. (eds.), Designing Personalized User Experiences in eCommerce, 119—140.

mobile networks) and anytime the pace completely selected by the customer. (Hiltunen et. al 2002.)

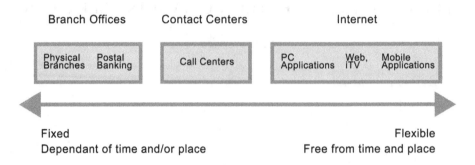

Figure 1. *Banking channels according to a "freeness" scale*

Internet banking is part of a multi-channel banking strategy. This generally means that customers are offered several channels from which they may select the one that pleases them the most in a given situation and need; for example, from regular branch office to IVR (Interactive Voice Response) telephone services and to online web services.

Internet banking has emerged in the last ten years, but similar interactive services were in place even before the Internet became widely available. PC based, desktop banking applications working with modem connections have existed much longer than the Internet, as we know it today. Today, the most common way of utilising the Internet channel in banking is through web-based interactive banking services, accessed either with personal computers or PDAs (Personal Digital Assistant). Other variants of Internet banking today are mobile Internet services, using protocols like WAP (Wireless Application Protocol), GPRS (General Packet Radio Service) and Interactive television, using protocols like DVB-MHP (Digital Video Broadcasting - Multimedia Home Platform). As new technologies are developed, the number of different Internet banking variants increase. At the same time, as back-end systems get more and more flexible, the number of different banking services provided through the Internet channel also keeps increasing. We live in interesting times when it comes to Internet banking!

The latest trend in Internet banking is to integrate third parties into the electronic business. Typically, customers use banks to interact with a third party, for example to pay their bills. In this case, the Internet channel can also be used to do the complete transaction electronically, resulting in impressive cost and time saving, not only for the bank and its customer, but also for the other involved parties. In addition, the electronic business aspect of Internet banking is creating completely new types of services – services that do not exist in other banking channels – that can be offered to new customer segments and used to create new revenue.

One of the main motivations behind Internet banking is cost reduction. This does not just mean reducing the bank's costs, but also letting the bank's customers get the service cheaper than before, as a result of cheaper, more transparent processes and extensive competition in the markets. In addition to cost savings, Internet banking enhances the processes dramatically, making transactions faster and thus providing better service to customers. Internet banking has also been found to increase customer loyalty (Polatoglu & Ekin, 2001) and satisfaction (Mols, 1998). All in all, the more the customers choose to use the Internet channel in their banking, the better for both them and the banks. Obviously, the third parties involved also get the same benefits: improved efficiency and better customer service.

To make the customers choose the Internet channel in as many situations as possible, the Internet channel must be the best alternative for a given situation; as easy, compelling and convincing as possible. It also needs to be all this to as many users as possible.

There are many challenges and special issues to be dealt with in Internet banking. The technology used is crucial, not only because of security issues and the fact that mistakes are unacceptable in this area, but also because of the heavy volume of Internet service usage and the large backend systems. The software architecture and hardware used must perform. Security and performance aspects create demands and limitations on how the Internet services can be designed and also on how they can be presented to customers.

Existing local and international legislation control banking procedures, for example, the information that must be presented and the responsibilities each party must be able to fulfil. International standards, both official and unofficial, provide a framework that Internet banking must accommodate. For example, electronic invoicing and payment standards determine the format in which the payments are sent between banks. As new services and technological innovations are integrated into Internet banks, the flexibility and maintainability of the existing services becomes more and more important. One must be able to change, add and remove service components and utilise new technological features easily and cost-efficiently in order to develop the existing services effectively.

The competition in the markets is high, making "time to market" a crucial aspect when developing new services for the Internet channel. The same goes for the overall usability and appearance of the services and the pricing; it is easy to switch banks when most of the large banks offer similar services online, making the comparison easier than before.

For banks, one of the most promising outcomes of Internet banking is the cross selling of new services. The idea behind cross selling is to leverage the usage habit of customers already familiar with some of the services in Internet bank and offer new services to these people. The bulk of the service in retail Internet banking targeted to private customers is regular invoicing and account management services. Leveraging the usage habits of the mass of users – that use only these bulk services – to sell banking products that fulfil other needs of these users cost-efficiently and in a user-centered way online is one goal in future Internet banking.

2.1   Human Computer Interaction and Internet banking

Internet banking provides an interesting area for HCI (Human Computer Interaction) researchers and practitioners. There is a high interaction level in online banking services, when compared to many other Internet service genres, making the User Interface (UI)- and interaction design crucial and challenging. Many of the core tasks of Internet banking are mission critical; it is crucial not to make mistakes involving money. In order to get as many customers as possible to select the Internet as their channel in making business with or through the bank, the Internet service must provide quick, straightforward, pleasant and effortless service while preventing mistakes from happening, for example, by having precautions like asking for user confirmation and acceptance before transactions are completed. In addition to cognitive and efficiency issues, the Internet bank must also deal with the online trust experience, providing UIs that optimise the perceived trustworthiness; helping the customers to make decisions under varying degree of uncertainty. The list of critical HCI issues goes on and on. It is clear that HCI as a discipline and dealing with usability of the service is important to the success of the Internet bank.

Today's society presents a continuous flow of information from different sources in forms of direct and indirect marketing, news, TV, and Internet. This challenges our information processing capacity. In this time of information overload, Internet services in general must compete for people's attention, and at the same time, provide simple, easy to use ways to achieve the users' goals. (Harald, 2002) The winners of the competition must spare the target from unnecessary noise by offering only the relevant information and doing so in a visible way. But how does an Internet bank succeed in this when, at the same time, the number of services available is increasing rapidly in the electronic channels and more and more inexperienced users are adopting them?

A few years ago, the question from the customers' perspective was whether or not the services were available online. The most important thing was how many of the most important services were available, and in the beginning they were few. The first users of Internet banking were early innovators. These early adopters of new technology did not care much about usability or visual design aspects of the net bank; what was important was to have it working and available. Today, when most Internet banking customers are not technological enthusiasts or nerds, ease and intuitiveness becomes more critical. As the largest banks are starting to address usability and are not differentiating themselves in this area, the value-added capabilities, like electronic invoicing and third-party integration, will become the competitive and differentiating factor for them. More and better service is demanded from successful Internet bankers all the time.

According to Mattila, the main adoption driver for Internet banking is its independence of time and place, whereas the main adoption barriers are the lack of personal service and users' difficulties in using computers (Mattila, 2001). This makes lots of sense, when thinking about regular people, either being required to travel to a branch office to do their banking, stand in a line and deal with the branch personnel and then travel back versus simply logging in to a net bank and doing the same thing in seconds or minutes from the comfort of own home. If computers and the Internet are familiar to at least a basic level, choosing the most convenient channel to be used in most cases is easy.

According to Karjaluoto, existing online customers consider speed, security, ease-of-use, price and independence of time and place to be the most important characteristics of an Internet bank (Karjaluoto, 2002). He also states that non-online customers appear to value social contacts higher than online customers; this may be a key point when thinking about the challenges of getting the existing non-users to adopt the Internet for their use. Nordea research has noted that elderly customers unfamiliar with the Internet seem to have personal, friendly relationships with particular branch employees. They also have time available during office hours and do not see a problem in travelling to these persons with whom they like to do their banking. They have gotten used to personal service in the past and this habit is echoed in their current attitudes and values, making self-service feel hollow. This feeling of personal service is hard to translate to an Internet-based service design. In addition to customising services, personal service also includes the social aspect of visiting a branch office and dealing with a living person behind the counter.

The strategic importance of Internet banking to banks' business is very high and usability of the Internet banking services is an important competitive factor, making HCI issues very important to be dealt with properly.

2.2 Factors affecting Internet banking

As discussed above, several issues influence how Internet banking evolves and should be developed in order to succeed. These factors can be grouped into four main areas: user needs, market influence, business motivation and technology demands. An Internet bank should comply with all of the four areas in order to meet changing requirements. From an HCI point of view, however, some problems require novel solutions in order to ensure that services remain easy and satisfying to use.

Figure 2 below, illustrates the four main areas influencing Internet banking. The market influence contains factors in the bank's external environment, to which banks have a limited possibility to influence. These factors include legislation and standards, the cruel reality of business, competition in the marketplace and the importance of possessing efficient time to market capability. The business needs area contains important issues for profitable banking. These are the motivation factors behind a bank's decision to go into Internet banking: reducing costs, improving efficiency, increasing revenues by generating more sales, cross selling and increasing customer satisfaction by offering convenient services to customers. Customers, on the other hand, need different things than banks, or at least their view of the needed factors is different. Customers want to have usable, accessible services that they feel comfortable using and trust to be secure. They value the freedom created by the Internet banking and the speed of doing their banking. Technology factors make Internet banking possible – and limit the design. Performance is a key issue, as is security and backup systems. Technological systems must also be easy to maintain and develop: it should be easy to add new services to the Internet bank.

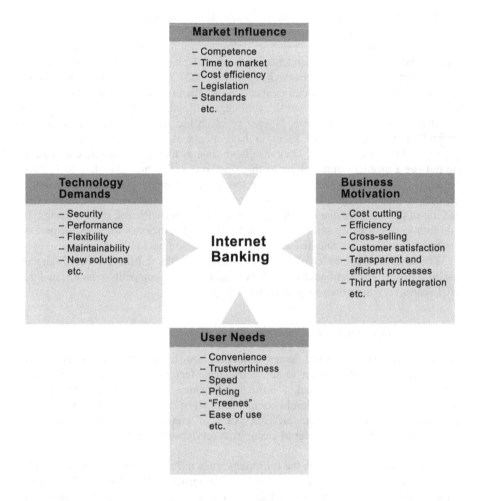

Figure 2. *The four areas influencing Internet banking*

2.3 Nordea and Internet banking

Nordea is the leading financial services group in the Nordic and Baltic Sea region. The Nordea Group has more than 10 million customers, 1,288 branches and is present in 24 countries. Currently (in late 2003) Nordea has approximately 3,6 million online customers, both private and corporate. The adoption of the Internet channel has been rapid and the pace does not show any signs of slowing. Nordea has succeeded not only in getting the early innovators to adopt the service, but also to compel the majority of "regular" people, who are not enthusiastic about new technologies as such. Crossing this chasm between attracting the minority of technology oriented people and majority of the rest of us is indeed one tollgate differentiating those who succeed in providing Internet services from those who quickly die out. (Moore, 1991, 1995.)

Nordea has succeeded in electronic banking by being at the front of technological development and by taking the customers' point of view when offering services via electronic channels. Services are offered through branches, call-centres and Internet; it is up to the customer to decide which channel to use in any particular context. Services offered through the Internet are easy, straightforward, secure and intuitive to use; this has led to a adoption of Internet as the channel for everyday banking and customer habits that have been building for as long as the World Wide Web has been available. There are also several external factors in Nordea's main market area (the Nordic countries) that have contributed to the rapid adoption of Internet banking, for example, good technical infrastructure, high average education and long physical distances.

As the adoption of Internet banking increases and reaches the majority of the population, new user needs emerge. With millions of online customers, Nordea must be able to serve a variety of customers, ranging from the early innovator type to those with limited Internet competence. The variance in the online customer base increases as the service adoption rises. At the same time, technological innovation makes it possible to provide more and more banking services online, so the overall complexity of Internet services keeps increasing. Together these two phenomena create an HCI challenge that must be addressed to satisfy all kinds of online customers. One possible answer is personalization.

3. PERSONALIZATION IN INTERNET BANKING

3.1 Defining the term in the context of Internet banking

Marketing experts Don Peppers and Martha Rogers first used the term personalization in a 1993 book called "The One to One Future". The book discussed the possibility of super-optimised selling by targeting each customer individually. Around 1995, technology-oriented marketing specialists coupled Peppers and Rogers with the Internet and concluded that online commerce would be one-to-one marketing's killer app. (Peppers, 1993.)

However, the idea of modifying content or the means to offer content targeted to the needs of individuals or groups has a much older history. Even the first radio receivers allowed channel selection and volume adjustment, newspapers and books have been targeted to special audiences during their existence and military propaganda has used sophisticated means to deliver messages according to the target audience and context ever since Julius Caesar. In a sense, the philosophy of personalising communication forms and modalities is a fundamental part of inter-human communication. We adjust our non-verbal communication according to audience feedback coupled with the content of our message. In addition we can adjust our appearance as well as possible beforehand – by, for example, selecting appropriate clothing.

There are some definitions that are easier to apply to this broad idea of personalising in the Internet context: *Personalization* refers to any process that changes the functionality, interface, information content, or distinctiveness of a software system to increase its relevance to an individual. The process can be initiated and carried out either by the user or by the system itself (Blom, 2000); this distinction is sometimes referred to as customisation and personalization (or the other way around – usage is not completely systematic) or explicit and implicit personalization.

The incorporation of personalization techniques in the field of electronic banking is not new. Nordea, for example, allows its customers to modify their personal settings for the Internet bank and for WAP services. Extranet services – targeted at private customers – modify their content for the specific customer using it. Nordea has also done work to increase the accessibility of its online services, e.g., by providing a text-only version of its Internet bank.

Personalizing the experience of a one-time user makes little sense. The cost (in time and effort) of customising a one-time experience would far outweigh the benefits. Implicit personalization requires that the computer system have a history with the user. A one-timer has no history.

Personalization, then, only makes sense for returning, frequent users. An obvious requirement is that the system is able to identify the user; this happens when the user logs in to the service. Luckily, the users of Internet banks are all "frequent" users in the sense that they are identified and they do not just happen to drop by the banking service.

In a personalization sense it should be possible for the customers to personalize the Internet bank, but then they'll have to supply more information to have a one-to-one relationship with the bank – otherwise the banks cannot know the needs of the customers in sufficient detail. Privacy concerns must be addressed before the users are willing to give us the information necessary for good personalization (Nielsen, 1998). Again, banks are lucky in this respect: banks know a lot about their customers and do not need to ask for the same things again in order to personalize most things.

Good personalization requires the system to know a lot about the user. In addition to the privacy issue, this also is in direct conflict with the paradox of the active user where people are more motivated to start using things than to take the initial time to learn about them or to set up a lot of parameters. Web users are impatient and want to get something useful out of a site immediately: they typically don't want to spend time setting up complex personalization features. (Nielsen, 1998.)

Although Nielsen generalized his comments to typical web users in a typical context, the same can very well be thought to be the case also for Internet bank users; they have a goal and want to reach that – using the service, fast!

Part of the privacy issue is how comfortable the user is with sharing personal information with the bank online, in addition to the financial information already possessed or derived by the bank. Many of the services provided by the bank are personal in nature and relate closely to planning one's life and life status. How easy is it for the bank to recognize status changes (death of spouse) or changes of plans (divorce)? Issues like that are so personal that great delicacy is called for. If an Internet banking application tries to sell life insurance to the spouse just passed away, "One-to-one communication" is not the first concept that springs to mind.

3.2 Reasons to personalize

As stated above, personalization refers to any process that changes the functionality, interface, information content, or distinctiveness of a software system to increase its relevance to an individual. What the bank gets out of a properly personalized application is different from what the user gets out of it.

Benefits for the bank:

- More loyal customers. People are likely to remain loyal to a personalized service and to stay on the site longer (Nielsen/Net Ratings, 2000).
- Selling more (both cross-selling and selling more of one service). In banking it's generally estimated that the cost of selling to a new customer is ten times higher than selling to an existing customer.
- Competitive edge. Personalization is a marketing issue in Internet banking - losing initiative to a competitor means losing business.
- Increased trust. Providing what the user personally needs will increase trust, enabling deeper benefits for both sides.

Benefits for the user:

- Saved time. A well-personalized application will generate shorter task completion times.
- Added value from services. Correctly targeted content can lead the user to adopt services, such as online investing, that are better suited to her tasks.
- Financial and other benefits. Correctly targeted content can also lead the user to adopt products or services that generate benefits such as better insurance coverage.
- Increased trust. Fulfilment of needs as promised will increase trust, enabling deeper benefits for both sides.
- Improved user experience. A feeling of being in control of the environment increases satisfaction and productivity (Spolsky, 2001).
- Reduced cognitive workload in using the service, resulting from reduced "noise" and complexity in the UI when the bank is able to present only the relevant content or services.

What is really fascinating and interesting is that most of the issues above are really only the different sides of the same coin. Personalization in Internet banking context seems to be a real win-win situation, where the goals for the service provider meet exactly the ones of the user.

3.3 Reasons not to personalize

Personalization can be a powerful tool when used correctly. But it can easily be misapplied, particularly if one has a shaky grasp on the (quite serious) limitations of present-day personalization technology. Here are some issues to consider:

Drawbacks for the bank:

- Cost. Personalization is an expensive and laborious process to implement. "The average personalization system costs about $1.5 million, no matter what the size of the site," says Michele Rosenshein, an analyst with Jupiter Communications (Eads, 2000).
- Uncertainty of success. Success of personalization is hard to measure and thus difficult to argue for. The success of a personalized system is hard to prove with immediate testing, as even the system often has its cold start time. On the other hand, in the long run the amount of increased revenues or decreased costs generated by personalization is hard to prove, as there are many other contributing factors.
- Technological limitations. Integrating existing systems to create a data warehouse for personalization is a task of its own, as is implementing the personalization engine, the "brain" that directs personalization correctly.
- Lack of knowledge. Lack of information of individual buying preferences, reactions, and interests, cross-referenced with more general properties such as demographics etc., will make starting to build a personalized system harder. This will also make the cold start time longer.
- Usage uncertainty. If the chances are that only a small fraction of the users will personalize the site, is it worth the cost and effort?
- Performance. Especially if integrated with legacy systems, response times will increase as a function of the complexity of the personalization. Speed is one of the key issues in Internet banking, as in any other web site.

Drawbacks for the user:

- Lack of trust. However trustworthy a partner the bank is, there are still people who unwilling to trust any additional information to it.
- Betrayal of trust. Any bad subjective experience from betraying trust (for example the feeling of being spammed) from an Internet application will degrade the trust in all other applications.
- Lack of value received. Poorly functioning personalized applications that do not deliver the promised added value will create a more negative attitude towards personalization in general.
- Cold start time. Too long cold start times (the time required by the system to collect a sufficient amount of initial information) might make a personalized service appear ineffective, thus not delivering the promised added value, causing customer disappointment.

It's no wonder, then, that many companies are reluctant to invest too heavily in personalization. The unequivocal success stories are few and far between. However, we believe there are benefits to be achieved, and good techniques for doing that.

4. HCI RELATED CHALLENGES FOR PERSONALIZATION IN INTERNET BANKING

A good feature in an online service is pointless if not used. This is a challenge for communication strategies in general – how to inform customers about new features in a way that encourages them to try them out? It is also a challenge to the interaction and user interface design processes; how to make personalization so intuitive, attractive and easy to use that customers (including Internet novices) try it out, succeed in using it and are amazed at its possibilities? There is plenty of HCI research on similar issues, but not specifically in the context of electronic banking.

Ways to make personalization functionality easy to access and use should be studied with a variety of different user types. Personalization of the service should feel attractive and easy for both expert and novice users, even though the attitudes and needs of these user segments differ from each other. Studying the differences might answer the interaction design question on how to implement the personalization in the service. Particularly interesting to study are the possibilities of personalization to create a subjective feeling of personal service to customers in a banking context while still letting the user feel in control.

There are many methods for studying the impact of personalization. Several of them have been used in Nordea, ranging from qualitative usability tests to quantitative survey research and data mining. We have found that the most appropriate way of using the methods is to incorporate them in a complementary fashion. The real challenge lies in the ability to integrate the pieces of information each methodology gives rise to and to transfer this knowledge into user-friendly and efficient design. We are also looking forward to the emergence of a personalization research forum, one that would explicitly adopt the perspective of the user in striving for beneficial personalization technologies.

4.1 Cross selling and task completion

Remus Brett calls for online banking to sell, urging banks to shift their Internet strategy focus from cutting costs to generating revenue by extending business with those who are ready to buy online and piecing together online tools to create a seamless buying cycle. (Brett et al., 2002.) While facilities for buying exist, personalization can greatly aid in the completion of purchasing transactions. Adapting offerings to the customer's online buying experience will improve sales: start with low-complexity products such as savings accounts or frequently purchased products such as car insurance, and move gradually to more complex and less frequently purchased products such as mortgages. (Brett et al., 2002.) This way the user's confidence, experience and trust in the application will increase hand in hand, allowing further-reaching decisions with higher monetary value to be made. In other words: leverage existing usage habits to introduce other, more complex products to be purchased online.

Generating revenue is an important factor for the bank, but it can't be over-favored at the expense of core task usability. Nordea has identified several task-related segments among the online bank users, such as users that use the online bank only to pay bills, and ones that use it mostly to manage investments. It has also been noted that these segments rarely overlap. To ensure that a message or an offer really hits the target, it must be targeted according to the customer needs. Customer needs are, however, challenging to understand and apply in the process of targeting. This process consists of different levels of information that must be integrated before the information can be utilized in targeting. After the targeting has been completed, it must be carefully made sure that the message will not impede the customers' ability to complete the tasks they want to get done. One of the most common issues that come up in our usability tests is that a customer says, "I just want to pay my bills and be gone". Anything that prevents him from doing so is obviously bad for the overall impression of application quality, thus affecting the level of trust and from that the likelihood of a future purchases.

At least two levels of issues must be taken into account when creating targeted offerings: the actual offer and its visual presentation. It is rather straightforward to see what could be offered; or the other way around, what should *not* be offered to a particular customer. If a person already has a life insurance or an investment agreement, it should not be offered to him again! Naturally, a bank knows what products a customer has purchased or what agreements exist, and they can easily be applied in targeting. Certain demographics can give hints about what services could be of use to the person, and selecting the most likely ones would form the space from which the targeted offers could be then selected to give the best fit. However, the question of how concretely to present the offerings is a more complex, or better, more delicate issue; it makes all the difference if a person feels the offering to be either "just another add" or "a helpful hint meant just for me". And as we know, feelings and emotions are both difficult to predict and hard to manage.

4.2 Designing personalizable user interfaces

When putting the personalization into practice, we believe it's important not only to implement the most complex solutions, but also the simplest ones, designing from the bottom up. There are a number of interface issues, such as providing for flexibility and scalability and terminal device independence, which will already provide valuable personal features not only to Internet banking but also to any other Internet service. The best thing about these features is that the extra cost of implementing them is relatively low or negligible.

There are a number of ways of implementing the actual customization or personalization features. When considering which ones to use, one should utilize a proven set of design guidelines – working in compliance with such a set it is much easier to weigh the benefits and costs of using a given technique. For Internet banking design guidelines we have prioritized trust, intuitiveness and consistency, speed, and efficient communication.

4.2.1 Designing from the bottom up

The user experience of an application with personalization is a multi-faceted entity. Considering the user experience from the start, from the user's end, the first point of interaction is the terminal device itself. With multi-channel applications we in Nordea give the user the possibility to choose the type of device used for the task at hand. All online services should be highly usable with both mobile and fixed devices. Narrowing the scope, when the device is chosen, there is still lot to consider before the user experiences will include content that is fully targeted by utilizing information from the Customer Relationship Management (CRM) database.

Most terminals have device-dependent possibilities for customizing the application use. Unfortunately often in web applications, the use of these options is limited. The most basic way a PC user hopes to customize his HCI is by selecting the hardware, such as the screen size and input device type. While this selection is vital and quite limited for people with disabilities, it is also significant for normal, able-bodied users (Pilgrim, 2002).

Personalization features should not impede implementing the application in a generally proper way. And accessibility options, flexible layout, scalable font size and browser independence included to facilitate personalization should be implemented creatively in the graphical design, to contribute to the general quality and appearance of a site – the site doesn't need to be boring or ugly.

Flexible layout

Taking advantage of the extra euros spent on a larger screen is quite often prevented by over-wary web design. Using a flexible (often also called fluid or liquid, i.e. using the whole browser window width) page layout (see Figure 3) instead of a fixed layout (often centered or left-aligned) can be argued to reduce the cognitive workload by reducing vertical scrolling and allowing UI elements to be presented in a way that uses all available space. By using a flexible layout the user interface is allowed to spread out to more relaxed and spacious form instead of a packed and cramped one, and flexibility also facilitates font scaling better. Flexible layout has been argued for both from usability and visual design aspects. (Nielsen, 2000; Veen, 2002.). The reason why fixed layout is often favored is the fact that it always looks the same, regardless of the end terminal qualities, e.g. screen resolution. UI elements look the same and stay in the same places when viewed with different resolutions. On the other hand, the fixed layout will cause scrolling with small resolutions and leave available space unused with bigger ones. This approach is obviously easier for the designers, but does not provide optimal screen real estate usage for the users.

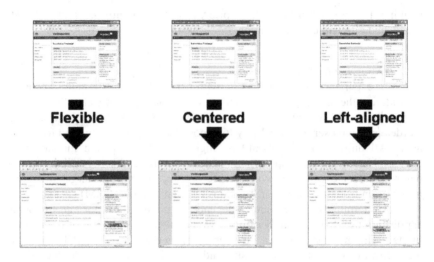

Figure 3. *Illustration of the effects of the different layouts*

Font size scaling

Technology allows the user to be artificially prevented from using the browser's font size scaling options, which might lead to reading problems or discomfort (Pilgrim, 2002). As rudimentary as it is, we believe both the font size scaling and layout flexibility are good ways for the user to customize the application, and thus affect positively to his user experience. And sometimes these rudimentary issues are not just 'nice to have' but in fact enabling factors, such as print large enough to read. As age does not seem to be a barrier to the adoption of Internet banking (Mattila, 2001), the effects of aging, such as degrading eyesight, should be taken into account. In fact, considering the advantages of the Internet channel and its location independence, elderly people will potentially benefit a lot from adopting it in their daily banking. However, text size is not a problem only for the elderly; eyesight has been found to start degrading at the age of 40.

Browser selection

The second layer where a selection takes place in the web is the browser. Application users have personal preferences, but the selection may also be based on necessity. Here again the special browsing devices for the disabled, such as the Braille devices (tactile devices for reading the Braille dot type) and screen readers are a factor. Providing for different browsers is neither hard nor expensive, all that is necessary is simple and valid HTML or XHTML code (Pilgrim, 2002). The business incentive for doing this is that interfaces facilitating for this kind of browsers are also quite usable with mobile devices too, thus providing for the multi-channel approach.

Use of both the keyboard and the mouse

HTML and XHTML also have simple but often-neglected features, the access key and tab index, that greatly add to the usability of a keyboard as a pointing device. Access key (HTML attribute 'accesskey' supported by the major browsers) allows the designer to set a key that, when pressed together with the ALT key, directly accesses the object, either activating a link or setting a focus to a text box, for example. While this technique has limitations (dependence of the natural language, for example), it can still aid in designing more usable and accessible user interfaces. Tab index (HTML attribute 'tabindex') enables us to set the order of tab stops, making it easier to navigate with tab from control to another. Both of these features are in general use in Windows applications.

4.2.2 Design guidelines for Internet banking success

Designing for online banking is similar to designing for any other application; having good and concrete guidelines help to hit the right target in the first attempt. Every bank offering Internet services is likely to have their own visual guidelines, but they are not enough. In addition to graphical guides, there is a need for more abstract set of rules, often called as usability guidelines that outline the "philosophy" of designing the services. For example, Serco Usability Services has created a set of general and public usability guidelines for online banking design (Serco, 2002). Together with academic research, like Karjaluoto's and Mattila's research for Internet banking adoption reasons, they can be used to elicit personalization features that would help make the application even more successful.

Trust

Trust is one of the main factors for a successful online bank. Quite often financial institutions command a strong presence of trust – "It's like putting money in the bank" – but it is also important not to damage that feeling with inappropriate design or implementation. For example, using a too small font size might give the user the feeling there's too much information or that he's presented with the "small print". Presenting outdated information or including a "fun" area in an online bank can also erode the confidence. Something as small as providing alternative points of contact such as telephone numbers and address details will increase the credibility and give a feeling that a service is given "all the way through".

From a personalization viewpoint it is even more interesting how an individual's feel of trust can be increased with subtler design-related actions targeted for creating a specific emotion. Somewhat striking research claims that using a 3D clipart half the size of the screen and cool, pastel tone colors with no background will elicit a greater extent of trustworthiness (Kim & Moon, 1997). While individual designs do vary (especially culturally), we feel that personalization of the elements can have a significant effect on the interface's ability to create trust.

Information is both a key asset in personalization and a major point of uneasiness regarding trust. Therefore, to encourage trust, the information must be handled properly. While banks do posses a quantity of personal information on the customer by the nature of the business, it is still important to clearly state what additional information is collected. It is a good practice to state what this information is used for and that it is not used for anything else than what the user consents to. As an addition it may even be trustworthy to let the user modify or delete the information.

Preventing errors that result from mistakes by the user or misunderstandings regarding the result of users actions is important to generate a feeling of trust towards using an Internet bank. Providing a consistent arsenal of acceptance and confirmation practices ensure that users make few critical mistakes and learn that "no money gets taken from their account" without their final confirmation of the transaction. This feeling of trust allows users to try out new, often complex services without constant fear of buying something they do not really want.

Intuitiveness and consistency

Internet bank service design must be both intuitive and consistent. Intuitiveness means that new users immediately recognize the meaning of the user interface elements and processes; that the logic behind the service design matches their inner, mental models as well as possible. Consistency of the design, on the other hand, helps users to learn to use the variety of features in the services; when they grasp the logic of one of the features, they benefit from a "positive transference" in learning to use the other features, because all the features work in a similar way. Intuitiveness in the ways personalization is presented and sticking with the same logic throughout the service is important. That helps the users understand the possibilities and the logic of the personalized elements as well as to identify them after learning what they are there for.

Speed

One of the greatest reasons for online banking adoption, speed, must not be compromised. Direct access to the desired task must be guaranteed without teaser marketing or loading delays because of unnecessary graphics. Personalization and customization can be used to present the important tools such as direct access to pay bills or to make investment transactions clearly on the front page, to affect the nature and amount of marketing material presented, and to adjust the amount of "eye-candy" in the interface. On many Internet sites, the service provider's revenue model is in direct conflict with user needs, and thus with the reasons users want the service in the first place. For example, a news portal offers up-to-date news, but makes money by presenting readers blinking and flashing banners that compete for their attention and clutter the looks of the service. Users might even be forced to go through irrelevant pages in order to get what they really want; news articles in this example. Such a situation simply cannot provide both optimized usability and optimized revenues at the same time.

Efficient communication

Content of graphics and pictures, particularly images of faces, and writing style can influence users' reactions towards an application. Potential customers can be alienated by a presentation style they feel is targeted at a different group of people, and elderly people can be put off by "young" faces.

Using professional terms is often risky. The expertise level of the customers will affect how much they use the jargon of the trade. Banking business professionals have their own vocabulary, and even non-banking people dealing actively in stocks have a different vocabulary from the ones using the Internet bank only to pay bills. Sometimes this is hard to remember on the business side. Personalizing communication down to the level of terms and vocabulary is effective in a complex trade like banking.

4.2.3 Presenting customization

Nordea has many years of experience with customer-initiated customisation. It is, for example, possible to define a personal start page (the page where you go after login) and to freely name accounts according to their use in the Internet bank. These facilities, however, haven't been widely used, even though customers have a positive attitude towards them.

Teaching customers to utilize user-initiated personalization functionalities is important to allow them to benefit from it and realize its value. Past studies (Willcocks & Plant, 2001; Nunes & Kambil, 2001) imply that most users benefit from the personalization features of online services. Why is it, then, that they are so rarely used? The question is not "would you customise a web application" but "why don't you customise it". Do the benefits gained seem small compared with the trouble of customising the service? Are the features too difficult to find, use or learn? Or do the users simply not care, i.e., the service is "good enough" out of the box?

Our extensive user testing implies that the drive to "just pay my bills and get out" is so great that most users rarely even consider improving the Internet banking application by customizing it. The most important thing that matters to a strong majority of Internet bank customers is that the link for making the payment is clearly visible in the same place and paying the bill is easy, efficient and straightforward. An Internet bank is not something that a majority of users spend time primarily browsing around nor use for long enough stretches of time that they feel any great need to improve the interaction. Many users also don't intuitively seem to expect to find customisation possibilities in an Internet bank.

In order to get customisation features into real use, active education is required. The users must be presented with clear – but unobtrusive! – hints about the personalization possibilities. It must be clearly communicated that the customisation features are personal ("Own shortcuts" or "My shortcuts" instead of "Shortcuts") and using them must be easy and intuitive, with the benefit clearly illustrated. Many cases also call for easy access to a "Back to default settings" option, as some users are clearly afraid of loosing something or ruining the application if they meddle with it. Finances are such a serious issue that users want to avoid all risk of error.

Finding good approaches to active education is hard. A careful balance between the attention value and amount of distraction from the task itself must be reached, remembering also the cross sales content. The solution must be simple and elegant, so as not to harm the impression of trustworthiness of the application. And on top of that, using more flexible and more enabling tools like Flash, Java applets and ActiveX is often impossible due to the high security requirements in applications handling monetary transactions.

In a customisable Internet banking application, a fitting agenda for a user test would include 1) the task and the user interface, 2) the application's ability to cross-sell and 3) the users' ability to learn to customise. The balance of these three things will display the success of implementing the design guidelines, success of balancing the cross selling and task completion, and the ability of the users to make use of the features designed for them to make the application even more usable. A design is flawed if customisation is *needed* to make the service usable in the first place, but even the best out of the box service can be made better with proper customisation.

4.2.4 Presenting personalization

Banks typically offer different sets of financial services and products to different kinds of customers; a typical customer uses only a small subset of what is available. Making that subset more accessible than the rest of the products would make the whole online service easier to use and, at least to some extent, respond to the barrier of lacking computer and Internet skills. The next step would be to manage to associate each subset of services with the appropriate target.

Banks leverage existing customer relations by offering new services to existing customers and by promoting adoption of the Internet channel for other service areas. Although these business objectives may well be aligned with customer needs, the presentation of such targeted content elements often misses its target or adds unnecessary complexity to the service, thus making the service more difficult to use. Therefore, targeted content must be targeted correctly, and its presentation must not impede the usability of the service. Targeting of content, whether it is a direct offer or just a piece of information, must satisfy customers' needs in order to benefit both the bank and its customers.

Technologically speaking, adaptivity is possible with cutting edge content management tools connected to CRM databases and engines that compile the user interfaces from components case by case, depending on the customer's own settings and terminal device used. However, as the whole idea of the adaptivity is customer convenience, ease of use and hitting the right target with the provided content, it is crucial to know what the appropriate way to achieve this really is. As with the content customized, also the content personalized must be transparent to the user, enabling him to correct, undo or ignore any changes the personalized system presents him. The content and the changes can be presented in a variety of different ways, some of which are presented below (Kobsa et al., 2001):

Smart forms

A smart form is a form that has been partially pre-filled by the system, using personal information provided by the user earlier. For a web application this is an easy feature to accomplish, as a user database should be used for authentication all way through the application. In Internet banking context this is very beneficial, as the bank already has much of the information, and what's lacking the users often present willingly due to the trustworthy nature of the application.

Page variants

Page variants means having different personalized versions of all pages with personalized content. Technically this is simple, as only the page selection is required, but it requires a lot of background work since all individual pages must be written separately. In Internet banking this is generally a usable technique for larger customer segments, say to provide a separate entry page for a few large customer groups.

Fragment variants

Fragment variants technology consists of variable fragments (for example an image or a paragraph of text) with personalized content included in a static page frame. This requires dynamic generation of web pages at runtime, but is more flexible and reusable than page variants. Of all the different possibilities described here, fragment variants is the easiest to implement with a modern content management system. Fragment variants are a good way to provide more personal information than page variants and can generally be used to provide targeted information for smaller groups. In addition to that, better coverage can be reached by using a few different fragments per page.

Fragment coloring

With fragment coloring the content of the personalized page remains unchanged, but the content is highlighted differently for different user groups. Highlighting can be used, for example, to mark some content either important or irrelevant to the user. An advantage of this system is that errors in assessing the user group have less effect as all the content is visible, but for the same reason this can be used only in cases where the variation between groups is relatively low. Fragment coloring is best used with larger stretches of text, and thus is not very usable in Internet banking. From a layman's perspective, all terms and conditions could use some highlighting for the important pieces, but as the bank is the provider of the services and also legally responsible, it is hard to format the legalese to more and less important pieces. Product descriptions, however, do benefit from using fragment coloring.

Adaptive stretchtext

Adaptive stretchtext is a system where expandable and collapsible text is included in the normal content. Stretchtext pieces are generally very short, from a few words to a single sentence. For Internet banking, the same limitations and benefits apply as with fragment coloring.

Adaptive natural language generation

Adaptive natural language generation techniques create alternative text descriptions for different user groups, adapting to the user's goal and knowledge as well as experience. Pages with adaptive stretchtext need to be linguistically well formed in all possible stretch variations, and natural language generator can smooth the expression out. For Internet banking, the same limitations and benefits apply as with fragment coloring.

Authorization-based display of content or services

The majority of Internet banking services in the market offer only simple forms of personalization, such as authorisation-based services (the customer gets to see and use only the services mentioned in her agreement) and some minor, authentication-based pieces of personal information, such as personalized greetings displayed after logon. We are not aware of any electronic banking service that fully integrates unified customer databases with banking services and marketing content. Authorization-based display of content and services is quite often used as the "poor man's personalization" in order to give an idea of personalized content. However, it can be also used to generate revenue by displaying only the services the customer specifically has signed for, while separate services have their own fees. As a cross-selling angle from banking perspective authorization-based display is often used to provide a user a demo of a service not currently subscribed to.

Adaptive user interfaces

Continuing the train of thought of designing for personalization from the bottom up, the user interface's adaptation to different terminal devices (laptop, mobile browser, smart phone, PDA, PC etc.) is worth attention. Issues such as smaller screen size or interaction device type (keyboard vs. number pad vs. stylus) can be tackled with well-designed adaptation to for example simplified user interface. User interface adaptation can also be done to better fit a given UI solution to the needs of a specific user segment. For example, an UI design that works best for elderly users who do not posses high Internet competency would most probably differ from the one meant for the hardcore professional day trader. The extent to which user interfaces can meaningfully be adapted to users varies, as does the technology behind it. The same logic as mentioned before is also useful in this context: either the user could select the preferred UI alternative or the system could learn from the user to offer the best one or make the selection based on login and demographic information. The business case for developing adaptive user interfaces that adapt to users in the context of Internet banking is, however, rather questionable and thus is not experimented in customer services.

4.3 How to hit the target with personalization

There are many ways of targeting content and the best approach may be situation-dependent. To ensure that it hits the target, a message or an offer must be targeted according to the customer needs. Customer needs are, however, difficult to understand and apply in the process of targeting. This process uses different levels of information that must be integrated before the information can be utilized in targeting.

The information sources include demographics, market research, data mining of usage patterns and customisation choices (log files), customer behaviour in traditional businesses, attitudes, interests and life events, customer programmes, and customer feedback. These information channels must be integrated before being used as a basis for personalization. Combining all this to simple-enough-to-use form has not been researched much in the banking field. In particular, the academic world lacks a profound and unified model of customers and their contexts of use.

Once the customers have been classified, the next logical step would be to understand the distinctive needs of each customer type, or profile. This task requires us to combine information from multiple sources to gain a holistic understanding of the needs of a particular customer type and to model that understanding in a useful way. In addition, needs change over time, as new behaviour patterns are learned and new technologies emerge. Understanding the customers is therefore an ongoing process.

Important information can also be acquired directly from the customer, but it is important that the initial interview or the start-up procedure is not too long and cumbersome – only two to three core questions should be used (Kobsa et al., 2001). The user can be also prompted to answer a slightly more comprehensive query if an incentive, such as better service or some extra added value service, is offered. That information, however, must be sufficient to start to generate the profile together with the compiled information and the information the bank already has on the customer. In this aspect Internet banking has it easy, since the user's birth date, address and some of her financial interests (providing that, for example, advanced investment tools are sold as a separate packet included in the same application, available for an extra fee) are already known, and some conclusions of her financial status can be drawn. With this wealth of information, the real personalization process can begin.

5. CONCLUSION

Personalization is without a doubt a promising area that might be able to answer some of the burning questions that Internet banking must deal with today and even more in the days to come. The possibilities of personalization are not yet fully utilized, nor is there sufficient hands-on experience or research-based knowledge about the most advanced ideas of how to personalize Internet banking services.

Personalization in Internet banking, as discussed above, is not simple to design or implement. The importance of hitting the right target in both selecting the things to be personalized and the way of presenting them visually are delicate matters. If not done right, they might compromise the most important customer values: speed, efficiency and trust.

Internet banking provides a very interesting area to be studied from an HCI perspective, because of its numerous special characteristics and heterogeneous user population. The importance of successful HCI management is also of tremendous importance to the success of the services, making it financially meaningful to practice high-class HCI activities. Including personalization into this context creates interesting and important area for study.

6. REFERENCES

Baker, A. (2001). *Meaningful personalization*, http://www.merges.net/theory/20010402.html

Blom, J. (2000). Personalization – a taxonomy. *Extended Abstracts of CHI'00 Conference on Human Factors in Computing Systems, Hague, Netherlands: 313-314.*

Brett, R., Favier, J., O'Connell, P. and Hadzi-Stevic, M. (2002). Making Europe's Online Banking Sell, *Forrester*, June.

Eads, S. (2000). *The Web'sStill-Unfulfilled Personalized Promise*, http://www.businessweek.com/bwdaily/dnflash/aug2000/nf2000084_506.htm

Harald, B.(2002). Unpublished interview.

Hiltunen, M., Laukka, M., and Luomala, J (2002). Professional Mobile User Experience, *IT Press.*

Karjaluoto, H. (2002). Electronic Banking in Finland: consumer beliefs, attitudes, intentions, and behaviours. Unpublished report, Jyväskylä: University of Jyväskylä.

Kim, J., Moon, J (1997). Emotional Usability of Customer Interfaces – Focusing on Cyber Banking System Interfaces. Unpublished report, Seoul, Yonsei University.

Kobsa, A., Koenemann, J., and Pohl, W. (2001). *Personalized hypermedia presentation techniques for improving online customer relationships.* Cambridge University Press.

Mattila, M. (2001).Essays on Customers on the Dawn of Interactive Banking. Unpublished report, Jyväskylä: University of Jyväskylä.

Moore, G. (1991). *Crossing the Chasm.* HarperBusiness.

Moore, G. (1995). *Inside the Tornado.* HarperBusiness.

Mols, N. (1998). The behavioural consequences of PC banking, *International Journal of Bank Marketing*, 16 (5), 195-201.

Nielsen, J. (1998). Alertbox October 4, http://www.useit.com/alertbox/981004.html

Nielsen, J. (2000). *Designing web usability.* New Riders Publishing, Indianapolis.

Nunes, P. and Kambil, A. (2001). Accenture Institute for Strategic Change. *Harvard Business Review*: 55, April.

Peppers, D. and Rogers, M. (1997) *The One to One Future. Building Relationships One Customer at a Time.* Doubleday.

Pilgrim, M. (2002). Dive Into Accessibility, http://diveintoaccessibility.org/

Polatoglu, V. N. and Ekin, S (2001) An Empirical Investigation of the Turkish Consumers' acceptance of Internet Banking Services. *International Journal of Bank Marketing*, 19 (4), 156-165.

Serco (2000).How to Design On-line Banking and Insurance Services: Usability Guidelines. Unpublished report, Serco Usability Services.

Spolsky, J. (2001). *User Interface Design for Programmers.* Apress.

Veen, J. (2002) Inside Web Design, *IT Press.*

Willcocks, L. and Plant, R. (2001). Pathways to E-Business Leadership: Getting From Bricks to Clicks, *MIT Sloan Management Review*, Spring.

DADONG WAN

PERSONALIZED UBIQUITOUS COMMERCE: AN APPLICATION PERSPECTIVE

1. INTRODUCTION

1.1 The Rise of Ubiquitous Commerce

To many people, the term "e-commerce" conjures up the image of the dot com madness of the late 1990's. As we know well by now, Amazon.com has not made brick-and-mortar bookstores obsolete; neither did electronic exchanges replace physical supply chains. However, e-commerce as a utility function has become an integral part of as well as a permanent fixture to businesses of all sizes, large and small. With the proliferation of devices such as cell phones and personal digital assistants (PDAs), as well as digital cameras, embedded microprocessors, miniature sensors, radio frequency identification (RFID) tags, and wireless networks like 802.11 and Bluetooth, we are currently witnessing a trend in which technology is moving away from desks into our pockets, purses and even onto our walls and furniture. Traditional products ranging from cars, refrigerators, to toys and alarm clocks also begin to acquire computing, sensing, and communications capabilities. In short, technology is increasingly blending into our everyday environments, following us every step of the way, creating a world that is always on, always active and always aware. We coin the term "ubiquitous commerce," or u-commerce for short (Gershman, 2002), to refer to this new reality, which promises, and perhaps ultimately demands, that businesses be available at the times and places where people use these products and services rather than just through the Web or at physical stores. This emerging reality also presents a new set of challenges and opportunities, and redefines what we mean by personalization.

1.2 Personalization for Ubiquitous Commerce

The Web is a highly customisable medium. Many Web-based applications support some level of personalization. My Yahoo, for example, allows us to explicitly select and customize content types, sources, and presentation formats. Amazon.com recommends books and music that are potentially of interest to us based on our past purchasing history. While features like these are useful, they are far from adequate to many people for three important reasons. First, most of these

141

Clare-Marie Karat et al. (eds.), Designing Personalized User Experiences in eCommerce, 141—160.

customisations are based on the static profile specified by the user, e.g., My Yahoo preferences. As these preferences change, the user must remember to explicitly make corresponding changes to the system. In the real-world, however, few users are disciplined enough to do so. As a result, these profiles often become obsolete and useless very quickly. Second, while past transactions reveal much about our interests, the current representation of such history is fragmented. Amazon.com, for example, might make excellent recommendations of books and music based on what I've bought from them during the past six months. However, their recommendations could be totally off mark by not taking into account of my purchases from other stores, especially their competitors, both online and offline. Perhaps most importantly, most existing e-commerce applications have little or no awareness of the current tasks in which the user is involved. As a result, they cannot adapt their offerings dynamically to the present need of the user. For example, Amazon.com may recommend a new childcare book because I bought a similar book two months ago. However, what they may not realize is that I'm currently involved in a home improvement project and thus more interested in books on this topic.

In the world of ubiquitous commerce, user task context is more readily available, and thus may be used for further personalization of services. One very common type of context, for example, is the user's real-time location. With inexpensive Global Positioning Systems (GPS) built-into cars, cell phones, PDAs, and other products, it is now possible to provide a wide range of location-based services, ranging from navigation and roadside assistance, to personalized advertising and shopping. A roadside billboard owner, for example, may dynamically change the advertising message based on the number of cars currently passing by, the type of car, and even the type of driver. This is made possible by integrating real-time context information from various sources, including GPS embedded in those vehicles. As sensors like GPS, RFID, and digital cameras become ubiquitous, more user context will be available electronically. This in turn will open the door to a new generation of ubiquitous commerce applications that support a much richer and more personalized experience.

Thus, personalization in ubiquitous commerce involves more than just static user profiles and online transaction histories. It calls for automatic sensing of the user identity, the task, and the surrounding physical environment in which the current task is taking place. As illustrated by the applications described throughout this chapter, the novel use of sensors and personalized devices is essential to seamless tracking of dynamic user contexts in the physical world and, ultimately, to achieving a higher level of personalization.

1.3 The Organization of this Chapter

For the remainder of this chapter, we will describe four research prototypes of personalized ubiquitous commerce: MAGIC MEDICINE CABINET, ONLINE WARDROBE, REAL-WORLD SHOWROOM, and VIRTUAL HANDYMAN. Each of these applications addresses a different task domain, and thus provides its own unique set of features. One common thread among them is that they all attempt to create a new kind of commerce experience, especially on the personalization front, by integrating a number of emerging technologies, including RFID, biometrics, speech, wireless networks, mobile devices, miniature cameras, and Web services. Collectively, these prototypes highlight some important trends in personalization; they also paint our vision for future e-commerce. While some of these technologies are not widely adopted yet, we believe most of them will be in 3-5 years. Just like concept cars, our focus here is primarily to show what is possible in terms of new user experience and business opportunities when some of these new technologies come together. We recognize that privacy issues are ultimately important to considering personalized systems, but we will not address this topic in great detail in this chapter.

2. MAGIC MEDICINE CABINET

2.1 Introduction

In recent years, we have heard much about smart appliances, such as Internet microwaves and refrigerators. Most of these appliances, however, are little more than their traditional counterparts with an Internet connection—a connection whose utility is dubious at best. There is almost no integration between the newly added functionality and what the appliance already does. For instance, with Web browsing available through a microwave front panel, one can perform many functions we use our desktop computers for: home banking, electronic shopping, and even online gaming. But despite the versatility, these functions have little to do with what the microwave's function: speed cooking and reheating of food. We believe that closer integration between the traditional use of an appliance and Internet capabilities related to that use will result in smarter appliances.

We view healthcare in two distinct terms: *informational* and *physical*. Activities such as finding out the side effects of a particular drug, or scheduling an office visit with one's physician, fall into the first category. Taking a pill or measuring one's blood pressure is a physical activity. With the advent of the Internet, we have witnessed an explosion of healthcare information. According to a recent survey, two-thirds of Internet users use the Web to search for health information (Williams, 1997). While the increasing accessibility of health information is essential to the future of healthcare, it represents only one part of the equation. To achieve the dual purposes of lower cost and higher quality of care, consumer-initiated physical care, especially at home, must be encouraged and explicitly supported. Our goal here is to create an application that enables better consumer-centred situated care by integrating the growing array of Internet resources with home health appliances.

2.2 The Prototype

MAGIC MEDICINE CABINET (MMC) (Wan, 1999) is a smart appliance that supports both informational and physical aspects of consumer healthcare. It embeds a number of technologies that, together, enable consumers to perform routine physical care, such as ensuring that you take the right medication, tracking vital signs, accessing up-to-date personalized health information, and interacting with online care providers, including physicians, hospitals, and pharmacists. Our implementation incorporates the following capabilities:

- *Face recognition*: The build-in camera (see Figure 1) and face recognition software enables the medicine cabinet to automatically recognize the person in front of it, and respond with proper services.

- *RFID-based smart labels*: Drug products stored in the medicine cabinet have smart labels attached to them, which lets the cabinet know its contents and in particular which bottles are being removed and returned.

- *Vital sign monitors*: One can use these monitoring devices to track a wide range of health indicators, such as blood pressure, heart rate, body weight, and cholesterol level.

- *Voice synthesis*: This allows auditory output to supplement what's shown on the cabinet display.

MMC has an embedded Mini-ITX system with Morex 2677 computer and Internet connection. As shown in Figure 1, the prototype looks much like a conventional medicine cabinet. One big difference is that the left panel of the cabinet has a built-in LCD display. The user interacts with MMC through its touch-sensitive screen, voice output, and the cabinet display.

Figure 1. MMC knows what medication is in the medicine cabinet, and warns you if you accidentally pick up the wrong bottle.

2.3 *A Usage Scenario*

Johnny, a 12-year old 6th grader, suffers from a severe allergy problem. In the morning, Johnny gets up and heads to the bathroom to get ready for school. As he picks up his toothbrush from the bathroom countertop, he hears a pleasant voice from his medicine cabinet:

"Good morning, Johnny. I have an allergy alert for you."

Johnny looks up at his medicine cabinet display, and sees the pollen count in his area is dangerously high. He also sees big red flashing letters on the cabinet display reminding him to take his allergy medication.

Johnny opens the cabinet door, reaches on to the shelf, and picks up a medicine bottle:

"Wrong…you've picked up Liptor instead of Claritin!"

Johnny puts the bottle back and picks up another one:

"Great…now you have the right medicine."

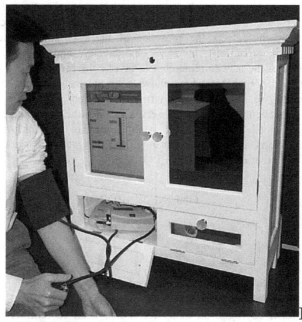

Figure 2. MMC not only reminds but allows you to measure your blood pressure and other vital signs and, if necessary, share that information with your care providers securely over the Internet.

That evening, Johnny's father, Dan, happens to come in front of the medicine cabinet. MMC senses Dan's presence, and reminds him to measure his blood pressure. Dan opens the cabinet door and slips the cuff around his arm (see Figure 2). His medicine cabinet tells him that his blood pressure has gone a bit high since the previous reading, and suggests that he consult with his doctor. If he is so inclined, Dan can schedule an office visit with his family doctor right there through his medicine cabinet!

2.4 Discussions

MMC embodies several novel personalization features. Unlike health portals such as WebMD, which sits far away from their users in the virtual world, MMC resides in the everyday space of its user, i.e., home. The medicine cabinet is traditionally a bathroom fixture for a reason: the bathroom is a highly frequented quarter in the house where many daily personal care activities take place. MMC takes advantage of the situated nature of the medicine cabinet, and extends it from a passive storage space into an interactive appliance. Because of that, the application is capable of sensing the user situation as it happens, e.g., time of the day, and offers them personalized information and reminders of actions at the point of need. The user thus does not have to break away from their normal activity flow to benefit from these services. Second, by using biometric sensing, e.g., face recognition, MMC automatically detects the presence of the user and initiates appropriate interactions. This proactivity increases spontaneity, and reduces the cognitive burden required of the user to remember to invoke the service. And finally, similar to (Want, et al, 1999), MMC shows how to bridge the gap between the physical world in which we live, and the virtual world on which we are becoming increasingly dependent. The prototype serves as a healthcare appliance that provides everything we need for individual healthcare: the right information, timely reminders of actions, vital sign monitoring, and the gateway to doctors, hospitals, pharmacies, and other care providers.

3. ONLINE WARDROBE

3.1 Introduction

In the world of shopping, retailers are confronted with two challenges: (1) how to use what consumers already own to help with what they are about to buy; and (2) how to transform buying from being an end in itself to reinforcing a long-term relationship between retailers and their customers. Today, people going to retail stores cannot bring the content of their living room, refrigerator, or wardrobe with them to the stores. As a result, they have to remember exactly what they already have so they avoid buying duplicate products or products that do not go well with what they already own.

By comparison, online stores such as Amazon.com can more easily track what their customers have bought. Based on this information, they are able to personalize their offerings. However, even these stores have no means of telling what their customers are buying from their competitors. The lack of access to their customer's complete, up-to-date buying history, which we call "buyer context" (Wan, 2000), prevents consumers from having richer shopping experience and better relationships with retailers.

With technologies like radio frequency identification (RFID) tags and electronic product code (EPC) (Auto-ID Centre, 2000) it becomes increasingly feasible to keep track of buyer context. Lauded as the next generation bar code, EPC promises a fine-grained addressability of physical objects. While the bar code tracks products at the SKU or group level, the EPC's 96-bit code allows the unique identification of every individual product ever made. More importantly, the new product code may be embedded in tiny, inexpensive chips, which may in turn be manufactured into products themselves or affixed in their packages. Such tags require no line of sight, and are capable of communicating remotely using radio frequencies without human intervention. This unique ability makes it possible to automatically track the whereabouts of a product in real-time. The ubiquitous use of such tags will allow dynamic linking between physical products and the vast amount of online information about them. Ultimately, the convergence of RFID and EPC technologies and smart appliances will extend the Internet from the world of bits into the world of atoms. As a result, it will become possible to capture the rich context of people's day-to-day activities. The ready availability and easy access to such contexts opens up new ways by which businesses and their customers relate to each other.

3.2 The Prototype

ONLINE WARDROBE (Wan, 2000) is a prototype that shows how a traditional bedroom fixture like the wardrobe can be transformed into a new channel for interactive services. Its thrust is not that it offers yet another way of browsing the Web from your home. Rather, ONLINE WARDROBE provides a new kind of interface, i.e., the physical interface, to the online marketplace. Specifically, an embedded RFID sensor enables the wardrobe to detect what clothing products you own. It also detects what is being added or removed. With this capability, you can shop interactively from online stores by using what is in the wardrobe as the shopping context. For example, if you want to buy a dress shirt, you first pull out the pair of pants and jacket with which you would like to wear it. ONLINE WARDROBE uses the selected pants and jacket as the constraints to search online stores. It then returns a list of shirts that best match with the criteria. Depending on the search result, you may choose to tighten the constraints by pulling out additional pants you want the new shirt to go with, or broaden the search scope by dropping the jacket.

ONLINE WARDROBE also provides a new channel to the everyday space through which retailers and consumers can interact spontaneously and continuously. For example, when you bring home a brand new jacket you've just bought, ONLINE WARDROBE immediately recognizes it as a new arrival, and asks you whether you are interested in other products that would go well with the new jacket. Today, people already trust their grocers to automatically replenish their groceries by granting them remote access to their refrigerators. In the future, we will see consumers allowing their favourite department stores to access what they have in their wardrobe so these stores can deliver exactly what their customers need at their doorsteps even before their customers realize they had a need.

Figure 3. As a physical interface to online stores, ONLINE WARDROBE has a built-in touch sensitive LCD, voice output, and an RFID sensor for detecting its contents.

To facilitate the interaction between the consumer and the online marketplace, ONLINE WARDROBE introduces four constructs:

- *My Wardrobe*: It corresponds to what you already have in the physical wardrobe. You may browse it and find out when and where a product was purchased, and how much you paid for it. You can also view products from the current marketplace that are similar to what you have. When you take out a product from the wardrobe, or put in a new one, *My Wardrobe* is updated instantly to reflect the current state of the physical wardrobe.

- *My Wish-List*: It contains the products you do not own but would like to. ONLINE WARDROBE periodically suggests products that may be of interest to you based on what you already have and what is on-sale in the marketplace. You may choose to buy the recommended products, ignore them, or, defer the decision by placing it on the *My Wish-List*.

- *My Store*: It contains a personalized list of merchandise from various online stores that ONLINE WARDROBE deems relevant to you based on such criteria as what you already have, your preferences in style and colour, season and price. ONLINE WARDROBE continuously updates *My Store* to reflect the current offerings from the marketplace.

- *The Market*: It consists of a listing of online stores that offer products typically found in your wardrobe. At times you may want to shop in the open market, as opposed to just those in *My Store*. In its idle mode, ONLINE WARDROBE also randomly displays products from *The Market*.

ONLINE WARDROBE is equipped with an embedded computer, Internet connection, and an RFID sensor. All apparel products in the wardrobe are affixed with tiny Texas Instruments' Tag-It^{tm} smart tags that uniquely identify each of them. As shown in Figure 3, ONLINE WARDROBE looks just like an ordinary wardrobe. You interact with it through the touch-sensitive screen on the left, voice output, and the physical products in the wardrobe.

3.3   A Usage Scenario

After a quick shower in the morning, Dave pulls out a pair of casual pants and a shirt out of his wardrobe, and is ready to put them on. Then, he hears a voice from the wardrobe:

"Good morning! Dave. Don't forget you have a client meeting today. What you've picked is a bit too casual. You may want to consider some alternatives."

As he glances at the wardrobe screen, Dave notices his morning schedule, including an important client meeting, and his selected attire (see Figure 4). Embarrassed by his own selection, he touches on the "Suggestion" button on the screen. In response, ONLINE WARDROBE brings up a recommendation that matches well with Dave's activity on that day. It also reminds Dave to remember to bring an umbrella, since it will be raining.

Later that evening, Dave checks in again with his ONLINE WARDROBE to find what it has in store for his upcoming vacation with his family. Since he had planned the vacation about two months ago, his wardrobe has been continuously monitoring market activities from various retailers. In response to Dave's request, his wardrobe comes back with a customized list of what to pack as well as what to buy in getting ready for the vacation.

3.4   Discussions

ONLINE WARDROBE provides two unique personalization features. First, it takes advantage of a situated nature of the wardrobe to bring personalized shopping from a store into your own bedroom. As such, it represents a new channel through which consumers and retailers can interact with each other. By using ONLINE WARDROBE, consumers may selectively make available the content of their wardrobe to certain trusted merchants. In return, they receive personalized offerings and timely reminders about products of interest. Because the wardrobe is in the everyday space, retailers can more easily deliver products and services to where their customers are, instead of having to lure them to their stores.

ONLINE WARDROBE also shows how to use buyer context to enhance the shopping experience. As one purchases apparel products tagged with RFID chips, it is quite easy to build a virtual wardrobe, called *My Wardrobe* here, which represents your buyer context for clothes shopping. When a new product is bought and added to the wardrobe, *My Wardrobe* is automatically updated. As a result, it stays synchronized with the physical content of the wardrobe. Preferred retailers may be granted access to this buyer context, and use it to recommend appropriate products. Since the buyer context is available virtually, consumers can take it with them when they shop in stores. For example, when they visit in a brick-and-mortar store, they can bring up the content of *My Wardrobe* through an Internet connected kiosk. This buyer context would put the sales associate in a much better position to assist the customer. Alternatively, the kiosk application may automatically figure out what products the customer needs to look at based on what the customer already has and the store's current stock by programmatically applying a set of codified fashion rules.

Figure 4. ONLINE WARDROBE makes personalized recommendations on what to wear on a given day based on a person's schedule, weather, the current wardrobe content, and history.

4. REAL-WORLD SHOWROOM

4.1 Introduction

Despite recent growth in online retailing, shopping, as we know it, has not changed much. We still go to *stores*, online or offline. Shopping is a distinct activity. It is also an orchestrated process by the retailer to maximize sales and efficiency. The retailer maintains control over what to sell and how to sell it. For example, if a retailer wants to promote a product, he might place it more visibly on the shelf next to the checkout counter or on the Web site's front page.

Two subtle problems exist in such a seller-centred approach. Since it is difficult to accurately predict potential market demands, retailers often stock more merchandise than they eventually end up selling. This practice, while widely accepted, leads to sub-optimal business performance because of inventory tie-up and inevitable markdowns. Moreover, customers must also spend extra time searching through a large array of products in order to find the few they really want. In many cases, this requirement leads to frustrated customers and lost sales.

As consumers, on the other hand, our needs for new products often arise serendipitously during our daily activities. For example, you are attending a party at a friend's house. You see a blue-stripe couch in their family room. Suddenly, you realize you need the exact couch for your own house! Today, when we encounter situations like this, we simply push what comes to us into our short-term memory, hoping we still remember it when we later visit a physical store or a Web site. For many people, such a time may never come. When it does come, we'd be lucky if we still remember what we set out to buy.

To address these two problems, we developed REAL-WORLD SHOWROOM, a research prototype that allows consumers to access real-time product information and to shop *as* they encounter these products during their normal course of activities. Its aim is to transform the world around us into a product showroom and our mobile devices into personalized checkout counters.

4.2 The Prototype

Imagine you're sitting in a café and a man passes by in a particularly sharp sweater. Rather than just admire his taste and wonder where he bought it, you pull out your PDA or cell phone, and press a button. Instantly, you have access to all the information about the sweater, including its brand, similar products, availability, and price (see Figure 5.) By pressing another button, the very sweater is yours, and will be on your doorstep next day.

Sounds like a science fiction? Not if you had REAL-WORLD SHOWROOM. The central tenet underlying this prototype is that, *commerce and consumer interactions take place serendipitously, when and where people see and use products, not just in a store or at a Web site.* To enable this spontaneous shopping experience, we link together two technologies: wireless devices and RFID tags. More specifically, we use a PDA equipped with an RFID reader and wireless Internet connection. The products in the surroundings are tagged with RFID chips. When you see a product that appeals to you, e.g., the lawn mower your next-door neighbour is using, you approach the product, point the device directly at it from a short distance away, and press a button. Immediately, all the relevant information is retrieved from a number of online sources and displayed on your PDA. With a few more button presses, you can buy the product, all without ever giving up whatever you happen to be doing at the time. With REAL-WORLD SHOWROOM, you can also easily verify the authenticity of the product in front of you, since the information stored in RFID tags is unique to each product, and almost impossible to tamper with. Just as the tags can distinguish between a coffee machine and a necktie, so can they easily tell a fake Versace sweater from the real thing. Furthermore, REAL-WORLD SHOWROOM allows you to find out the entire product history. Such a capability is especially useful for products that are sensitive to their physical environments, such as pharmaceuticals, wines, and perishable goods.

Figure 5: REAL-WORLD SHOWROOM in Action

Our initial prototype is implemented on a Visor Prism, using an RFID Springboard module from ID Systems, Inc. (See Figure 5.) This PDA has one expansion slot, which is used for RFID. As a result, this version doesn't provide real-time wireless Internet connectivity. Instead, all the product information is stored in a database on the Visor itself. The initial database includes several dozens of products, such as clothing and furniture. All products have Texas Instruments' Tag-It RFID tags embedded. The database contains product information such as manufacturer, description, style, price, and availability. A production version of this application would require a server-based component, which performs real-time aggregation of product information from various sources on the Internet.

4.3 Discussions

REAL-WORLD SHOWROOM demonstrates two intriguing personalization capabilities; it shows how ubiquitous RFID tags and wireless mobile devices together can help transform the world around us into a personalized product showroom, and our PDAs or cell phones into personalized checkout counters. As consumers, this new environment enables us to see products in their real usage context and decide whether we want to buy them. Once we choose to buy a product, we can act on this intention instantly by simply pressing a few buttons on our PDA.

In essence, we integrate everyday activity as part of shopping context. Put differently, with this application, shopping now becomes an integral part of what we do, rather than a distinctive activity. There is no more need to accumulate or remember a long list of things to buy, nor make separate trips to the mall or Web sites.

With REAL-WORLD SHOWROOM, consumers are no longer just consumers; they also become the agents or personalized billboards for the products they use. Presumably, our family and friends exert even more influence on us than those celebrities in terms of what to buy. This has some interesting business implications. For example, if you buy a sweater because you like it when you see your friend Dean wearing it, Dean might get a commission. To retailers, their existing product owners now become channels for marketing and sales. And those owners are motivated to wear or use the merchandise so as to increase their commissions.

5.   VIRTUAL HANDYMAN

5.1 Introduction

For most people who happen to be homeowners, home is perhaps the single most important physical asset and the biggest investment in their lifetime. It is also the place where they spend many of their waking hours engaging in a broad range of activities: entertainment, work, learning, and maintaining or decorating the space itself. Thus, it comes as no surprise that the home is a huge market for technology products and services, including telephones, television, fax machines DVD players, smart appliances, game consoles, home computers, digital cameras, cable modems, and so on. Despite the high penetration of such technologies and the increasing availability of wireless home networks (e.g., 802.11b) and broadband Internet access, direct virtual services to consumer homes still barely exist.

Just imagine a homeowner trying to install a lighting fixture. It doesn't go smoothly, so he needs expert assistance. What would he do? First, he'd look for help, possibly in a thick phone book or perhaps through a keyword search on the Internet, or ask a neighbor. He'd assess the possibilities (e.g., home improvement and hardware stores, private contractors, handymen) and make a choice. Then he'd make a call, try to describe the problem, and decide what to do. Maybe he'd take notes and go back up the ladder to give it another try. Maybe a repairman would eventually come to the house, lend a hand, and present a bill.

The above scenario represents a typical call for "micro services" – services that come at a highly granular level in terms of duration and cost. These services share three common characteristics. First, they involve a layperson and an expert. The task typically requires asymmetric collaboration between the two parties. While the first step in any service involves finding an appropriate service provider for the problem on hand, the difference is that the discovery cost for micro services is very high relative to the total cost for rendering the service. In the above scenario, for example, it may only take the electrician ten minutes to show the homeowner how to install a lighting fixture, but it would take much longer to find an electrician who is available and willing to provide such a service. And finally, micro services require a high degree of spontaneity. In the above example, if getting the service requires the homeowner to go out of their way, e.g., waiting for 3 hours or learning a new application, chances are that the person would not end up using the service.

To addresses these unique challenges of micro services, we propose the concept of "micro services on tap," which allows spontaneous service delivery by integrating several technologies, including miniature wireless cameras, Web services, wireless networks, and speech interface.

5.2 Delivering Micro Services on Tap

Here, we define services as composed of five distinct components: *discovery*, *invocation*, *interface*, *administration*, and *delivery*. The first step in any service involves discovery, or finding an appropriate provider based on the type of task on hand, and the price, availability, reputation, and technical capabilities of the service provider. Then, the service requestor and the provider must connect together, either face-to-face, or through telephone or another communications channel. In the case where the interaction is mediated by computer applications, these applications must also be linked up properly. Once the two parties are brought together, the user must describe the task and the help needed. Only then, can the provider render the required service. To conclude the process, the provider must get paid, and feedback may be gathered about the quality of service so future users may benefit.

It is worth noting that, four out of the five components above are fixed overhead, which means that, they are required for any service, large or small. The time and cost associated with accomplishing these steps are often independent of the size of services delivered. For example, fixing a malfunctioning electrical outlet may take an electrician five minutes. However, to find an appropriate electrician, and to bring him to one's home would take much longer and cost quite a bit more. To make micro services economically viable, we must reduce the relatively high overhead cost associated with providing such services, in particular, the cost related to discovering an appropriate service provider for the task at hand, and interfacing the novice who performs the task and the expert who is supposed to help. Two key technologies, Web services and miniature wireless cameras (e.g., camera phones), provide great promise in accomplishing these goals.

Web Services are emerging open standards that enable applications of different sources, e.g., languages, platforms, and organizations, to find, link and interact with one another over the Internet, sharing data and performing tasks, all without human intervention. One important component of Web services is Universal Description, Discovery, and Integration (UDDI) (UDDI, 2002), which provides a standard framework for application publishing, discovery, and dynamic integration. With UDDI, it is possible for applications to automatically find and talk to each other, and thus greatly reduces the cost of discovery. Going back to the earlier scenario, the electrician may register his application in a centralized UUDI registry. When a home owner needs such a service, his application can search the registry, and automatically talk to and invoke the application when a right match is found.

One way to take advantage of the increasing availability of inexpensive miniature cameras is to use them as the remote eyes for the service providers at a different location. For example, to fix your leaking kitchen sink, you get connected over the Internet with a plumber at the other end of town. Through a miniature camera you have in your shirt pocket or a flashcam (see Figure 6.), the remote plumber is able to see with his own eyes exactly what's going on, and helps you fix the problem in just a few minutes. In situations like this, the interactions between a layperson and an expert could otherwise be difficult, because they tend to use different terminologies even when they are talking about the same thing. As the saying goes, "a picture is worth a thousand words." By using direct sensing through remote cameras, the level of time, effort, cost and, possibly, frustration is greatly reduced. As a result, it enhances the experience for both parties.

Figure 6. On the left, a 900 MHz miniature wireless camera (courtesy of Super Circuits, Inc.) in a shirt pocket allows hand-free operations. On the right, the flashcam has built-in flashlight, wireless camera, and laser pointer.

5.3 The Prototype

VIRTUAL HANDYMAN is a research prototype that was developed to support micro services on tap for home improvement tasks. The prototype consists of three modules: *user*, *provider*, and *marketplace*. The three applications run on separate machines connected to a local area network. The user application includes a wireless microphone and a wireless miniature camera that measures .88 x .57 x .92 (inches) and with a range of up to 750 feet line of sight. We also custom built a flashcam (see Figure 6) that combines illumination, wireless video, and pointing device into a convenient form factor that can be used when working in poorly lit areas. The wireless camera and flashcam enable the provider at a remote location to see what the user is up to, and to give advice accordingly. The wireless microphone (i.e., Sony WCS-999) allows the user to freely roam around the home and still be able to interact with the application on a home computer via speech recognition and synthesis.

Imagine that Randy is trying to replace an existing electrical outlet in a bathroom with a GFCI outlet. After purchasing all necessary supplies from a local hardware store, Randy is ready to embark on the task on his own. He turns off the switch on the main switchboard, opens up the socket, takes out the old outlet, and suddenly finds himself lost. He desperately needs some help. Below is a sample dialogue between Randy (R) and VIRTUAL HANDYMAN (V), as he seeks for help via a wireless microphone:

R: *I need some help in installing my electrical outlet.*
V: *Do you want an electrician?*
R: *Yes.*
V: *I've found two service providers: Excel Home Centre and Jack's Electrical Shop.*
R: *Tell me more about Excel Home Centre.*
V: *Excel Home Centre offers virtual installation services for the products sold in its stores free of charge.*
R: *Connect me to Excel Home Centre.*
V: *Please wait while I'm binding to Excel Home Center...*

When Randy's request arrives at Excel Home Centre, the service provider is alerted through a pager-like device. He then walks over to a store kiosk or an in-vehicle PC. By simply entering the service ID, he immediately gets connected to the user. Figure 7 shows the view from the Excel Home Centre. The screen displays the recent history with the customer and a live view of Randy's task environment.

At the heart of VIRTUAL HANDYMAN is the marketplace application, which includes a private UDDI registry and a custom taxonomy for home improvement. For our prototype, the registry contains a dozen businesses and services. The Web services interface is implemented using Microsoft UDDI Server SDK. Aside from UDDI functions, the module integrates speech engines (e.g., IBM Via Voice and AT&T Natural Voices) so the user can use voice to interact with the system, as illustrated in the dialogue above. The module also includes a simple task model about home improvement so that it can map the user task at hand to a specific type of service. For example, when the user mentions the word "electrical outlet" or "lighting fixture," it knows that he is performing an electrical job, and thus replies, "Do you want an electrician?"

To complement the mobile solution, we also built an online workbench (see Figure 8) with an embedded camera, microphone array (Andrea DA-400), LCD display, and Internet connection. When a user carries out a task on the workbench (e.g., repairing a small appliance or creating a blueprint) and needs help, he can call up a service, just as described above. This time, however, he doesn't need to wear a microphone or camera, since both are built into the workbench. As a fixed-location interface to the service provider, the workbench can afford much richer experience.

For example, if needed, the provider can direct the user to an instructional video or a Web page about a task, which is shown on the LCD display.

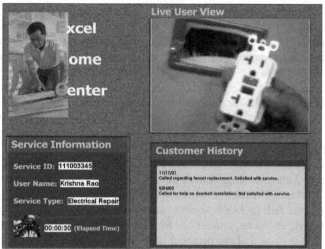

Figure 7. A service provider's screen shows a live view of the customer's task environment.

Figure 8. The online workbench (with built-in camera, microphone array, LCD display, and Internet connection) offers a fixed location interface between the user and the service provider.

5.4 Discussions

VIRTUAL HANDYMAN demonstrates how situated sensing (e.g., speech recognition, speaker identification, and wireless cameras) can help enable a new level of personalization and a new class of services, i.e., micro services on tap, through just-in-time personal interactions. First, it uses speech recognition to automatically activate the custom task model and the service provider list. For example, when the user mentions the word "electrical socket," it responds with a list of electricians instead of plumbers. Second, it relies on speech to identify who the current user is. Once the user is identified, it retrieves the preferences of that user (e.g., price, vendor reputation) from the database, and uses them to further narrow down the appropriate service provider. Third, it employs wireless cameras to enable the remote service provider to directly see the context in which the user is carrying out a task. As a result, the user doesn't need to spend much time describing the situation. Services are discovered dynamically through Web Services and delivered automatically over the Internet. In so doing, the system offers the consumer more convenience, lower cost, empowerment, and better overall experience. At the same time, it provides businesses such as retailers a new option to connect with their customers, and enhance their bottom lines through additional revenue streams.

While VIRTUAL HANDYMAN focuses on home improvement tasks, the approach can be generalized to other service areas, such as cooking, fashion, personal security, travel, shopping, and so on, where personal interactions between a novice and an expert is needed. Take personal fashion, for example. With a smart wardrobe like (Wan, 2000) in your bedroom, any time you need advice on what to wear, your wardrobe can, *in real-time,* find and connect you to a live fashion advisor, who may help you select the best outfit for your specific occasion. Since the fashion advisor can see what you're wearing through the built-in camera, and what you have in the wardrobe through the embedded RFID sensor, you don't need to waste any time explaining or describing them. The service is fast, personal, and can be called upon any time.

Take travel as another example. Imagine you're standing in front of an ancient monument in a foreign country. You'd like to know its rich history but you don't speak the language. Now, you pull out your camera phone, which also is equipped with locationing capability. By pressing a few buttons, you get connected to a live tour guide, who knows not only your language, but also where you are, what you're facing, and everything about the monument. You two spend next 15 minutes together, virtually. The cost is minimal, and the experience is seamless.

In sum, micro services on tap, as illustrated by VIRTUAL HANDYMAN, are all about being able to easily and spontaneously discover and interact with people who could be helpful for a specific situation. They necessitate automatic detection of the user's current task context, and require situated sensing. With the proliferation of broadband wireless networks, Web services, and sensors like inexpensive miniature cameras, GPS receivers, RFID tags, and speech recognition, we expect such services to become even more widely available in the near future.

6. CONCLUSIONS

In this chapter, we introduced four research prototypes of ubiquitous commerce: MAGIC MEDICINE CABINET, ONLINE WARDROBE, REAL-WORLD SHOWROOM, and

VIRTUAL HANDYMAN. Together, these applications highlight what we see as four important personalization trends in e-commerce: *physicalization, in-context, real-time,* and *micro services*. First, e-commerce activities no longer just take place inside a computer or through a mobile device like a cell phone or PDA. Increasingly, they happen in the physical world around us, embodied in familiar objects and products. The automobile is an early example of this trend, where computing and communications technologies help transform cars from a means of transportation to a channel for a wide range of services, including navigation, shopping, safety, and so on. Similarly, familiar fixtures like medicine cabinets, wardrobes, and workbenches begin to acquire new commerce capabilities, and emerge as physical portals for various online services. This physicalization trend calls for an interface that goes beyond traditional keyboards and mice. As illustrated in MAGIC MEDICINE CABINET and ONLINE WARDROBE, the new interface needs to incorporate other modalities such as speech and touch. More importantly, it also needs to use biometrics, such as face recognition and speaker identification, to automatically initiate necessary interactions. In doing so, it helps reduce the user efforts, and increase spontaneity and the level of personalization.

With the proliferation of cheap sensors ranging from RFID and GPS, to miniature video cameras and microphones, it is increasingly feasible to track physical activities of a user and related contexts, including transactions in the physical world, movements, locations, and immediate surroundings, and automatically generate the corresponding "virtual double" (Ferguson, et al, 2002) with little or no additional cost. These virtual doubles typically serve as two types of context: *user* and *task*. A good example of user context is *My Wardrobe,* which is the virtual double of all your apparel shopping activities, a complete transaction history from both online and brick-and-mortar retailers. In VIRTUAL HANDYMAN, a picture of your half-finished electrical socket represents a task context. As demonstrated in these prototypes, the ready availability and accessibility of these virtual doubles, when and where we need them, greatly enhances our experience in the physical world.

As shown in REAL-WORLD SHOWROOM and VIRTUAL HANDYMAN, e-commerce has moved into real-time. This implies that businesses need to not only deliver their services at speed, but be capable of sensing what the customers' needs are long before the customers realize it. With MAGIC MEDICINE CABINET, for example, a preferred healthcare provider can intervene in real-time when the reading of an individual's vital signs exhibits any abnormality. The other implication of real-time commerce is that businesses must learn how to bring their products and services into their customers' daily space so that they can meet their customers needs as these needs arise, just in time and in place.

Finally, e-commerce is primarily about services and, increasingly, micro services. While the need is always present, it is not economically viable in traditional commerce to offer micro services. With essential infrastructure such as Internet and Wi-Fi hot spots already in place, some attractive business capabilities begin to emerge. As demonstrated in VIRTUAL HANDYMAN, technologies like Web Services, 802.11 networks, camera phones, speech recognition, and inexpensive video cameras are making the interaction with micro services much easier. Instead of keyboards and mice, consumers can now interact naturally with appropriate service providers, just in time, and from the comfort of their current task settings, including their homes. The combination of the economic viability and the ease of interface is bound to accelerate the continuing uptake of micro services.

7. REFERENCES

Auto-ID Centre. "The Networked Physical World: Proposal for Engineering the Next Generation of Computing, Commerce, and Automatic Identification." MIT-AUTOID-WH-001. December, 2000. For more information on Electronic Product Code, see www.epcglobalinc.org.

Ferguson, G., et al. "Reality Online: The Business Impact of a Virtual World." *Outlook* (Special Edition), September, 2002.

Gershman, A. "Ubiquitous Commerce: Always On, Always Aware, and Always Pro-Active." 2002 *Symposium on Applications and the Internet (SAINT)*, January 28 - February 1, 2002, Nara City, Nara, Japan. For more information on ubiquitous Commerce, see accenture.com/ucommerce.

UDDI, "The Evolution of UDDI." July 2002. For more information on UDDI, see www.uddi.org.

Wan, D. "Magic Medicine Cabinet: A Situated Portal for Consumer Healthcare." *First International Symposium on Handheld and Ubiquitous Computing*, September 27-29, 1999, Karlsruhe, Germany.

Wan, D. "Magic Home: Exploiting the Duality between the Physical and the Virtual Worlds." *Conference on Human Factors in Computer Systems (CHI 2000) Extended Abstracts,* April 1-6, 2000, The Hague.

Wan, D. "Magic Wardrobe: Situated Shopping from Your Own Bedroom." *Second International Symposium on Handheld and Ubiquitous Computing*, September 25-27, 2000, Bristol, UK.

Want, R. et al. "Bridging Physical and Virtual Worlds with Electronic Tags." *Conference on Human Factors in Computer System.* May 15-20, 1999, Philadelphia, Pennsylvania, USA.

Williams, T. "There's No Place Like Home Healthcare." *Healthcare Informatics* (October, 1997).

RICHARD HALSTEAD-NUSSLOCH

SELF-SERVICE, PERSONALIZATION AND ELECTRONIC GOVERNMENT

A Little History, a Few Issues, and a Small Number of Solutions

1. A LITTLE HISTORY: FROM SELF-SERVICE TO E-SERVICE

1.1 Post-World War II America—The Advent of Self-Service Shopping

Preface Many things occur in cycles: night and day, sleep and awake, the seasons, business, and buying. Some cycles are physical, others are behavioral, still more cultural. My motivation in writing this chapter is to show that electronic personalization (e-personalization) can be seen as a cycling or recycling of approaches to shopping developed for the post-World War II US economy. Starting with a short history of the last half of the Twentieth Century, I trace the development of shopping, as we know it today: individual, with tremendous pleasure potential, and an experience that can be actual or virtual. Because it started with self-service, a context and a set of benchmarks has come to e-personalization in virtual shopping from its roots in actual shopping. These are covered not only to better understand successful e-personalization today but also bridging understanding of electronic government (e-government) in the USA as a cousin (but not a sibling) of electronic commerce (e-commerce).

My father and his father were Main Street merchants. My grandfather's general store[1] was in a small Minnesota town and sold groceries and clothes or "dry goods" as they were called in the early 1900's. My grandfather served his customers by dispensing groceries from bulk containers that sat on the store floor. These containers were moved around the store according to the season. For example, during the winter holiday and baking season, walnuts and dates were placed in the front of the store for convenient access. During the hot summer, such baking items were kept in the back of the store if kept at all. It goes without saying that shoppers

---

[1] Those readers who are fans of Garrison Keillor's "A Prairie Home Companion" radio show have a head start on this historical sketch.

Clare-Marie Karat et al. (eds.), Designing Personalized User Experiences in eCommerce, 161—183.

needed to know what they wanted, because things were not put on display. A clerk
served every customer and in every transaction found and chose the items "desired."
Although customers received personal attention and service, they could not easily
browse to shop as in almost every store today. And the clerk was involved in and
created context for all service.

In the late 1930's, my father joined my grandfather in the business. Although
World War II brought rationing to everyone including our family business, it also
brought the USA out of its Great Depression. The rationing meant that demand for
commercial goods grew and remained high during and after the war. The increased
logistics capability achieved during the war meant that the goods could be readily
supplied in individual units or packages. In response during the 1950's my father
limited the business to groceries and innovated self-service. Instead of a clerk
dispensing bulk groceries on demand for each customer, goods were packaged ahead
of time into consumable portions. Packages were made increasingly more colorful
and attractive. They were organized onto display shelves, where like goods were all
placed together, e.g., the baking section. Customers then browsed the packages.
Self-service was the advent of *shopping as we know it today*.

Figure 1. *My Family's Grocery Store in 1959*

1.2 Self-service and personalization—What was innovative in the 1950's

I learned the basics of business and HCI working in my father's grocery store. A highlight of this experience was seeing both the producer and consumer sides of the shopper's "user interface" (UI). I watched my father and his staff build, test and refine what amounted to new UI tools (Karat, Karat, and Ukelson, 2000) for self-service that would make every customer feel that the shopping experience was designed for him/her personally. I saw delight when they felt success and also frustration and intense determination whenever they realized that significant refinement was required. I saw customers absorbed by the brilliant colors of the groceries, especially fresh fruits and produce on display in contrast to the snow-white, dazzling drabness of the Minnesota January. Being in the front of the store[2], the produce case caused the customer to shed hats, scarves and gloves to fully see, hear, smell, and feel the fruits of warmth from California or Florida. Many would dwell for minutes working the produce from one end to the other to finally select just a couple oranges and a lemon. Nonetheless, it served the purpose of a graceful transition into a personalized shopping mindset--"what looks good to me today?"--inducing many customers to remain in the store and shop for a long time.

Self-service brought many innovations into commerce, and has changed commerce forever.   Some of these changes are in the foundation of HCI, e-commerce and personalization, including:
- The customer is the best arbiter of his/her needs, including always being right and well informed. Customers do not want to be "handled" by sales personnel who feed them only filtered information and the products the sales staff chose.
- Consumers want and producers must do or die:
   a) More control in transactions and also to feel always in control
   b) To serve themselves and choose specific items after testing them
   c) To find what they want and do so comfortably
- Self-service displays (the UI tools) must *connect items to the customer:*
   a) Activating her/his needs and knowledge
   b) Using recognition-based cognition, not recall
   c) Producing both organization and "emotionalization" of the UI by
      1. Placing items in attractive and colorfully labelled packages
      2. Grouping items in natural or intuitive categories, e.g., fruits are together, seasonings are next to meats (and perhaps also in spices)
- The self-service stimulus environment aimed to trigger each customer's *need* response, while making sure that (s)he felt in control in the shopping experience.

The self-service environment aimed to amplify a positive personal experience for every customer while also utilizing mass communication to achieve economical viability. Given the reality of a small town, the store staff also aided personalization

---

[2] The produce did not start in the front of the store. After my father realized the value that feeling and experiencing fresh produce had for both customers (they liked to see and feel what fresh tastes were available) and the business (customers quickly came into a shopping mood), he placed the self-service produce case up front as the first main event.

by setting items aside known to be favorites of selected customers. For example, one widow always wanted three plump pink grapefruit, and the produce man always came through for her. In the self-service of my father's store, personalization was accomplished primarily on a mass-communication plane, but also for individual customers. It was done without IT and in the context of a business model that not only provided value for both customers and the store, but also provided some "glue" to hold the community together.

1.3 Successful personalization in self-service, e-tailing, and e-service

The above list of innovations also shows qualitative criteria to define successful personalization in self-service shopping. Success is when customers always feel right, knowledgeable, comfortable, and in control and where the shopping environment connects items to customers to trigger recognition responses of their needs. In short, the most successful self-service shopping is often an intense and unexpected experience of one's most personal needs. Think about shopping trips where you have found absolutely smashing clothes or the perfect food or beverage and have shared your delight in your find with friends and family. Self-service not only changed commerce forever by making it more personal, it also prepared the way for e-commerce.

What was transformational about the move to self-service commerce in the 1950's? To me, it was the beginning of shopping as a personal and fulfilling human activity that people *did for themselves at their own pace and largely for self-fulfillment*. Self-service both enabled and required *personalization*. No longer could customer loyalty be built on the person-to-person interactions with a clerk. Non-human system components needed to be designed to support personalization in real-time as customers shopped. It was also a beginning of human-system interaction design because designing effective self-service meant meeting effective UI design principles:

a) The customer (or user) is sentient, right and knowledgeable and therefore is to be kept in central focus.
b) Items need to be displayed (in the UI) to activate in customers minds the connections between those items and their current needs and goals.
c) The self-service store is an (user interaction) environment designed to keep customers active on their own and feeling in control of their actions.

The changes made in the move to self-service commerce not only were precursors of HCI, but they brought about shopping as we know it--something that is personal and bedrock to the point of being *de facto* an unalienable right for those of means in today's consumer culture. Self-service was a cultural transformation as well as changing business models and commerce.

Definitions of self-service, e-tailing, and e-services will help understanding of how they apply to personalization. As above, a self-service store puts the customer in control and also in an active position for shopping and business transactions.

Self-service customers have roles in the store, making them unpaid "employees." Thus, the UI design of the self-service store is key.

An e-tail store is a web site that functions as a (retail) store on the web. These web sites merely "webify" a mail order catalogue and allow purchase and payment on-line. Rust and Kannan (2003) further characterize e-tailing as porting retail self-service onto the web in a de-contextualized fashion, where neither the new IT environment nor the newly possible business models created by the web are taken into account and fully exploited. Based on factors such as cost reduction and efficiency, the focus in e-tailing is inward. Rust and Kannan go further to distinguish an e-service store or business as fully accounting for and exploiting the new IT and business model enabled by the web.

In e-services, the emphasis is on outward factors such as revenue expansion and customer satisfaction. With respect to personalization, self-service is a fundamental business process enabling personalized shopping, e-tailing is the initial implementation of self-service on the web and is focused inwardly on making the technology work, e-services refine this initial attempt and focus outwardly towards building customer bonds and loyalty (equity) with the business.

Self-service, e-tailing, and e-services all brought the customer into the business process and gave them scripted roles and expectations that previously were filled by a professional staff member. The British situational comedy, "Are you being served?" illustrates to a hilarious extreme the roles filled by clerks prior to the arrival of self-service. Much of the funny business in this show comes from deciding what merchandise is to be displayed where, who on the staff is responsible for the merchandise, and how customers are passed up and down the pecking order formed by the store staff. This show illustrates shopping prior to the advent of self-service and I refer the interested reader to view it for that purpose.

Taking a phone order in the family grocery store illustrates the situation pre-self-serve. The customer was responsible for making a list and calling the store as in Table 1. The answering store staff member took the order and most often then fulfilled it. Some of the order takers further specialized in specific customers, knowing, e.g., that when Mrs. Smith ordered a loaf of bread it actually meant the largest loaf of white bread instead of the smallest loaf of whole wheat. As shown in Table 1, this meant that the store took the major responsibility for selecting items. The store staff would check-out, package and deliver the order to the customer, who would pay for it upon delivery or add it to their credit account with the store. The customer might specifically request a clerk or an item, but the store staff did most of the personalization in this case.

As described above, this changed in large measure with self-service. For purposes of illustration, assume that Mrs. Smith has given her husband a short shopping list (bread, milk, butter, and cookies) to pick up after he visits the barbershop next to the store. Going to the bread rack, he sees the large-loaf white bread and picks up a loaf. Although customers still are responsible for need identification in self-service, the store's display of items often makes this a recognition task as opposed to a recall task. Walking over to the cookies, he sees many varieties that the Smiths like, so he chooses two packages on sale. Noticing a new variety is also on sale, he picks up a package to try. Going over to the dairy case, he completes shopping by picking up the butter and milk. The cottage cheese is too tempting, so he picks up a package and also grabs a can of cling peaches on the way to the check-out. This illustrates that self-service shopping is closer to heuristic-guided search than a fixed-path process.

Table 1 *Roles for the Customer (C=major, c=supporting), Store (S=major, s=supporting), and Web Store (W=major, w=supporting) in Four Shopping Scenarios*

Shopping Action	Pre self-service-- phone order	Self- service-- store	e-tail-- Web Van	e-services-- Amazon
Need identification-- making a list, seeing needed item	C	C	C	C-w
Travel to or communication with store	C	C	C-w	C-W
Selection of items-- category, brand and instances	S-c	C	W-c	C-W
Purchase/Checkout-- scanning items, totalling cost, etc.	S	S-c	W-C	W-C
Payment	C-s	C-s	C-w	C-w
Packaging and shipping from store to home or use location	S-c	C-s	S-w	S-w-c
Personalization-- routes, short cuts, routines, suggestions, profiles	S-c	C-s	C-w	W-c

Table 1 shows that self-service brought the largest changes in shopping actions to the stages of item selection, packaging and shipping, and also personalization. Self-service shoppers wholly participated in the logistics of shopping, made their own selections, choose their own routes through the store, and developed shopping routines and habits that were pleasing to them. This added new opportunities for making shopping pleasurable, and also put the shopper in the driver's seat for personalization making self-service also *self-personalization*. There were also a couple things in it for the seller-- customers started doing some of the logistic tasks of shopping, and a non-personnel asset (store design or UI design) became as or more important than staffing. In short, self-service often resulted in a big win for both the merchant and customers.

Table 1 also shows that e-tailing represents a half-step back to the pre-self service style of shopping. Consider for example the now defunct Web Van. Instead of phoning in an order, customers would access the Web Van web site and place an order. Largely, the rest of the transaction more closely matches that of the pre-self service scenario than self-service. Selection of items in e-tailing is driven by the web store, which also takes care of the shopping logistics as prior to self-service. As in self-service, e-tail customers drive their own personalization, but they do so in a virtual environment without physical cues, conventional landmarks, or versioning history[3]. E-tailing might make shopping on-line more akin to the work of deciphering the store's web site than the pleasure of seeing "what I might want that's for sale" in a self-service situation. In contrast to the self-service example above, there is little opportunistic selling and impulse buying in e-tailing.

Although not fully realized as of yet, many potential improvements are possible through e-services. Considering Amazon as a leading prototype for an e-service based business, we see the customer unburden or assisted in all of the shopping actions of Table 1. The current version (December 2003) of the Amazon.com web store assists the customer in identifying needs and the means of connecting those needs with the appropriate sections of the web store through the opening page, which invites the customer to search, browse, or view recommendations. Regardless of which style of web shopping taken, the selection of items proceeds as collaboration between the customer, who drives, and the web pages that keep appropriate context and focus in the customer's field of view. Personalization is accomplished through web technology, but involves the customer in ever enriched roles. Through cookies or after logging on, many web pages in an Amazon transaction display how the store has personalized shopping, using purchase history, navigation bread crumbs, and collateral marketing. The personalizations mostly appear as softly stated, meaningful recommendations and there is always an obvious way to change or back out, e.g., a button labelled "change payment method." Amazon.com illustrates many of the features of an e-service based store while simultaneously providing best practices of self-service in a virtual environment. It utilizes personalization and information integration to enrich and enliven that sparse and limited virtual environment. It is a quality shopping experience as a result.

With respect to the HCI of e-personalization, examining why e-tailing has largely failed is informative. Many reasons have emerged to explain the lack of success for e-tailing. I suggest that being in a virtual environment has degraded online shopping in e-tail stores to a largely unfulfilling experience for many customers. For example, the span of items that fits on a web page is small compared to the same span in a shopper's field-of-view from anywhere inside the average retail store today. The limits for the customer are reminiscent of the limiting factors in my grandfather's store, e.g., needing a clerk to find things. Thus, e-tailing is a step backward in commerce. Many sites that implemented e-tailing have ported self-

---

[3] Perhaps web sites should add an equivalent to the phone-based caveat--"please read the site carefully as some of our link options and choices have recently changed."

service retail concepts and business processes without the benefit of the physical contextual cues of the store. This makes shopping demand more and higher cognitive processing from the shopper than just tooling the cart down the aisles at half or less attention.

Given these severe HCI limitations inherent in e-tailing and that today, e-commerce is maturing from e-tailing into *e-services*, a comparison of self-service and e-services will be informative. Although informally defined above, there is not a universally accepted and formal definition of an e-service (Stafford, 2003). E-services embody major extensions of both the business model and IT architecture from self-service and e-tailing. Personalization plays a pivotal role in these extensions. We can start to understand e-services and personalization by examining similarities and differences about customers as they serve themselves on the web in an e-service environment.

Rust and Kannan describe the changes in customers' roles and how sellers regard them as e-services grow. For example, advertising in e-tailing gives way to two-way dialogue in e-service; 1:1 marketing replaces mass marketing; customization is the way instead of commodities; customer equity and profitability replace brand equity and product profitability. These changes from a naïve e-tailing to a more enlightened (and profitable) e-service roughly correspond to the three areas of change that came with self-service, which are summarized below in Table 2.

What is successful personalization? In self-service, successful personalization meant that each customer felt safe, knowledgeable and in control shopping in our store, found and purchased what he or she wanted, and kept coming back. In e-commerce today, Riecken (2000) describes personalization as being all about building customer loyalty. Major differences between self-service and e-service occur in the increased complexity of the business model and IT requirements. Still, e-commerce personalization aims towards a meaningful 1:1 relationship between the customer and the store or web site. It requires understanding each customer's needs. The business must map and satisfy simultaneously the customer's goal and the business' goal in their respective contexts. Table 2 reflects my definition for successful personalization from both the self-service and e-service environments.

Table 2. *Parallel Transitions in Self-Service and Personalized E-Service*

Self Service Store	E-Service Web Store
The customer is right, knowledgeable, and feels in a safe environment	The business must understand and attend to each customer's needs
The displays (UI tools) connect items to the customers and their needs	The business must map and satisfy both the customer's goal and the business's goal in their respective contexts.
The shopping experience must keep the customer actively engaged on his or her own, feeling in control, and returning to shop	The customer and business build a meaningful 1:1 relationship, leading to customer loyalty

Summary Although the move to self-service that took place fifty years ago was more "trial-and-error," than today's systematic development of e-services, the same fundamental transitions took place. Customers and businesses alike adopted new roles, which essentially made *the customer an integral part of the business*. Customers came to like their new, active role called *shopping* and flocked to stores in the 1950's and then to the web in the 1990's. That customers feel that self-service and e-service shopping is *personalized* is key to continued commercial success.

In parallel, the current adoption of e-services into government has enabled every citizen to take a "Main Street" seat at the table of government. Applications of IT have begun to shrink the gaps between governments and the governed in terms of increased access to information, increased performance of governmental services, and citizen participation in government (Marchionini, Samet, and Brandt, 2003). In the retrospective of seeing self-service and personalization brought to Main Street, I turn now to discuss the prospective possibilities for e-personalization in electronic government.

2. ELECTRONIC GOVERNMENT AND ELECTRONIC COMMERCE

2.1   Why and what is e-government[4]?

Unlike commerce, government did not go through a deep transformation to self-service during the post-war 1950's. But with the advent of the web came a natural pressure to change and with the 1990's started the provisioning of governmental functions through e-services, or *e-government*. This follows Marchionini, Samet, and Brandt (2003), who describe e-government as the "application of IT to government service" and distinguish *digital government* as "the larger concept of government that depends upon IT to achieve basic missions." This distinction is, in their terms, "lexically arbitrary, but serves to distinguish R&D specifically aimed at creating techniques for applying IT to government operations." Seeing value in this distinction, I will continue to use it, and refer to the larger IT concepts, methods and R&D domains as "digital" as in digital government and the actual applications of IT with the e prefix, such as "e-government" or "e-services."

2.2   What are the major differences and similarities between e-government and e-commerce?

E-commerce has major roots in the self-service movement in retail commerce. Customer confidence is thus at the heart of e-commerce. Customers must feel that their private information will be protected. In online transactions, encryption will be used to prevent fraud. Data used to electronically maintain the 1:1 relationship will be kept secure and used only for the stated purposes. Customers need to feel that

---

[4] Due to multiple reasons, my discussion of government and e-government focuses on the USA.

information they yield will be used to mutual benefit, e.g., through personalization. In e-commerce, the attitudinal trend is towards the *privacy* of personal information.

E-government has grown up differently, having passed over the self-service movement with the possible exception of mail transactions. Only recently have governmental bodies, such as the post office, established "retail" outlets with self-service. Similar to e-commerce, e-government requires citizen confidence about private information, and more. Government in general has a wider range of accountability and openness requirements. Governmental record-keeping requirements are detailed and have a long history. All levels of government require that citizens be able to request and have reasonable access to public records. E-government must facilitate and maintain the public record and its access that are inherent in open government. In e-government, the attitudinal trend is towards *keeping fastidious records* and the *openness* of all information, which includes personal information. With respect to personalization, e-government is different from e-commerce in the mix of private and public information held in its records.

Major differences with respect to personalization between e-government and e-commerce thus include less governmental experience in self-service, long standing requirements for governmental accountability, openness and record keeping, and a mix of governmental records heavily weighted towards being open and away from being private.

E-commerce and e-government have a common direction towards a set of common goals and models. Both aim towards direct connection and communication by relying on the web and other IT for customers and constituents to serve themselves. Both aim to increase efficiency and capabilities of the staff and thereby better serve and provide better value to customers and constituents. Although from different angles, both are converging on a "value-chain" business model. Since sales in commerce and politics in government have always been "high-touch" and personal activities, e-personalization plays an ever-increasing role in both sectors.

2.3   How does personalization play a role in e-government?

The Preamble to the U.S. Constitution reads, "We the people of the United States, in order to form a more perfect union, establish justice, insure domestic tranquillity, provide for the common defense, promote the general welfare, and secure the blessings of liberty to ourselves and our posterity, do ordain and establish this Constitution for the United States of America." Although at a very lofty level, the Preamble touches many points of personalization, specifically insuring domestic tranquillity and securing the blessings of liberty to ourselves and our prosperity. Witness the many public servants that in the 1990's embraced and promoted the incorporation of e-services into government. These included many that were effective in bringing about e-government from both the left and the right perspectives (Vice President Gore, Speaker Gingrich, etc.). E-government has come about in large measure through vision of our leadership as they saw a better future for our Republic. Indeed, President Bush has carried this forward with a strategic plan[5] built on the vision of "e-gov: my government, my terms." Three guiding principles underlie this plan:

1. **Citizen-centered**, not bureaucracy or agency-centered
2. **Results-oriented**, producing measurable improvements for citizens
3. **Market-based**, actively promoting innovation

Looking at it from a value-chain perspective, governments contribute value in terms of linking individuals, businesses, and organizations to a union or *community*. That community should be centered on citizens, and not the government (nor business nor any other organization for that matter). Citizens need to see and experience actual (measurable) improvements through e-government. E-government needs to be market-based and active in promoting innovation and continuous improvement to learn its way through problems. Personalization techniques along with the personal information collected along the way can greatly aid the implementation of these principles and speed the production and delivery of benefit to citizens.

Furthermore, the rhetoric and the resources used in the 1990's emphasized making government more *personal* in e-government. The rapid development of the Internet infrastructure to reach all the US and governmental e-services such as Thomas[6] were promoted and funded by the government. These were both enablers and examples of what leaders across the political spectrum envisioned: a government that was more approachable for each citizen personally through electronic means. In its foundation and original lofty visions, e-government was intended to be personalized, meaning that personalization plays a fundamental role in e-government, that is, without personalization, e-government does not exist.

Personalization is key to ensure that we do not end up with what Speaker Gingrich has called e-bureaucracy (Hasson, 2003). E-bureaucracy is the old business model of government poorly ported to (obsolescent) IT. By researching personal preferences in government and parallel business services, we can implement e-government that is better centered on citizens.

In sum, one of the most successful of e-services in government that relies on personalization is the online renewal of driver's license and motor vehicle tags. Many states now offer renewals over the web, when they involve no changes of personal information. The renewal process is started when the appropriate state agency sends a renewal notice to the driver or vehicle owner at the current address. The person accesses the web address on the notice, enters authorization codes from the notice and verifies information. If all personal information is as recorded in the database feeding the web site, the renewal transaction is completed with payment. The new license or tags are sent to the address on record. If information has changed that needs verification, e.g., address, the transaction is halted and the driver

---

[5] http://www.feapmo.gov/resources/e-gov_strategy.pdf

[6] Thomas at http://thomas.loc.gov/ covers U.S. Federal legislative information on the Internet. It serves as a portal to much if not all of the business of the U.S. Congress, e.g., the on-line Congressional Record.

or owner must travel to an agency office to verify the change. For the vast majority of straightforward renewals, the transaction is completed in about 5 minutes. This usually represents a saving of a few hours of effort for each transaction and increases citizen satisfaction. For driver's licenses, many states require the driver to come in every other renewal for an eye exam and a new photo, thus updating all personal information. This example illustrates that if the personal information on file is correct, an effective e-service can be put in place. Furthermore it illustrates the value and necessity of keeping one's personal information current in such state agencies. It provides a good benchmark for a positive role of personalization in e-government.

2.4 What are the major personalization issues in e-government?

A colleague recently shared that it seems that citizens have come to expect "*anonymous convenience*" in e-commerce and e-government. That this combination is difficult if not impossible to deliver illustrates that there are major issues in coming down off the lofty e-government mountain into the realm of implementation. They are major for two reasons: 1) because they must be resolved for effective e-government, and 2) because they are both large and complex. Of these issues, I discuss here four issues: digital or electronic identity, electronic records, privacy and security, and regulations.

One's electronic identity, *e-identity* here, refers to the pieces of personal information needed to complete a specific electronic transaction. It is in some ways related to personal identity, which is a construct of many flavors, including psychological, business, security, information-technology etc. From the perspective of social psychology, one's identity is projected to others through a process such as impression formation, where perceptions of another are integrated into a whole memory trace representing one's identity in another person. Similarly, one's e-identity is formed in part by data traces from personalization episodes and significant electronic records, such as a credit report, as well.

E-identity is the locus of many issues in e-government and personalization because personalization traces contribute to one's e-identity and the government is the originator of most if not all of the fundamental identity records. The management of ones e-identity is a central issue in e-government. Additional issues include ownership, marketing, and mining of the personal information and data traces in e-identities. How vital records are handled illustrates major e-government issues in e-identity. Birth, marriage and death certificates are example vital records, which are managed most often through counties for collection and at the state level for storage and distribution. Such certificates form the core of every citizen's identity and are thus at the root of our e-identity too. The birth certificate is required to obtain a social security card, passport, employment, bank account, school enrollment, etc. Marriage (and divorce) certification is central for verifying eligibility for benefits. Our heirs will need a death certificate to collect their benefits and inheritance. In today's hurried and mobile society, it would be often convenient to utilize an e-service for such certifications or even to order the appropriate certificate. But currently, no state is doing e-certification or fully using an e-service for order processing. A few states are moving closer by accepting third-party online payment, but virtually all require a signed application from an eligible party to obtain certified copies of vital records, especially birth certificates. As tempting as it might be to turn the ordering of vital records over to an e-service, keeping a wholly manual set of steps in the process provides an important safeguard against automated fraud, namely time and trouble. Although it might be very convenient, an e-service offering one-click ordering of all vital records for a family might open a Pandora's Box of automated fraud through identity theft. The time and trouble of working through one of the private or public information integration web sites for vital records are at this time worth the protection against automated fraud. Even though one needs to follow the procedure of each state, and wait for the certificate to arrive, it is something we normally have to do just a few times in our lifetime. So the example of vital records serves to illustrate the issues of how critical are our identities and also how not automating the distribution of such certificates through an e-service affords all citizens some level of protection.

Electronic records or *e-records* are collections of electronically stored information that have meaning in terms of legal status or business process. They are lifeblood of e-commerce and e-government. A central issue is what constitutes an e-record in e-commerce and e-government. Is the printout of a browser screen a bona fide record? Additional issues of e-records include their authenticity, preservation, and security.

Some businesses work to protect the *privacy and security* of customers seeing it as key to maintaining a positive 1:1 relationship. Others see that information as a marketable asset, which is to be bought and sold to the full extent allowed by their policy and law. In personalization, privacy and security are thought of as overlapping. Privacy refers to controlling access to personalized data and records. Security refers to the trust level that individuals have that their personal data and information will be well used and well protected.

In e-government, I see that the most significant issue in privacy and security is the extremely complex set of trade-offs created by terrorism, information warfare and fraud. For example, the Federal E-Gov Enterprise Architecture Guidance stipulates[7] the following set of seemingly competing actions be taken to handle privacy:

> "[Government] agencies that implement Privacy Sensitive data in their IT systems should be held accountable for effectively securing them from inappropriate use, while at the same time efficiently sharing them for purposes such as homeland security, and reducing needless burdens upon the public to supply the same data to multiple stovepipe systems (in accordance with the Paperwork Reduction Act of 1995)"

Any single one of the three actions mandated is technically complex and involved, making their combination a technical problem that will likely far exceed the scope of the Y2K event. Politically, each one of these creates a significant

---

[7] Pages 13 and 14 of E-Gov Enterprise Architecture Guidance (Common Reference Model) Draft Version 2.0, 7/25/02, http://www.feapmo.gov/resources/E-Gov_Guidance_Final_Draft_v2.0.pdf

information battlefield, and their combination ensures politically charged debate and information warfare for at least the next generation.

One example showing an outer edge of these trade-offs in privacy and security covers the new and very popular government web sites of parolee and sex offender registries. Users can see who on these registries lives in their zip code(s) or towns. For the agency that operates it, the web site affords an inexpensive and easy way to maintain and update the registry. For citizens, having the registries on the web affords easy access to information on offenders and parolees that is e-personalized to their area. For everybody involved questions arise about what is truly private information about the offenders and what should be made public. For example, for offenders, name, address, a photo, the offense, the period of inclusion on the registry, etc. are not considered private and regularly included on the web site. Extraneous and very key private items, such as social security number, place of employment, health status, etc. are secured and not available on the web.

Much *government regulation* has been considered and some has been put in place to deal with the downsides of e-personalization. Although this regulation offers potential protection, it comes up against the new reality that wanted e-services but also unwanted criminal acts alike occur at machine speed. Add in cases of mischief and one can easily see the difficulties faced trying to draft and then implement regulation for e-personalization. Still, citizens expect anonymity and/or privacy, and regulation is the way Americans have come to deal with failures to deliver on those expectations.

Regulation's purpose is to remedy issues, some of which are described above. However, such cures sometimes create other issues through unintended consequences. One of the main areas of concern in e-personalization regulation is *information integration* or the bringing together of disparate pieces of personal information. Within governmental units there exist more pieces of personal information, but also more regulations on its use. Consequently a market has grown for private information integrators, which are somewhat less stringently regulated.

One recent controversy in my home state of Georgia concerned participation in a private database that would potentially integrate all Georgia citizens' personal data. Although it was decided against doing so, the deliberations raised the need to establish balanced regulations for the storage and use of personalization data, regardless of whether a private or public organization held them. A similar controversy is now arising between a major private information integrator and the community of professional private investigators. The information integrator has just announced the availability of integrated personal data so that businesses can pursue their own background checks. The private investigator community is questioning the wisdom of loosening the restrictions on access and use of such sensitive data, citing that most businesses do not have individuals with sufficient expertise to adequately interpret such data and also identify many critical backgound deficiencies.

Core issues and questions in regulation include: Do data gleaned through a personalization process belong in an information integrator's repository? Where is the balance among private interests, public interests, security and privacy? How should this balance be attained? What are the appropriate standards of professional conduct?

Another related issue is whether e-government should be regulated to use or perhaps not to use e-personalization information it has on a citizen or constituent. For example, many states run lotteries, which are very lucrative. Should the lottery send citizens who regularly check the lottery web site spam encouraging purchases? Should the lottery web site make recommendations to users based on the click stream and history of use? If a specific lottery client is identified, should her tax records be accessed to help focus targeted marketing? All these examples and questions serve to illustrate the tough decisions that government must make to regulate e-personalization both for itself and corporate entities as well. Without enlightened, balanced and well-thought regulation and self-regulation, we are at risk of automating troubles and turmoil into chaos.

Summary: E-government lags behind e-commerce in some facets including personalization, in part because of minimal experience in self-service. Nonetheless, e-government is quickly catching up. In some areas of personalization, including privacy, security, record keeping, openness, etc., e-government has considerable experience. Still, there are major issues that effective personalization in e-government (and e-commerce) faces. Primary among these are digital and e-identity, e-records, and the regulation of personalization. These issues are clear indicators that the citizen expectation of anonymous convenience through the web is unrealistic and that this is largely because that the e-personalization that enables convenience necessarily means a loss of anonymity.

3. THE PRIMARY PERSONALIZATION ISSUE IN E-GOVERNMENT: ONE'S DIGITAL OR ELECTRONIC IDENTITY

3.1 What is e-identity?

Following the tradition we have observed about uncertainty and arbitrariness in a field's initial lexicon, Emily Frye (2003) has described digital identity as having no single legal definition, but a concept based on three IT characteristics. According to Frye, *digital identity* is:
1. A set of pieces of information about a person
2. Where that information is needed to conduct a particular [IT] transaction
3. Not fixed, but varies according to the requirements of the transaction.

Considering these three characteristics of digital identity as the initial definition of a larger IT concept, I will define e-identity as an instance of a digital identity. That is, in providing the IT to complete a transaction requiring pieces of information about a person, that aggregate of personal information is that person's electronic or *e-identity* for that particular application. Thus, "digital identity" will be used for discussions of policy formation, IT design, etc., and "e-identity" will be used for specific applications, such as one's e-identity for buying items on amazon.com or renewing one's drivers license with the state's department of motor vehicles' web site.

3.2 What are the e-identity issues for e-government and personalization?

There are many issues about e-identity and these issues interact in complex ways. Focusing on those issues central to personalization in e-government, I suggest the following issues are key:

What personal information is fundamental to digital identity? The Federal Enterprise Architecture quoted above talks about "Privacy Sensitive data elements" (PSDE), which implies that a set of personal data is fundamental to our digital identity and privacy. What should be included in the PSDE set? Should name, address, social security number be included as PSDEs? What should be the requirements for PSDEs, when release of the set is sufficient to do harm to individuals? This issue and these questions were largely taken up in a bill (S. 2201) introduced by Senator Hollings in 2002. That this bill received so much comment and open debate underscores the difficulty of this issue.

A related question is whether this PSDE should be gathered into a single repository to provide directory services for all citizens. This could be through an e-government or an e-commerce e-service. For example, state departments of motor vehicles could do so, as could many corporations using proprietary or open-source directory services technology.

Who owns that information? What markets are possible? What roles, responsibilities and rights do all parties have in digital identities? Attitudes towards digital identity differ from the U.S. to the E.U. Roughly speaking, in the U.S., "possession is nine-tenths of the law" with respect to digital identity and data from personalizations; whereas in the E.U., the person whose identity has been "digitized" is given the nod of ownership (and control). This has created markets for information from our digital identities, e.g., for a small sum one can buy the social security number of elected officials and many other U.S. citizens too. Roles, responsibilities, and rights are in a state of high fluctuation now, as government struggles with legislation and regulation, and business struggle with policies and procedures for personalization and identity that are both competitive and protective.

One set of related questions includes whether governmental bodies who issue fundamental identity records and documents (birth certificates, driver's licenses, passports, etc.) can or should participate in the markets that have grown up surrounding personal and identity information. Similarly, what role should e-government play in digital certificates and identity authentication and management? Is an e-government just another consumer, or should it use its position as an originator of digital identity information to also be a (paid) supplier? Likewise, should e-government services that utilize personalization contribute information to citizen's digital identities, similar to reporting credit information to a credit bureau? Many questions surround the value of personalized information in, e.g., digital identities and the production and marketing of that information, especially concerning the role of e-government.   These are among the most difficult of questions.

How can digital and electronic identity be effectively managed and utilized? Identity management and utilization is an operational area that has significant ties to personalization.   For example, credit card companies routinely call customers whenever their IT identifies a card-use pattern falling outside of the personalized profile.   When an e-service receives a request for something requiring authorization, e.g., a logon, it needs to verify and authenticate that the requester is whom he, she, or it asserts as an identity.   When someone's digital identity changes or contains an error, (s)he needs a way to change it and/or it needs to be changed through personalization processes.   Again, questions about the role of e-government as producers and/or consumers of digital identity management and the place for personalization in identity management are just now being raised.   I believe that *trust* will be a deciding factor in determining the entities that will manage e-identities.

Summary: Digital and e-identity is my choice for the most critical personalization issue now associated with e-government.   If any organization, especially a government, can not quickly and accurately identify its constituents, it is ineffective.   Furthermore, if an IT entity, such as e-government, can not do so or can not authenticate requests for service, it is dangerous.   Personalization will play a major role in digital identity through use behavior, user preferences, biometrics, etc.

4.   PERSONALIZATION ISSUE: DATA, INFORMATION AND RECORDS

4.1   What are differences between personalization data, information and records?

Personalization *data* refers to that data created and stored during a personalization transaction.   These data might or might not be identifiable to a person, and they might be distributed across multiple machines, e.g., in cookies on the browser and data records on a server.   In general these data elements taken by themselves are not very significant nor deeply interpretable.

These data become *information* when they are labelled and then grouped or aggregated together in a meaningful way.   For example, grouping together a name, address, date of birth, and credit card data provides identity information.   Another meaningful group of data would be a click stream showing that a user looked at tents, sleeping bags, and a first aid kit.   The information here is that the user is shopping for a camping trip.

This information becomes a *record* when it has a business-policy or legal status. For example, identity information and a click stream indicating approval of a credit card payment provides a record of authorizing payment for a purchase.

These three levels imply different levels of value and use. Having a database without knowing the keys and field names is fairly useless. Just try to interpret your browser cookies by looking at the data alone. Value and utility come with information and records because fields are labelled and grouped meaningfully. Records have additional value because of their authority to verify actions and/or events, especially in court. What are the important issues for e-government and personalization of these three levels?

How should one's base digital identity be provided and maintained in the context of personalization? Is this an e-government or an e-commerce function? In order to get a digital identity today, one first needs an identity. The foundational cornerstones of everyone's identity come from government. These include birth (and death) certificates, driver's licenses, social security cards and numbers, passports, voter registration cards, etc. A verification chain can be followed from most any form of identity issued to an official government-issued record or document, e.g., birth certificate. Currently, only government-issued identification is accepted as base identification. So, in the future electronic realm, how will that be done? Will vital records departments start collecting different personal information, e.g., epithelial cells for DNA, for stronger and more computable digital identities in the birth certificate? Will commercial firms step into this chain? Who will pay for maintenance and use of the base records (and samples)? Will subsequent records resulting from personalization be linked to the base records? There are many issues and possible touch points between an individual's personalization history and base records.

In e-government, what constitutes a record? How often have you been told to print out a web page to verify your transaction? If later an error invalidates the transaction, or data is lost and the transaction disappears from the database, is your screen-print a valid, legal record? Is there a critical level of personalized data in a screen-print or any other record to link you to a transaction record, e.g., an email address? Because e-identity is by definition transitory, questions about the role of personalized data in records need resolution.

Summary: By themselves and without labels or other bases of interpretation, personalization data seem to be of little to no value. But, when appearing as labelled and in meaningful groups, personalization information has value. Personalization and identity records are most valuable, having business or legal status.

5. REGULATIONS FOR PERSONALIZATION IN E-GOVERNMENT AND E-COMMERCE IN THE UNITED STATES

5.1 What are some primary U.S, regulations that pertain to personalization?

There is good news and some uncertainty about privacy and access of personalized information. The good news is that considerable attention is being paid to privacy and access. The uncertainty is in the cost and effectiveness of the approach taken: government regulation.

Numerous government regulations concerning privacy and access to personalization and identity information have recently been considered and some have been enacted. At the base of these regulations is the Privacy Act of 1974 (5 U.S.C. § 552A). This law regulates the keeping and use of records maintained on individuals in the areas of education, medical, financial, criminal, and employment. It stipulates requirements for keeping, use, matching, disclosure, access, review, and amendment of records.

Twenty years later, update of the regulations began in the context of increased IT capability and differentiated needs within different domains. More and better IT spawned a regulation for "Fraud and Related Activity in Connection with Computers" (18 U.S.C. 1030). This regulation does at least two things important to personalization: First, it explicitly protects data, information, and services on computers by restricting access only to those that are authorized. Second, it also begins to define levels of risk associated with unauthorized access. In 2003, the General Services Administration has further defined (GSA 2003-N02) regulations for access by requesting comment on an "E-Authentication Policy for Federal Agencies." The policy is based on assurance levels, which are associated with a level of risk the government agency is willing to accept. The assurance level is defined by "how much confidence the relying party has that the electronic identity credential presented is done so by the person whose identity is asserted by the credential." This proposed regulation clearly takes electronic personalization to a most serious level by establishing a process for credentials based on e-identity.

The recognition that different needs exist in different domains has spawned specific regulations in the areas of education through FERPA (20 U.S.C. § 1232g; 34 CFR Part 99), medical records through HIPAA (Public Law 104-191), and financial through the Gramm-Leach-Bliley financial modernization act of 1999 or GLB (Federal Trade Commission). Special protection is afforded to children using computers through COPPA (Federal Trade Commission). All of these regulations are directed at electronic and personal information, and must be taken into account by any organization (and sometimes individuals too) that pursues electronic personalization. In all the regulations, the spirit and intent is to increase levels of privacy and security of e-personalization for all citizens. It is too early in the process to tell what if any refinements might be required to meet that intent.

5.2 What can the e-personalization community do in terms of regulation?

At this early stage, I suggest that our community would be wise to do three things about regulation: 1) education, 2) evaluation, and 3) consultation. First, we should educate ourselves about the importance of e-personalization (through e-identity) to the continued integrity and viability of the national and global IT infrastructure. The regulations, policies, and procedures *are required for continued survival and prosperity*. We should also educate the IT security and privacy community about our potential to contribute to the cause. In our community's vast experience with users, we know that if there are two ways to achieve a goal and one is intuitive and natural while the other is bureaucratic and arbitrary, the intuitive and natural will be more effective, because it will be used. Through evaluating regulation in terms of good old usability, we can make a valuable contribution. This contribution is better communicated through consultation empasizing solutions.

6. TECHNOLOGY FOR E-GOVERNMENT--A SMALL NUMBER OF POSSIBLE SOLUTIONS

6.1 *Personalization and E-Identity Commerce--Opt-In or Opt-Out?*

A major discussion point about markets of personalization information is whether organizations holding that information should use an opt-in or an opt-out process for sharing or selling that information. The opt-in process requires the subject of the personalized information to explicitly consent to sharing or sale of that information. Opt-in is used in the E.U and in Canada more and more now. The opt-out process requires the subject to explicitly request removal of the personalized information from sharing or sales. In the opt-out process, an individual's consent to share the personalized information is implied. Opt-out is used in the U.S.

My personal preference is for the opt-in process. My background in self-service, where the customer needs to maintain control and experimental psychology with the protocol of "informed consent" is strongly expressive here. Still, the opt-out is the way of the land in the US. In that light, I suggest the personalization community work towards developing tools and processes that allow individuals to easily identify where they have left personalized traces and also automatically opt-out, should that be their desire.

6.2 *Group Identities or Profiles*

In many electronic transactions, either party does not require highly personalized or specifically identified information be retained. For example, requests for information about products or planning board meeting schedules require only categorical information to complete. For these instances, I suggest the personalization community develop group identities or profiles. These can unburden the user and the organization alike from the worry and overhead about giving and using personalized information. Furthermore, a group e-identity implies a lower level of risk than an individual e-identity, which is in parallel with the current e-government authentication process.

6.3 *"Personalization" Crumbs*

Navigation crumbs have become mainstays of good web UI design. They make obvious where a user has been and provide controls to easily return to a previous point. It would be good if personalization traces were made equally obvious. Our CHI 2003 Workshop suggested the personalization community might develop a facility to display "personalization" crumbs and I agree.

6.4 e-Identity and e-Personalization Education and Browsers

Currently, one's e-identity information dwells in the "land of mystery" for most citizens. First of all, many web users do not realize that personalized traces are kept throughout the web, including in cookies on own machines. Once awareness is achieved, obtaining specific information on one's e-identity is possible, but not straightforward. Through a fee-based service, one can search through e-records on one's self. A spy-ware or ad-ware checking program on one's PC can reveal and stop some of the hidden programs that share your personalized information with organizations.

I suggest a good role for the personalization community is to develop awareness and education programs for e-identity and e-personalization. Supporting the education with tools, such as an e-identity browser, would greatly help.

6.5 Effective Protocols and Best Practices for Managing E-Personalization and E-Identity

Following along the path of making user citizens aware and knowledgeable of e-personalization, our community's action to develop professional practices will be very valuable. What matters here is effectiveness in e-personalization transactions more so than if it is achieved through an e-government regulation or an industry best practice implemented throughout e-commerce. I suggest that our e-personalization community is positioned to lead the development of best practices.

7. CONCLUSION: A GOAL AND STRATEGY FOR PERSONALIZATION IN E-GOVERNMENT

7.1 What should be our goal for personalization in e-government?

I suggest a good goal for personalization in e-government is to form a better sense of community. Utilizing personalization techniques, we can knit our community together electronically to effectively "form a more perfect union, establish justice, insure domestic tranquillity, provide for the common defense, promote the general welfare, and secure the blessings of liberty to ourselves and our posterity" as stated in the Preamble. This is a tall order, but after all in setting a goal we should aim high.

Before proceeding to a few details, a cautionary note is in order. As in the popular "Star Wars," the force of personalization has its potential dark side also. Safeguards must be put in place to ensure that personalization in e-government is done with trustworthy integrity, and that it does not produce extreme imbalances such as in the Holocaust (Black, 2001) or the McCarthy era or the Stasi (Ash, 1998). Everyone should take responsibility for these safeguards, including IT professionals who implement personalization.

For this goal, e-government can learn much from e-commerce. Many goals of the e-service type of e-commerce aim toward establishing community (Rust and Kannan). Establishing a 2-way dialogue, focusing on satisfaction, building customer equity and increasing information flows are all oriented towards creating a community of loyal customers. For example, pick a make of automobile and do a Google on that name plus "owner." For many, but not all makes, one will find numerous communities of interest that focus on the brand fostering increased loyalty and interest.

Although such approaches in electronic community building might degenerate into informal blogs if left on their own, though minimal foresight, planning and methodology, an effective and learning e-community of interest can be formed. For example, an electronic version of Thomas Jefferson's Assembly could be easily implemented. As reported by Holzel (2003), Donald Anderson has used Assemblies to effectively build communities that solve local problems. These communities work through 1:1 and small group discussions on community and personal problems and roll up their results to larger groups. Every citizen has an opportunity to participate and the consensus and decisions move up to ever-larger groups. With e-services, this roll-up can be automated, presented in standard reports and made public. The process with its solution-oriented outcomes, could become as commonplace as following one's favorite TV shows, sports teams, or news stories. Such e-communities could facilitate problem solving and community development. One specific and high-profile implementation of this goal is Internet voting. Today, we can not have a trustworthy election using Internet voting. The means we have for using personalized information and digital identities is not up to the task of authentication of citizens for voting on the Internet. But, Internet voting is technically possible, and will rely on personalization in e-government. When we are able to authenticate adequately to hold elections on the Internet, we have achieved a better sense of community through e-government.

This goal aims towards bringing out the best in e-government and e-commerce, where personalization is done in a context of providing value to individuals, to businesses, and to the community. As we develop personalization techniques, we should try to do things for individuals, businesses or organizations, and the community as well.

Ultimately the goal is to move personalization towards trust and support of governmental or public "community" motives as well as private "profit" motives.

7.2 Suggested strategy for personalization in e-government

The strategy I suggest is to extend the e-business context of the Personalization Value Space that is at the foundation of this book to include community and governmental characteristics (see Chapter 2). Just as Johnson and Johnson mobilized on community safety factors over immediate profit to handle the Tylenol crisis, community-oriented factors should be included in the e-business context.

By expanding the context in which personalization techniques are applied to individual characteristics, more public and community aspects are included. Then, personalized e-commerce can more easily take a civic-minded path down "Main Street" USA and potentially create Main Streets worldwide.

8. REFERENCES

Ash, T. *The file: A personal history*. New York: Vintage, 1998.

Black, E. *IBM and the holocaust.* New York: Crown, 2001.

Federal Enterprise Architecture Project Management Office. *E-Gov Enterprise Architecture Guidance* http://www.feapmo.gov/resources/E-Gov_Guidance_Final_Draft_v2.0.pdf, 2002.

Federal Enterprise Architecture Project Management Office. *Implementing the President's management agenda for e-government*. http://www.feapmo.gov/resources/e-gov_strategy.pdf, 2003.

Frye, E. personal communication, 2003.

Hasson, J. Gingrich blasts TSA, e-bureaucracy. *Federal Computer Week*, June 11, 2003. http://www.fcw.com/fcw/articles/2003/0609/web-gingrich-06-11-03.asp

Holzel, D. The assembly man. *Michigan Today*, Fall 2003, Vol 35, No. 3. http://www.umich.edu/news/MT/03/Fal03/assembly.html

Karat, J., Karat, C., and Ukelson, J. Affordances, motivation, and the design of user interfaces *Communications of the ACM*, August 2000, Vol. 43, No. 8, pages 49-51.

Marchionini, G., Hanan, S., and Brandt, L. Digital government. *Communications of the ACM*, January 2003, Vol. 46, No. 1, pages 25-27.

Riecken, D. Personalized views of personalization. *Communications of the ACM*, August 2000, Vol. 43, No. 8, pages 27-28.

Rust, R., and Kannan, P. E-service: A new paradigm for business in the electronic environment. *Communications of the ACM*, June 2003, Vol. 46, No. 6, pages 37-42.

Stafford, T. E-services. *Communications of the ACM*, June 2003, Vol. 46, No. 6, pages 27-28.

9. LAWS AND REGULATIONS CONCERNING PERSONALIZATION

Federal Trade Commission. *Privacy regulations, including Children's online privacy protection act (COPPA) and The Gramm-Leach-Bliley financial modernization act of 1999*. http://www.ftc.gov/privacy/

GSA 2003-N02. E-Authentication policy for federal agencies: request for comments. *Federal Register*, Vol. 68, No. 133, Friday, July 11, 2003, 41370-41374.

Public Law 104-191 *Health insurance portability and accountability act of 1996 (HIPAA)*. http://aspe.hhs.gov/admnsimp/pl104191.htm

5 U.S.C. § 552A. *The privacy act of 1974*. http://www.usdoj.gov/04foia/privstat.htm. 1974.

18 U.S.C.§ 1030. *Computer fraud and abuse act*. http://www.usdoj.gov/criminal/cybercrime/1030_new.html

20 U.S.C. § 1232g; 34 CFR Part 99. *The family education and privacy act (FERPA)*. http://www.ed.gov/offices/OII/fpco/ferpa/index.html

CAROLYN BRODIE, CLARE-MARIE KARAT AND JOHN
KARAT

CREATING AN E-COMMERCE ENVIRONMENT WHERE CONSUMERS ARE WILLING TO SHARE PERSONAL INFORMATION

1. INTRODUCTION

In this chapter we describe how the personalization of commercial websites affect the decisions made by IT professionals interested in purchasing new IT equipment and obtaining support for equipment they already have. In the last few years, there has been a growing interest among both researchers and e-Commerce companies in collecting and using personal information to tailor site visitors' experiences on the website. Proponents of personalization have argued that if personal information is collected about individuals it can be used to improve the customer experience and better target marketing efforts, and therefore, increase the likelihood that customers will purchase from the e-Commerce company (Fichman and Cronin, 2003). Although many different policies and features have been recommended by researchers and implemented by e-Commerce companies (Rossi, Schwabe, and Guimaraes, 2001), no one knows what the value of personalization is to either the creators of an e-Commerce website or the people who visit it (Fink, and Kobsa,, 2000), (Hagan, Manning, and Souza, 1999). In this chapter, we present the results of a study designed to determine the relative values of personalization features and policies and the affect of the implementation of the highly valued policies on website visitors' willingness to share personal information with the website in exchange for personalized services.

1.1 Personalization, Personalization Policies, and Personalization Features

"Personalization" can mean many different things. Personalization has been a catch phrase for such diverse functionality as customization of one's home page, user interest modeling and information filtering based on explicitly entered and implicitly

185

Clare-Marie Karat et al. (eds.), Designing Personalized User Experiences in eCommerce, 185—206.
© 2004 *Kluwer Academic Publishers. Printed in the Netherlands.*

collected data, collaborative filtering techniques, and dynamically generated content (Barrett et al, 1997), (Kobsa, Konenemann, and Pohl, 2001), (Manber, Patel, and Robison, 2000), (Sarwar et al, 2001), (Schafer, Konstan, and Riedl, 1999), (Anupam, Hull, Kumar, 2001). For the purposes of this chapter, we define *personalizing a website* to mean using personal information about an individual to tailor the experience for that individual on a website. Further, we define a *personalization policy* as a decision made by an e-Commerce company involving the handling of personal data on the company's website. Generally, a personalization policy applies to the whole site. Examples of policies include the degree of visibility and control over personal data that is given to website visitors. In contrast, a *personalization feature* is a method for collecting and using personal information in order to tailor a website visitor's experience on the website. A single personalization feature provides functionality for a particular task on the site. Examples of personalization features include collaborative filtering and adaptive navigation.

Although many different approaches have been used to gather data from users, ranging from collecting implicit data (such as click stream data) to asking visitors to fill out lengthy questionnaires about themselves, potential customers often show their distrust of websites by disabling cookies on their computers and entering incorrect personal data into online forms (Hagan, 2000). Researchers have identified issues that affect website visitors' attitudes towards e-Commerce websites. Ackerman, Cranor, and Reagle (1999) identified several factors influencing whether or not individuals would share personal information with websites. They found that people are concerned with knowing how their data will be used, the types of data being collected, whether the website is run by a trusted company, whether they can find out what information the company is storing about them, and whether they can remove themselves from mailing lists. Similarly, the Australian Office of the Federal Privacy Commissioner conducted a large study of the factors that affect whether or not individuals are willing to share information with a business or other organization (Office of the Australian Federal Privacy Commissioner, 2001). They found that it is important to individuals that they understand how their data will be used and to have control over who has access to it. Jarvenpaa, Tractinsky, and Saarinen also found that knowing that a merchant has a good reputation tends to increase customer willingness to use personalized functions (1999). In contrast, researchers have reported conflicting results regarding the affects of guarantees of privacy (i.e. privacy statements and privacy seals) on sharing personal information (Palmer et al, 2000), (Turow, 2003). Our goal was to extend the study of customer attitudes towards the use of personalization e-Commerce websites by exploring how a computer manufacturer's choice of personalization policies and features affect visitors' willingness to share personal information with the company.

1.2 Overview

During this project, researchers worked with the developers of a large computer company's website. This company wanted to increase customer satisfaction regarding the site and revenue generated from the site by providing a personalized experience for their customers. We focused the work on individuals interested in making business purchases of computer equipment and support for their companies (B2B). The reason we chose this group is that personalization is most useful for repeat customers, and businesses tend to purchase computer equipment much more often and in greater volume than do individuals for their home use. If we had been working with an e-Commerce company in another domain, such as clothing sales, we would have targeted individual consumers (B2C) rather than business buyers. Our goal was to determine the personalization features that were likely to bring the biggest return on investment by increasing customers' abilities to achieve their goals, thereby leading to greater customer satisfaction and number of purchases on the website.

1.3 Costs and Benefits of Personalization

There are costs and benefits to personalization both for e-Commerce companies that implement personalization and for their customers who use it. E-Commerce companies must invest in the design and implementation of personalization features as well as in the added infrastructure costs involved in storing and protecting personal data. The main benefit of personalization for e-Commerce companies is the potential to increase revenue from the website by providing services and advertising that are targeted at an individual customer's needs and desires. For potential customers of e-Commerce sites, the cost of using a personalized website can be measured in both the time and inconvenience involved in entering personal information into the website and their degree of discomfort regarding sharing personal information with the company in order to use personalization on the site. Personalization can benefit individuals if it allows them to accomplish their goals on an e-Commerce site more quickly and easily or with fewer errors. To make investments in personalization of websites pay off for companies, a large percentage of site visitors must be willing to share personal information with them. However, the necessary customer confidence is not always easily gained. During these studies, there were three policies that we hypothesized to be very important to the use of personalized e-Commerce websites. These include 1) the website visitor owns the data in his profile; 2) the visitor is only asked to provide the personal information needed to use the particular feature in which she is interested (Permission Marketing); and 3) a website visitor's level of identity can vary over time and appropriate support is provided for the different levels of identity. Each of these will be discussed in more detail below.

1.3.1 Ownership of Data
In the past many companies viewed the data they collected about visitors to their website as something the company owned and could use in any way it liked. This

view has been changing for some time. Both social and legal pressures in Europe, North America, and elsewhere in the world have forced companies to view personal data as being owned by the subject of the data. Given this trend, we wanted to test the value of the policy that customers own their own data to see how important it was to e-Commerce customers. By "own their own data" we mean that customers can view, edit, and delete information about themselves, their purchases, and their actions on the website at any point in time and can easily understand how the information that is collected will be used by the e-Commerce company. We were interested to see if this policy was valued by website visitors or if they would consider this an inconvenience.

1.3.2 Permission Marketing

Permission Marketing (Godin, 1999) is the concept that a customer's profile is built slowly over time as the individual develops trust in the e-Commerce company. The customer is only asked to provide the information needed to enable specific services and receives immediate value for all the information that she provides. Many personalized websites today require that anyone who wants to use any personalization features on the site must register by filling out lengthy questionnaires. Given Hagan's findings that people often defeat the purpose of these forms by entering incorrect information (2000), we wanted to see if only asking for the information needed to provide an immediate service to website users would increase their willingness to share data.

1.3.3 Levels Of Identity on an E-Commerce Website

The levels of identity concept defines the degree of personal information to which a website has access based on the type of relationship between the e-Commerce company and the customer at any given point in time (Schaffer, 2001). According to Schaffer's definition this ranges from no information (visitor is *invisible*) when a user has cookies turned off, to knowing which of several possible roles an individual was using during any given session (visitor has *differentiated roles*). Roles a user might have include a home and work role or perhaps multiple work roles. We expected to find that visitors to the site progressed from being virtually *invisible* to the website to being *identified* as an individual with a profile to being *associated* with an organization or team to finally having *differentiated* roles defined with separate profiles for each role. In our study, we wanted to observe the preferred level of identity of participants from those listed in Table 1.

2. METHODOLOGY

2.1 Approach

To understand how the choice of personalization policies and features could affect users' willingness to share data with the website we first developed a master list of possible policies and features by reviewing the literature and conducting heuristic evaluations of several current e-Commerce websites that sell computer equipment. We then conducted an iterative series of user studies to progressively refine and identify the list of the highest value policies and features.

Table 1. Levels of Identity on a Website

Level of Identity	Description
Invisible	An individual who has not only not registered with the site, but has his cookies turned off so that the website cannot detect whether he has ever visited before.
Anonymous	An individual who has cookies enabled, but has not registered on the site.
Identified	An individual has registered with the site, providing personal information in exchange for the use of personalization features.
Associated	An individual has both registered with the site and indicated that she is associated with a particular team or organization.
Differentiated	An individual who has created multiple profiles on the website for different purposes (e.g. home and business, different business roles).

2.2 Potential Personalization Features and Policies Studied

Because the overall goal of this research was to determine what personalization features were valuable to business customers interested in purchasing and supporting IT equipment and how this affects customers willingness to share personal data, we started by compiling a list of potential personalization features and policies that could be implemented on the site. We created this master list from the personalization and adaptive hypermedia literature (Kobsa, Koenemann, and Pohl, 2001), conducting heuristic reviews of several computer manufacturers' websites, discussing current research projects in our own organization involving personalization, and interviewing the executive stakeholders from within the e-

Commerce company we were working with. We used as many sources for identifying potential features as possible so that we would have a very broad prospective regarding personalization. While constructing the initial list we did not consider the feasibility of implementing the personalization features in the initial list. Seventy-five potential policies and features were identified. Many of the features that we considered are in use today (e.g. collaborative filtering and recommender systems) while others are still research initiatives (e.g. inferring the website visitor's mood and changing site behavior accordingly).

We grouped the seventy-five possibilities into fourteen categories of similar features. Because we do not have room to present the complete list here, Table 2 shows the list of major categories. Our goal was to study as wide a range of personalization features as possible. However, we hypothesized that having a central place on the website around which all the personalization features could be accessed and all personal data found would be valuable to website visitors. We chose to use the construct of a *Personal Book (Berreby*, 1999) to test this hypothesis. The Personal Book is a personal space on the website which is created when a visitor chooses to register with the site. It is available from any page on the site and provides the visitor with both constant access to his or her profile and quick links to all of the other personalization features, such as a list of purchased products that allows users to track transactions, find compatible accessories, find replacements for discontinued items, and see a history of their IT purchases. Figure 1 shows the Personal Book used in the prototypes. Other personalization features available through the Personal Book include the ability to filter products based on user needs, and the ability to indicate items that the user may wish to purchase in the future so that he or she is notified of special offerings involving those products. Policies tested include: 1) the website visitor owns the data in his profile; 2) Permission Marketing; and 3) a website visitor's level of identity can vary over time and appropriate support is provided for the different levels of identity.

2.3 User Studies

The first two studies were conducted using group sessions (similar to design walkthroughs) and the third involved sessions with individual participants. The policies that we tested were the same in each of the studies, but the list of features included in the second and third studies was adjusted based on the results of the first and second studies.

2.3.1 Study Participants

Participants in the first study were responded to a request for study participates who had purchased a laptop, desktop, or server within the last year that was sent to other employees who worked for the same company as the researchers. They were given a lunch certificate redeemable at the company cafeteria as compensation. An external vendor recruited participants for the second and third study through the use of user profiles. These study participants were drawn from a population of people who all were experienced both with the World Wide Web and with the purchase of servers, desktop computers, and laptop computers for business purposes. People in this population purchase IT equipment from the web themselves, but sometimes also enlist technical assistance from others. Study participants were paid between $150 and $200 for taking part in the two-hour session. New groups of target users were recruited for each study.

2.3.2 Procedure

The experimental procedure for both group and individual sessions began with a pre-session questionnaire to collect demographic and job-related information.

Studies 1 and 2

In the group sessions (Study 1 and 2), the experimenter then read three task scenario scripts to participants accompanied by the presentation of a storyboard prototype. Each scenario involved a fictitious manager, Pat User. The first scenario concerned buying a server and a mix of desktop and notebook systems for a new department of ten people who were beginning a new project. The second scenario was about upgrading the server to handle the workload of an additional 10 people and buying additional desktop and notebook systems for them. The third scenario focused on buying accessories - in this case zip drives - for Pat's entire department. Each scenario was presented using a storyboard approach where participants saw screen shots and heard how Pat User used different personalization features to complete tasks.

Each scenario presented between 5 - 13 personalization features (e.g., presentation of accessories constrained to those compatible with a selected machine previously purchased; presentation of servers compatible with previously determined business characteristics when searching for servers). Each scenario presentation was about 20 minutes long and involved presentation of about 10 screen shots. Following the presentation, the experimenter facilitated a five-minute discussion with the participants covering the features presented. Comments were recorded on flipcharts in the room. Participants then completed a post-scenario questionnaire and gave their individual ratings for each personalization feature covered on a 7-point scale ranging from "Highly Valuable" to "Not at all Valuable" and design comments in writing. After the third scenario, participants filled out a post-session questionnaire which asked them to identify the most and least valuable features (in relationship to their jobs) from the entire set of three scenarios and to indicate whether or not the inclusion of the personalization features that they found most valuable on the website would make them more likely to visit and purchase from the site.

In Study 1, there were a total of 5 two-hour sessions with between 3 and 5 participants in each session. In total, 20 individuals participated in the study. The participants were all employees of the same company as the researchers and had all participated in the purchase of a server, desktop, or laptop computer in the last year.

Table 2. *The Fourteen Categories of Personalization Features Identified*

Feature Category	Definition
Personal Book (portal)	Area of the website, available from any page on the site, where all personalized data & functions available.
Universal Profile	Personal available and used throughout the site.
Subscription-Based Services	All services to which a user must indicate an interest in to receive.
Service and Support	Features that provide information and services related to supporting previously purchased products.
Recommendations Based on Profile Data	Features that make product recommendations that are based on personal information in the profile. (e.g. collaborative filtering)
Adaptive Presentation Tailored to User Characteristics	Features that modify the content of the web pages depending on the user characteristics or context.
Personal Preferences in Page Layout or Format	Features that allow users' to customize the website
Adaptive Navigation	Features that modify the content of web pages depending on user profile, pages visited during session, emotional state, or current task or context.
Live Help or Sales Support	Live help in the form of instant messaging, phone or email in which the technical representative has access to the customer's profile and the pages visited during the session.
Feedback that System "Recognizes" a Repeat Visitor	Features that provide the customer with indications that the site remembers him

Transaction History	Features that provide the visitor with easy access to a history of past purchases, support obtained, etc.
Loyalty Programs, Incentives	Rewards type programs
Future Purchase Considerations	Features that assist visitors with making future purchases (e.g. individualized catalogs, wish lists, etc)
Your Store, Built by an Expert	Customer catalog or pages built by an industry expert using group profiled

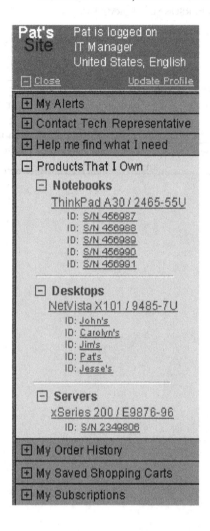

Figure 1. Personal Book from the Study 3 Prototype

To ensure that we had a wide range of features included in Study 1, we chose at least one item from each of the fourteen categories shown in Table 2. Because we did not have the resources to test all seventy-five features and policies, we filtered the list based on the feasibility of implementing the feature and the ease in which we could create a scenario in which the feature and policies were useful. We constructed three realistic scenarios each of which highlighted a subset of the 22 features and policies that were tested. We chose to use three scenarios so that we could present and discuss each scenario and have time for both the post scenario and the post session questionnaires in two hours.

In preparation for Study 2, we reviewed the results of Study 1, and made several small adjustments to the study, including adding 6 features that were suggested by participants in the first study and making small changes to the questionnaires, storyboards, and presentations. During the study, 5 two-hour group sessions were held with between 2 and 6 participants in each session for a total of 23 participants. Twenty-eight features and policies were tested. Participants were recruited by an agency outside of the company employing the researchers. The agency used screening questionnaires similar to those used in Study 1. The participants recruited were either IT decision makers or Business Unit Executives from a range of different types of companies.

Study 3

In individual user sessions (Study 3), six task scenarios about Pat User were provided in written form to the participant, and he or she completed the tasks using interactive personalized prototypes. The order of the presentation of tasks was counterbalanced using a Latin squares design. An example of a task was "purchase additional memory for the laptop computers you bought last month". The participants were encouraged to "think aloud" as they completed tasks. Each scenario included the use of between 3 and 4 features (21 features and policies were tested in total). During the individual sessions, participants read the scenario description and then attempted to complete the task described using a prototype system (described in Section 2.4). After each scenario, subjects filled out a questionnaire asking about their reactions to the features presented in the scenario. Following the discussion period with the facilitator, participants filled out a post-scenario questionnaire about the features in the scenario. The participants were asked for written ratings and comments. At the end of both group and individual sessions, participants completed a post-session questionnaire form and were debriefed before receiving payment. The post-session questionnaire asked the participants to rank order least and most favoured features across the scenarios, and they were also asked about expected future interactions with a personalized site.

During Study 3, 22 individual sessions were held. Participants were recruited by an agency outside of the company that employed the researchers. The agency used the same screening questionnaires as in Study 2.

2.4 Prototypes Employed in User Studies

During the course of the three studies, the manner in which the personalization features were presented to users evolved. In Study 1 and Study 2 we used a storyboard with a script to guide groups of participants through the use of the personalization features. The changes to the prototype made between Study 1 and Study 2 were based on an analysis of the results to Study 1. In Study 3, we developed a mid-level fidelity prototype that looked like a real website except that not all of the links were active. It allowed individual participants to complete a series of tasks relating to the research into and purchase of IT equipment as if they were on a real website. Although both the fidelity of the prototypes and the personalization features presented evolved through the three studies, the features in all the studies were presented within the central concept of the Personal Book (shown in Figure 1). Because of this central organization of features the prototypes used in all the studies had many similarities. For illustration purposes, we will show how the prototype used in Study 3 could be used to accomplish a portion of one of the tasks participants completed as part of the study. In this scenario, the participant, acting as the manager of a department, needs to buy additional memory for the department's desktop computers. When the participant begins the task, she sees the page shown in Figure 2.

The "personalization" area in the upper right of the page, shown in Figure 2, makes it clear that the site knows the user and gives her access to her Personal Book by clicking on the "open" link. When the user clicks on this link, the Personal Book, shown in Figure 3, is opened. The open Personal Book overlays a portion of the current website page. This is illustrated in Figure 2 by the dotted line box and can be hidden (closed) at any time so that the entire page is again visible. The Personal Book is the central area for all personal data and personalized functionality. By clicking on the different tabs, the user has access to the corresponding functions and all related personal data. In order to find compatible memory for her desktops, the user would click on the "Products that I Own" tab to see a list of the products that have been purchased, as shown in Figure 4. The participant can then click on any of the desktop computers listed to find compatible memory. Each of the scenarios included in the studies allowed participants to try a different set of personalization features in similar ways.

3. RESULTS

The results of the three studies provided a wealth of data. We collected several types of data including participant ratings of personalization features and both written and verbal participant comments. During each study, participants were asked to rate each feature presented on a seven-point scale that was anchored on the high end by "Highly Valuable" and "Not Valuable At All" on the low end. The average ratings for features and polices over the three studies ranged from 4.4 to 6.4 with 7 being the highest possible and 1 the lowest possible score.

Figure 2. *Prototype of the e-Commerce website with the Personal Book closed.*

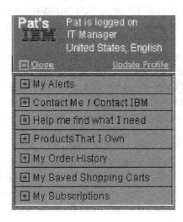

Figure 3. *Opened Personal Book from the Prototype. This window appears in the personalization area of the page as shown in Figure 2 by the dotted lined box.*

Figure 4. *Personal Book is opened to the "Products I Own" section. See Figure 1 for an easier-to-read view of this section of the Personal Book.*

We did not employ a statistical cut-off point for determining when to call a policy or feature highly rated versus not highly rated. We looked for natural and large breaks in the data and used those as determination points. Based on the results of the three studies, the highest rated policies and features are listed in Table 3. Table 3 shows the actual text used in the questionnaires given to participants, however it is important to note that each of the features had been demonstrated in the design sessions or used by the participants in the individual study. Overall, the ratings were similar in all three studies. The average ratings for the features listed in Table 3 from Study 2 and 3 are shown in Table 4. The ratings of Study 1 are not included because the participants were employees of the same company as the researchers rather than IT and business area executives recruited by a separate company.

We also collected verbal and written comments on the policies and features during the design walkthrough sessions in Study 1 and 2 and the individual sessions in Study 3. The comments were transcribed and analysed using conceptual analysis methods. We found that the same kinds of comments were repeatedly made about the features. Although we did not have room to include all of these comments in this paper, paraphrased versions of the comments made about features that participants found to be useful are shown in the last column of Table 4. The numbers next to the comments represent that comment's frequency for each feature.

Table 3. *The 12 Highest Rated Personalization Policies and Features*

1. You control all the data kept in your profile and can review and edit it at any time.
2. You can get automatic support updates for the products you own.
3. You can view your purchase order history.
4. You can use the "Help me find what I need" function to help you filter through product choices and make purchase decisions.
5. You can be provided with alternative recommendations for items that are listed on your "Products I Own" page or that are in saved shopping carts and are no longer available.
6. You can view a list of the products you purchased on the site and elsewhere.
7. Once you have logged in, it is clear that the system knows who you are.
8. You can create a wish list that contains items you may be planning to buy in the future if resources allow or there is a special offer.
9. A personal "myXXX" site is created for you when you provide information about yourself.
10. You can save shopping carts with price quotes, availability dates, and contact information in them.
11. You can track the status of your transactions on the xxx .com site.
12. You are asked to provide only the information needed to allow you to access a feature that helps you complete a particular task.

Finally, the post-session questionnaire used in all three studies included questions that elicited participants' attitudes regarding future visits to and purchases from an e-Commerce company website that had implemented the personalization features that they had identified as most valuable. When participants were asked, "If the features you indicated as of highest value to you were implemented on the ibm.com site, would you be more likely to use the site?" all of the participants in both Studies 2 and 3 indicated that they would be more likely to visit the site. The modal response to the follow-up question of how often they thought they would visit the site was "10+" more times during the course of a year. The average response across the participants was 4.3 in Study 2 and 4.0 in Study 3 where 4 represented 5-10 visits and 5 represented 10+ visits. When participants were asked, "If these features were implemented on the ibm.com site and IBM had a product that met your needs, was available, and was within your budget, would you be more likely to purchase from the site?" 22 out of 23 participants in Study 2 and all 22 participants of Study 3 indicated that they would. One participant responded "Maybe". The participants' modal and mean response regarding the number of additional purchases in a year was the range 3-4 purchases. The modal response in terms of the amount of the purchase was in the $5001 - $10,000 range. The mean across participants was 5.8 in Study 2 and 5.7 in Study 3 with 5 representing $2501-$5000 and 6 representing $5001-$10,000.

During the course of the project, we identified three personalization policies that we hypothesized were related to visitor willingness to share personal data in order to use personalized functionality. Two of these items were among the personalization policies that we presented to participants: the website visitor owns his own data and the website visitor is only asked to provide the data needed for a particular feature (permission marketing). The third personalization policy is the idea that users would choose to have an ever-increasing level of identity on the site as they came to trust the e-Commerce company. This we tested through the analysis of the comments we received throughout all of the studies. After analysing the results of the studies, we found that the policies we had hypothesized as affecting customer willingness to share personal information do, although not always in the ways we had thought. We found that the choice of personalization features is also important; website visitors will use personalization when they feel that it provides them as much or more value as it does the e-Commerce company. Each of these areas is discussed in more detail below.

3.1 User Control of Data

Participants in our studies rated controlling their personal data as the most valuable of the features tested. Over three quarters of the comments received about this policy indicated that participants valued it because it gave them more control over the data collected about them and how it was used. In the words of one of the participant, "It makes me feel comfortable to be in control of my information. It makes me feel I can trust a company that is not looking to control or sell my information."

3.2 Only Asked to Provide Information Needed for Task at Hand

There is a potential cost for website visitors when they have complete control of their data. They may have to spend time filling out lengthy forms every time they want to change their data. One personalization policy that can mitigate this risk is that website visitors are asked to provide or update only the information needed for the task at hand (permission marketing). Our participants told us that they want to decide for themselves what features provide enough value to make sharing personal information worth it. As one user told us, "I have no time or desire to enter a lot of personal information – only what is needed and only entered once".

3.3 Support for Varying Levels of Identity

Another method visitors have for controlling their experience on a website is by changing their level of identity on the site. We expected visitors' level of identity on the site to increase monotonically from invisible to associated and differentiated. However, we found that while users did transition from one level of identity to another, it was not in the manner we expected. Instead of a steadily increasing level of identity on the website, participants reported that they want to choose the level of identity based on the task they need to accomplish at a given point in time. For example, participants in our study reported times in which they browsed on certain

Table 4. *Results from Study 2 and 3 on the 12 Highest Rated Personalization Policies and Features (from 28 total in Study 2 and 21 total in Study 3). Bolded entries represent policies and non-bolded entries represent features.*

Personalization Features	Study 2	Study 3	Types of Comments
1. User Control of Data	**6.4 +/-0.8**	**6.4 +/- 0.7**	**Gives me control 77%; Makes it easy 19%; Saves me time 4%.**
2. Automatic Support Alerts	5.9 +/-1.1	6.2 +/- 1.1	Helps me do my job 53%; Saves me time 27%; Gives me control 12%; Reassures me 4%; I don't like it 4%.
3. Order History	6.1 +/-1.0	6.1 +/- 0.7	Makes my job easier 100%.
4. Help Me Find What I Need	5.6 +/- 1.0	6.1 +/- 1.5	Makes my job easier 58%; Saves me time 37%; Reassures me 5%.
5. Suggest Product Alt.	5.6 +/-1.0	6.0 +/-0.9	Makes my job easier 62%; Saves me time 38%.
6. List of Products You Own	5.5 +/- 1.0	6.0 +/-0.8	Makes my job easier 53 %; Saves me time 37%; Reassures me 10%.
7. Login Feedback	5.6 +/-1.4	5.8 +/-1.1	Saves me time 39%; Makes my job easier 46%; Reassures me 15%.
8. Wish List	5.1 +/-1.8	5.8 +/-1.1	Makes my job easier 88 %; Design comments 8%; Saves time 4%.
9. Personal Site	5.4 +/-1.1	5.6 +/-1.2	Makes my job easier 50%; Saves me time 25%; Gives me control 13%; Didn't notice 12%.
10. Saved Shopping Carts	5.6 +/-1.1	5.6. +/-1.1	Makes my job easier 85%; Save me time 15%.
11. Transaction Tracking	6.2 +/-0.9	5.6 +/-1.3	Makes my job easier 79%; Saves me time 21%.
12. Only Info Needed	**6.0 +/-1.0**	**5.5 +/-1.1**	**Saves me time 73%; Gives me control 27%.**

areas of e-Commerce websites to learn more about a new product, technology or service without knowing if they would ever come back to this part of the site or make use of the information they were viewing. They did not want implicit data such as the pages they visited collected and added to their profiles or used to modify navigation until they gave permission to collect that data. The participants in the study told us that they did not believe that the information collected during this kind of a session could be used in anyway that would be helpful to them with the possible exception of during the same session in which the data was collected. One participant summed up these feelings by saying that he did not want all this data "cluttering up" his profile. In this case, the issue with sharing personal information was not related to the usual security and privacy issues that have been traditionally discussed, but with the ability of website developers to create useful functionality.

However, there were also situations in which participants saw great value in being identified on the site. Once the participants started a task (discussed during Study 2 and observed during Study 3) in which individual personalization features can be helpful to them, they chose to identify themselves by logging on to the site. For example, when a user has narrowed her purchasing decision down to a few choices, but has questions that are specific to her organization she may choose to contact the company's technical support desk via instant messaging. Many participants felt that if the company's technical support person could then have access to both the page at which the potential buyer is looking and past purchases they could provide more meaningful information. In this case participants observed that being identified on the site could be very helpful. Participants saw this scenario as saving them time and helping them to prevent mistakes (reassuring them about their purchases).

3.4 Provide Value to Customer

In addition to a website visitor understanding that she knows what data is in her profile, how it will be used, and how she can change or delete it, there is one more important consideration when determining whether or not to share personal data with an e-Commerce website. Participants in our studies told us that they were interested in personalization features that helped them in their jobs in some way, rather than just providing the e-Commerce company with data to make it easier for the company to send unwanted marketing information. During each of the studies we asked participants to indicate the most valuable and second most valuable features presented in each scenario and to tell us why they were valuable. These comments were grouped by feature and then by similarity to other participants' comments regarding that feature. These comments are reported in fourth column of Table 4.

We found that all of the features that were rated most positively generally received similar types of comments from participants. These comments show that website users want features that help them to do their jobs better or faster. The participants in our study were either business area executives or IT professionals. They told us that they are very busy and value anything that helps them to be proactive in preventing problems altogether or solving problems that do occur more quickly. They identified ways in which the personalization features we presented could help with both of these issues. For example, participants identified three of the top rated features as helping them to be proactive in preventing problems or saving them money. These include Automatic Support Alerts, Wish Lists, and the constrained search on the "Products I Own" lists. The Automatic Support Alerts were seen as helpful because they alerted users to the existence of security patches as soon as they became available. The Wish List, with which users could indicate that they would like to receive emails about special offers involving a particular product, was seen as potentially saving them money by notifying them of special prices only on items in which they were interested. Likewise, the "Products that I Own" list was seen as a way of preventing mistakes in the accessories ordered by providing users with the ability to find compatible accessories. Participants told us that this reassures them that they buying accessories that will work with the equipment they already own.

Participants also reported that features that helped them to solve problems more quickly were helpful. For instance, they told us that having a Transaction History that allowed them to easily find out the status of products that did not arrive when expected was very useful. They also liked the ability to obtain recommendations about replacements for products that are no longer available. Overall, participants told us that in order to share the personal information needed to use personalized functions provided by an e-Commerce company, they must feel that the company is doing more than just protecting their data – it must also be providing them with functionality and services that they value.

4. DISCUSSIONS AND CONCLUSIONS

Overall, we found that the choice of personalization policies and features implemented on an e-Commerce website does affect website visitors' willingness to share personal information with the site. In these studies, we told participants to assume that data held by the e-Commerce company was kept secure. Given that starting assumption, all of the participants in Study 2 and 3 told us that they would be more likely to use the site if the personalization features and policies that they found most valuable were implemented. From the results of these studies we conclude that website visitors are more willing to share information when they have confidence that the e-Commerce company will 1) protect their information from theft by others (provide security), 2) not allow the information to be used in ways they did not intend (protect privacy), and 3) provide value to their customers through the use of shared information (make it worth the visitor's while).

The first two points reduce the costs of using personalization by making users feel comfortable that their data will be protected from others and not misused by the e-Commerce company itself. Many factors influence the first two points such as the reputation of the merchant and the quality of the site itself (Jarvenpaa, Tractinsky, and Saarinen, 1999), (Palmer, Bailey, and Faraj, 2000), and (Princeton Survey Research Associates, 2002).   In our studies we found that the choice of personalization policies implemented also affected website visitors' willingness to share personal data with an e-Commerce company. When visitors feel they own their data and can control when it is collected and used by choosing their level of identity on the site, it is easier for them to feel that their data will not be misused. These findings confirm the results of the study conducted by the Australian Office of the Privacy Commissioner (2001) that showed that having control of one's data and understanding how it would be used greatly increased customer trust of the business or organization with which the individual shared data.   This also confirms the prediction made by Kuhlen (1998) that an open information policy is important to the development of trust in complex computer systems.

Although the original idea behind permission marketing (Godin, 1999) was that customers would develop trust in a business slowly as they continued to receive value for each piece of information they provided, this concept actually has multiple advantages for website visitors using a personalized site. It not only saves them the time of having to fill out a long form when they first register with the site, but it also increases the amount of control they have on the site. They can choose which personalization features provide value to them and only provide the personal information needed to enable those functions.   Without this policy, users of e-Commerce company websites who want access to even one of the personalization functions may be forced to provide the personal information needed for all personalization functions available on the site whether or not they use the functionality.

Given that website visitors feel their data is secure and private, which reduces the costs to them of using personalization, the choice of features implemented is important in determining the value of personalization to them and therefore the costs that they are willing to tolerate. Website visitors want personalization features that make their lives easier in some way. Our participants rated highly features that saved them time, reassured them that they were doing the right thing, or made a job easier for them.

Although we studied a particular e-Commerce domain, a company that manufactures and sells computer equipment and a particular group of users, web-savvy business area and IT executives, we believe that the personalization policies that we found affected user attitudes towards sharing personal information with the e-Commerce company also would apply to a much broader e-Commerce audience. We hypothesize that any group that frequently visits an e-Commerce company's website for the purpose of researching and buying products or getting support for currently owned products would be more likely to share personal data with an e-Commerce company if 1) they own and control their data, 2) are asked to provide only the information needed for the features they actually use at the point they first use them, 3) can decide their level of identity on the site based on their current task, and 4) are provided with personalization features that are valuable to them in the tasks they are trying to accomplish. However, additional studies must be performed to actually determine the relative value of various personalization features in different domains and with different types of users. We plan future studies in which to test our hypotheses regarding personalization policies and features to identify what personalization features are valuable to different kinds of repeat site visitors in different domains.

5. REFERENCES

Aberer, K. and Despotovic Z., (2001). "Managing Trust in a Peer-2-Peer Information System", *Proceeding of the 2001 Conference on Information and Knowledge Management,* pages 310-317.

Ackerman, M. S., Cranor, L. F., and Reagle, J. (1999). "Privacy in E-Commerce: Examining User Scenarios and Privacy Preferences" in *Proceedings of the 1st ACM Conference on Electronic Commmerce,,* Denver, Colorado, pages 1-8.

Anupam, V., Hull, R., Kumar, B. (2001). "Personalizing E-commerce Applications with On-line Heuristic Decision Making" in *Proceedings of the Tenth International World Wide Web Conference,* May, p. 296-307.

Barrett, R., Maglio, P., and Kellem, D. (1997). "How to Personalize the Web" in the *Proceeding of the 1997 Conference on Computer-Human Interaction* (Atlanta, Georgia), p75-82.

Berreby, D., (1999). Getting to Know You, Special Report: The Rise of E-Business, *IBM Research Magazine,* N1.

Finchman, R. G. and Cronin, M. J. (2003). "Information-Rich Commerce At a CrossRoads:Business and Technology Adoption Requirements". *Communications of the ACM* Vol. 46, #9 pages 96-102.

Fink, J., & Kobsa, A., (2000). A review and analysis of commercial user modeling servers for personalization on the World Wide Web. *User Modeling and User-Adapted Interaction,* 10, p209 - 249.

Garfinkel, H. "A Conception of, and Experiments With, "Trust" as a Condition of Stable Concerted Actions" in O. J. Harvey (Ed.), Motivation and Social Interaction", Ronald Press, New York, 1963:187-238.

Godin, S., (1999). *Permission marketing: turning strangers into friends, and friends into customers,* MuSimon and Schuster.

Hagen, P. R., Forrester Report, (2000). "Personalization Versus Privacy", November.

Hagan, P. R., Manning, H., & Souza, R., (1999). The Forrester Report: Smart Personalization. 1 - 18. Cambridge, Massachusetts: Forrester Research, Inc.

Jarvenpaa, S., Tractinsky, N., and Saarinen, L., (1999). "Consumer Trust in an Internet Store: A Cross-Cultural Validation", *Journal of Computer-Mediated Communication* 5 (2) December.

Kobsa, A., Koenemann, J., & Pohl, W., (2001). Personalized hypermedia presentation techniques for improving online customer relationships, *The Knowledge Engineering Review* 16(2), 111-155. http://www.ics.uci.edu/~kobsa/papers/2001-KER-kobsa.pdf.

Kuhlen, R. "Trust: A principle for Ethics and Economics in the Global Information Society", (1998). Presented at the Second UNESCO Congress for Informational Ethics, Monte Carlo, Monaco 1-3 October.

Manber, U., Patel, A., and Robison, J., (2000). Experience with Personalization on Yahoo! When Designing Web Personalization Products, Make Sure you Address All your Users in *Communications of the ACM,* V43, N8, August, p35-39.

Office of the Federal Privacy Commissioner, (2001). Privacy and the Community. Published survey research available at http://www.privacy.gov.au/, July.

Palmer, J. W., Bailey, J. P., and Faraj, S., (2000). "The Role of Intermediaries in the Development of Trust on the WWW: The Use and Prominence of Trusted Third Parties and Privacy Statements", *Journal of Computer-Mediated Communication* 5 (3) March.

Princeton Survey Research Associates (2002), "Research Report A Matter of Trust: What Users Want from Web Sites" Available at: http://www.consumerwebwatch.org/news/1_TOC.htm

Rossi, G., Schwabe, D., and Guimaraes, R. (2001). "Designing Personalized Web Applications" in *Proceedings of the Tenth International World Wide Web Conference,* May, p.275-284.

Sarwar, B., Karypis, G., Konstan, J., and Riedl, J., (2001). "Item-Based Collaborative Filtering Recommendation Algorithms" in *Proceedings of the Tenth International World Wide Web Conference*, May, p. 285-295.

Schafer, J. B., Konstan, J., and Riedl, J. (1999). "Recommender Systems in e-Commerce". In *Proceedings of the ACM Conference on Electronic Commerce* (EC-99). Denver, Colorado.

Schaffer, J.S., personal communications (2001).

Strader, T. J. and Ramaswami, S. N. (2002). "The Value of Seller Trustworthiness in C2C Online Markets", *Communications of the ACM* Vol45 #12 pages 45-49.

Turow, J. (2003). *Americans and Online Privacy: The System is Broken.* Philadelphia: Annenberg Public Policy Center.

GERALD HÄUBL, BENEDICT G. C. DELLAERT,
KYLE B. MURRAY, AND VALERIE TRIFTS

BUYER BEHAVIOR IN PERSONALIZED SHOPPING ENVIRONMENTS

Insights from the Institute for Online Consumer Studies

1. INTRODUCTION

One of the most exciting aspects of electronic shopping environments (such as online stores) is that they allow firms to create *personalized customer interfaces.* That is, user interfaces of commercial web sites can be designed to be adaptive to the specific interests, needs, and preferences of individual shoppers at particular points in time. In principle, such personalization can yield a unique user interface for each customer, based on what the site knows, or is able to infer, about that particular shopper.

As a research group, the authors have been working on advancing our understanding of buyer behavior in such personalized electronic shopping environments. This is important from both a scientific and an applied standpoint. In terms of basic research, there is a need to develop and test theories of human decision making in personalized information environments. From a more applied perspective, it is important to understand how shoppers respond to various aspects of interface personalization.

In what follows, we discuss the key insights to date from an ongoing program of research on buyer behavior in personalized electronic shopping environments. We present selected findings from a number of experiments that we have conducted, and the collective results are based on primary data obtained from a total of more than 2,000 study participants. This research program has been carried out with the support of the Institute for Online Consumer Studies (IOCS) – a laboratory for computer-based experimental research in the area of consumer decision making.[1]

The findings we present show how various forms of personalization affect buyer behavior in electronic shopping environments, and they can be categorized into three

---

[1] The Institute for Online Consumer Studies (www.iocs.org) is also a platform for internet-based scientific experiments in the areas of consumer behavior and human decision making.

Clare-Marie Karat et al. (eds.), Designing Personalized User Experiences in eCommerce, 207—229.

major research questions. The first two of these questions relate to two of the most common types of personalization and how these affect the way in which buyers make their purchase decisions:

1. What are the effects of *personalized product recommendations* on various aspects of buyer behavior in electronic shopping environments?
2. How does the availability of *personalized product-comparison tools* affect shoppers' decision processes and choice among competing online stores?

Our third major research question extends the perspective of the work to intertemporal buyer behavior and focuses on how personalized shopping environments can influence repeated purchase decisions and, in particular, buyers' decisions to continue shopping at a particular vendor:

3. What are the roles of experience-based interface-specific user skills and interface personalization in the development of *customer loyalty*?

For each of these themes, we present insights from multiple empirical studies. We focus on the key insights from the relevant streams of work and, in the interest of brevity, refrain from discussing individual studies in great depth. However, we always cite the original papers on which particular findings are based, and encourage interested readers to refer to these sources for a much more detailed discussion. One manifestation of this approach is that we do not report specifics with respect to data analysis and hypothesis tests. Note however that, unless explicitly stated otherwise, all effects or differences reported here are statistically significant at levels well beyond conventional standards (e.g., p<.05 or p<.01).

2. PERSONALIZED PRODUCT RECOMMENDATIONS

A key feature of electronic shopping interfaces is that they can easily be personalized based on information about individual visitors' preferences. One of the most promising potential benefits of such personalization is that it allows prospective buyers to screen large sets of products very efficiently and effectively (e.g., Alba et al., 1997). A common example of personalization in the context of customer interfaces is the presentation of a set of available products in the form of a list in which products are sorted in descending order of their predicted attractiveness to the shopper. We refer to the arrangement of products in this fashion as *personalized product recommendations* (PPRs). Some real-world examples of PPRs include consumer product recommendations based on other buyers' behavior, typically using collaborative-filtering techniques (e.g., amazon.com), and based on consumers' explicit input regarding their own preferences in terms of product features, which is sometimes referred to as content-based filtering (e.g., activebuyersguide.com). The research findings reported here pertain to the latter type of PPRs.

In our research, we have experimentally examined the effects of such personalized recommendations on buyer decision making. In this section we report on some of the advantages and disadvantages of PPRs to buyers. The main results cover three related areas. First, at the decision outcome level, we find that shopping with PPRs tends to yield important benefits to buyers, in particular in terms of reduced search effort, as measured by the number of alternatives examined and the amount of time spent searching, and improved decision quality (Häubl and Trifts, 2000). Second, at the decision process level, our results show that PPRs significantly affected several aspects of the buyer search process (Dellaert and Häubl, 2003; Häubl and Dellaert, 2003). We have found that, at any given stage of buyers' search through a lists of products, their decision whether or not to continue the search and their choice of their most preferred product are affected by the presence of PPRs. Third, our research shows that the preference elicitation algorithms used to generate PPRs affect buyer product preferences, and that this influence can persist into future purchase decisions that buyers make, even when they are shopping without the assistance of PPRs at that point (Häubl and Murray, 2003).

2.1 Assisting Consumers Through Personalized Product Recommendations

In research designed to examine the benefits to buyers of receiving PPRs, Häubl and Trifts (2000) conducted a large-scale experiment in which consumers were asked to shop for a backpacking tent and a mini stereo system in an (experimental) online store. A total of 54 products were available in each product category. Participants were assigned randomly to one of two experimental conditions – to shop either with or without PPRs. The recommendations in the PPR treatment were based on subjective preference information provided by the participants in terms of six features ("attributes") for each product category. In the PPR condition, products were sorted in descending order of attractiveness to the buyer. In the No-PPR treatment, subjects were taken directly to a hierarchically structured list of products, arranged alphabetically by brand. To make the task more consequential, all participants entered in a lottery in which they could win one of the two products they selected in the experiment plus a cash prize equal to $500 minus the price of the product they selected. The analysis involved a comparison of buyers' decision-making effort and decision quality across the PPR and No-PPR conditions.

The results of the experiment demonstrated that, with the assistance of PPRs, buyers were able to make decisions with significantly less effort than they did without such assistance. In particular, participants who shopped without PPRs looked at the descriptions of an average of 11.65 products, while those who did receive PPRs inspected only 6.58 alternatives on average (see Figure 1). That is, this type of personalization of the customer interface reduced the extent of product search that consumers engaged in by almost 50 percent.[2]

---

[2] Similarly, the availability of PPRs reduced the overall duration of consumers' shopping trips by about 50 percent.

GERALD HÄUBL, BENEDICT G. C. DELLAERT,
                      KYLE B. MURRAY, AND VALERIE TRIFTS

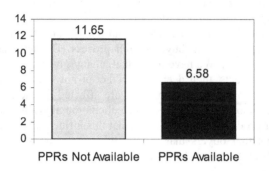

Figure 1. *Search Effort: Number of Products Examined*

In addition to drastically reducing consumer search effort, the PPRs also led
shoppers to make substantially better purchase decisions. For example, about 65
percent of the study participants who shopped without the assistance of PPRs chose
one of six target products that had been designed to be objectively superior to all
other available products (see Häubl and Trifts, 2000 for details). In comparison, 93
percent of those consumers who had received PPRs ended up choosing one of these
six alternatives, thus making an objectively good purchase decision (see Figure 2).
In sum, these results demonstrate not only that PPRs can benefit consumers, but that
they may do so by both reducing the amount of effort it takes a consumer to make a
purchase decision *and* improving the quality of these purchase decisions.

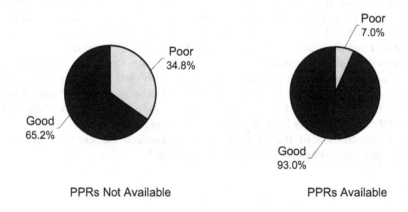

Figure 2. *Decision Quality: Choice of Product*

2.2 Personalized Product Recommendations and Consumer Search Processes

We further investigated these decision-outcome effects of PPRs in research that explored the more detailed process of buyers' step-by-step decisions when shopping with the assistance of PPRs (Dellaert and Häubl, 2003). In general, PPRs present buyers with a decision environment that is considerably different from more traditional settings such as retail stores or retail catalogues. Understanding the detailed decisions that buyers make when going through a list of PPRs can help explain buyers' product choices and decision effort, as well as how these outcomes may change depending on the particular technology used for generating PPRs.

In our research, we conducted a controlled computer-based experiment in which participants were randomly assigned to either a condition with PPRs or one without PPRs. Participants shopped for a product in one of two categories – mini stereo systems or weekend holiday home rentals – depending on which of these product categories they had greater interest in. In this study, all participants provided subjective preference input in terms of six product attributes and price. Subsequently, they were presented with a list of 500 hypothetical products. In the PPR condition, the products were listed in descending order of the shopper's anticipated preference. In the No-PPR condition, the list represented a randomized ordering of the products. Participants were asked to search for as long as they liked, and to eventually select their most preferred product from the list. The participants in this study were members of a large ongoing consumer panel in the Netherlands.

We examined various aspects of consumers' product-search and choice behavior in connection with PPRs. First, at the level of overall decision outcomes, we observed benefits of the presence of PPRs similar to the ones discussed above. In addition, we obtained interesting results about buyers' responses to PPRs in terms of their decision-making process. In line with the normative economic theory of search (e.g., Weitzman, 1979), we observed that shoppers tended to search less if the decline in product utility in the list of recommendations was steeper.

Another finding from the Dellaert and Häubl (2003) study is that PPRs increased the degree to which consumers relied on heuristics when making their step-by-step decisions in searching through the list of recommended products. A key explanation for this finding is the increased level of decision difficulty, which is due to the fact that it is harder to choose among recommended products (which tend to be of high and similar attractiveness to the shopper) than among randomly selected products (which tend to be more dissimilar). The intuition behind this finding is that it is difficult for a consumer to pick one of two products when the latter are approximately equally attractive overall but differ on several attributes (Shugan, 1980). Our result is also consistent with the notion that, as decision difficulty increases, consumers tend to more readily use simplifying heuristics (Payne, Bettman, and Johnson, 1988; Simon, 1955).

2.3 Influencing Consumers Through Personalized Product Recommendations

Yet another area of our research (Häubl and Murray, 2003; Murray and Häubl, 2004) has addressed the question of whether the particular nature of the process by which PPRs are generated might influence consumers' product choices, and perhaps even their long-term preferences, in a category. The key manipulation in this study was that the process by which PPRs were generated was selective in that it was based on only a subset of the relevant product features. We examined this in the context of consumers' preferences for backpacking tents. Pre-tests had indicated that most consumers consider two product features, a tent's durability and its weight, to be of greatest importance in this product category. During the preference-elicitation phase of the PPR process, study participants were asked to express their subjective importance of only one of these two primary product attributes along with that of several other attributes, and the subsequent PPRs were based on consumers' preference in terms of that set of attributes. To counterbalance this manipulation with the specific attributes used, the PPR process included durability (but not weight) for half the subjects and weight (but not durability) for the other half.

Participants were provided with PPRs based on their subjective preference, as revealed during the preference-elicitation phase. They then completed a simulated shopping trip for a backpacking tent. Their task was to select their most preferred product from a carefully designed set of 16 backpacking tents that was "efficient" in the sense that better levels of one attribute tended to be offset by worse levels of another (i.e., negative inter-attribute correlation). In particular, the product assortment was constructed such that none of the products had the most desirable level of both primary attributes. Two of the tents had the best level of durability (but not of weight), two other products had the most attractive level of weight (but not of durability). As a result, shoppers were forced to choose which of the two primary attributes they would obtain the most desirable level on.

The results of this study illustrate a powerful effect of PPRs on consumers' choices. If the selective inclusion of attributes in the PPR process had no influence on purchase decisions, the extent to which an attribute drives product choice would be independent of whether or not it was used in generating the PPRs. However, 71 percent of the participants in this study selected a product that was superior on the primary attribute that had been included in the process of generating the PPRs, while only 29 percent selected an alternative that was superior on the other primary attribute – i.e., the one that had not been included in the PPR process. Thus, simply including a particular product feature in the process of generating PPRs caused that feature to become more important in consumers' purchase decisions.

After performing several unrelated tasks, the same participants were asked to complete a series of preferential-choice tasks. No PPRs were provided at this point, and subjects were asked to choose their preferred product from each of twelve sequentially presented pairs of backpacking tents.[3]   Interestingly, we found that consumers' choices were still mostly driven by that primary attribute that had been included in the PPR process during the earlier shopping task, irrespective of whether that attribute was durability or weight. This demonstrates that the influence of PPRs on consumer preferences can persist into future shopping episodes, even ones taking place in environments that do not involve any form of personalization.

2.4 Section Summary

Our research to date has shown that PPRs can significantly improve buyer decision making both in terms of quality of purchase decisions and the amount of effort required to reach them. We also conclude that PPRs provide some new risks for error in buyer decisions. In particular, we have found that buyers may rely more on simplifying decision heuristics (e.g., merely counting the number of features on which one product outperforms another) when faced with PPRs and that a buyer's preference structure may be affected significantly by the way in which his or her preferences are elicited in the PPR process.

3. PERSONALIZED PRODUCT-COMPARISON TOOLS

The facilitation of side-by-side product comparisons is another aspect of personalization that our research has addressed. In this section, we examine the effects of two types of personalized comparative product displays on consumer decision making in electronic shopping environments. First, we discuss relevant findings by Häubl and Trifts (2000) on the effects of using a *comparison matrix*, an interactive tool that organizes information about considered products in an alternative-by-attribute matrix, on various aspects of consumer decision making. Basic forms of this type of tool are implemented on many online shopping sites, allowing consumers to make side-by-side comparisons among those products that they are most interested in. Second, we present insights from a study by Trifts and Häubl (2003), which focused on the effects of the provision of direct access to *uncensored competitor price information* by an online retailer on consumer preference for that firm relative to competing vendors. While there are many third-party tools for systematic cross-vendor comparisons (e.g., shopbots), the number of such tools that are located *within* a retail site and provide personalized comparisons with competitors' offerings is limited (but see, e.g., www.progressive.com). Our empirical evidence suggests that both of these types of personalized product-comparison tools tend to be highly beneficial to shoppers and can, therefore, be used effectively by vendors in managing their customer relationships.

---

[3]   The first six of these pairs included the tent that the subject had selected in the earlier shopping task along with different, previously unavailable alternatives. The final six choice sets consisted entirely of backpacking tents that had not been available in the initial shopping task.

3.1 Using Comparison Matrices to Personalize Information Presentation

A *comparison matrix* (CM) is a tool designed to assist consumers in making side-by-side comparisons among a set of considered products in an electronic shopping environment. The study by Häubl and Trifts (2000) provides insights into the effects of using a CM on various aspects of consumer decision making, particularly the quality and the efficiency of purchase decisions. The central thesis of this research is that such a personalized decision aid will benefit consumers by allowing for a shift in emphasis from memory-based to stimulus-based purchase decisions in the sense that it becomes less important for consumers to remember specific pieces of attribute information about products (see Alba et al., 1997). Overall, the empirical evidence reported by Häubl and Trifts (2000) supports this prediction.

The CM was implemented as an interactive display format in which product information was presented in an alternative-by-attribute matrix. It was designed to facilitate side-by-side comparisons among selected products. While viewing detailed information about an alternative in the electronic shopping environment, shoppers could choose to have that product added to their personal CM. (It was also possible to delete products from the CM). The display format was interactive in that consumers were able request at any time that all products in the CM be sorted by any attribute.

While Häubl and Trifts (2000) examined the impact of the availability of a CM on several aspects of consumer decision making, we focus here on (1) the set of products that a shopper considered seriously for purchase and (2) the quality of the consumer's ultimate purchase decision. Participants were assigned randomly to one of two experimental conditions – to shop either with or without the assistance of a CM (for a description of the shopping task, see Section 2.1). After completing their purchases, all participants were presented with a list of the products they had inspected in each of the two categories and asked to indicate which of these products they had considered seriously before making their purchase decisions (i.e., their "consideration sets").

The results show that consumers who had access to a CM had smaller consideration sets than those who shopped without the assistance of such a product-comparison tool. The mean number of products considered seriously for purchase was 3.77 when participants did not have access to a CM, and only 2.19 when they did (see Figure 3).

Number of products considered seriously for purchase

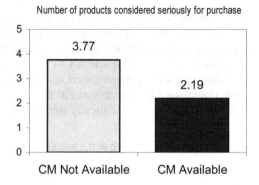

Figure 3. *Comparison Matrix and Consideration Set Size*

In addition, the availability of a CM led to a higher quality of consumers' consideration sets, as measured by the proportion of seriously considered products that are "nondominated" – i.e., that are in the set of six target products designed to be objectively superior to all other available products (details of this method of measurement are provided in Section 2.1). The mean share of nondominated products in shoppers' consideration sets was 57.2 percent without a CM, and 68.4 percent when a CM was available (see Figure 4). Thus, the availability of a CM caused the set of products that were considered seriously for purchase to be smaller, but of higher quality.

Share of considered alternatives that were nondominated
(mean ratio)

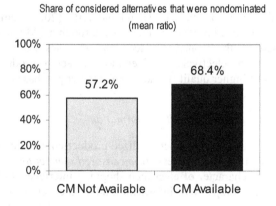

Figure 4. *Comparison Matrix and Consideration Set Quality*

The CM also had a positive effect on the quality of shopper's purchase decisions and on their confidence in their product choices. Consumers who were able to use a CM on their shopping trip were significantly less likely to abandon their initial choice during a subsequent switching task than were those who had no such assistance. (Switching to another product during this task was viewed as an indicator of poor decision quality.)   The share of participants who switched to another, previously available, product was 44 percent for those who shopped without a CM and only 38 percent for those who had access to a CM during their shopping trip (see Figure 5). The availability of a comparison matrix also led to a small increase in the share of subjects who purchased a nondominated alternative, a second measure of decision quality, but this effect was not statistically significant.

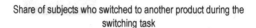

Share of subjects who switched to another product during the switching task

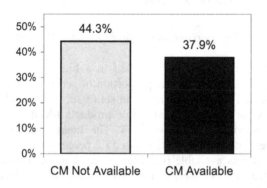

Figure 5. *Effect of Comparison Matrix on Decision Quality*

In sum, the results of the study by Häubl and Trifts (2000) demonstrate that the availability of personalized product comparisons through a CM allows consumers to be more focused in their purchase decision processes (i.e., to have smaller consideration sets), to selectively consider more attractive products (i.e., to have consideration sets of higher quality), and to make better purchase decisions.

3.2   Facilitating Access to Competitor Information

Another stream of research on personalized product-comparison tools focuses on a retailer's provision of direct access to *uncensored competitor price information*. Due to the dynamic character of electronic shopping interfaces, online retailers are able to provide such comparative information about their competitors interactively (i.e., in response to a consumer's actions), directly (i.e., without filtering or censoring), and in a highly personalized manner (i.e., only for the specific products that a shopper is interested in). If the technology that enables cross-vendor price comparisons were incorporated into an online retailer's site, as opposed to shoppers having to use a third party intermediary (e.g., a shopbot), consumers should attribute the benefits of using this comparison tool to the retailer. In particular, consumers may infer that a vendor that deliberately exposes itself to comparisons with its competitors intends to assist them in making a well-informed purchase decision.

Trifts and Häubl (2003) examined the effects of an online retailer's provision of access to uncensored competitor price information on consumers' perceived trustworthiness of, and long-term preference for, that vendor. They propose that the act of providing such information can be conceptualized as a type of market signal that conveys information about unobservable qualities of the firm to potential customers (Kirmani and Rao, 2000; Spence, 1974). By reducing the information asymmetry between the firm and its customers, such a signal is a type of communication openness that should have a positive effect on trust (Morgan and Hunt, 1994). Furthermore, since providing direct access to uncensored competitor information would only be a profitable signal for sellers that occupy an objectively attractive market position,[4] consumers may infer that a retailer that facilitates such access to uncensored information about its competitors' prices is attractive, and prefer it over one that does not.

In their paper, Trifts and Häubl (2003) also propose that consumers will make different causal attributions (Kelley, 1973) as to the motivations of the firm facilitating such comparisons depending on the firm's objective market position. That is, if no external factors can account for such actions, consumers will seek to explain the vendor's actions by examining its internal disposition (Prabhu and Stewart, 2001). They propose that there will be a moderate range of objective market positions in which the positive effect of providing access to competitor price information on consumer preference is strongest, because consumers are likely to infer more altruistic motivations on the part of a moderately attractive firm, compared to one that occupies a clearly superior objective market position.

The study involved consumers' evaluations of an online bookstore. Participants were told that they had been assigned to one of several retailers, and that their task was to evaluate it based on a search for a sample of books. In fact, all subjects completed the task for the same store and considered an identical set of books.[5] Participants were required to search for eight specific book titles (provided by the experimenter) in order to form an overall impression of the retailer. In addition to the focal vendor's online store, participants also used an independent source of comparative price information, which was provided by the experimenter and described as an unbiased and accurate tool for online price searches. Upon completion of each book search within the focal retailer's store, subjects were automatically transferred to a different web site, on which an alphabetical list of seven retailers carrying this book – the focal retailer plus six competitors – was generated dynamically. They were asked to check each vendor's price for the book, which required clicking on the name of each store on the list. For each of the eight books, participants were asked to record, on a paper form, the focal retailer's price

---

[4] For example, vendors who offer either identical products at lower prices than their competitors or objectively superior products at comparable prices.

[5] This was done to provide a credible experimental task and yet ensure that all subjects were exposed to stimulus worlds that were identical – apart from the factors that were manipulated experimentally.

and whether or not each competitor's price was lower than, equal to, or higher than the focal vendor's price.

Subjects were randomly assigned to one of six experimental conditions in a 2 (provision of access to competitor information) × 3 (objective market position) between-subjects design.

The *provision of access to uncensored competitor price information* by the focal online retailer (no or yes) was manipulated in the following manner. In the *no-access* condition, only information about the focal vendor's own offering was available. By contrast, in the *access* condition, that retailer also provided a list of all major online vendors that offered the target book at the lowest available price that day. Whether or not the focal retailer itself was included in this list for a particular book depended on its market position (see below). Participants were told that the information provided by the focal retailer was obtained in an automated, systematic search of the major competitors' online stores, and that this information was updated daily.

The *objective market position* of the focal retailer (unfavorable, moderate, or favorable) was manipulated by varying the latter's prices for the eight products, while holding the prices of the six competitors constant. The *favorable* market position was constructed such that the focal vendor had the lowest available price for each of the eight products. In each instance, the retailer was tied for the lowest price with three of its competitors. In the case of a *moderate* market position, the focal retailer was tied for the lowest price for four of the products, but was dominated on price by some competitors in connection with the other four products. The *unfavorable* market position was constructed such that the focal vendor was dominated on price by some competitors in connection with all eight products. In the three treatments of objective market position, the focal online retailer's average price across the eight product searches was either lower than that of any competitor (favorable), equal to the market average (moderate), or higher than that of any competitor (unfavorable).

After the eight price searches, participants were asked to rate their perceived trustworthiness of and preference for the focal online retailer (using 0-to-10 scales). They then completed two pairwise choice tasks in which they were asked to choose between the focal retailer and one of the two strongest competitors for their next book purchase. For each choice set, subjects also indicated the strength of their relative preference by stating how many percentage points of a price discount the less preferred retailer would have to offer them to make that vendor equally attractive to the one they chose. These decisions were tied to a probabilistic monetary incentive designed to increase the validity of the findings by making the shopping task more consequential (see Trifts and Häubl, 2003 for details).

Facilitating access to competitor information increased the perceived trustworthiness of the focal online retailer – the mean ratings for the no-access and access conditions were 5.93 and 6.83, respectively. Moreover, while this effect on perceived trustworthiness was strong when the retailer's objective market position was either unfavorable or moderate, it was much smaller, and not statistically significant, for the objectively superior vendor (see Figure 6).

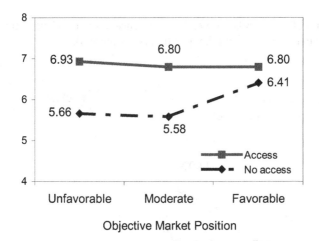

Figure 7. *Perceived Trustworthiness of Focal Retailer*

Consumers' choice of vendor was also affected by whether or not the focal online retailer provided access to uncensored information about its competitors' offerings. In particular, when the focal vendor was moderately attractive in terms of objective market position, it was chosen by a much greater number of shoppers for their next book purchase in the access condition (44 percent) than in the no-access condition (15 percent). The results of a mediation analysis indicate that the provision of access to competitor information affects store choice almost entirely through its effect on perceived vendor trustworthiness (see Trifts and Häubl, 2003 for details). By contrast, facilitating access to competitor information did not have a significant effect on store choice at either the unfavorable or the favorable level of objective market position (see Figure 7).

In addition to selecting their preferred vendor, participants also indicated the strength of their preference by stating how many percentage points of price discount the less preferred retailer would have to offer them to make that vendor equally attractive to the one they did choose. These percentages were converted into a graded-paired-comparison score through multiplication by either +1, if the focal retailer was preferred, or -1, if the competitor was preferred. The resulting score represents the extent of relative preference for the focal online retailer.

The findings in terms of relative preferences corroborate those based on raw choices. Providing access to uncensored competitor information had a strong positive impact on consumer preference for the focal vendor when the latter's objective market position was moderate. In this case, relative preference for the focal retailer was stronger by an average of 8 percentage points (of price discount) when it facilitated access to competitor information than when it did not. Furthermore, a mediation analysis showed that providing access to competitor information influenced retailer preference almost entirely via its effect on perceived trustworthiness, which is consistent with the results based on choice shares. Access provision had no effect on relative vendor preference at either of the extreme levels of the focal retailer's objective market position (see Figure 8).

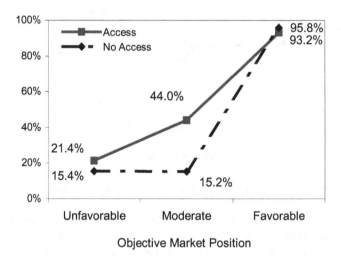

Figure 8. *Choice Share of Focal Retailer*

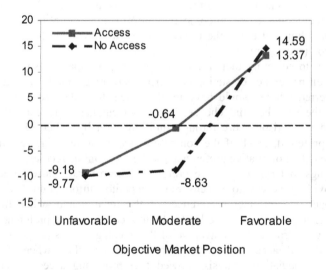

Figure 9. *Relative Preference for Focal Retailer*

3.3 Section Summary

The findings presented in this section indicate that the availability of personalized product-comparison tools can have a profound impact on consumer behavior in electronic shopping environments. In particular, our research on comparison matrices shows that the presentation of product information in interactive alternative-by-attribute displays facilitates in-depth product comparisons and benefits consumers by helping them focus in on a smaller set of more attractive products and, most importantly, make better purchase decisions. Moreover, we have demonstrated that online retailers can benefit significantly from providing shoppers with personalized access to uncensored information about competitors' offerings, in terms of both perceived trustworthiness and consumer choice.

4. PERSONALIZATION AND CUSTOMER LOYALTY

A key benefit to vendors of providing buyers with a personalized shopping environment is the latter's potential to increase customer loyalty. This is no small matter considering that in the online world the competition is "only a click-away." In fact, early internet pundits argued that the ease with which online shoppers can switch from one electronic store to the next would lead to a state of intense competition that would drive prices and profits to rock-bottom levels (Bakos, 1997).

However, recent research has indicated that, over time, online consumers can grow to be very loyal shoppers (Brynjolfsson and Smith, 2000; Johnson, Bellman, and Lohse, 2003). This occurs because, even though it is easy to navigate from one internet vendor to the next, buyers prefer to shop using interfaces that they are experienced with. In particular, once a buyer has learned to use one electronic interface, the time and effort required to make a purchase using that interface is greatly reduced. As a result, buyers are hesitant to switch to another interface where they would have to learn new skills and invest more time and effort to complete the same task. This type of loyalty is often referred to as *cognitive lock-in*, and it differs significantly from traditional notions of loyalty because it does not require a positive attitude towards the product, high levels of satisfaction with the product, or objectively superior product functionality. Instead, lock-in as a result of brand-specific training depends only upon the relative cost, in terms of time and effort, of learning to use a competitor.

A significant amount of research on the psychology of human-computer interaction has examined the processes by which individuals learn to execute complex sequences of actions, and how these behaviors can become automated to the point where they no longer require conscious control of the required individual cognitive and physical processes (see Card, Moran, and Newell, 1983; Salthouse, 1986). The *principle of least effort* (Zipf, 1949) has long recognized that people attempt to achieve the results they desire with a minimum amount effort. Having repeatedly practiced completing a task, such as buying a CD online, consumers acquire skills and knowledge that allow them to complete the task with a minimum amount of effort by merely repeating what they did in the past. Specific skills have been acquired that allow buyers to be more efficient when using the interface that they have previously used. As a result, the consumer is able to make similar purchases in the future with less effort, which creates a cost of switching. When the cost of switching is high enough, the buyer becomes *locked in* to the incumbent interface, unable to switch to competitors without paying a substantial price in terms of new skill acquisition (Shapiro and Varian, 1999; Wernerfelt, 1985).

The ability to complete purchases quickly has been cited as one of the primary advantages of the internet. Bellman, Lohse, and Johnson (1999) surveyed 10,180 internet users on a number of issues related to web-based activity. With regards to internet shopping, they concluded that "consumers shop online or use online services to save time" and that "convenience, rather than cost savings, may be a key benefit offered by successful online stores (p. 38)." It is not surprising then that a large portion of internet users can be described as "simplifiers" – i.e. users whose primary goal is to simplify their lives and save themselves time. In fact, simplifiers account for 29 percent of internet consumers and over 50 percent of all online transactions (Forsyth, Lavoie, and McGuire, 2000).

4.1 The Importance of Skill Transferability

From the customer's perspective, rather than searching the entire marketplace in an attempt to make the best possible decision, it is often more efficient to repeat behaviors that previously led to satisfactory outcomes (Stigler and Becker, 1977). This is due to the fact that, for the vast majority of behaviors, repetition results in improved performance. Psychologists studying the effects of task repetition have found that it results in a type of learning that consistently adheres to the *power law of practice* – task completion time decreases as a power function of practice (see Newell and Rosenbloom, 1981). For a buyer who repeatedly uses a particular interface to make purchases this implies that his/her skill level at using the interface increases with each visit, although at a decreasing rate. As the buyer moves along this learning curve, the utility of the interface increases. The development of skills that are *specific* to one interface – i.e., that cannot be transferred to other interfaces – results in a preference for that interface relative to other, competing interfaces. This is also consistent with the user-skills theory of brand loyalty, which asserts that switching costs increase, and the probability of continued search decreases, as a function of the development of non-transferable skills (Wernerfelt, 1985).

A growing body of research examining human behavior in electronic environments supports the user-skills theory, and finds that the development of non-transferable skills can have a strong effect on buyer preferences (Johnson et al., 2003; Murray and Häubl, 2002, 2003). In a recent laboratory experiment, Murray (2003) randomly assigned participants to one of two experience conditions. The conditions were defined by the amount of practice that each participant would have with an incumbent interface (Figure 9) before being exposed to a competitor interface (Figure 10). In one condition, respondents used the incumbent interface to complete 1 task before using the competitor, and in the other condition respondents used the incumbent interface 6 times before being exposed to the competitor.

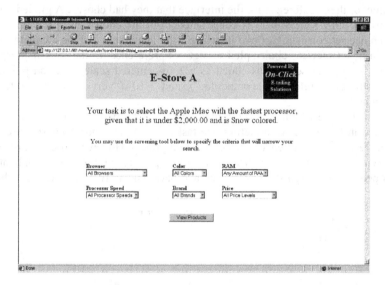

Figure 10. *Incumbent Interface from Murray (2003)*

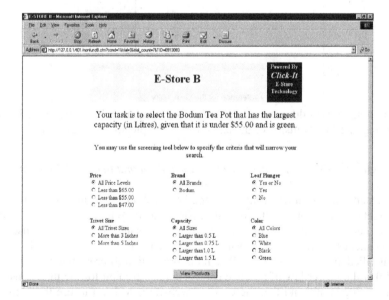

Figure 11. *Competitor Interface from Murray (2003)*

After using the competitor interface, all participants were required to choose which of the two interfaces they would like to use for an additional trial, and to rate the extent of their preference for the interface that they had chosen. A graded-paired-comparison (GPC) measure was constructed from the choice and preference data. For a choice set consisting of two interfaces (the incumbent and the competitor), the GPC variable (interface choice plus strength of preference for the chosen alternative rated on a 10-point scale) was coded as a zero-centered scale with end points -10 ("very strongly prefer the competitor") and +10 ("very strongly prefer the incumbent").

The difference in interface preference between the two experimental groups is illustrated in Figure 11. Completing one task with the incumbent interface resulted in no difference in preference between the two groups. However, after completing 6 tasks with the incumbent interface, a strong preference for the incumbent has developed, even though the only difference between the two interfaces is whether

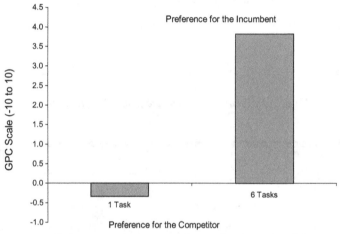

radio buttons or pull-down menus are used for navigation. The differences between competing interfaces outside of the laboratory are typically much greater.

Figure 13. *Extent of Experience with Incumbent and Interface Preference*

In a study of consumer behavior on the World Wide Web, Johnson et al. (2003) found that online shopping sites that are easier to learn to use (i.e., have the steepest learning curves) exhibit the highest rates of purchasing. These authors used data from a panel of 19,466 online consumers. For each household in the panel, software was installed on their home PC that monitored all web-browsing activity. They found that the power law of practice can accurately account for the time consumers spend visiting a site, and that the easier a website is to learn to use the higher the probability of purchase. Based on this result, one of the most valuable assets that a web site can develop is a navigation design that allows for the rapid learning of non-transferable user skills – i.e., skills that are specific to its interface.

4.2 The Role of Personalization

Given the emphasis that online buyers place on the ability of electronic interfaces to save them time and simplify their lives (Bellman et al., 1999; Forsyth et al., 2000), it should not be surprising that personalization has the potential to further enhance customer loyalty. One of the key strengths of personalization is its ability to reduce the time and effort required for the buyer to make a purchase decision (Häubl and Trifts, 2000). This suggests that, by personalizing an electronic shopping environment, the vendor should be able to increase the switching cost for the customer, because personalization results in an even greater reduction in time and effort than experience with an interface alone could provide.

The battle between Barnes and Noble and Amazon.com over Amazon's "one-click" technology is a good example of how important personalization is in increasing ease of use and improving customer loyalty among commercial web sites (Cox, 2002). The one-click feature personalizes the purchasing process for Amazon's customers by allowing them to store their credit card and shipping information. When customers find an item that they wish to purchase, they can simply use the one-click button to activate the automated checkout process. This, of course, substantially reduces the time and effort required to make a purchase at Amazon's site, and it has been successful enough that when Barnes and Noble attempted to implement a similar technology in their online store, Amazon initiated a patent infringement lawsuit. As a result, the rather simple combination of web technologies that made "one-click" viable creates a personalized interface that adds substantial value to the customer's shopping experience and underlies a business process that is a competitive advantage for Amazon.com.

4.3 Evidence from Consumer-Agent Interaction

Recent research examining the interaction between consumers and electronic agents that produce personalized product recommendations provides some additional insight into the value that a personalization tool can provide to a buyer over repeated shopping trips. The findings of a study by Häubl and Murray (2003) are relevant in this regard. The authors compared two groups of participants in a computer-based shopping experiment. One group was assisted by an electronic recommendation agent on each of eight shopping trips, while the other group completed all eight trips without any such assistance.

The data from this experiment that are most pertinent to this discussion are the measures of how effective the personalized environment (i.e., the condition in which participants were assisted by a recommendation agent) was in reducing consumers' search effort over the 8 shopping trips as compared to the condition without personalization (i.e., without agent assistance). This research extends the work by Häubl and Trifts (2000), which focused on a single interaction between a shopper and an electronic recommendation agent, by examining the effects of repeated interactions with such a tool on consumer decision making. In particular, the authors were interested in whether or not the effort required by the consumer to make a good decision would continue to decrease as experience with the agent increased. The key measure of expended search effort was the number of products for which a shopper

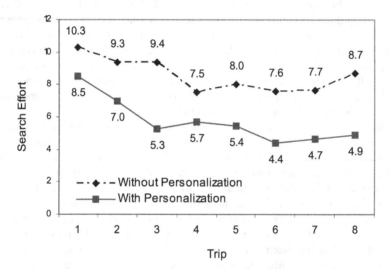

inspected detailed product information before making a purchase decision. A total of 16 products were available on each of the 8 shopping trips. Figure 12 shows the mean number of products inspected on each shopping trip in the two conditions.

Figure 14. *Information Search Effort With and Without Personalization*

The personalized product presentation format provided by the recommendation agent resulted in a substantial reduction in the extent of consumer product search. In addition, shoppers' search effort was further reduced with increasing experience. Given the preceding discussion of the powerful impact that ease of use has on buyer behavior, personalization technologies clearly have significant potential to enhance the ability of commercial web sites to cultivate customer loyalty in a systematic manner. As a result, the capability to create personalized shopping environments is of fundamental value to e-commerce firms.

4.4 Section Summary

The focus of this section has been on the development of customer loyalty as a function of shoppers' repeated interaction with an electronic shopping environment, and on the significant potential of personalization to further increase the loyalty of shoppers to a particular online store. We have highlighted the central role of interface-specific user skills as a basis for customer loyalty, and have discussed relevant empirical evidence to support our ideas.

5. CONCLUSION

We have provided an overview of the findings from a research program that is aimed at enhancing our understanding of buyer behavior in personalized electronic shopping environments. Based on empirical evidence from a several experiments, we have discussed insights relating to different forms of personalization, particularly tools that generate product recommendations based on customer preferences and tools that facilitate side-by-side comparisons of products. We have examined the effects of these different technologies on various aspects of consumer behavior, including (1) the overall extent of product search, (2) aspects of the step-by-step decision processes involved in product search (3) the focusing on a small number of attractive products, (4) the quality of consumers ultimate purchase decisions, (5) the susceptibility of consumer preferences to external influence, (6) the perceived trustworthiness of online vendors, (7) the acquisition of interface-specific user skills, and (8) the development of customer loyalty. The findings we have reported show that the personalization of shopping interfaces can have tremendous benefits for both buyers and sellers.

While the research summarized here represents a step towards understanding the effects of personalization on buyer behavior in electronic shopping environments, much work remains to be done in this area. Of the many promising avenues for future research, we would like to highlight one in particular. We believe that there is a need for a comprehensive framework for personalized customer interfaces that addresses the questions of (1) when to personalize an interface and when not to, (2) to what extent to personalize an interface, (3) which elements of an interface to personalize, and (4) what information, and what models of human behavior, to use as a basis for personalization. Such a framework should integrate normative approaches to the design of intelligent user interfaces with psychological aspects of customer behavior in personalized environments, such as those discussed here.

Our goal has been to provide a concise overview of the insights from our ongoing research program. We have focused on the key findings, and have deliberately provided only a degree of detail about individual studies that we deem necessary for readers to appreciate our results. For a much more detailed discussion of the theoretical ideas, research methods, and results pertaining to specific studies, we refer interested readers to the original papers, which are cited here.

6. REFERENCES

Alba, Joseph, John Lynch, Barton Weitz, Chris Janiszewski, Richard Lutz, Alan Sawyer and Stacy Wood (1997), "Interactive Home Shopping: Consumer, Retailer and Manufacturer Incentives to Participate in Electronic Commerce," *Journal of Marketing* 61 (July), 38-53.

Bakos, J. Yannis (1997), "Reducing Buyer Search Costs: Implications for Electronic Marketplaces," *Management Science*, 43, 12, 1676-1692.

Bellman, Steven, Gerald L. Lohse and Eric J. Johnson (1999), "Predictors of Online Buying Behavior,"
    Communications of the ACM, 42, 12, 32-38.
Brynjolfsson, Erik and Michael D. Smith (2000), "Frictionless Commerce? A Comparison of Internet and
    Conventional Retailers," *Management Science*, 46, 4, 563-585.
Card, Stuart K., Thomas P. Moran, and Allen Newell (1983), *The Psychology of Human-Computer
    Interaction*, Hillsdale, NJ: Lawrence Erlbaum Associates.
Cox, Beth (2002), "One Settlement Over One-Click," AtNewYork.com, (March 7), (accessed August 21,
    2003), [available at http://www.atnewyork.com/news/article.php/987061]
Dellaert, Benedict G. C. and Gerald Häubl (2003), "Consumer Product Search With Personalized
    Recommendations," working paper, Maastricht University.
Forsyth, John E., Johanne Lavoie, and Tim McGuire (2000), "Segmenting the e-market," *McKinsey
    Quarterly*, 4, 1-4.
Häubl, Gerald and Benedict G. C. Dellaert (2003), "Electronic Recommendation Agents and Tourist
    Choice," in: K. Weiermair and C. Mathies, eds., *Leisure Futures*, New York: Haworth Press, in
    press.
Häubl, Gerald and Kyle B. Murray (2001), "Recommending or Persuading? The Impact of a Shopping
    Agent's Algorithm on User Behavior," in: M. Wellman and Y. Shoham, eds., *Proceedings of the
    ACM Conference on Electronic Commerce (EC'01)*, New York, NY: Association for Computing
    Machinery, 163-170.
Häubl, Gerald and Kyle B. Murray (2003), "Preference Construction and Persistence in Digital
    Marketplaces: The Role of Electronic Recommendation Agents," *Journal of Consumer Psychology*,
    13, 1, 75-91.
Häubl, Gerald and Kyle B. Murray (2003). The Double Agent: Potential Benefits and Pitfalls of an
    Electronic Agent's Recommendations, working paper, University of Alberta.
Häubl, Gerald and Valerie Trifts (2000), "Consumer Decision Making in Online Shopping Environments:
    The Effects of Interactive Decision Aids," *Marketing Science* 19, 1, 4-21.
Johnson, Eric J., Steven Bellman, and Gerald L. Lohse (2003), "Cognitive Lock-In and the Power Law of
    Practice," *Journal of Marketing*, 67 (April), 62-75.
Kelly, Harold H. (1973), "The Processes of Causal Attribution," *American Psychologist*, 28, 107-128.
Kirmani, Amna and Akshay R. Rao (2000), "No Pain, No Gain: A Critical Review of the Literature on
    Signaling Unobservable Product Quality," *Journal of Marketing*, 64, 66-79.
Morgan, Robert M. and Shelby D. Hunt (1994), "The Commitment-Trust Theory of Relationship
    Marketing," *Journal of Marketing*, 58, 20-38.
Murray, Kyle B. (2004), "Experiencing Quality: The Impact of Practice on Customers' Preference for and
    Perceptions of Electronic Interfaces," in: S. Krishnamurthy, ed., *Contemporary Research in E-
    Marketing*, Vol. 1, : Hershey, PA: Idea Group, in press.
Murray, Kyle B. and Gerald Häubl (2002), "The Fiction of No Friction: A User Skills Approach to
    Cognitive Lock-In," *Advances in Consumer Research*, S. M. Broniarczyk and K. Nakamoto, eds.,
    Valdosta, GA: Association for Consumer Research, XXIX, 11-18.
Murray, Kyle B. and Gerald Häubl (2003), "Skill Acquisition and Interface Loyalty: A Human Capital
    Perspective," *Communications of the Association for Computing Machinery*, 46, 12, 272-278.
Murray, Kyle B. and Gerald Häubl (2004), "Processes of Preference Construction in Agent-Assisted
    Online Shopping," in: C. Haugtvedt, K. Machleit and R. Yalch, eds., *Online Consumer Psychology:
    Understanding and Influencing Behavior in the Virtual World*, Mahwah, NJ: Erlbaum, in press.
Newell, Allen, and P. S. Rosenbloom (1981). Mechanisms of Skill Acquisition and the Law of Practice,
    in J. R. Anderson (Ed.), *Cognitive Skills and Their Acquisition*, Hillsdale, NJ: Erlbaum, 1-55.
Payne, John W., James R. Bettman, and Eric J. Johnson (1988), "Adaptive Strategy Selection in Decision
    Making," *Journal of Experimental Psychology: Learning, Memory and Cognition*, 14, 534-552.
Prabhu, Jaideep and David W. Stewart (2001), "Signaling Strategies in Competitive Interaction: Building
    Reputations and Hiding the Truth," *Journal of Marketing Research*, 38, 62-72.
Salthouse, T. A. (1986), "Perceptual, Cognitive, and Motoric Aspects of Transcription Typing,"
    Psychological Bulletin, 99, 303-319.
Shapiro, Carl and Hal R. Varian (1999), *Information Rules*, Boston, MA: Harvard Business School Press.
Shugan, Steven M. (1980), "The Cost of Thinking," *Journal of Consumer Research* 7, 99-111.
Simon, Herbert. A. (1955), "A Behavioral Model of Rational Choice," *Quarterly Journal of Economics*,
    69 (Feb.), 99-118.

Spence, Michael (1974), *Market-Signaling*, Cambridge MA: Harvard University Press.

Stigler, George J. and Gary S. Becker (1977), "De Gustibus Non Est Disputandum," *American Economic Review*, 67, 76-90.

Trifts, Valerie and Gerald Häubl (2003), "Information Availability and Consumer Preference: Can Online Retailers Benefit From Providing Access to Competitor Price Information?," *Journal of Consumer Psychology*, 13, 1, 149-159.

Wernerfelt, Birger (1985), "Brand Loyalty and User Skills," *Journal of Economic Behavior and Organization*, 6, 381-385.

Zipf, G. K. (1949), *Human Behavior and the Principle of Least Effort*, Cambridge, MA: Addison-Wesley.

7. ACKNOWLEDGEMENTS

This research was supported by the Canada Research Chairs program, the R. K. Banister Professorship in Electronic Commerce, a Petro-Canada Young Innovator Award, several University of Alberta faculty fellowships, the Social Sciences and Humanities Research Council of Canada (INE research alliance grant 538-02-1013 & standard research grant 410-01-1332), and the Teradata Center for Customer Relationship Management at Duke University.

FRANCESCO RICCI AND FABIO DEL MISSIER

SUPPORTING TRAVEL DECISION MAKING THROUGH PERSONALIZED RECOMMENDATION

1. INTRODUCTION

1.1 Travel decision making

Travel planning is a multi-faceted decision process consisting of choosing a destination and grouping together tourism products and services (attractions, accommodations, and activities) closely related to the destination (Dellaert, Ettema, & Lindh, 1998; Jeng & Fesenmaier, 2002; Moutinho, 1987).

The complexity of the concepts used and of the decision process involved in travel planning poses challenges for the design of usable and effective decision support tools. For instance, the terms *destination* and *travel plan* refer to fuzzy concepts that lack a commonly agreed definition. Furthermore, the spatial extension of a destination is known to be a function of the traveler's distance from the destination area. Italy could be a destination for Japanese, but a European traveler may focus more specifically on a particular region, such as Tuscany.

Moreover, a travel plan may vary greatly in its structure and contents, and different strategies can be used to construct it. For instance, some people may search for pre-packaged solutions (all-inclusive) while "free riders" may prefer to select each travel component separately. It is possible to start from a destination and then to search for other items (for example in a nature-oriented leisure holiday) or, alternatively, to focus on a particular activity or event (e.g., a conference or an exhibition) and then extend the plan taking into account the constraints brought about by this event. The same person may use different strategies in different contexts.

Travel decision making is one of the most comprehensively investigated areas in tourism research. In particular, many conceptual approaches to travel destination choice have been proposed. These approaches can be classified into four different frameworks: (1) choice set models (Crompton & Ankomah, 1993; Um & Crompton, 1990), (2) general travel models (Woodside & Lysonski, 1989), (3) decision net models (Fesenmaier & Jeng, 2000), and (4) multi-destination travel models (Lue, Crompton, & Fesenmaier, 1993). This literature classifies the variables used to predict the destination into the two broad categories of personal features and travel characteristics. Personal features include socioeconomic factors as well as

231

Clare-Marie Karat et al. (eds.), Designing Personalized User Experiences in eCommerce, 231—251.

psychological and cognitive traits. Travel characteristics comprise the situational variables that shape the travel, such as travel purpose, length the travel, distance to the destination, and travel group composition.

Despite the richness of travel decision making literature, only a very limited number of contributions have dealt with the topic of integrating decision models into travel recommender systems. This might be because the majority of existing models are based on traditional studies of consumer behavior, which are not focused on web technology or on travel interactive decision aids. These studies provide only general and limited guidance, because they do not take into account the unique characteristics and constraints associated with each specific communication medium and support tool. Therefore, trying to fill the gap between the travel decision models and "digitized" decision behavior is a valuable but difficult task, which requires the design and test of new models and aids.

1.2 Recommender systems

A recommender system helps the user to make choices when there is no sufficient personal experience of the available options. These kinds of systems can aid the consumer in various ways. They can simplify the information search process and facilitate the comparison of products (e.g., activebuyers.com), report the reviews of other users (epinions.com), or exploit the consumers' history to suggest products similar to those purchased in the past or previously selected by users with a similar buying behavior (Amazon.com).

eCommerce web sites make use of recommender systems to suggest interesting and useful products and to provide consumers with information that is intended to support their decision processes (Kobsa, Koenemann, & Pohl, 2001; Schafer, Konstan, & Riedl, 2001). Recommender systems are mainly required in order to cope with information overload and lack of user knowledge in a specific domain. In general, they try to optimize some cost-benefit trade-off (for example, between the usefulness of the recommendation and the users' search and interaction costs).

Building real world recommenders demands a concerted effort and requires careful elicitation of user requirements, task analysis, development and tuning of the recommendation algorithms, and the design and testing of the graphical user interface.

Recommendation technologies are based on the implicit assumption that users' needs and preferences can be mapped into product selections, by employing the appropriate algorithms and the knowledge embedded in the system (Ricci, 2002).

Burke (2000) describes three different types of recommendation approaches: (a) collaborative-filtering or social-filtering, (b) content-based, and (c) knowledge-based. Here we will consider only the collaborative and the content-based methods, because they are integrated in our hybrid approach.

In the content-based systems, the user expresses some preferences on a set of products. Then the system retrieves from a catalogue the items that share common features with the products that have been judged interesting by the user. The results are typically sorted according to the degree of match with the user's preferences.

The major drawback of the content-based approach is its excessive compliance with the preferences specified by the user, leaving no room for variability regarding the suggestions (O' Sullivan, Wilson, & Smyth, 2002).

In the collaborative-based approach (Breese, Heckermann, & Kadie, 1998), the system collects users' ratings on the suggested products and on the previously purchased items to infer any existing similarity between users. In this way the system can suggest to the user a set of novel products, which have been positively rated or previously bought by similar users. Collaborative approaches are effective in suggesting interesting items. Moreover, the quality of the recommendation improves over time, as new ratings are collected. On the other hand, collaborative-based methods require a huge number of ratings before producing satisfactory recommendations and they are not able to take into account specific (session-dependent) needs, since they uniquely rely on the users' past behavior and do not make any attempt to adapt the recommendations to the session-specific consumer's requirements. Collaborative filtering can be directly applied only to frequently purchased products (books, movies, or CDs). Other kinds of products (e.g., travel, cars) are far less amenable to a collaborative-based recommendation, especially as they are not purchased so often. Hence, the system cannot have an appropriate list of personal ratings and past ratings may not provide enough knowledge to predict the user's future choices.

1.3 Challenges for a travel recommender system

An effective and usable travel decision aid should flexibly support a range of different users' needs and various specific planning strategies. Conventional recommendation technologies have applied only general methods. Therefore, the main problem is to devise travel recommender systems that are able to satisfy the travelers' unique requirements by taking advantage of the knowledge and findings of travel decision theory. In our opinion, these systems should attempt to satisfy the following requirements:

- Products may have a complex structure, and the final recommended item should be a coherent aggregation of more elementary components. For instance a trip may be composed of a flight, an accommodation, and a ticket for a match.
- Both short-term preferences (related to a situation-dependent goal) and long-term stable preferences should influence the recommendation. Given that short-term preferences often arise from compelling needs, they should have greater weight than long-term preferences. For instance, if the user is currently searching for a business flight, the system must lessen the influence of a previous history of 'no frills' flights.
- The cognitive effort that the user devotes to the information search should be reduced but, in any case, the recommendations must satisfy the user's explicit preferences.
- The user and the system should collaborate in a mixed-initiative fashion, and each one must contribute what it does best. In particular, the user should be

allowed to keep control of the interaction and to make informed choices, while the system must provide the relevant information (by offering easy ways to explore the option space and effortless means to specify and modify the information search).

- The lack of an initial database of user interactions or of a set of sales records should not prevent the application of the system support. Furthermore, both occasional and registered users should be able to obtain valuable recommendations.

Bearing in mind these requirements, we have conceived a methodology to support the information search and choice processes in the travel domain, based on the analysis of the travel decision making literature and of the existing recommendation technology. This methodology encompasses both the interaction design (i.e. how the interaction is structured and sequenced) and the different kinds of support provided in the different interaction stages (i.e. the specific decision aid provided for each interaction step). The interaction design cannot be considered as neutral, but it is always a means of shaping the decision process according to our hypotheses about the appropriate ways to aid the user. In our case, we have tried to support a two-stage decision process, with an initial noncompensatory screening of the options and a subsequent choice phase focussed on a set of attractive alternatives. This process may sometimes result in sub-optimal choices (Edwards & Fasolo, 2001), but it is coherent with the user's choice strategies when the initial number of options is high (Payne, Bettman, & Johnson, 1993). Moreover, it allows for a reduction in the cognitive effort associated with the specification of preferences and with the information search.

In section 2 we will present the interaction design and in section 3 the technologies that we have developed to enable the proposed interaction. Section 4 illustrates the pilot evaluation of the NutKing prototype. Finally, in section 5, we will discuss issues related to the topic of personalized decision support in the travel domain and sketch some directions of our future work.

2. INTERACTION DESIGN

In this section, we will first describe the interaction design in abstract terms. Then we will provide a concrete example in order to make the stages that the user goes through more explicit. The example describes a real interaction session with a system prototype (NutKing), which is a specific implementation of our support methodology. In the next section we will present the techniques used to provide specific aids in the different interaction steps and we will summarize their theoretical underpinnings.

A recommendation session is divided into three stages:

- *Stage 1: Acquisition of travel preferences.* The system asks the user to provide some information about personal and travel characteristics. These features include group composition, means of transport, type of accommodation, budget, travel period, knowledge of the destination area, and preferred activities. These characteristics are considered as predictors of the user's decision behavior by the models of destination choice. They are called *collaborative features* and used by the system to retrieve similar *recommendation sessions* from a case base. The retrieved cases will be used, in the subsequent stages, to generate recommendations and to sort the results of the user's searches.

- *Stage 2: Search for travel products.* The user starts the process by seeking a destination or a product (accommodation, event, sport activity) that satisfies a set of requirements (for example, a destination close to a lake with golf facilities, or a budget hotel near the city center). The *content features* are used to define these requirements. When the search is successful, the system presents a set of results that satisfy the requirements. When the number of results is high, the system asks the user to provide some additional content features in order to winnow out the less interesting products (*tightening* of the query). In the case of a search failure (no results), the system asks the user to withdraw some content features, suggesting a set of minimal query modifications that will produce some results (*relaxation* of the query).

- *Stage 3: Choice.* In the last stage, the results obtained from a successful query are sorted and presented to the user. The recommender system finds similar recommendation sessions, employing all the collaborative features previously entered by the user. After the retrieval of a small set of similar sessions, the system sorts the list of results according to a specific similarity ranking criterion, which takes into account the agreement between the users' travel preferences (see section 3). The aim of this operation is to highlight products that are potentially interesting, because they are similar to those selected by other users in similar recommendation sessions. Once the items have been presented to the user, their features can then be carefully examined and the user may decide to add some products to a shopping cart (called *travel plan*). Obviously it is possible (and quite frequent) that the user cycles through the second stage (search) and the third stage (choice), modifying the search criteria and examining new sets of results.

Our approach enables content features to dominate the selection process and to determine which items will compose the choice set. But the collaborative features are exploited to rank the set, highlighting the most attractive items.

A quite different way to use the system is to exploit the so-called *complete travel recommendation* function, which produces results in the form of whole travel packages (see section 3). In our prototype, this option is currently available as an alternative to the search for travel products (stage 2).

We will now present an example to illustrate our abstract description. Imagine you are a European tourist, mainly interested in culture and nature. You are planning your first trip to Trentino (a region of northern Italy), and decide to use the NutKing system (http://itr.itc.it) to find some advice regarding this trip. After a welcome page, the recommender asks you to provide some information about your travel preferences (Figure 1). You are required to fill out a form, and the collaborative features are thus acquired (stage 1).

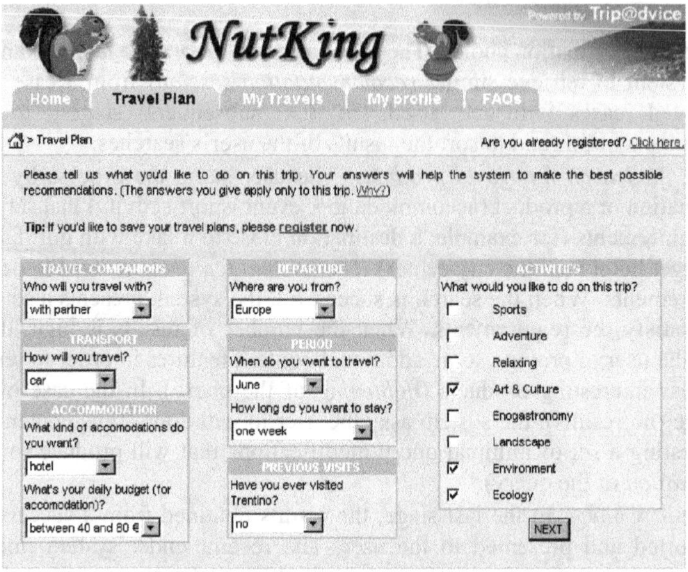

Figure 1. *Acquisition of travel preferences*

During stage 2 you start searching for travel items. After deciding that you will visit Trento, you seek a particular type of accommodation in the Trento area (for example a hotel between 2 and 4 stars, within a given price range: figure 2 on the left). The search produces 16 results and the system suggests that some constraints could be added (tightening), while also providing a list of content features that may be specified (figure 2 on the right).

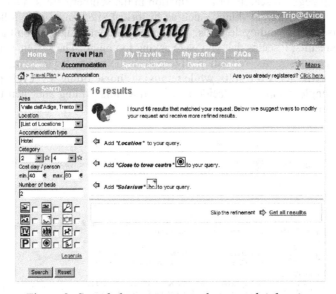

Figure 2. *Search for an accommodation and tightening*

You decide to add the following constraint: the hotel should be near the city
center. The search is performed again and it produces eight results, which are sorted
according to the system ranking criteria (stage 3: figure 3). After a careful
examination of the information available on the various options, you add a hotel to
your travel plan.

Figure 3. *List of results*

Now you begin to search for a destination in the southern areas. You would like it to offer many different things, such as historical sites, museums, folklore, jazz music, horse riding, and cycle paths. You specify a query (figure 4 on the left), but you get no results: it seems that you were asking too much! The system suggests you remove some constraints (relaxation: figure 4 on the right). If you avoid specifying the area you will get two results, while removing 'horse riding' or 'cycle paths' will produce a single result. You decide to withdraw horse riding and then the city of Rovereto shows up.

Figure 4. *Search for a destination and relaxation*

Figure 5 depicts the structure of the interaction in stages 2 and 3.

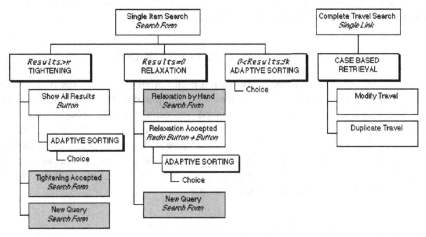

Figure 5. *The possible NutKing interaction paths (stages 2 and 3). The shadowed boxes mark the system intervention. The gray boxes indicate the composition of a new form-based query or the modification of one previously formulated.*

In stage 2, the user has two main options. The first one is to request a complete travel recommendation by following a link. Alternatively, it is possible to compose a query to seek a specific type of travel item (a location, an accommodation, an event, sports). This single item search is performed by supplying content features in specific search forms.

If a complete package is requested, the suggested travel items can be modified or duplicated, in order to transfer some information to the user's personal travel plan.

When the user searches for a single item, the search can produce three possible outcomes: (a) no results, (b) more than k results (k is a threshold with a default value of 10), and (c) a number of results between 1 and k (inclusive).

If the recommender realizes that the query will not produce any results, it suggests to the user to relax some constraints. This can be done simply by selecting the preferred suggestion or by refining the query by hand on the single item search form. Alternatively, the user can enter a new query (i.e., a query that cannot be considered as a relaxation of the previous one).

If the query produces many results, the recommender proposes to the user some ways to tighten the search. After the tightening suggestion, the user can choose from three options: (a) follow the system advice and modify the query accordingly, (b) display all the results, or (c) formulate a new query (i.e., a query that cannot be considered as a tightening of the previous one).

The search results are always sorted according to the specific similarity measure employed by the system, and they are subsequently presented to the user (three items per page).

Finally, the user examines the result pages, acquiring information about the options, and an item can be selected to be added into the travel plan.

A typical interaction session is composed of several queries, and each unsuccessful query can be refined in an iterative way.

3. RECOMMENDATION METHODOLOGY

Trip@dvice, the proposed recommendation methodology, satisfies the requirements summarized in subsection 1.3, while also supporting the interaction process described above. It integrates case-based reasoning (CBR), cooperative query answering, and collaborative filtering. The logical architecture of the recommendation methodology is shown in Figure 6. The recommendation manager is the entry point for all of the recommendation functions and is accessed via the graphical user interface. The other modules will be described in the following sections, starting with the case-based reasoner.

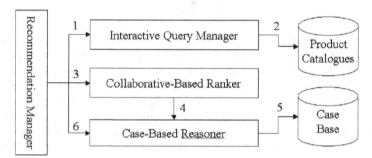

Figure 6. *Logical architecture of the recommender system*

3.1 Recommendation sessions as cases

CBR is a multi-disciplinary research area, focused on the exploitation of past experience encoded in the form of cases (Aamodt & Plaza, 1994; Aha, 1998). There are at least two different conceptions of CBR: it is regarded as a plausible high-level model for cognitive processing (Kolodner, 1993) or as a computational paradigm for problem solving (Aamodt & Plaza, 1994). We adopt the latter view, referring to CBR as a problem solving paradigm that relies on the specific knowledge gathered by solving practical problems. In CBR, a case comprises two main components: the problem and the description of the solution. The basic assumption of CBR is that similar problems share similar solutions. In our approach, a case models a unique user-system recommendation session and it comprises:

– the travel preferences provided by the user in the first stage of a recommendation session (i.e., the collaborative features);
– the products chosen by the user and belonging to the travel plan;
– the user's profile, composed of some demographic and personal data (age, gender, nationality, address, etc.); this is available only if the user is registered.

In our model, the collaborative features provided by the user (and the user profile)
describe the "travel problem" that the user "solved", whereas the chosen products
represent the solution. A set of recommendation sessions involving many different
users is stored in the case base, while the catalogues of tourism products and
services (attractions, accommodations, activities) are stored in several databases.

A straightforward application of classical CBR solves a recommendation
problem by searching for similar recommendation sessions. This means that the
problem definition (collaborative features) is used to retrieve cases (matching), and
that the system suggests to the user products which are contained in the retrieved
cases. In our system, this simple approach is adopted in the *complete travel
recommendation* function. This function is implemented by asking the CBR
manager to create a case, initialized with the user-provided collaborative features.
The newly generated case represents the current recommendation session (arrow 6 in
figure 6) and it is used to retrieve a set of similar cases from the case base (arrow 5
in figure 6).

This approach has limitations. First, the products found in the retrieved cases may
be temporarily unavailable: the suggested hotel may be fully booked and a given
event may have already taken place. Second, this approach does not consider
specific user preferences (for example, the user may be interested in a budget hotel
close to the city centre). Searching for cases with additional constraints (containing
only the available products with the desired features) would almost certainly
produce a failure, unless the case base contained a wide range of offers. This ideal
condition seems very difficult to attain, because it requires devoting a long time for
the acquisition of cases (bootstrap) before the system can deliver useful
recommendations.

Therefore, we have decided to use in a different way the implicit preferences that
derive from similar cases. In our approach, these past recommendation sessions are
utilized to rank the results of the searches that the user has performed in the product
catalogues (the details of the ranking algorithm are described in section 3.3). In the
current implementation, the system dynamically builds a user model for each
recommendation session. This model comprises a set of cases retrieved from the
case base. These cases own vectors of collaborative features similar to the vector
representing the current case. The similarity between the current case and a retrieved
case is defined by a heterogeneous distance metric that is computed as a weighted
sum of local distances (i.e. feature differences, Ricci et al., 2003). At present, the
user profile is not taken into account in the generation of the user model but we are
planning to expand the approach to include these personal features.

3.2 Interactive query management

The goal of the cooperative query answering research area (Gaasterland, Godfrey, &
Minker, 1992; Godfrey, 1997) is to create systems that attempt to understand the
meaning of a user query, suggest or answer related questions, and produce an
answer from the available data or give an approximate response.

In our approach, we apply some methods borrowed from this area when a user is searching for products that satisfy some preferences expressed using descriptors of the product (the content features specified in the second stage of the process previously described). For instance, if the user is looking for a budget hotel close to the center of the city of Trento, the Interactive Query Manager Module (IQM) performs the following steps before displaying any recommendation:

1. IQM searches for all those hotels that satisfy the user-specified constraints (arrow 2 in figure 6).
2. IQM analyses the result set.

   a) If no result is found, the system computes an alternative version of the user query for each specified content feature, relaxing the constraints contained in the initial user query. Hence, in the example mentioned before, two queries are generated: the first relaxes the budget condition while the second relaxes the preference on the hotel location. Then the system offers the user a choice among the relaxed queries that result in a non-void set of items. This choice is presented with the explanation that it is not possible to satisfy all the constraints specified in the initial query, but that there is the possibility to find some products that partially satisfy the original request (Ricci, Mirzadeh, & Venturini, 2002). The aim of the relaxation function is to maximize the probability of finding some results, taking into account both the user's preferences and the composition of the product catalogue.

   b) When a query produces too many items (above a threshold value) it is assumed that the user will not browse the entire result set to locate the most interesting items. Therefore, we have designed a system function that explains this situation of potential information overload and lets the user choose between displaying all the results and tightening the original query. In this last case, the system suggests some tightening options by identifying new product features that are potentially interesting but not yet specified. For instance, if the user searched for a hotel in Trento, the system asks the user to specify the desired values for an additional content feature, as there are many hotels in Trento. It does this by displaying a list of alternatives (for example, the price range, the category, or the distance from the city center). The list of the features that can be used for tightening a specific query is established by an unsupervised feature selection method that combines the information gain of a feature and its popularity (Ricci et al., 2003). Those features most frequently used in queries of the same type as the one currently specified are selected as candidates, if they have not been already specified. Otherwise, the system selects the unused feature with the highest entropy value. Entropy is a measure of "disorder" of the feature values: the higher the entropy the more uniform is the distribution of values. Hence, assigning a value to the feature with the highest entropy will make it more likely that the new result set will be smaller. For instance, if only half of the hotels are close to the city center but almost all of the hotel rooms are equipped with a TV, then the user will be asked to specify a value for the "close to center" feature.

The proposed interactive query management function enables the user to perform a more efficient search from the available options, implementing a mixed-initiative scheme. The system is better suited to compute the alternative successful relaxations or the best candidate features for query tightening, while the user can choose which query change is more satisfying.

3.3 Collaborative-based sorting

A custom implementation of the collaborative filtering approach is applied in order to present the result list of products obtained from a user query. This function is used at the beginning of the third interaction stage (choice) after the potential intervention of the cooperative query answering methods (in the second stage).

In classical automated collaborative filtering the system rates the products which have not yet been judged by the user by taking a weighted average of the ratings of similar users (Breese, Heckerman, & Kadie 1998; Schafer, Konstan, & Riedl, 2001). The weights in this approach are the similarity values, where the similarity between two users is computed by taking the correlation of their ratings.

In our approach, we want to support even users who have no rating history or who are not interested in logging into the system. Moreover, the travel decision choice literature points out that the specific features of the current travel plan should be appropriately taken into account. For the above reasons, the preferences associated with the specific travel products that the user is currently searching should play a prominent role. On the other hand, as the success of the recommender technology demonstrates, it would seem useful to exploit also the implicit knowledge that derives from the information about similar users. As previously described, we have combined the two approaches: after the user has obtained a reduced set of candidates through a content-based search, the collaborative-based ranking method is applied. The reduced set of options loosely corresponds to the *late consideration set* of the choice set models (Crompton & Ankomah 1993; Um & Crompton 1990): the decision maker will acquire information about a subset of these options that, given the current constraints, are deemed attractive (the *action set*).

The collaborative-based ranking is computed in the following way. A small set of recommendation sessions (cases) is retrieved using a similarity function that takes into account only the collaborative features of the current case (arrow 4 in figure 6). These sessions have similar values for the predictive features and therefore they should provide good recommendations for the current case. The rationale is that since the current session and a retrieved session both share the values of the predictive features (problem definition in CBR terminology) they should also share the recommended solution (i.e. the destination or the tourism products contained in the travel plan). The items of the reduced set of candidates that are more similar to the items contained in the retrieved sessions are considered as good recommendations. These items are presented to the user in a sorted list. The order of the list reflects the estimated values of the recommendations for the user, and these recommendation values are displayed explicitly on a graphical five-point scale.

The reduced set of candidates is actually sorted according to a score function (Ricci et al., 2003) that is computed by multiplying the session similarity (between the current case and one that has been stored) by the item similarity (between an item in the reduced set and an item in a similar case). For both the similarity functions we have used the Heterogeneous Euclidean Overlap Metric (HEOM) as a basis (Wilson & Martinez, 1997). The distance between two n-dimensional vectors including both numeric and symbolic features, $d(v,u)=d((u_1, ..., u_n), (v_1, ...v_n))$, is computed as the square root of the sum of squares of the local feature distances $d_i(u_i,v_i)$. The local distance is given by the module of the difference of values for numeric features and by the equality test, $d_i(u_i,v_i)=0$ if $u_i=v_i$, for symbolic features. HEOM distance is normalized and ranges between 0 and 1, whereas similarity is computed as $1-d(v,u)$.

4. PILOT EVALUATION

We will now describe the first pilot evaluation of the system prototype, outlining the main results and empirical findings, and focussing our attention on a detailed analysis of user-system interaction.

This study provided three main contributions:
— it gave some preliminary indications regarding the specific strengths and weaknesses of the system, and on the interaction design;
— it suggested some hypotheses that were able to promote our understanding of the user-system interaction;
— it provided significant methodological feedback, which will help us to plan further evaluation studies.

4.1 Pre-evaluation qualitative assessment

In accordance with the viewpoint of user-centered design, we took into account the users' needs from the first stages of development. System requirements were derived from the analysis of the travel decision making literature and from the identification of usage scenarios.

A series of qualitative evaluations (cognitive walkthroughs, heuristic evaluations, and detailed analyses of the interaction structure) have been carried out in various development stages by different experts, promoting significant changes to the design of the system and of the user interface.

4.2 Evaluation goals and system limitations

The NutKing prototype has been evaluated in order to acquire some preliminary feedback on the system efficiency and effectiveness, and to obtain some indications on the quality of the interaction design. We were also interested in obtaining some evidence on the statistical power of the tests and on the evaluation procedure, which is useful for blueprinting further experimental studies.

It should be noted that the NutKing user interface was a prototypical version that had never undergone an empirical test. Furthermore, the case base of the system was very small (35 cases). These cases had been generated by a group of expert and naive users.

The NutKing product catalogues were comprised of locations (220 records and 26 attributes), accommodations (1618 records and 20 attributes), sport activities (1624 records and 7 attributes), events (3286 records and 5 attributes), and cultural attractions (538 and 3 attributes). These data types are views over an Oracle database listing more than 100 tables, developed by the regional destination management organization (APT Trentino).

4.3 Experimental design and procedure

Using a between subjects design, the participants were randomly assigned either to the NutKing+ or to the NutKing- group. The first group (n=16) used the full functionality recommender (NutKing+), while the second group (n=19) interacted with a baseline system (NutKing-), deprived of the interactive query management and of the adaptive sorting functions. The two system variants (and interfaces) were very similar and the interaction flow was basically the same: a cycle of preference acquisition, query generation, and product choice.

The participants, students and office workers of the University of Trento, had to plan a vacation in Trentino, searching for appropriate travel items and selecting a set of products. Given the exploratory nature of the study, there were no specific constraints on the accomplishment of the task and all of the participants were familiar with the target area. The participants were told only that the experiment was about "travel planning" and that they could work at their own pace. They were not given any hint as to the type of system that they would use, and we tried to avoid generating any kind of expectation or Hawthorne effects (Shadish, Cook & Campbell, 2002).

The experiment was preceded by a training period (about 10 min), during which the participants were allowed to freely explore the system and to read the on-line explanations. After the experimental session, the participants completed a tailor-made evaluation questionnaire, and they were asked to express their comments and observations on the system.

The two main hypotheses were as follows:

– (H1) the NutKing+ system will be able to provide useful recommendations (the items selected by the NutKing+ participants will be placed closer to the top of the result list than the items picked up by the NutKing- participants);

– (H2) the use of the NutKing+ recommender produces an improvement in search and decision efficiency (provided that there are a similar number of items collected in the travel plans, the number of queries and the total amount of time taken will be lower in the NutKing+ system).

4.4 General results

The results of the experiment are summarized in table 1.

The participants of both groups specified a similar amount of input information (on identical forms). Both the mean number of collaborative features (NutKing+: M=11.5, SD=2.1; NutKing-: M=12.3, SD=1.4) and the mean number of query conditions (NutKing+: M=4.4, SD=1.1; NutKing-: M=4.7, SD=1.2) are very similar. t-tests with separate variance estimation and Mann-Whithney U tests did not show statistically significant differences. Also taking into consideration that no clear differences were found in the type of information specified, it appears that the system type did not affect the query generation process.

Table 1. Mean scores for the two NutKing variants. The variables marked with * are associated with statistically significant differences (p<.05).

Variable	NutKing+	NutKing-
Number of collaborative features	11.5	12.3
Number of query conditions	4.4	4.7
Number of queries	13.4	20.1
Number of results *	9.8	42
Number of pages displayed	71.3	93.3
Session duration (min)	31	28.5
Number of items in the travel plan	4.1	5.8
Mean position of the selected items in the result list *	2.2	3.2

NutKing- users formulated more queries than NutKing+ users, but this difference is not statistically significant. The Levene test showed that the variance in the number of queries is significantly lower for the NutKing+ system (F(1,33)=4.29, p<.01; NutKing+: SD=9.25; NutKing-: SD=19.17). The mean number of results produced by NutKing- is greater than the mean number of results produced by NutKing+ (t(33)=2.05, p<.05). A similar trend is observed in the mean number of pages displayed by the two systems, and the variance of the number of results is again significantly lower in NutKing+ than in NutKing- (Levene test: F(1,33)=18.39, p<.0001).

Despite some differences in the queries and in the results, the session duration is not significantly different in the two conditions. Therefore, it seems that NutKing+ users have spent more time examining information rather than composing queries or moving through the pages. Thus we obtained some partial indications that NutKing+ can promote efficiency (H2), but it can be hypothesized that the time saved is devoted to a deeper analysis of the information and to the choice processes.

The travel plans assembled using the two systems are composed of a similar number of items, but the mean position of these items in the result list is significantly closer to the top in NutKing+ (t(141)=1.96 p=.05 with log transformed data). In general, the participants tend to select the upper items in the result list. However, in accordance with H1, NutKing+ participants picked those items with higher recommendation rankings.

4.5   User-system interaction

We analyzed the NutKing+ log data, our main goal being to try to understand if the interaction design was appropriate and to acquire some indications relating to the participants' interaction strategies. We took into account 216 queries (all those queries with complete information) and summarized the observed interaction paths (figure 7).

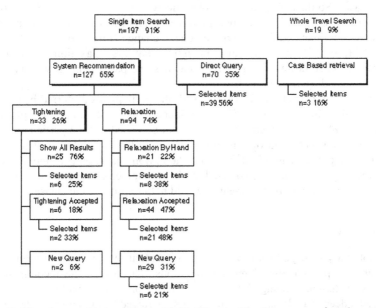

Figure 7. *The observed interaction with NutKing+. The frequency of each action and its occurrence percentage, computed in relation to the alternative actions, are presented inside the action box. The frequency of item selection (i.e. adding an item to the travel plan) and the item selection percentage after each specific action are shown below the corresponding action box.*

The complete travel recommendation function was rarely used (19 queries, 9%). Furthermore, the travel product suggested by the system was accepted by the participants in only 3 cases, and the difference between the proportions of selected items after a single item search and after a complete travel request is statistically significant (single item=.42, complete travel=.16, $p<.05$). We can formulate many hypotheses to explain these results. The more reasonable are as follows: (a) an inadequate interaction or interface design (i.e. the complete travel recommendation was not apparent in the interface or its meaning was not made clear), (b) the unsatisfying nature of the specific system suggestions with regard to the whole travel search, and (c) the participants' general unwillingness to rely on the suggestion of a complete travel package. Further experiments should contrast these hypotheses, given that the participants' free observations did not provide specific indications.

The single item search was quite frequent (197 queries; confidence interval for the proportion: $.87 \leq .91 \leq .94$), and it was repeated in an iterative way until the travel plan was deemed complete.

The system proposed a query change in 65% of single item queries. In the majority of cases, the initial request was too specific (74%), and the users accepted the system's relaxation hint. This subsequently led to the selection of a travel item in 31% of cases. So the participants accepted the system suggestion, and this proved to be useful: the proposed relaxations produced a significantly higher proportion of item selections than a different type of query change (relaxation=.45; other query change=.21, $p<.05$). It should also be noted that the relaxation interaction has probably not been designed perfectly, because some participants have relaxed their queries 'by hand' (cf., section 2).

The tightening function was rarely used: the participants preferred being able to examine all the results (95% confidence interval for the proportion: $0.59 \leq 0.76 \leq 0.88$). Again, many hypotheses can be raised: (a) the participants do not want to winnow out good options without having the possibility to actually view them, (b) the participants like to explore the option space, and (c) the participants avoid the cognitive effort associated with the tightening operations. As in the previous case, only additional research would help to provide the answer.

4.6 Discussion

The pilot study provided some weak indications that the NutKing+ variant appears to be able to provide useful recommendations. The use of the recommendation-enhanced system also changed the users' information-seeking patterns and probably produced a deeper analysis of the information retrieved from the search. In any case, the real effectiveness of the decision support provided by the system must be further investigated through more powerful tests, encompassing a broader and more detailed set of measures (for example: more detailed log data, satisfaction ratings on the products, high-quality post-study questionnaires). The execution of web experiments (Birnbaum, 2000) as a complement to the traditional laboratory study could help us to increase the external validity of the evaluation, even if this approach will require solving many methodological and technical issues.

Specific indications have been acquired on the support functions. The relaxation support seems to be useful, but it requires a better interface design. The tightening support and the complete travel recommendations should probably undergo a deeper reconsideration, once a complete understanding of the reasons underlying their low usage rate in our specific decision environment is established.

5. CONCLUSIONS AND FUTURE WORK

Our experience shows that it is possible to design personalized applications for the travel domain. It is quite a difficult task, but the potential benefits could be very high, given the huge variability of users' preferences in this domain.

We have built a prototype system that is able to satisfy a series of basic requirements (including some partial form of personalization), and we are currently improving its design and exploring alternative recommendation possibilities. We decided to follow this 'requirement-oriented' approach (instead of adopting a model-based approach) because of the existence of many problems that must still be solved in order to be able to fully specify other kinds of decision aids for the tourism domain. The first problem is the lack of detailed knowledge about the users' interactive information search processes and decision behaviors. We do not have sufficient knowledge of the tourists' decision processes to be able to fully specify satisfying descriptive models. This knowledge should concern a detailed analysis of the ways in which different types of tourists use the different media and decision aids in their travel planning efforts. A second problem is related to the difficulty of translating some existing general-purpose prescriptive approaches into real decision aids. In order to do this, we will need to apply a trusted normative model, such as the multiattribute utility theory (Keeney & Raiffa, 1976). These normative models are not easily applicable to the travel domain and their 'embodiment' in this domain will require the solution of complex problems (for example, the selection of the attributes for shaping the travel decision problem). Therefore, we have devoted most of our efforts to the reduction of the search and interaction costs and we have attempted to exploit the implicit knowledge stored in memorized recommendation sessions.

Some significant lessons learned from the design of the NutKing system and from the review of the first pilot evaluation are as follows:

- The design of a travel recommender system requires taking into account preferences regarding different types of products. Much attention should be given to the interaction design in order to keep the multiple-item search process as simple as possible and to allow a seamless integration of the explicit preferences and of the collaborative recommendations.

- The real usefulness of the main support functions should be empirically tested. In our pilot study we observed that some functions were rarely used (tightening and complete travel recommendation). Our current evidence is solely observational, but experimental tests could be performed to analyze the usefulness of specific system functions.

Our future work will follow three main directions:

- We will improve in various ways the recommendation technology described in this paper, increasing its degree of personalization. For instance, we will enable the learning (adaptation) of the feature weights used in the similarity measures, employing a punishment/reward algorithm (Ricci & Avesani, 1999). Moreover, we will try to offer a seamless support to users who adopt different decision styles (Fesenmaier, Ricci, Schaumlechner, Wöber & Zanella, 2003).

- The potential of different methods will also be explored. In particular, we are interested in some approaches deriving from the behavioral decision making literature (Edwards & Fasolo, 2001) that prevent the users from adopting suboptimal noncompensatory decision strategies. As we have just pointed out, applying these approaches to the tourism domain will require specific research effort and carefully designed support tools.
- Finally, we are currently trying to define an integrated approach for the evaluation of recommender systems and decision-facilitating web sites for consumer decision making (Del Missier & Ricci, 2003). This approach will be based on a principled integration of focussed experimental tests of specific interface and system components, simulations, laboratory experiments within a context-matching approach (Payne, Bettman, & Schkade, 1999), and web experiments (Birnbaum, 2000). The insights acquired from the layered evaluation method will be taken into account in the design of the experiments (Karagiannidis & Sampson, 2000). A preliminary step will be the identification of the appropriate evaluation dimensions for the different types of decision aids (Yates, Veinott, & Patalano, 2003).

6. ACKNOWLEDGEMENTS

The research was supported by CARITRO Foundation, European Union (contract DieToRecs IST-2000-29474), and a grant from Provincia Autonoma di Trento (Indirecs project).

REFERENCES

Aamodt, A., & Plaza, E. (1994). Case-based reasoning: foundational issues, methodological variations, and system approaches. *AI Communications*, 7, 39-59.

Aha, D. W. (1998). The omnipresence of case-based reasoning in science and application. *Knowledge-Based Systems*, *11*, 261-273.

Birnbaum, M. H. (2000). *Psychological experiments on the Internet*. San Diego: Academic Press.

Breese, J., Heckerman, D., & Kadie, C. (1998). Empirical analysis of predictive algorithms for collaborative filtering. *Proceedings of the Fourteenth Conference on Uncertainty in Artificial Intelligence*, 43-52.

Burke, R. (2000). Knowledge-based recommender systems. In J. E. Daily, A. Kent, & H. Lancour (Eds.), Encyclopedia of Library and Information Science, Vol. 69, Supplement 32. New York: Marcel Dekker.

Crompton, J. L., & P. K. Ankomah. (1993). Choice set propositions in destination decisions. *Annals of Tourism Research*, *20*, 461-476.

Del Missier, F., & Ricci, F. (2003). Understanding recommender systems: Experimental evaluation challenges. *Proceedings of the Second Workshop on Empirical Evaluation of Adaptive Systems*, 31-40.

Dellaert, B. GC., Ettema, D. F., & Lindh, C. (1998). Multi-faceted tourist travel decisions: a constraint-based conceptual framework to describe tourists' sequential choices of travel components. *Tourism Management*, *19*, 313-320.

Edwards, W., & Fasolo, B. (2001). Decision Technology. *Annual Review of Psychology*, *52*, 581-606.

Fesenmaier, D. R., & Jeng, J. (2000). Assessing structure in the pleasure trip planning process. *Tourism Analysis*, *5*, 13-17.

Fesenmaier, D. R., Ricci, F., Schaumlechner, E., Wöber, K., & Zanella, C. (2003). DIETORECS: Travel advisory for multiple decision styles. In A. J. Frew, M. Hitz, & P. O'Connors (Eds.). *Information and Communication Technologies in Tourism 2003* (pp. 232-241). Springer-Verlag.

Gaasterland, T., Godfrey, P., & Minker, J. (1992). An overview of cooperative answering. *Journal of Intelligent Information Systems, 1*, 123-157.

Godfrey, P. (1997). Minimization in cooperative response to failing database queries. *International Journal of Cooperative Information Systems, 6*, 95-159.

Jeng, J. & Fesenmaier, D. R. (2002). Conceptualizing the travel decision-making hierarchy: a review of recent developments. *Tourism Analysis, 7*, 15-32.

Karagiannidis, C., & Sampson, D. (2000). Layered evaluation of adaptive applications and services. In P. Brusilovsky, O. Stock, & C. Strapparava (Eds.), *Adaptive hypermedia and adaptive web-based systems*, Lecture Notes in Computer Science, Vol. 1892, (pp. 343-346). Springer-Verlag.

Keeney, R. L. & Raiffa, H. (1976). *Decisions with multiple objectives: Preferences and value trade-offs.* New York: Wiley.

Kobsa, A., Koenemann, J., & Pohl, W. (2001). Personalised hypermedia presentation techniques for improving online customer relationships. *The Knowledge Engineering Review, 16*, 111-155.

Kolodner, J. (1993). *Case-Based Reasoning.* San Mateo: Morgan Kaufmann Publishers

Lue, C. C., Crompton, J. L., & Fesenmaier, D. R. (1993). Conceptualization of multi-destination pleasure trip decisions. *Annals of Tourism Research, 20*, 289-301.

Moutinho, L. (1987). Consumer behavior in tourism. *European Journal of Marketing, 21*, 2-44.

O' Sullivan, D., Wilson, D., & Smyth, B. (2002). Improving case-based recommendation, a collaborative filtering approach. *Proceedings of the Seventh European Conference on Case-Based Reasoning*, 278-291.

Payne, J. W., Bettman J. R., & Johnson, E. J. (1993). *The adaptive decision maker.* New York: Cambridge University Press.

Payne, J. W., Bettman, J. R., & Schkade, D. A. (1999). Measuring constructed preferences: Towards a Building Code. *Journal of Risk and Uncertainty, 19*, 243-270.

Ricci, F. (2002). Travel recommender systems. *IEEE Intelligent Systems, 17*, 55-57.

Ricci, F., & Avesani, P. (1999). Data compression and local metrics for nearest neighbor classification. *IEEE Transactions on Pattern Analysis and Machine Intelligence, 21*, 380-384.

Ricci, F., Mirzadeh, N., & Venturini, A. (2002). Intelligent query managment in a mediator architecture. In T. Samad & V. Sgurev (Eds.), *First International IEEE Symposium on Intelligent Systems* (pp. 221-226). IEEE Press.

Ricci, F., Venturini, A., Cavada, D., Mirzadeh, N., Blaas, D., & Nones, M. (2003). Product recommendation with interactive query management and twofold similarity. *Proceedings of the Fifth International Conference on Case-Based Reasoning*, 479-493.

Schafer, J. B., Konstan, J. A., & Riedl, J. (2001). E-commerce recommendation applications. *Data Mining and Knowledge Discovery, 5*, 115-153.

Shadish, W. R., Cook, T. D., & Campbell, D. T. (2002). *Experimental and quasi-experimental designs.* Boston: Houghton Mifflin.

Um, S., & Crompton, J. L. (1990). Attitude determinants in tourism destination choice. *Annals of Tourism Research, 17*, 432-448.

Yates, J. F., Veinott, E. S., & Patalano, A. L. (2003). Hard decisions, bad decisions. On decision quality and decision aiding. In S.L. Schneider & J. Shanteau (Eds.). *Emerging perspectives on judgment and decision research* (pp. 13-63). New York: Cambridge University Press.

Wilson, D. & Martinez, T. (1997). Improved heterogeneous distance functions. *Journal of Artificial Intelligence Research, 11*, 1-34.

Woodside, A. G., & Lysonski, S. (1989). A general model of traveler destination choice. *Journal of Travel Research, 27*, 8-14.

MARCO DEGEMMIS, PASQUALE LOPS ,
GIOVANNI SEMERARO, MARIA FRANCESCA COSTABILE,
STEFANO PAOLO GUIDA, AND ORIANA LICCHELLI

IMPROVING COLLABORATIVE RECOMMENDER SYSTEMS BY MEANS OF USER PROFILES

1. INTRODUCTION

Nowadays, users are overwhelmed by the abundant amount of information created and delivered through the Internet. Especially in the e-commerce area, catalogues of the largest sites offer millions of products for sale and are visited by users having a variety of interests. In this field, it is well known that the process of buying products and services often implies a high degree of complexity and uncertainty. It is of particular interest to provide customers with personal advice (which reflects their individual interests) and *proactive* support to experience an effective navigation and improve searching in online product catalogues. Thus, Web personalization has become an indispensable part of e-commerce. Users value personalization because it makes the site easier to navigate and use. Sites value personalization because it creates a relationship that keeps the users coming back (Andersen et al., 2001).

One type of personalization that many Web sites have started to embody is represented by *recommender systems*. Such systems take input directly or indirectly from users and, based on user needs, preferences and usage patterns, they make personalized recommendations of products or services, thus giving users easing the information search and decision processes. The recommender systems are used to either predict whether a particular user will like a particular item (*prediction problem*), or to identify a set of N items that will be of interest to a certain user (top-N recommendation problem) (Sarwar et al., 2002). Recommender systems have been revolutionizing the way shoppers and information seekers find what they want, because they effectively prune large information spaces and help users in selecting items that best meet their needs and tastes.

There are two frequently used approaches for performing recommendations: a content-based and a collaborative one. In the first approach, the content (i.e., text) plays an important role: the system suggests the items similar to those the user liked based on the content comparison. In contrast with the content-based approach,

253

Clare-Marie Karat et al. (eds.), Designing Personalized User Experiences in eCommerce, 253—274.
© 2004 *Kluwer Academic Publishers. Printed in the Netherlands.*

which can be successful applied to a single user, a collaborative approach assumes that there is a set of individuals using the system: user advice is based on the item ratings provided by other users.

In a content-based system, the items of interest are defined by their associated features. This type of recommender learns a profile of the user interests based on the features present in the items the user has rated. The main weakness of this approach is that the learning method employed is limited by the features explicitly associated with the items. On the other hand, the greatest strength of collaborative techniques is that they rely only on user ratings and are completely independent from any machine-readable representation of the items being recommended.

Hybrid recommender systems combining both techniques have also been proposed to gain better performance with fewer of the drawbacks of any individual technique (Burke, 2002). Collaborative systems actually represent the state-of-the-art of recommendation engines used in most commercial e-commerce sites. The approach we propose in this paper aims at improving collaborative techniques by means of user profiles that store knowledge about user interests. Profiles are inferred from the analysis of transactional data (browsing and purchasing history of users), without considering any content, and are exploited to discover for each user a set of "nearest neighbors" to compute collaborative recommendations.

The main goal of this work has been to identify some objective measures for evaluating the quality of recommendations a system provides to the users. The metrics we propose are used to asses the actual improvement of the proposed hybrid approach with respect to a pure collaborative approach to recommendations. This has been achieved through an intensive experimental session described in the paper.

The chapter is organized as follows: Section 2 describes some related work on recommender systems. Section 3 provides a general description of the most frequently approaches used in the recommender systems, i.e. collaborative and content-based ones. It is also described a possible way to combine the approaches in order to improve the entire recommendation process. Section 4 gives a description of the two systems, namely User Profile Extractor (UPE) and Profile Extractor (PE), we integrated to build a hybrid recommender system called $U(PE)^2$. Sections 5 highlights the importance of evaluating recommendations. Section 6 presents the experimental work performed to evaluate the possible improvement of $U(PE)^2$ system with respect to UPE Finally, conclusions are drawn in Section 7.

2. RELATED WORK

The literature on recommender systems distinguishes primarily between the collaborative and content-based approaches and also considers the combination of the two as a more accurate approach (Balabanovic and Shoham, 1997; Konstan et al., 1998; Pazzani, 1999). Examples of such hybrid systems include *Fab* (Balabanovic and Shoham, 1997) and *Ringo* (Shardanand and Maes, 1995).

Fab maintains user profiles based on content analysis, and directly compares the profiles to determine similar users for collaborative recommendations. Items are recommended to a user both when they score highly against that user profile or when they are highly rated by a user with a similar profile.

Ringo is similar to *Fab* except that, during a similarity assessment among users, the system selects profiles of users with the highest correlation with an individual user. *Ringo* compares user profiles to determine which users have similar tastes. Once similar users have been identified, according to a classical collaborative approach, the system predicts how much the user may like an item that has not yet been rated by computing a weighted average of all the rates given to that item by the other users that have similar tastes.

In general, a well known limitation of the content-based approach is that it provides only a limited understanding of users behavior: recommended items are determined exclusively in terms of the attributes (for example, keywords) of the previously considered items. This strategy does not take into account other "behavioral" factors determining the preferences the user. Examples of behaviors are: "when purchasing beer, John Doe usually buys chips" and "On weekends, John Doe usually spends more than $50 on groceries."

In our opinion, behavioral factors should be considered in order to produce hybrid recommender systems exploiting behavioral profiles, that model the user's actions, not only content-based profiles.

Tuzhilin and Adomavicius (1999) state that: "In order to provide more accurate recommendations, it is necessary to base them on a thorough analysis of the *on-line behavior of the user* that is much broader than the behavior captured by current content-based filtering systems". Rules describing the on-line behavior of a user can be learned from the analysis of his/her transactional history using various data mining methods and can be included as a part of that user's profile. *Behavioral profiles* can describe much richer types of user behavior than user profiles from the content-based approach, but they do not provide any recommendations by themselves. Therefore, it is important to couple the behavioral profiling approach with other techniques.

We consider the integration of behavioral profiles and collaborative methods into one integral approach because, in our opinion, customer recommendations should be based on understanding behavior of that customer and on the preferences of similar customers. In our approach, rules describing the customer behavior are used in order to discover preferences of users, for example product categories. In a book recommending context, rules could be used in order to determine whether a user is interested in a specific book category. A simple example of such rules is: "Customers that buy at least 3 books belonging to the *horror* category are interested in that book category".

Preferences are stored in personal profiles exploited to group customers having the same interests. Our idea is that profiles could drive the collaborative method by reducing the set of users on which the algorithm is applied only to users interested in the same product categories. Combining behavioral profiles with collaborative methods is similar to some attempts made to improve the process of building a neighborhood of likeminded customers. The neighborhood generation scheme usually uses Pearson correlation or cosine similarity for computing the distance between consumers based on their preference history (Shardanand and Maes, 1995). Sarwar et al. (2002) described a method that partitions the users of a collaborative filtering system using a clustering algorithm, and uses the partitions as neighborhoods. The authors show that clustering-based neighborhood provides comparable prediction quality as the basic collaborative filtering approach and at the same time significantly improves the online performance.

Instead of using clustering to build the neighborhoods, we rely on a supervised machine learning technique that classifies each user as interested or not interested in one or more product categories. Given a fixed set of *n* product categories, we define *n* binary classification tasks, one for each category. At the end of the learning phase, *n* binary classifiers are obtained. For a user, the output of each classifier is used to determine the list of product categories he/she is interested in. Each "product category" classifier is a model for the class "users interested in that category". For example, if the current user is classified as interested in the product category "horror books", then he/she will be considered in the class "users interested in horror books".

Our idea is to compute collaborative recommendations after this classification step, separately on each class.

3. DIFFERENT APPROACHES TO RECOMMENDATIONS

Many of the largest e-commerce Web sites are using recommender systems to help their customers find products to purchase. A recommender system learns from customers and recommends products that customers will find most valuable among the available products. There are many different techniques for implementing recommender systems (Burke, 2002; Resnick and Varian, 1997; Schafer, Konstan and Riedl, 1999; Terveen and Hill, 2001):

- *Collaborative* filtering is the most successful recommender system technology to date, and is used in many recommender systems on the Web. The main idea of collaborative filtering is to recommend new items of interest for a particular user based on other users' ratings. These systems recommend products to a customer based on the correlation between that customer and other customers who showed interests in those products, i.e. who have purchased products from the e-commerce site.
- *Content-based* recommender systems suggest items based on their associated features. A pure content-based recommender system is one in which recommendations are made for a user based solely on a profile built by analyzing the content of items which that user has rated in the past.
- *Demographic* recommender systems aim at categorizing the user based on personal attributes and make recommendations based on demographic classes. Demographic techniques form "people-to-people" correlations like collaborative ones, but use different data. The benefit of a demographic approach is that it may

not require a history of user ratings of the type needed by collaborative and content-based techniques.

- *Knowledge-based* recommender systems attempt to suggest items based on inferences about a user's needs and preferences. In some sense, all recommendation techniques could be described as doing some kind of inference. Knowledge-based approaches are distinguished in that they have functional knowledge: they have knowledge about how a particular item meets a particular user need, and can therefore reason about the relationship between a need and a possible recommendation.

3.1 COLLABORATIVE/SOCIAL FILTERING SYSTEMS

Collaborative filtering is a type of recommender system that works by finding patterns of agreement among users of the system, leveraging the tastes and opinions about quality of all of the users to help each user individually. The main features of this techniques is to use the judgment of the group of users with similar tastes. The user judgment is given by taking implicitly into account parameters such as style, importance or novelty of an item. Typically, for each user a set of "nearest neighbor" users is found whose past rates have the strongest correlation. Rates for unseen items are predicted based on a combination of the rates known from the nearest neighbors. In Section 4.1, the technique of collaborative filtering we have implemented is illustrated in more detail.

Pure collaborative techniques provide recommendations without taking into account specific characteristics of the content the user is dealing with. However, there are cases in which collaborative recommendations may not be appropriate since the content plays an important role in the decisional process of the user, as in the case of non standardized products (such as travel, cameras, cars, etc.). This is discussed in (Ricci and Del Messier, 2004).

Collaborative filtering has a number of advantages over content-based methods:

- The knowledge engineering problem associated with content-based methods is relieved, since explicit content representations are not needed.
- The quality of collaborative filtering typically increases with the size of the user population, and collaborative recommendations benefit from improved diversity when compared to content-based recommendations.

However collaborative filtering does suffer from a number of significant downsides:

- It is not suitable for recommending new items because these techniques can only recommend items already rated by other users. If a new item is added to the content database, there can be a significant delay before this item will be considered for recommendation. Essentially, only when many users have seen and rated the item will it find its way into enough user profiles to become available for recommendation. This so-called "latency problem" is a serious limitation that often renders a pure collaborative recommendation strategy inappropriate for a given application domain.
- Collaborative recommendation can also prove unsatisfactory in dealing with what might be termed an "unusual user". There is no guarantee a set of

recommendation partners will be available for a given target user, especially if there is insufficient overlap between the target profile and other profiles. If a target profile contains only a small number of rates or contains ratings for a set of items that nobody else has reviewed, it may not be possible to make a reliable recommendation using the collaborative technique.

– Collaborative filtering systems require a lot of computational resource with the increasing of the number of users and items involved into compute.

3.2 USER KNOWLEDGE

Personalized systems get preferences through interactions with users, keep summaries of their preferences in a user model, and utilize this model to adapt themselves to generate customized information or behavior. A key issue in the personalization of a Web site is the automatic construction of accurate machine-processable profiles. A profile is a collection of information about an individual; it enables the recognition of the user, and generates predictions as to why he or she did something, and what he or she wants to do next.

User profiling is typically either knowledge-based or behavior-based. Knowledge-based approaches engineer static models of users and dynamically match users to the closest model. The knowledge about users can be acquired in different ways. Generally, it could be acquired through questionnaires, where users select different content types and services from a list of predefined choices. However, this approach does not take into account the dynamic nature of user preferences. This implies that users must manually update their profiles when their interests change. These limitations clearly call for alternative methods that infer preference information implicitly and support automated content recommendation.

Behavior-based approaches use the users' behavior itself as a model. Machine learning techniques are being used to recognize the regularities in the behavior of customers interacting with e-commerce Web sites and to infer a model of the interests of a user, referred to as *user profile* or *user model*. The user model is a collection of information about an individual and should be able to recognize the user, know why he or she did something, and guess what he or she wants to do next.

We have decided to adopt a behavior-based approach for automatically acquiring knowledge about the user's preferences, in the sense that machine learning techniques have been used in order to discover patterns and regularities in the transactional data describing the users' behavior. The goal of this analysis is to induce a binary model able to distinguish what users find interesting and uninteresting. For example, a possible outcome of the learning process is a general model of "users interested in horror books" in terms of number of searches performed in this product category or number of purchased horror books.

3.3 INTEGRATING COLLABORATIVE RECOMMENDER SYSTEMS WITH USER KNOWLEDGE

User models have been used in *recommender systems* for content processing and information filtering. It could be useful to develop methods for integrating behavioral profiling with collaborative filtering into one integral approach. In particular, the approach we propose integrates collaborative techniques with user profiles inferred from the analysis of transactional data (browsing and purchasing history of users) without considering any content.

There are two main alternatives to accomplish this task:
1. *Profiles Drive Collaborative Methods*. Profiles are used to reduce the set of items that should be used for the computing recommendations. This means that standard collaborative methods will be applied, but they will work on a smaller consideration set of data. We expect this to increase the performances of the overall technique in comparison to the stand-alone collaborative filtering method.
2. *Profiles Are Used After Collaborative Filtering*. Standard collaborative filtering techniques are used to generate a preliminary set of possible recommendations. Then, profiles are exploited to re-rank the set of the recommended items or to prune some of the items that were preliminarily recommended.

Our approach exploits alternative 1, but it reduces the set of users on which the algorithm is applied instead of reducing the set of items. In Section 4.3 we will give more details about the adopted approach.

4. PERSONALIZATION SYSTEMS

The increasing need to analyze customer behavior (especially on the Web) in order to enhance customer loyalty (and to convert visitors to buyers) has produced several technologies attempting to tackle the problem, such as clickstream analysis tools, recommender systems, data mining tools, profiling systems. These technologies could be grouped under the heading of "personalization systems", because the idea behind them is that by better understanding users, online retailers can provide them with a more personally relevant online experience.

In previous work, we have developed two personalization systems, each exploiting a specific technique for providing recommendation: UPE, described in Section 4.1, is a collaborative filtering recommender system, and PE, described in Section 4.2, is a user profiling tool.

4.1 UPE

UPE (User Profile Engine) is a recommender system that provides personalized suggestions (recommendations) about pages users might find interesting in a product catalogue on the Web (Buono et al., 2002). The user profiles managed by UPE have a static component and a dynamic one. The static component consists of a set of information that identifies each user and does not change (or changes rarely). For example: name, nationality and type of user. The information sources come primarily from the registration forms that some users are required to fill. The dynamic component of user profile is the changing part of user data. The set of user preferences is part of the dynamic profile. UPE obtains this information by using different type of ratings: *explicit ratings*, i.e. the user explicitly indicates what he or she thinks about an item; *implicit ratings*, obtained by tracking user navigation. For the latter, system considers as interesting the following events: access to a Web page, print and/or save action, download of specific files included in download areas, image zooming, etc.

Even if explicit rating is fairly precise, it has disadvantages, such as: 1) stopping to enter explicit ratings can alter normal patterns of browsing and reading; 2) unless users perceive that there is a benefit providing the rates, they may stop providing them. Implicit rating is much more difficult to determine. Oard and Kim (1998) divide implicit rating into three categories: rates based on examination, when a user examines an item; rates based on retention, when a user saves an item; rates based on reference, when a user links all or part of an item into an other item. Even if implicit ratings are difficult to determine, they have the following advantages: 1) every interaction with the system (and every absence of interaction) can contribute to implicit rating; 2) can be gathered for free; 3) can be combined with several types of implicit ratings for a more accurate rating; 4) can be combined with explicit ratings for an enhanced rating. Indeed, the method that is quite effective is a mixed technique that exploits implicit and explicit rating and we implemented it in UPE. However, especially in the case of sites with many pages, we can be in a situation that some pages have not been evaluated by the current user (neither explicit nor implicit ratings are available). To overcome this situation, UPE uses an algorithm of collaborative filtering (Breese et al., 1998). It predicts user interests on an item (i.e., a Web page of a product, a single product or a service) not evaluated by taking into account the historical data set on rates of a user's community stored into a database of existing rating provided by other users. Such a database is a set of rates $u_{i,j}$, corresponding to the evaluation of user i on the item j. If I_i is the set of items on which user i has expressed a rate, then it's possible to define the average rate for user i as:

$$\bar{u}_i = \frac{1}{|I_i|} \sum_{j \in I_i} u_{i,j} \tag{1}$$

It is also possible to compute the evaluation of the current user(indicated with u_a) based on information on the current user and on a set of weights calculated from the user database. We can assume that the predicted rate of current user expected for item j, i.e. $p_{a,j}$, is a weighted sum of rates of other users:

$$p_{a,j} = \bar{u}_a + k \sum_{i=1}^{n} w(a,i)(u_{i,j} - \bar{u}_a) \tag{2}$$

where n is the number of user in the database with non-zero weight. Weights $w(a,i)$ can reflect distance, correlation, or similarity between each user i and the current user. K is a normalization factor such that the absolute values of the weights sum to unit. In our case, the weight $w(a,i)$, which reflects the degree to which the current user a and the user i are related, is the Pearson's correlation coefficient:

$$w(a,i) = \frac{\sum_j (u_{a,j} - \bar{u}_a)(u_{i,j} - \bar{u}_i)}{\sqrt{\sum_j (u_{a,j} - \bar{u}_a)^2 \sum_j (u_{i,j} - \bar{u}_i)^2}} \tag{3}$$

where summations over j are calculated on all items which have been evaluated by the users a and i.

As it is well known, these algorithms are useful but also very time consuming. Some heuristics are used to reduce the algorithm complexity. For example, UPE does not re-calculate all the weights $w(a,i)$, but does it only for those pairs of correlated users, in which at least one of the two users has interacted with the Web site and has modified a number of rates higher than a certain threshold.

4.2 PE

Among issues the personalization community must deal with, the following are of special importance: how to provide personal recommendations based on a comprehensive knowledge of who customers are, how they behave and how to extract this knowledge from the available data and store it in user profiles? To address these issues, we have adopted an approach that uses information learned from transactional histories to construct individual profiles. The advantage of using this technique is that profiles generated from a huge number of transactions tend to be statistically reliable.

The process of learning customer profiles is performed by the PE (Profile Extractor) personalization system (Semeraro et al., 2003), which employs supervised learning techniques to automatically discover users' preferences from transactional data recorded during past visits to the e-commerce Web site. In Business to Consumer (B2C) e-commerce, items are grouped in a fixed number of categories. For example, at Amazon.com books in the catalogue are organized in many subject categories. PE is able to analyze data gathered from sources such as data warehouse or transactions in order to infer rules describing the customer/user behavior. Rules are exploited to build profiles containing preferences such as the product categories the user is interested into. Some preliminary work is needed to establish a formal description of the features and attributes that are needed to accomplish the given task; we can use the results to define the representation language of the entire learning framework. From our point of view, the problem of learning user's preferences can be cast to the problem of inducing general concepts from examples labelled as members (or non-members) of the concepts. In this context, given a finite set of categories of interest $C = \{c_1, c_2, \dots c_n\}$, the task consists in learning the target concept T_i "users interested in the category c_i". In the training phase, each user represents a positive example of users interested in the categories he or she likes and

MARCO DEGEMMIS, PASQUALE LOPS ,
GIOVANNI SEMERARO, MARIA FRANCESCA COSTABILE, STEFANO PAOLO
GUIDA, AND ORIANA LICCHELLI

a negative example of users interested in the categories he or she dislikes. We chose
an operational description of the target concept T_i, using a collection of rules that
match against the features describing a user in order to decide if he or she is a
member of T_i. The complete set of attributes (transactional data about customers)
used to represent the examples is listed in Table 1.

Table 1. *Description of the attributes used to represent examples. <CategoryName>
denotes each one of the eleven product categories used in our experimentation,
namely Underwear, Furniture, Pet Supplies And Products, Household Articles,
Kitchen Utensils, Sanitary Articles, Electronics, Hardware, Jewelry, Informatics,
Babyhood.*

Attribute	Description
User_id	Unique identifier of each user
Gender	Gender of the user
Birth_date	Birth date of the user
City	City of the user
Id_content_category	Explicit interest category of the user
Shop<categoryname>	Number of products, in a specific category, purchased by the user
Addcart<categoryname>	Number of products, in a specific category, added to the cart by the user
Dwlinfo<categoryname>	Number of information on the products, in a specific category, downloaded by the user
Dwlsrch<categoryname>	Number of product pages, in a specific category, the user browses after a search
Dwlpag<categoryname>	Number of product pages, in a specific category, the user browses
Zooming<categoryname>	Number of zoom on products, in a specific category, the user does

This information, as depicted in Figure 1, is arranged into a set of unclassified
instances (each instance represents a customer). The subset of the instances chosen
to train the learning system has to be labeled by a domain expert, that classifies each
instance as member or non-member of each category. The training instances are
processed by the Profile Extractor, which induces a classification rule set for each
product category (Figure 2). The rules are used to classify each user, as interested or
not interested in each product category, on the basis of his/her transactional data
(Figure 3).

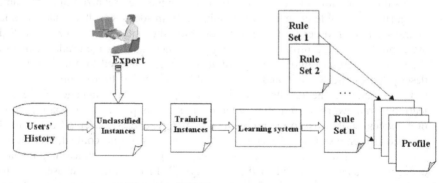

Figure 1. *The learning process*

There are 8 rules extracted for class Kitchen Utensils:

If addcart_Kitchen Utensils > 13.0
   and Gender = M then
   Class: yes
Else if addcart_Elettronics <= 5.0
      and dwlpag_Hardware <= 2.0
         and Gender = F then
      Class: no
Else if zooming_Household Articles > 18.0 then
   Class: yes
...
Otherwise Class: no

Figure 2. *An example of classification rules for the "Kitchen Utensils" category*

Profile for User: 7

GENDER	M	class_Sanitary Articles	yes	0.6666	no	0.3334
BIRTH_DATE	1974-03-10	class_Kitchen Utensils	yes	1.0	no	0.0
CITY	plain	class_Household Articles	yes	0.7902	no	0.2098
ID_CONTENT_CATEGORY	Sanitary Articles	class_Underwear	yes	0.6702	no	0.3298
shop_Sanitary Articles	1	class_Furniture	yes	0.9902	no	0.0098
addcart_Sanitary Articles	0	class_Pet_Supplies_And_Products	yes	0.6018	no	0.3982
dwlinfo_Sanitary Articles	2	class_Hardware	yes	0.0	no	1.0
dwlsrch_Sanitary Articles	1	class_Informatics	yes	0.0038	no	0.9962
dwlpag_Sanitary Articles	0	class_Babyhood	yes	0.0	no	1.0
zooming_Sanitary Articles	10	class_Jewelry	yes	0.0025	no	0.9975
shop_Kitchen Utensils	13	class_Electronics	yes	0.3333	no	0.6667
addcart_Kitchen Utensils	18				
dwlinfo_Kitchen Utensils	20				
dwlsrch_Kitchen Utensils	19				
dwlpag_Kitchen Utensils	1				
zooming_Kitchen Utensils	8				
shop_Household Articles	0				
addcart_Household Articles	10				
dwlinfo_Household Articles	5				
dwlsrch_Household Articles	3				
dwlpag_Household Articles	0				
zooming_Household Articles	5				
shop_Underwear	8				
addcart_Underwear	0				
dwlinfo_Underwear	2				

Figure 3. *An example of a user profile*

More precisely, the architecture of the PE is made up of several sub-modules:
- *XML I/O Wrapper*, which is the layer responsible for the extraction of data required for the learning process.

- *Rules Manager*, which is implemented through one of the WEKA (Frank and Witten, 1998) classifiers. The learning algorithm adopted in the rule induction process is PART (Witten and Frank, 1999), which produces rules from pruned partial decision trees.
- *Profile Manager*, which classifies each user on the ground of the users' transactions and the set of rules induced by the Rules Manager. The classifications, together with the interaction details of users, are gathered to form a *user profile*.

4.3 INTEGRATING UPE AND PE: U(PE)^2

We have already discussed in the previous sections the advantages of hybrid recommender systems that integrate collaborative methods and knowledge based methods producing behavioral profiles. Our idea is to produce a hybrid method by integrating behavioral profiles inferred by PE and the collaborative method implemented by UPE into one integral approach in an attempt to demonstrate that it outperforms the pure collaborative filtering method. The resulting system U(PE)^2 implements a cascade hybrid method: profiles inferred by PE are exploited to group customers having similar preferences. In our case, preferences are the product categories the customer is interested in. Our idea is that profiles could drive the collaborative method by reducing the set of users, on which the algorithm is applied, only to users interested in the same product categories. PE is applied first to identify distinct groups or "classes" of users. For example, users can be grouped as interested in a particular "content category". Then, the collaborative filtering algorithm is applied to each group of users. In this way, it is possible to improve computational performance by carrying out parallel computation for each group of users. We actually use PE to classify registered users and assign them to the content categories of their interest; we then apply collaborative filtering algorithm to the users of each class, in order to generate recommendations that fit their interests.

5. EVALUATING RECOMMENDATIONS

Useful recommendations have the potential of increasing Web site's usability, since their objective is to allow users to perform their tasks and achieve their goals with less effort, experiencing a higher satisfaction. There are two main aspects related to the evaluation of recommendations:
- measuring the quality of recommendations in order to make a comparison among different systems;
- the analysis of the impact of the recommendations from the point of view of the user, i.e. their effectiveness on user experience with the system.

The first aspect is more technical and needs the definition of metrics to measure the quality of a recommender system. To this purpose we have used the metrics described in Section 6.2. Such metrics are also used to establish whether a recommender system is better than another one.

The second aspect concerns the impact of recommendations on the users, i.e. whether the users appreciate the type of recommendations the system provides and the way they are presented. In fact, the main problem of most of today's Web applications is that they offer manifold navigation options and (usually simple) search functions, but leave it up to users to find their way through the many interface functions, understand them and interrelate them cognitively. Usually, users have to decide themselves which sequence of actions must be performed to solve a given task. The purchase process, for example, contains several complex search queries that must be constructed step by step. Users, especially beginners or occasional, are often daunted by the complexity of the functionalities provided by Web applications and thus need "proactive" support or advice from the system (the recommendations of product, actions, generic items, etc.) in order to fully utilize the range of functions available. This aspect is currently taken into account in our research work, but is not described here. The idea is to follow the approach adopted in (Semeraro et al., 2003), where an experimental evaluation is performed to compare two versions of the system: one with the personalization component, and the other without.

In this paper we focus on the first aspect because our goal is to evaluate the performance of the hybrid technique implemented by $U(PE)^2$ in terms of quality of recommendations and computational resources.

6. EXPERIMENTAL WORK

We have performed two experiments in order to compare the performance of the proposed hybrid recommender system $U(PE)^2$ with the system UPE.

- Experiment 1: evaluation of UPE implementing the classical collaborative filtering technique, described in Section 4.1.
- Experiment 2: evaluation of the hybrid system $U(PE)^2$ obtained integrating the behavioral profiles inferred by PE with the UPE collaborative method. The performance of $U(PE)^2$ has been compared with the UPE personalization system.

For both experiments we used historical browsing data from an Italian e-commerce company. This dataset contains information about 380 users on 154 catalogue products (products are grouped into 11 product categories, as listed in Table 3 of Section 6.3). The dataset contains explicit rates given by users and implicit rates computed by the system on the basis of the user behavior. Each action performed by a user on a web page, for example zooming on the picture of a product, corresponds to a rate. Both explicit and implicit rates vary from 0 to 5. In total, the dataset includes 9,073 rates. The average number of ratings per user is approximately 24. The dataset is represented as a user-ratings matrix, in which the columns represent the products and the rows the users. The sparsity of the user ratings matrix (defined as the ratio of not null ratings to all matrix size) is approximately 85%.

6.1 EXPERIMENT DESCRIPTION

For both experiments we divided the dataset into a training set and a test set by using 90%/10% training/test ratio (the training set is composed by 342 users and their ratings, the test set is composed by 38 users and their ratings). From each user in the test set, ratings for 25% of items were randomly withheld. Predictions were computed for the withheld items using each of the different algorithms.

Experiment 1

The dataset was converted into a user-product matrix that had 380 rows (i.e., 380 users) and 154 columns (i.e., products that were rated by at least one of the users). Predictions were computed for the withheld items using the pure collaborative filtering technique implemented by UPE. The quality of the predictions was measured by comparing the predicted values for the withheld ratings to the actual ratings, using several metrics described in the Section 6.2. The procedure was repeated 5 times selecting a different test set (the intersection of the five test sets was empty). This allows running 5 trials that are completely different. Finally, results were averaged over the 5 trials.

Experiment 2

The dataset was converted into 11 user-product matrices, each corresponding to a specific product category C_i in which PE classified the users. Each matrix had n_i rows (i.e., the number of users that PE has classified as interested in the category C_i) and 154 columns (i.e., products that were rated by at least one of the users). In this case, the UPE collaborative filtering was applied separately to each matrix. The quality of the predictions was measured by comparing the predicted values for the withheld ratings to the actual ratings for each matrix, using the same metrics of Experiment 1. As Experiment 1, Experiment 2 was performed 5 times by selecting each time a different test set, and results were averaged. Finally, results were averaged over all categories.

Experimental platform

All systems were implemented using Java. We ran all our experiments on a Microsoft (Windows 2000) based PC with Intel Pentium IV processor having a speed of 2 GHz and 512 Mbytes of RAM.

6.2 EVALUATION METRICS

Recommender systems research has used several types of measures for evaluating the success of a recommender system. We only consider the quality of prediction or recommendation, as we are only interested in the output of a recommender system for the evaluation purpose. It is, however, possible to evaluate intermediate steps (i.e.., the quality of neighborhood formation). Here we consider only two types of metrics for evaluating predictions and recommendations respectively.

To evaluate an *individual item prediction* researchers use several metrics. Statistical accuracy metrics evaluate the accuracy of a system by comparing the numerical recommendation scores against the actual user ratings for the user-item pairs in the test dataset. Mean Absolute Error (MAE) between ratings and predictions is a widely used metric. MAE is a measure of the deviation of recommendations from their true user-specified values. For the prediction of N items $(p_1,...,p_N)$ and a real evaluation of a user $(r_1,...,r_N)$, error $E = (|p_1-r_1|,...,|p_n-r_N|)$ is calculated. We can compute MAE by first summing the squared absolute errors of the N corresponding ratings-prediction pairs and then computing the average. Formally,

$$|\overline{E}| = \frac{\sum_{i=1}^{N} |p_i - r_i|^2}{N} \tag{4}$$

The lower the MAE, the more accurately the recommendation engine predicts user ratings. We used MAE as our choice of evaluation metric to report prediction accuracy because it is most commonly used and easiest to interpret directly.

Since the task was to identify or retrieve items preferred by users from a repository, traditional information retrieval measures were adopted, namely *Precision (Pr)*, *Recall (Re)* (Sebastiani, 2002). We have adapted the definition of recall and precision to our case as our experiment is different from standard IR in the sense that we have a fixed number of recommended items.

In the evaluation phase, the concept of *relevant item* is central. An item is considered as relevant by a user if the score he or she has given is greater than 2.5. An item is considered as relevant by a system if the computed numerical recommendation score is greater than 2.5. Our goal is to look into the test set and match items (products or contents, in our case) that both the system and the user deemed relevant. Let Rel_u be the set of test items the user deemed relevant and Rel_s be the set of test items the system deemed relevant. Items that appear in both sets are member of a set that is called *hit set* (Hit). In this context, it is possible to re-define recall and precision as follows:

$$Re = \frac{|Rel_u \cap Rel_s| = |Hit|}{|Rel_u|} \tag{5}$$

$$Pr = \frac{|Rel_u \cap Rel_s| = |Hit|}{|Rel_s|} \tag{6}$$

In other words, *recall* is the proportion of relevant items that are classified as relevant, and *precision* is the proportion of items classified as relevant that really are relevant. The fact that both measures are critical for the quality judgment leads us to use a combination of the two. In particular, we use the standard *F1* metric (Sebastiani, 2002), which gives equal weight to them both and is computed as follows:

$$F1 = \frac{2 \times Pr \times Re}{Pr + Re} \tag{7}$$

We also adopted the *Normalized Distance-based Performance Measure (NDPM)* (Yao, 1995) to evaluate the goodness of the items' ranking calculated according to a certain relevance measure. Specifically, *NDPM* was exploited to measure the distance between the ranking imposed on items by the user ratings (represented by $>_u$) and the ranking predicted by the system (represented by $>_s$). Given a pair of items (t_i, t_j) in the test set T of a user, we compute the distance between them according the following scheme:

$$\delta_{>_u>_s}(t_i,t_j)=\begin{cases} 2 \Leftrightarrow (t_i >_u t_j \wedge t_j >_s t_i) \vee (t_i >_s t_j \wedge t_j >_u t_i) \\ 1 \Leftrightarrow (t_i >_s t_j \vee t_j >_s t_i) \wedge t_i \approx_u t_j \\ 0 \Leftrightarrow otherwise \end{cases} \qquad (8)$$

The NDPM value over the test set T is computed by the following equation:

$$NDPM_{>_u>_s}(T)=\frac{\sum\limits_{i\neq j}\delta_{>_u>_s}(t_i,t_j)}{2\times n} \qquad (9)$$

where n is the number of item couples. Values range from 0 (agreement) to 1 (disagreement).

6.3 RESULTS AND DISCUSSION

In this section, we discuss our experimental results of integrating behavioral profiles which collaborative filtering methods. Results are mainly divided into two parts: quality results and performance results. In assessing the quality of recommendations, we first analyze the results obtained in Experiment 1 by UPE, and summarized in Table 2.

MAE	NDPM	Recall	Precision	F1-measure
0.421	0.066	0.942	0.905	0.923

Table 2 – Results obtained by UPE (averaged over 5 trials)

The most important observation from these results is the high accuracy that can be achieved by the system on the whole dataset in predicting the ranking of the products according to the customers interests (the NDPM value is close to 0). The low value of NDPM is not sufficient to guarantee good recommendation quality because it does not state whether the system is able to recognize *good* items to be recommended, i.e. *relevant* items. The high value of the F1-measure and the balance between recall and precision demonstrates that the list of recommendations presented to users by UPE contains relevant items correctly ranked. We recorded the time required to generate predictions for the entire dataset (380x154) and found that the process is computationally very expensive (5h 47min on average over the 5 trials).

In the second experiment, we examined separately the recommendation accuracy for users grouped according to their behavioral profiles computed by PE. Each group of users was considered as a different dataset: from the original dataset of 380 users, 11 datasets have been formed, one for each product category, according to the classification predicted by PE. For each dataset (product category), Table 3 reports the number of users that are classified as interested in that category, the number of users poorly, moderately, and strongly correlated, and the mean correlation value computed over each pair of users, in each dataset (product category). This coefficient, whose values vary between -1 and 1 (but we consider only the absolute value), represents the degree of association (similarity) between any two users and is computed by UPE according to Equation (3). A correlation coefficient between 0.3 and 0.6 reveals a moderate association, while values above 0.6 indicate a strong correlation. A correlation coefficient at zero, or close to zero, indicates no relationship. In Figure 4, we reported the $U(PE)^2$ values of MAE. In general the results are positive given the small number of users belonging to each category (from 35 users in the category "kitchen articles" to the 74 users in the category "underwear"). Only for two categories ("kitchen articles" and "jewelry") the value of MAE was over 2. In particular, the computed MAE for the category "kitchen articles" is greater than 8; in order to fully understand this result it is important to notice that this category contains the smallest number of users (35) and reported the lowest value of mean user correlation. For the users in the category "kitchen articles", the computed value was 0.42 against at least 0.49 achieved in all the other categories (see Table 3 for more details).

In general NDPM results are very positive (values do not exceed 0.2), showing a strong correlation between the ranking imposed by the users and the ranking computed by the system, although there is a high degree of variation between different categories. NDPM is better for users strongly correlated and belonging to "more populated" categories: the best values have been found in the categories "underwear" (74 users) and "hardware", which show the highest values of user correlation.

Table 3. *Statistics on the 11 datasets. The last row is referred to the entire dataset of 380 users.*

DATASET (Product Category)	NUM. OF USERS	U.C. <0.3	0.3<=U.C.<=0.6	U.C.>0.6	MEAN USER CORRELATION
UNDERWEAR	74	11 (15%)	10 (13%)	53 (72%)	0.50
FURNITURE	67	10 (15%)	14 (21%)	43 (64%)	0.51
PET SUPPLIES AND PRODUCTS	69	10 (15%)	16 (23%)	43 (62%)	0.51
HOUSEHOLD ARTICLES	68	12 (18%)	17 (25%)	39 (57%)	0.49
KITCHEN UTENSILS	35	9 (26%)	5 (14%)	21 (60%)	0.42
SANITARY ARTICLES	70	9 (13%)	24 (34%)	37 (53%)	0.50
ELECTRONICS	59	9 (15%)	7 (12%)	43 (73%)	0.49
HARDWARE	65	12 (19%)	8 (12%)	45 (69%)	0.52
JEWELRY	70	14 (20%)	11 (16%)	45 (64%)	0.51
INFORMATICS	65	9 (14%)	13 (20%)	43 (66%)	0.51
BABYHOOD	70	8 (12%)	12 (17%)	50 (71%)	0.51
ENTIRE DATASET	380	64 (17%)	41 (11%)	275 (72%)	0.65

For the F1 score, we consider the results presented in Figure 6 as very positive. Overall, 8 out of the 11 categories reported values that exceed 0.80, while only for one category ("kitchen articles" again) the system was not able to reach a value of at least 0.70.

The aim of the second experiment was to compare the results obtained by $U(PE)^2$ averaged over all the categories with the results obtained by UPE without considering the additional knowledge about users represented by behavioral profiles. To this purpose, we summarized the results obtained by both systems in Table 4.

As regards MAE, the value achieved by UPE is almost five times better than the value we registered for $U(PE)^2$. UPE outperforms $U(PE)^2$ both for NDPM and F1-measure. This result is to be expected, as the collaborative filtering algorithm implemented by UPE generates recommendations based on the strength of the association among users and it is adversely affected by reduced training sets containing poorly correlated users. Notice that only 3 product categories ("underwear", "electronics", "babyhood") reported at least 70% of users strongly correlated, as in the original dataset, and that the mean user correlation observed in each product category is always lower than in the entire dataset (see Table 3).

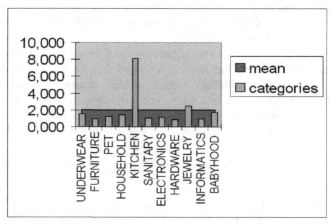

Figure 4. *$U(PE)^2$ MAE values for the 11 product categories*

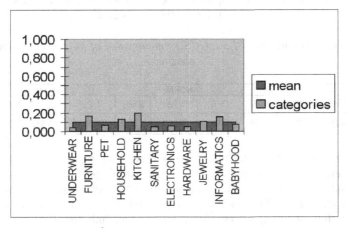

Figure 5. *U(PE)^2 NDPM values for the 11 product categories*

Nevertheless, the results achieved using behavioral profiles are satisfactory because NDPM is still very close to 0 and F1-measure shows a classification accuracy in recognizing relevant items that is almost 84%. This means that $U(PE)^2$ is able to recommend "good" items, although the individual item prediction gets worse.

The most important observation from the analysis of the results of the experiment 2 is that the number of neighbors and their correlation have a significant effect on the quality of recommendations: even if two users are interested in the same categories, we are able to produce good recommendations only if there is a strong association between them. This is probably due to the fact that behavioral profiles that classify a user as interested or not interested in a product category are not able to give information about the preferred items in a category. As a consequence, even if two users are interested in the same product category, their rates could be different and hence the prediction obtained by the system using their rates could be unreliable.

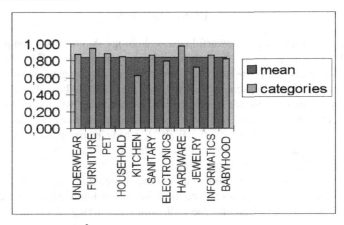

Figure 6. *U(PE)^2 F1-measure values for the 11 product categories*

GIOVANNI SEMERARO, MARIA FRANCESCA COSTABILE, STEFANO PAOLO
GUIDA, AND ORIANA LICCHELLI

Table 4. *Comparison UPE vs. U(PE)^2: mean value of MAE, NDPM and F1-measure*

MAE			NDPM			F1-measure		
UPE	U(PE)^2	|Diff.|	UPE	U(PE)^2	|Diff.|	UPE	U(PE)^2	|Diff.|
0.421	1.936	1.515	0.066	0.099	0.033	0.923	0.839	0.084

When we focus on performance issues (see Table 5), we find the main advantage of grouping users according to their behavioral profiles before computing recommendations: the total time requested by UPE to produce recommendation on the whole dataset of 380 users was 5h 47min, while the time requested by U(PE)^2 was 57min for computing recommendations and 1h 27min for classifying users into 11 categories. The total time for completing the process was 2h 24min.

Table 5. *Elapsed time for computing recommendations on 11 categories by U(PE)^2*

DATASET (Product Category)	COMPUTATION TIME(h.min.sec)
UNDERWEAR	0.06.23
FURNITURE	0.05.23
PET SUPPLIES AND PRODUCTS	0.05.45
HOUSEHOLD ARTICLES	0.05.38
KITCHEN UTENSILS	0.01.13
SANITARY ARTICLES	0.05.58
ELECTRONICS	0.04.21
HARDWARE	0.05.14
JEWELRY	0.05.55
INFORMATICS	0.05.19
BABYHOOD	0.05.54
AVG.	**0.05.21**

7. CONCLUSIONS

Recommender systems are a powerful new technology that allows a company to get additional value from its user database. These systems are rapidly becoming a crucial tool in e-commerce because they help the company by generating more sales, and conversely, they help users in finding items they want to buy. A real problem is that recommender systems are being stressed by the huge volume of user data in existing corporate databases, and will be stressed even more by the increasing volume of user data available on the Web. A strong research issue is to develop methods that can dramatically improve the scalability of recommender systems, still producing high-quality recommendations.

In this chapter, we have presented a new experimentally evaluated approach for collaborative-based recommender systems. It integrates knowledge about customers stored in behavioral profiles into the collaborative filtering algorithm in order to reduce the computational time required for generating the recommendation score of items.

The final goal of the work has been to identify some objective measures for evaluating the quality of recommendations a system provides to the users. For this purpose, we have presented a detailed analysis of a case study, the empirical evaluation of the $U(PE)^2$ hybrid recommender system. We have adopted metrics both to evaluate the goodness of the items' ranking and to evaluate the accuracy of the score prediction on a single item.

Our results have highlighted the actual improvement of the proposed hybrid approach with respect to a pure collaborative approach to recommendations. We can conclude that the proposed technique holds the promise of allowing collaborative-based algorithms to scale to large data sets, still producing high-quality recommendations.

8. REFERENCES

Andersen, V., Hansen, C.B., Andersen, H.H.K. (2001) *Evaluation of Agents and Study of End User needs and behaviour for E-commerce, COGITO Focus group experiment*, Risø-R-1264 (EN), CHMI-01-01, Risø National Laboratory, Roskilde, Denmark.

Burke, R. (2002) *Hybrid Recommender Systems: Survey and Experiments*. User Modeling and User-Adapted Interaction, Kluwer Academic Publishers, the Netherlands, 12, 331-370.

Balabanovic, M. and Shoham, Y. (1997) *Fab: Content-Based, Collaborative recommendation*. Communications of ACM, 40 (3), 66-72.

Breese, J.S., Heckerman, D., Kadie, C. (1998) *Empirical Analysis of Predictive Algorithms for Collaborative Filtering*. In Cooper, G. F., Moral, S. (Eds.): UAI '98: Proceedings of the Fourteenth Conference on Uncertainty in Artificial Intelligence, July 24-26, 1998, University of Wisconsin Business School, Madison, Wisconsin, USA. 43-52. Morgan Kaufmann.

Buono, P., Costabile, M. F., Guida, S., Piccinno, A. (2002) *Integrating User Data and Collaborative Filtering in a Web Recommendation Systems*. In Reich, S., Tzagarakis, M.M. and Debra, P.M.E. (Eds.), Hypermedia: Openness, Structural Awareness and Adaptivity, Lecture Notes in Computer Science, vol. 2266. 315-321. Springer, Berlin.

Frank, E. and Witten, I. (1998) *Generating accurate rule sets without global optimization*. In Shavlik, J. W. (Ed.): Proceedings of the Fifteenth International Conference on Machine Learning, July 24-27, 1998, Madison, Wisconson, USA. 144-151. Morgan Kaufmann.

Konstan, J. A., Riedl, J., Borchers, A. and Herlocker, J. L. (1998) *Recommender Systems: A GroupLens Perspective*. In Recommender Systems. Papers from 1998 Workshop. Technical Report WS-98-08. 60-64. AAAI Press.

Oard, D., and Kim, J. (1998) *Implicit Feedback for Recommender Systems*. In Kautz, H. (Ed.), Recommender Systems. In Proceedings of the AAAI Workshop on Recommender Systems, July 1998. AAAI Press.

Pazzani, M. (1999) *A Framework for Collaborative, Content-Based and Demographic Filtering*. Artificial Intelligence Review, 13 (5-6), 393-408.

Resnick, P. and Varian, H. R. (1997) *Recommender Systems*. Communications of the ACM, 40 (3), 56-58.

Ricci, F. and Del Missier, F. (2004) *Supporting Travel Decision Making Through Personalized Recommendation* In Karat, C.M., Blom, J., and Karat, J. (Eds.), Designing Personalized User Experiences for eCommerce, Kluwer.

Sarwar, B. M., Karypis, G., Konstan, J. and Riedl, J. (2002) *Recommender Systems for Large-Scale E-Commerce: Scalable Neighborhood Formation Using Clustering*. In Proceedings of the Fifth International Conference on Computer and Information Technology, December 2002, East West University, Bangladesh.

Schafer, J. B., Konstan, J. and Riedl, J. (1999) *Recommender Systems in E-Commerce.* In EC '99: Proceedings of the First ACM Conference on Electronic Commerce, November 3-5, 1999, Denver, CO. 158-166.

Sebastiani, F. (2002) *Machine Learning in Automated Text Categorization.* ACM Computing Surveys, 34 (1), 1–47.

Semeraro, G., Abbattista, F., Degemmis, M., Licchelli, O., Lops, P., Zambetta, F. (2003) *Agents and Personalisation for Developing Intelligent e-Business Applications.* In Corchuelo, R., Ruiz Cortés, A. and Wrembel, R. (Eds.), Technologies Supporting Business Solutions, Part IV: Data Analysis and Knowledge Discovery. Chapter 7, 163-186. Nova Sciences Books and Journals.

Semeraro, G., Andersen, H. H. K., Andersen, V., Lops, P. and Abbattista, F. (2003) *Evaluation and Validation of a Conversational Agent Embodied in a Bookstore.* In Carbonell, N. and Stephanidis, C. (Eds.)., Universal Access: Theoretica Perspectives, Practice and Experience, Lecture Notes in Computer Science, vol. 2615. 360-371. Springer, Berlin.

Shardanand, U., Maes, P., 1995. *Social Information Filtering: Algorithms for automating "word of mouth".* In Proceedings of the Conference on Human Factors in Computing Systems, May 7-11. 210-217, Denver, CO. ACM Press.

Terveen, L. and Hill, W. (2001) *Human-Computer Collaboration in Recommender Systems.* In J. Carroll (Ed.), Human Computer Interaction in the New Millenium. 223-242. Addison-Wesley, New York.

Tuzhilin, A. and Adomavicius, G. (1999) *Integrating user behaviour and collaborative methods in recommender systems.* In CHI' 99 Workshop on Interacting with Recommender Systems, May 1999, Pittsburgh, PA, USA.

Witten, I. H. and Frank, E. (1999). *Data Mining: Practical Machine Learning Tools and Techniques with Java Implementations.* Morgan Kaufmann Publishers, San Francisco.

Yao, Y. Y. (1995) *Measuring Retrieval Effectiveness Based on User Preference of Documents.* In Journal of the American Society for Information Science, 46 (2), 133–145.

EARL J. WAGNER AND HENRY LIEBERMAN

PERSONALIZED PRESENTATION OF POLICIES AND PROCESSES

1. INTRODUCTION

The web enables an organization to offer a unique interface to each of its customers. Personalization in e-commerce has traditionally focused on marketing products and services before a sale. By tracking a customer's purchases, software for personalization precisely identifies the customer's segment and offers narrowly focused product suggestions, through recommender systems, for instance. But what happens after the order is originally placed? A customer may have a problem with an ordered item and want to exchange it. Another customer may see an incorrect stock transfer and want to know its history across sites. In cases like these, there are further opportunities for personalized support beyond the original sale. The organization's policies themselves can be explained in reference to the customer's context. More importantly, the customer can benefit from personalized explanations of processes of the organizations with which he interacts.

2. CURRENT TECHNOLOGIES FOR CUSTOMER SERVICE

A customer's context changes in an important respect after performing an action, such as placing an order. Once the customer initiates the purchase, further interactions she has with the organization occur within the context of this ongoing process. A customer may want to switch a plane ticket depending upon the airline's policy but, in order to know what her options are, she must match the abstract policy description on the airline's web site with the concrete data of her purchase. Another individual may notice incorrect information about his status on his organization's intranet. To find out what happened, he may need to visit several pages to learn how it was set. To see the "big picture", he would have to understand the policies of his organization and determine how they were applied. A recent study by Jupiter Research noted that the more complex a product or service is, the more customers will value good support for it, with travel and financial services being among the most complex (Daniels, et. al. 2003). When something goes wrong, as in these

275

Clare-Marie Karat et al. (eds.), Designing Personalized User Experiences in eCommerce, 275—292.

cases, and customers' initial attempts to diagnose the problem fail, they contact an organization's customer support.

Even when it is effective, however, good customer support raises further problems. The customer has to spend time waiting on hold, provide identifying information and explain the problem (often to multiple people if it is escalated). All of this must take place before working with the customer support representative (CSR) to trouble-shoot the problem or even just discover what options there are for future action. From its perspective, the organization has to dedicate resources to a service with which customers are still often dissatisfied. Worst of all, the customer and CSR may spend time trying to diagnose a problem and discover that it was caused by a third-party. Then the customer has to start the process of diagnosis all over again with the other organization.

Most importantly, however, a perfect interaction with customer support by phone still lacks the benefits of a web-based interface. In order to resolve a problem, a customer must be sure to call during the hours support is offered, and have a block of uninterrupted time. The web, on the other hand, is always available and if some information is not immediately at hand, a decision can be postponed. Furthermore, it is often easier to understand complex information and learn procedures when they are presented graphically as well as with text (Mayer, 2001). A web site's slick presentation is wasted when the customer has to hear his options or receive instructions over the phone. In fact, all of the advantages of having information in a digital format are lost. With a digital version, the customer can see his options, save them for later, cut-and-paste them to a to-do list, print them out and so on.

Organizations have put a great deal of effort into developing sophisticated web sites for selling products and services. Recognizing the benefits of offering better support (and the associated opportunities for cross-selling and up-selling), many organizations have also invested in customer relationship management (CRM) systems for integrating and managing a customer's data. However, customer-facing interfaces for help remain fundamentally unchanged. One new trend is toward "customer self-service". Providing more sophisticated information and functionality on the web site is intended to enable customers to diagnose and resolve problems on their own. Because of the concept's appeal, it is expected that by 2005, more than 70% of customer service queries for information will be automated (Kolsky 2002a). Nevertheless, there is still a long way to go before the potential for self-service is realized. When facilities for self-service are offered, 46% of those who use them reported needing to complete inquiries via telephone, and only 26% found the information they sought (Kolsky, 2002b). Indeed, current tools for self-service continue to work at a somewhat superficial level. Information about policies is stored in a knowledge-base and found with a search engine. Alternately, detailed customer information is provided through billing and account applications. We can see the potential for improvement more clearly by focusing on these two technologies, knowledge-bases and account applications, that both reach deep into the organization.

In using a knowledge-base, the customer must search through a lot of explanations of policies and processes and determine which of them apply to the problem at hand. Why can't a customer simply ask "which of these apply to me?" Though organizations have records of their interactions with their customers, these records are not typically used to tailor the information they provide. For instance, whom the customer has to contact to modify a purchase that has already been made is only applicable after the customer makes a purchase. Information about making a new purchase is not considered useful when a customer is trying to resolve a problem with the current one. It's more helpful for a customer to see how an organization's policies apply to his case than to some arbitrary example. All of this is common-sense to people like customers and CSRs, but none of it is used to make the organization's web site help more effective.

The other important component of self-service is access to applications. A recent study found that three of the four most important features that customer look for in an online bank are self-service applications including online bank statements, transaction histories of 2 years or more, and the ability to change a billing address or stop payments on checks (Dhinsa, 2003). The study concluded that these services would maximize "real cost savings through contact-center productivity" and "provide experiences that deepen customer relationships over time".

An under-explored possibility exists for even more advanced self-service. When performing an action such as placing an order, a customer triggers a process that involves multiple parties, such as the vendor, the vendor's delivery service and the customer's bank. In a transaction like this one, the customer is the only entity that interacts with each of the others. Information that customers most desire from the vendor, such as updates on delivery delays (Daniels, et. al. 2003), often requires coordination among multiple sites. When sites don't have an existing relationship, important information cannot be provided. In conducting a study of web users, we found that most would like to be able to inspect a charge in their credit card transaction history to see the saved confirmation page for the purchase (Wagner, 2003). Supporting this feature, however, would depend upon either improbably close coordination among banks and vendors, or active information gathering on the customer's side. While the customer places the order, her steps would have to be recorded and the corresponding pages saved. After the purchase, these records would have to be matched with the appropriate charges in her transaction history at the bank. All of this would be tedious, if not overwhelming, for a person to perform. On the other hand, this painstaking work is a perfect fit for computer technology.

Software agents can act autonomously collect information about a user's transactions. An agent, working on the user's computer with the web browser, could automatically monitor the user's transactions and match them to pages in which relevant data appears, such as a credit card transaction history page. By inspecting the data, such as a charge, the entire record of the transaction could be accessed. A software agent acting in this way could offer an even greater level of personalization than any one site could by acting alone.

In the rest of this chapter we will further discuss these possibilities for personalization. We will see how policy information in knowledge-bases could be combined with a customer's account information to automatically generate "dynamic explanations" of their policies and the customer's options. We will then see how an agent can provide a "big picture" view of a customer's transactions, enabling him to more easily understand these processes and diagnose problems. First, however, we will discuss what both of these possibilities depend upon: a formal representation of an organization's policies and processes.

3. PERSONALIZATION THROUGH FORMAL PROCESSES

The promise of efficient, automated interactions among organizations through web-services is appealing. This has led to software vendors' development and standardization of languages for business processes including Business Process Execution Language for Web Services (BPEL4WS) and the Business Process Modelling Language (BPML). Formal descriptions of an organization's business policies and processes, at least the ones a customer interacts with, create new opportunities for help systems. Combining these descriptions with a customer's data enables the dynamic generation of explanations of the relevant policies involved. Examples within these "dynamic explanations" could illustrate a customer's options. Alternately, by sharing these descriptions in a standard format, the organization could enable its customers to compile the descriptions from multiple businesses and see an overall view of a process, even when it spans multiple sites. A customer could see the complete history of a purchase or other transaction and never have to bother with personally contacting each organization individually to assemble the record of the history. Of course, customers themselves are not likely to retrieve these descriptions themselves. Instead, we argue that a software agent, working with the web browser, could retrieve this information and help customers in diagnosing problems by themselves.

In the next section we will see how an organization's policies can be combined with a customer's data to more effectively explain the customer's options and even allow the customer to consider hypothetical cases that are difficult with current technology. We will then discuss an agent we've developed, Woodstein, that works with a user's browser to explain not just an organization's policies, but also the overall process a customer is involved in.

4. PERSONALIZED EXPLANATION OF POLICIES

Consider a situation recently faced by one of the authors. In planning a trip, he went to a discount airline's web site and ordered the cheapest ticket it offered for the dates he wanted to fly. A few days later, he realized that he'd have to arrive a day earlier. He wanted to know whether changing the ticket would be permitted, and what the associated costs or penalties would be. None of the information presented on his reservations page appeared relevant, however. He looked through the rest of the web site and found a policy web page that, if printed out, would be about twenty pages long. It described all possible options for all ticket types but, because he wasn't familiar with the details of his own ticket's category, he was still confused. He ended up calling customer support and asking for help. After waiting on hold, then explaining the situation to the CSR, he learned that he could change the ticket by paying an extra fee.

The customer would have preferred to quickly resolve the problem on the web, but had to resort to calling customer support for help. The most immediate problem was that the reservations page didn't explain his options involving the ticket. However, this page was designed for presenting just the information about his reservations in as simple a way as possible. From a design standpoint, presenting all possible policies for modifying reservations would be too cumbersome. On the other hand, the policy page was itself too unwieldy and it wasn't clear which policies were relevant. The situation might have been improved by including some information about the reservation options. However, we see the problem more broadly.

The essential problem is that abstract policies are difficult to understand. The customer knows about and can access his data. But it is often not clear how the customer's data interacts with the vendor's policies. What does it mean in relation to those policies? What options does the customer have? Policies are typically phrased as "When the customer purchased..." and "The customer has 14 days after..." Understanding these policies requires translating them into the customer's terms: "When you purchased..." and "You have until Thursday, May 29 to..." Figure 1 shows the set of policies for the customer's ticket class.

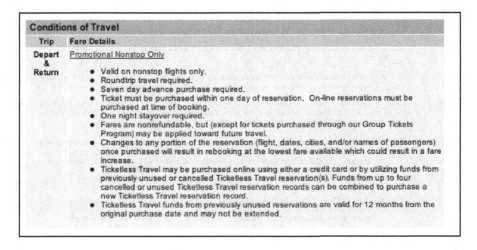

Figure 1. *Policies without Personalized Explanations*

Figure 2 shows the ticket policies supplemented with explanations computed from data about customer including information about his ticket. With an interface like this one, he could more easily understand the options and restrictions for the particular ticket he selected. Further, he could compare the policies associated with other types of tickets without having to figure them out for himself by re-calculating all of the data, such as dates or prices. Today, customers either piece together these explanations themselves, or receive them through customer support.

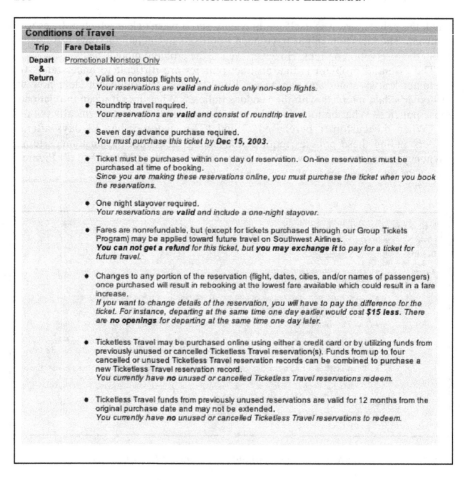

Figure 2. *Policies with Personalized Explanations*

Helping people learn about abstract concepts has been a focus in work on intelligent tutoring systems (ITSs) at the intersection of research in artificial intelligence (AI) and education (Forbus and Feltovich, 2001). An ITS explains the concepts of an area like algebra or physics and then gives the student problems to solve. It keeps track of information about the student, including the principles she has learned and those she still finds difficult. Based on this profile, it selects problems that best challenge her and further develop her understanding of the area.

Unlike learning in an academic environment, however, the type of learning that a customer is engaged in is extremely pragmatic and focused entirely on the problem at hand - completely different from the situation of a student studying algebra, for instance. A customer is interested in reaching his goals primarily and not in learning about the principles, in this case, the organization's abstract policies. Yet this is exactly what many organizations' web-sites demand. The customer had to find his concrete data, his ticket type, and match it with an abstract policy of the organization, its rule on exchanging tickets, in order to discover his options for satisfying his goal of changing his ticket.

Formal descriptions of policies offer the possibility of dynamically generated explanations like the ones above. Today, we have dynamically-generated data pages, such as the page the customer saw explaining his flight reservations. In the future, we will have dynamically-generated policy pages, in which policies are explained with examples featuring a customer's up-to-date data. Customers could use these examples to explore hypothetical possibilities such as "which ticket would I have to buy in order to be able to change the dates without penalties?", and later "how do I change the departure date for my ticket", or more generally, "what policies are active for the ticket I bought?"

This approach can enable more intimate personalization even beyond the context of the current purchase. In future purchases, the web site might remember that the customer had invoked particular policies in the past and highlight the items that provide the flexibility he may require. In our example, the system would note in the customer's profile that he had changed the dates for his reservation. For a future ticket purchase, it might suggest that he may want to select among the types of tickets that offer that as an option and present these ticket types more prominently.

This is exactly the sort of help the customer would receive from a good human agent. By combining representations of the organization's policies with the user's profile and account information, the web site could provide sophisticated recommendations and explanations both before and after the sale.

One possible concern with this approach would involve the privacy of the customer's data. Concerns about the privacy often focus on how user data is collected and how it is shared. In this case, data the user has already shared with the organization is used to generate explanations. Since this interaction only involves the organization and customer, no new problems are created.

Within an organization's systems, processes arise from interacting policies. For processes as well as policies, customers seek relevant information: "what happened in my case?", "how did my account get this status?", "what's going on here?" Customers can benefit from explanations of these processes, even when they don't have experience with formal representations of processes. Instead of interacting with these representations directly, they could turn to a software agent playing a role like that of a human agent that explains how a customer's data interacts with a vendor's policies and processes.

5. PERSONALIZED PRESENTATION OF PROCESSES WITH WOODSTEIN

Woodstein is a software agent that works with a user's web browser to answer questions like "how did that data get that value?" "why did that happen?" and "what's happening now?". It monitors a user's actions on the web, such as browsing an online retailer and adding items to a shopping cart, to create a record of the user's overall process, in this case, making a purchase. It is then able to answer questions about the history and current status of the process, as well as how data in the process was set.

Woodstein matches a user's actions to the steps of an abstract model for the process. Through this recognition behavior, it knows to look for more information about the process on other web pages and web sites, even if the user never visited them. By watching the user select a credit card and shipper for a purchase, Woodstein knows to go to the sites of the bank and shipper to retrieve the status of the purchase, including whether it has been paid for and delivered.

Later, when the user is looking at other pages with data about the process, such as the credit card transactions history page, the charge itself can be inspected. The history of the purchase process can be accessed and reviewed, making it convenient to understand the context of the data, the charge.

Woodstein explains the history of the data and actions of the user's process through multiple views. One view shows the history of a process and allows the user to revisit any point. When inspecting a data item, another view displays an automatically generated audit trail for it, enabling the user to jump among pages in which it appears. The user can inspect the charge amount in the transactions page and, in one click, view a saved copy of the order confirmation page featuring the purchase total.

In addition to providing views on the history of processes and data,   Woodstein also provides help in diagnosing problems when something goes wrong. When the user notices that something doesn't "look right", he can easily notify the agent. Woodstein responds by producing the record of the user's process of investigation. Through this assistance, the user is able to complain about the exact step or data that caused the error or created the unexpected result.

Woodstein's features can best be understood through an example. In the next section we will see how Woodstein:
- supports direct inspection of information in pages, when the user wants to know more about data and processes presented within them,
- explains the history of processes and data, through easily-understood views that visualize their relationships,
- shows all pages related to a user's action, including relevant pages retrieved by Woodstein that contain more information.

Problems arise because of mistakes by either the user or the web site, or because the user has an incorrect mental model of the process. It is important that the agent provides help in all cases, because when a problem symptom is found, it is not known what the source of the problem is or whether there even is a problem.

6. INSPECTING A PROCESS WITH WOODSTEIN

In this example we will see how Woodstein can support an individual accessing information on his organization's intranet. Although it could apply equally well to a company employee examining his health benefits, or his stock options plan, we will focus on a masters' student intending to graduate from the institute he attends. The student was sure to add himself to the list of graduating students earlier in the semester and he knows he's completed all other requirements for graduation. He knows that sometimes there are bureaucratic mistakes, however, so he goes online and checks the student information web site to verify that everything is OK. Upon loading the graduated degree audit page, however, he sees that everything is not OK; it appears he's not eligible to graduate (Figure 3).

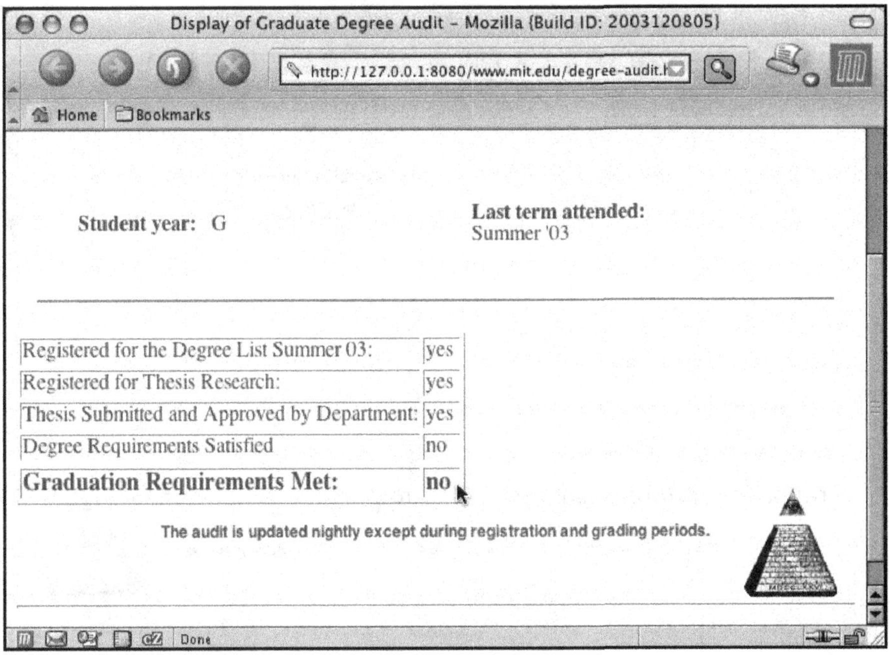

Figure 3. *Viewing the graduation degree audit page*

The user would like to know why he's not eligible. More specifically, he'd like to know what particular requirement was not satisfied and caused him to become ineligible. It looks like his degree requirements weren't satisfied, but that is still too general and he'd like to narrow down the problem even more. Without Woodstein, he'd have to contact the institute's administration then perhaps be told that he'd have to talk to his academic department, or some other unit for more information. With Woodstein, he is able to interact with the data item directly. While the user browses, Woodstein adds its icon to every page he sees. Now the user wants to inspect the graduation eligibility data directly, so he turns on Woodstein's inspector by clicking on the icon (Figure 4)

For every data item it found when analyzing the page, Woodstein converts the text of the item to a button. The user moves the cursor to the "no" button to the right of "Graduation Requirements Met" and presses down, causing its menu to appear (Figure 5).

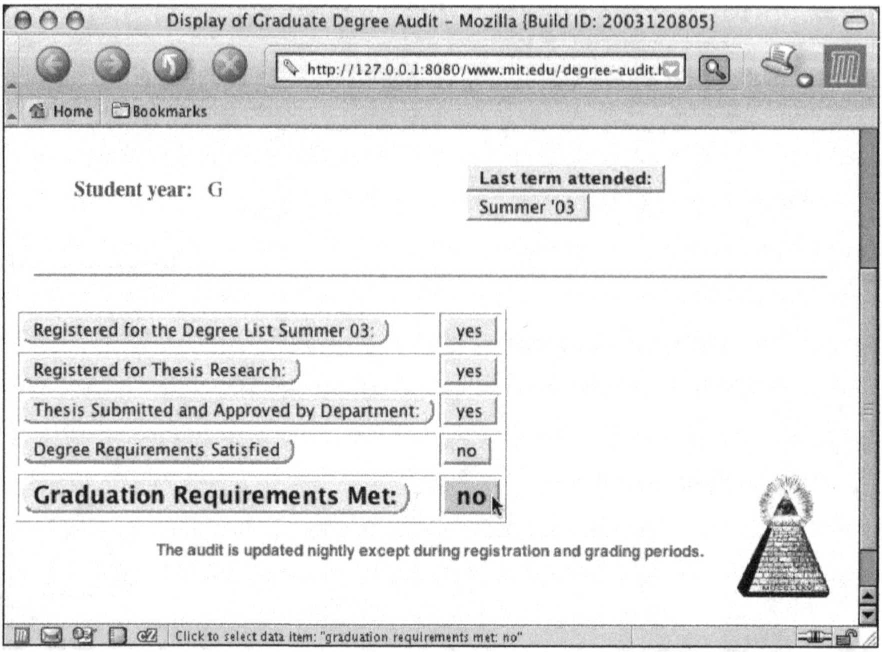

Figure 4. *Inspecting the graduation degree audit page with Woodstein*

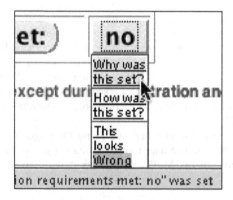

Figure 5. *Inspecting the "graduation requirements met: no" data item*

The student wants to know why his graduation requirements were not met, or in other words, why the "graduation requirements met" data item was set to "no", so he selects "why was this set?" Woodstein opens a new window to show the history of how the data item was set (Figure 6).

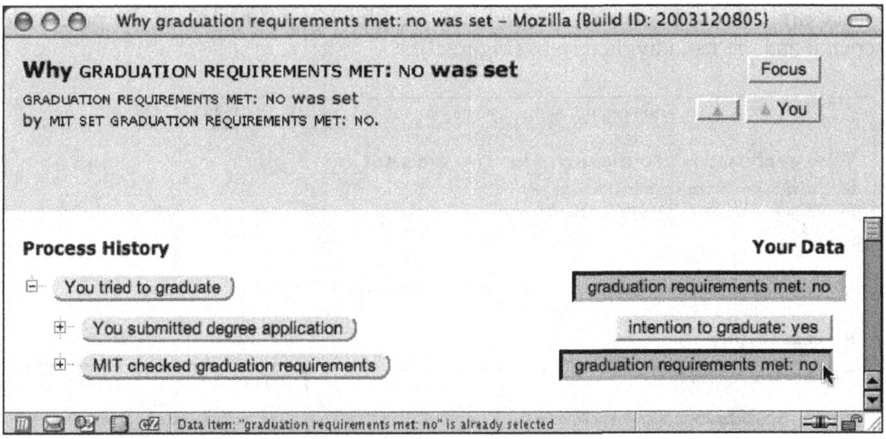

Figure 6. *Viewing why "graduation requirements met" was set to "no"*

This new window is Woodstein's "process history" view. It shows the history of the student's attempt to graduate with English descriptions of the processes and data involved. The top frame, in grey, explains some of the context of the data item he inspected. It was set as the result of the process: "Institute set graduation requirements". Below the top frame is a tree with the structured history showing the student's actions in attempting to graduate and the Institute's reactions. On the left are the steps of the process, while on right is the student's data resulting from the processes.

The student originally expressed his intention to graduate by submitting his application for an advanced degree. Woodstein created this record in response to that action. It re-constructed the steps in computing his graduation eligibility taken by both this site and other sites on the institute's intranet. Now the student is able to view the record to see what went wrong.

Woodstein manages "representations", or "reps" for both data and processes on the web. Data items include prices, quantities, and, as in this case, boolean values such as "yes" or "no". Processes are either user actions or web-site reactions. They have data items as inputs and set a single data item as a result. Whenever a data item appears in a page, as with the data item the student selected, Woodstein converts the actual data value, "no", to a rectangular button corresponding to the data and the label "graduation requirements met:" to a rounded button for the process that set the data item. Processes and data appear as buttons in Woodstein's views and any button can be inspected by pressing the mouse button down to choose from its menu, or by just clicking on it to select it. Since the student just interacted with the "graduation requirements met: no" data item, it is the currently selected rep described by the view; unlike other buttons, it appears pressed-in.

In looking at the process history tree, the student sees that he tried to graduate, but was unable. He sees that in the first step of this process he submitted his degree application. Woodstein confirms that this was successful because the site recognized his intention to graduate. The next step, the site's reaction, does not appear successful. To find out why, he clicks on the plus-box to the left of the process to open it and see its individual steps (Figure 7).

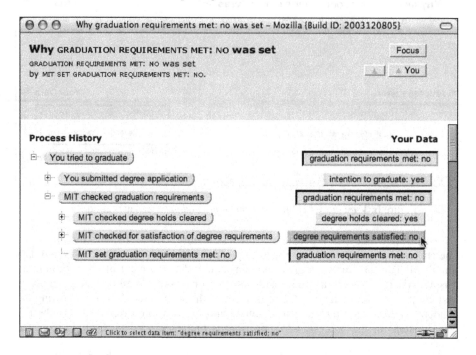

Figure 7. *Looking at the graduation requirements*

He can see that the institute checked whether any holds on his degree were cleared, and finds that they were. He also sees that his degree requirements were checked but that those requirements were not met. Because they were not met, his overall graduation requirements were not met. He clicks on the triangle to open the process of checking his degree requirements to find out more (Figure 8).

He sees that although his subject requirements were satisfied, and his residency requirement was satisfied, his thesis requirements were not satisfied, so he opens the corresponding process. "Drilling-down" even further, he discovers that his thesis title had not been provided (Figure 9).

Clicking on a rep's button causes Woodstein to load its saved page for the rep. The student clicks on "Institute checked if thesis title has been provided" to see the page Woodstein found that describes the rule (Figure 10). The student knows that he satisfied all of the details of this requirement, so he goes back to process history view and selects the "thesis title provided: no" data item. Its saved page is the page where it first appeared (Figure 11).

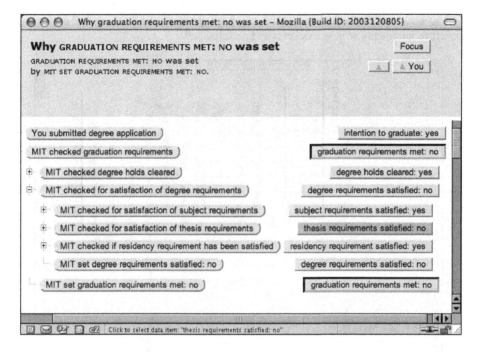

Figure 8. *Looking at the degree requirements*

The student knows that there is some problem, but this is as far as he can go. At this point, he wants to complain about the data item, so he presses down on it to bring up its menu and he selects "This looks Wrong" (Figure 12).

Woodstein creates a new mail window with an automatically generated complaint indicating the data item that looks wrong and the page that it appears on, as well as the student's path in finding it (Figure 13). The student could customize this email before sending it and re-submit his thesis title, for instance.

In this scenario we have seen how Woodstein can help a user inspect a data item in a page to see the overall process that includes it. With the steps of the process organized hierarchically, the user is able to drill down to quickly find the individual requirement that is not met. Finally, Woodstein enabled the user to easily generate a complaint about the incorrect data item.

In some cases, as with the policies of the airline in the previous example, a single site manages all of the user's relevant data and can generate a detailed list of how its policies apply to the user. In other cases, a site generates results using data received from multiple sites. In this case, the institute's administration had some information in about the student, and received some from the student's department, the library, health department, and others. Woodstein can play an important role here by compiling this information for the user and allowing him to see the overall history for the process and the role his data plays. Although a site can generate explanations about a limited set of policies, by presenting the process history, Woodstein enables the user to see the processes involving any of his data. Applied to the domain of airline tickets, Woodstein would enable the user to see the process that caused some fee to be added to his ticket as well as the page in which the fee is described, or the exact requirements of how a ticket may be exchanged.

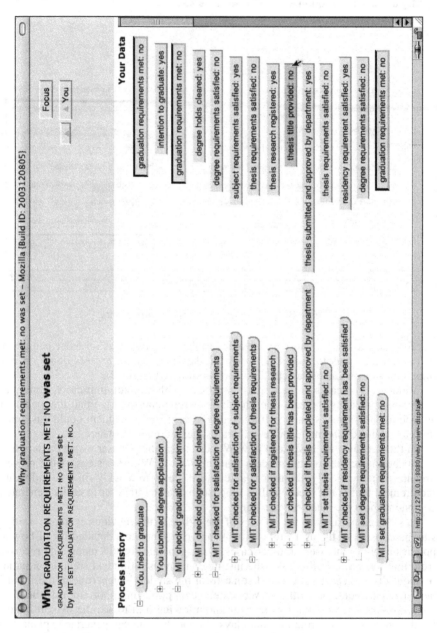

Figure 9. *Finding the unmet requirement*

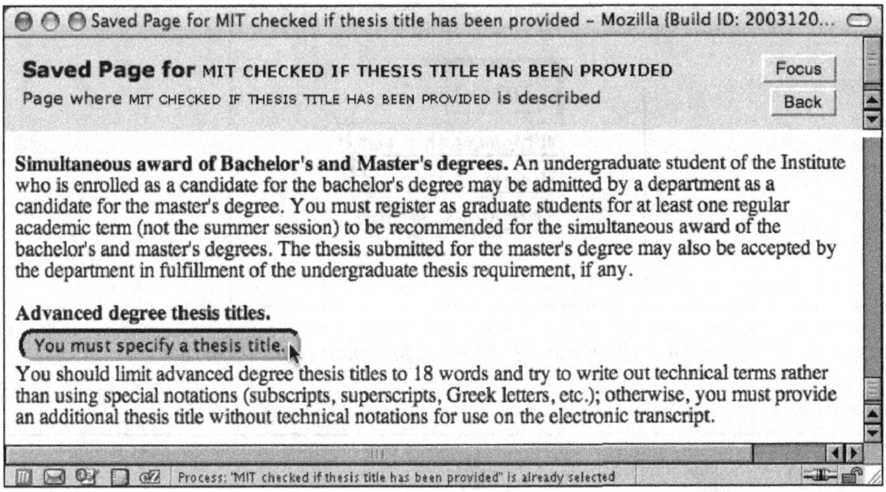

Figure 10. *Viewing the requirement that a thesis title be specified*

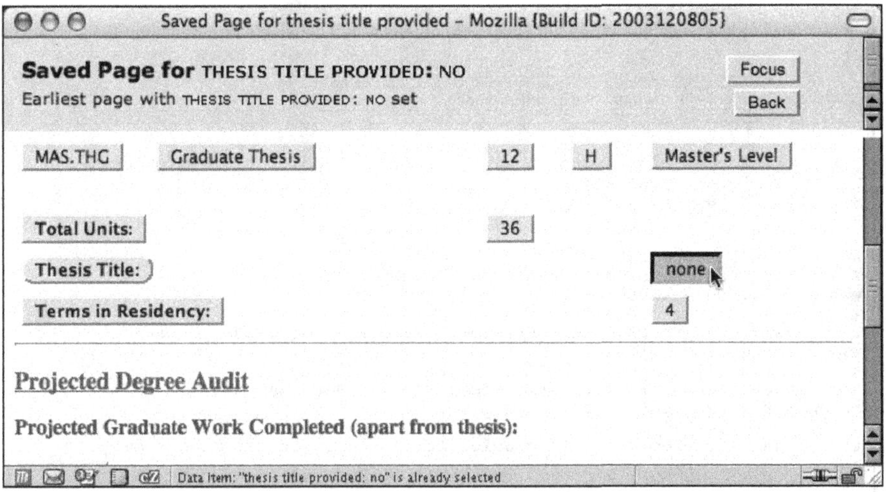

Figure 11. *Viewing the page with the incorrect requirement*

none
Why was this set?
How was this set?
This looks Wrong

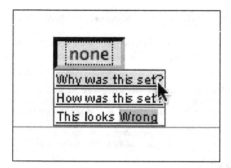

Figure 12. *Noting that the requirement looks incorrect*

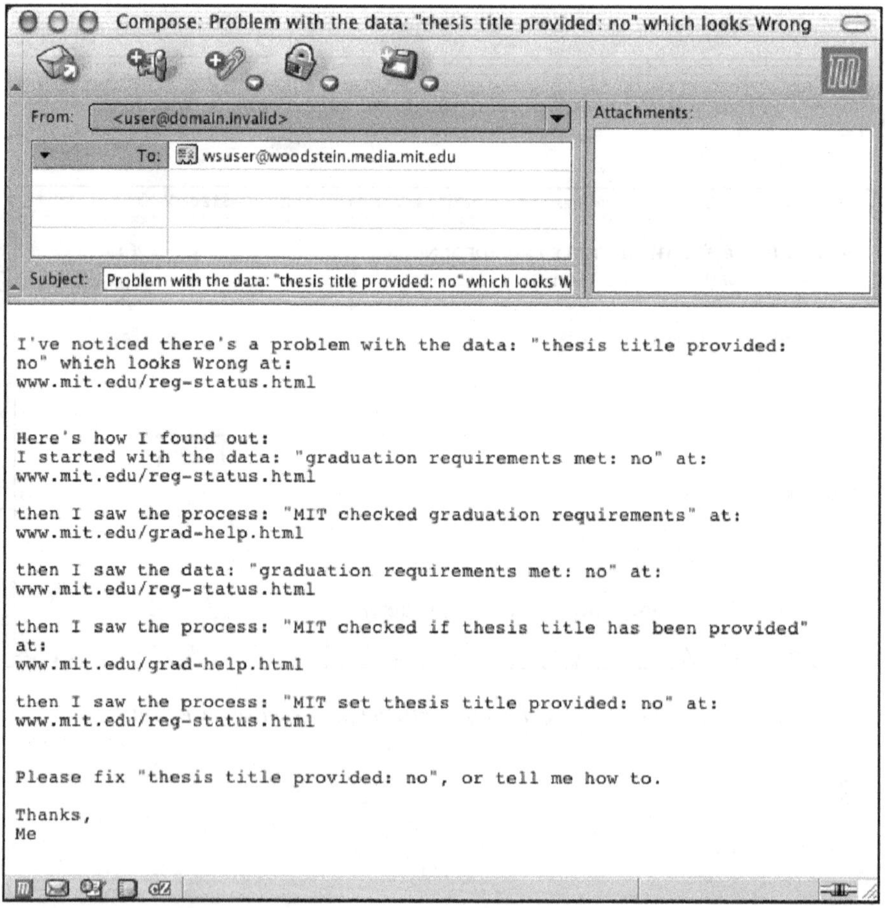

Compose: Problem with the data: "thesis title provided: no" which looks Wrong
From: <user@domain.invalid>
Attachments:
To: wsuser@woodstein.media.mit.edu
Subject: Problem with the data: "thesis title provided: no" which looks W
I've noticed there's a problem with the data: "thesis title provided: no" which looks Wrong at:
www.mit.edu/reg-status.html
Here's how I found out:
I started with the data: "graduation requirements met: no" at:
www.mit.edu/reg-status.html
then I saw the process: "MIT checked graduation requirements" at:
www.mit.edu/grad-help.html
then I saw the data: "graduation requirements met: no" at:
www.mit.edu/reg-status.html
then I saw the process: "MIT checked if thesis title has been provided" at:
www.mit.edu/grad-help.html
then I saw the process: "MIT set thesis title provided: no" at:
www.mit.edu/reg-status.html
Please fix "thesis title provided: no", or tell me how to.
Thanks,
Me

Figure 13. *Complaining about the incorrect requirement*

7. DETAILS OF WOODSTEIN'S OPERATION

Woodstein is implemented as a web proxy that stands between the user's browser and the web. It tracks user requests for pages, then analyzes and annotates the pages received, adding JavaScript to controls such as links to track user actions. It matches these actions through plan recognition to process descriptions in its library, such as a description including the steps of a purchase. It then instantiates this description to represent the data and sub-processes of the overall process. The agent simulates and verifies web site reactions and user data by autonomously retrieving related pages indicated by the process descriptions. Its views of process and data history are generated from the processes and data it represents.

Woodstein is a "proof-of-concept" system intended to demonstrate how the sorts of higher-level interactions with web pages and processes could be supported. More work would be required, however, to make it robust enough for everyday use. Importantly, it accepts generic process models for any processes associated with web pages, not just purchases. Examples in the domains we have discussed such as viewing the history of a credit card purchase and following the stock purchase and transfers have been accommodated with this approach.

Beyond Woodstein's applicability to multiple domains is the issue of the generality of its support within a domain. The current version of Woodstein requires specific models for particular complex actions. The graduation example illustrated a process particular to an organization, and information in pages related to the process are annotated. More common processes, such as purchases, could be described in a generic way. Thus an important area of future research is to extend Woodstein to both support these generic descriptions, and robustly extract information from unannotated web pages for common processes like these, perhaps even allowing end-users to train it to track simple processes.

Woodstein raises some issues regarding the privacy and security of a user's data. Additionally, there is the concern about the actions the agent performs on the user's behalf. Anticipating the last concern, we designed Woodstein to only perform information-gathering activities, such as logging-into and retrieving data from user accounts. It does not perform purchases or any other actions on behalf of the user, though scripting these activities is another area for future research. Woodstein also does not share a user's data with anyone other than the user; its role is to compile and integrate the user's data. One could imagine that sharing this information in a standard way might be useful to the user when he consults a CSR with her own copy of Woodstein. The user could say he investigated only so far into the processes of the organization, and the CSR could continue and inspect the processes more deeply. However, this too remains unexplored. Finally, there is the question of how secure the integrated user data is. We note that this data can be just as secure as user-names and passwords saved with the web browser. Security was not an explicit focus, though, and the potentially increased risks associated with integrating a user's data are unknown.

8. CONCLUSION

Research on personalization in e-commerce has often focused on marketing products and services to customers prior to a sale. Meanwhile, organizations have become interested in using the web to enable customers to solve their own problems. In this chapter, we have argued for greater personalization in self-service, both in explaining an organization's policies in the context of the customer's own data, and in enabling an agent working on behalf of the customer to collect and integrate information about his actions online.

We believe these techniques can provide help beyond just the domain of sales. As we noted before, people are often faced with abstract policies that make sense only when applied in concrete cases, preferably their own. They stand to benefit from clearer explanations from the organizations they interact with. These can include illustrations of the rules associated with an employee's benefits or, as we saw, even the processes involved in determining an individual's status within the organization. More broadly, there are many domains in which end-users can benefit from being able to inspect the history of information that affects them, such as, for instance, notations on their credit reports. All of this begins by combining user data with representations of organization policies for the users' benefit.

9. REFERENCES

Daniels, D., Matiesanu, C. and Schatsky, D. (2003) *Jupiter Consumer Survey Report: The State of Customer Service, 2003.* Jupiter Research.

Dhinsa, R. (2003) *Self-service: The New Category of Services to Facilitate the Adoption of Online Banking.* Jupiter Research.

Forbus, K. and Feltovich, P. (2001) *Smart Machines in Education.* AAAI Press.

Kolsky, E. (2002) *Is Self-Service the Panacea?* Gartner, Inc.

Kolsky, E. (2002) *The Six Steps for Web Self-Service in Customer Service.* Gartner, Inc.

Mayer, R. (2001) *Multimedia Learning.* Cambridge University Press.

Wagner, E. (2003) *Woodstein: A Web Interface Agent for Debugging E-Commerce.* MIT M.S. Thesis.

MARKUS STOLZE AND MICHAEL STRÖBEL

RECOMMENDING AS PERSONALIZED TEACHING

Towards Credible Needs-based eCommerce Recommender Systems

1. INTRODUCTION

Recommender applications are an important technology for online retailers who want to increase their sales by providing potential consumers with personalized product recommendations. Such interactive Business-To-Consumer (B2C) eCommerce systems help to convert browsers into buyers, increase cross sells, and build loyalty (Kobsa et al., 2001). Studies indicate that eCommerce sites that offer personalization convert twice as many visitors into buyers than sites that do not offer personalization (ICONOCAST, 1999, cited in Fink & Kobsa, 2000).

A typical recommender system comprises functionalities for product navigation and decision support. Today, several approaches exist (for an overview see Kobsa et al., 2001) to support a consumer in navigating through the product space of an electronic shop. From a historical perspective the early techniques modeled conventional paper-based catalogues, whereas the second generation of navigation aids introduced advanced search capabilities. Advanced B2C eCommerce systems aim to provide shoppers with an efficient and personalized shopping experience. Today, many of the technologies needed for building such systems are available as commercial software components. These include components for user profile management, rule-based content adaptation, product recommendations based on collaborative-filtering algorithms, and preference-based catalog search. A central question for developers of such advanced eCommerce systems is how to best use and combine these components. One of the design decisions is whether user profiles should be stored over multiple sessions, what functionality for profile management to provide to users, and which parts of the profile to re-use for a returning customer. Ricci and Del Missier (this volume), for example, base catalog queries on information gathered in the current session, and use stored profile information only for sorting the result set. Elsewhere (Stolze & Ströbel, 2001a) we have proposed a framework that allows users to manage and re-use multiple profiles relating to different roles. Here we focus on a different design issue, namely whether (and how) systems recommending technical products can benefit from querying potential

293

Clare-Marie Karat et al. (eds.), Designing Personalized User Experiences in eCommerce, 293—313.

buyers about their high-level needs instead of focusing exclusively on product features.

The potential of needs-based recommendation has been identified by a number of authors. Based on an analysis of interactions between buyers and human shopping assistants in real shops Grenci and Todd (2002) argued that consumers with limited knowledge of a product domain should be approached in a "solutions-driven" manner, which focuses on customers' needs instead of product features. This analysis is in line with observations made by Ardissono and Goy (2000) who found that people with limited domain knowledge searching for home phones feel well supported if they are presented with qualitative (instead of technical) product information.

However, there is also evidence of limited benefit of needs-based product recommendation of complex technical products. A recent study (Felix et al., 2001) showed that most consumers want to inspect technical features (e.g. the pixel resolution of a digital camera) in detail before they feel confident about their choice. These results are in line with observations reported by Spiekermann and Parachiv (2002), who found that consumers who perceived higher uncertainty preferred to perform a manual inspection of technical features, instead of relying on the (needs-based) recommendations by an automated shopping agent. The needs-based support was perceived by consumers as a service that helps them to obtain a short list of products quickly. It was not perceived as a recommendation that can be trusted without further inspection.

Closer investigation of the needs-based recommendation components in the two studies reveals that both employ the entered customer needs to compute a "match score" for each of the digital cameras in the catalog. Neither system, however, shows the user the numeric score nor how this score was computed from the base data. We believe that it is this lack of transparency that keeps users from perceiving the recommender system as being credible (Fogg, 2002). As a result users prefer the feature-based style of navigation where the relationship between their stated requirements (ranges of acceptable feature values) and the provided product descriptions is obvious.

The reported preference for automatic, needs-based components early on in the decision-making process, but for manual, feature-based exploration later in the process can be interpreted such that users feel insecure about what product features they should look for to accommodate their particular needs. Performing a needs-based session first lets them arrive at a set of products that prototypically show the range of feature values that match the stated needs.

We believe that users regarded the main benefit of the needs-based recommendation component to be that it provided them with contextualized information about what kind of products match their stated needs. However, simply listing examples without explaining why a given product fulfills the stated needs has two main disadvantages. First, customers have to form their own (possibly false) explanations of how their stated needs influenced the evaluation. Second, customers apparently feel that, without an explanation, they have no way to evaluate the appropriateness and credibility of the recommendations. This situation can be changed by providing customers with a comprehensible explanation of how the stated needs determine the way products are evaluated. The importance of providing explanations in eCommerce recommender systems has been discussed by Herlocker et al. (2000), who studied methods for generating explanations for systems using collaborative filtering mechanisms. Explanation methods derived from that work are now in operation at the Amazon Internet store (www.amazon.com). The importance of system transparency for fostering user trust has also been shown by empirical studies (Sinha & Swearingen, 2002; Zimmerman & Kurapati, 2002). Given these empirical results we conclude that an essential ingredient for enhancing consumer confidence will be to enable consumer learning by providing a guided transition from a needs- to a feature-oriented interaction.

In this paper we present an approach for interactive B2C eCommerce systems that support the required guided transition from a needs- to a feature-oriented interaction. The approach distinguishes between a model level and a system level (see Figure 1). On the model level, this approach suggests novel elements for the user and product representation to specifically address the learning aspect in the user conversation. On the system level, we introduce a needs-oriented, guided preference construction technique based on modeling an expected target group membership.

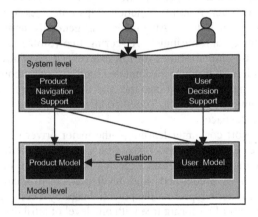

Figure 1. *Conceptual system overview.*

To demonstrate the application aspects of our approach, we continue to use the familiar example of shopping for a digital camera online. The remainder of this paper is organized as follows: in Section 2 the overall rationale and specific elements of the underlying user and product model are introduced. Section 3 then presents the different phases of the suggested product navigation and decision support approach. In Sections 4 and 5, technical aspects in these phases are explained in more detail. Section 6 outlines our prototype implementation. Finally, section 8 concludes this paper with a discussion of related approaches.

In summary, this paper proposes a new computational framework for credible needs-based eCommerce recommender systems. Instead of giving the user "expert advice" we aim to provide users with a personalized learning experience that supplies them with the information they need to decide and to convince themselves about what product best matches their current needs.

2. USER AND PRODUCT MODEL

For the following conceptual overview we assume the existence of an eCommerce system and define the potential consumers to be users of this system, who interact with the system through navigation aids.

Our approach focuses on attribute-based navigation. Within this navigation paradigm, the navigation options are driven by characteristics of the currently viewed product information, and not, for instance, by characteristics of the user's cluster as in collaborative filtering (Schafer et al., 2001). For attribute-based navigation, a model of the respective product domain is necessary that provides representations of the product information and user preferences. These representations are then used to support the consumer in navigating through the products of the online shop.

Typically, multi-attribute utility theory (Keeney & Raiffa, 19976) is used to represent the satisfaction that a person will get from a variety of different outcomes, such as buying a product. A utility function maps outcomes to utilities, which are values on a scale from 0 to 1. An outcome is generally assumed to consist of different values for certain attributes. A scoring tree (Stolze, 2000) with multiple levels of criteria assessing attributes (or lower-level criteria) allows the hierarchical aggregation of utilities to produce a cumulated score for an outcome. In our example scenario, the outcomes are digital cameras and their attributes are camera features such as pixel resolution and weight. Together, all outcomes and their attribute values represent the product space.

In order to support consumer learning—the major driver of our approach—the generic scoring tree evaluation model has to be extended in the following sense: we focus on the potential needs for, and expected benefits from, the desired product, and represent them as predefined, high-level product evaluation criteria in the scoring tree. These criteria represent the potential uses by a consumer.

These uses are part of a scoring tree with one level of attributes and two levels of criteria: a higher layer of potential uses, and a lower layer of feature preferences, which assess the attribute values of the products through utility functions (see Figure 2). Please note that one attribute can be assessed by multiple feature criteria (see for example the "battery size" attribute in Figure 2), and that one feature criterion might contribute to several uses.

In our model, every consumer is represented by an initial evaluation structure (scoring tree) based on uses, which includes default weights. In the course of an interaction, this model is customized for the interacting consumer.

The hierarchical structure of the model allows a system to explain to a consumer why a product can be recommended for a specific use. If a product achieves a high score for a specific use, the recommendation can be drilled down to the dominant features contributing the highest values or having the highest importance. The other direction is equally possible. Consumers can inspect the evaluation structure from the bottom, and investigate what specific uses a feature might have. Overall, this results in a homogeneous utility model that allows uses to be mapped to features and vice versa.

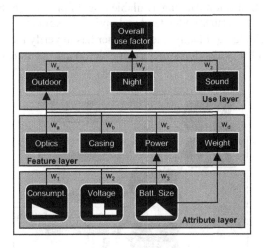

Figure 2. *Example of a scoring tree.*

Our user and product model is complemented with the notion of target groups. Target groups represent a cluster of consumers with a common evaluation structure. Examples of target groups in the domain of digital cameras are professionals (press or studio photographers), trend sport enthusiasts (snowboarders, mountain bikers), and new parents. In addition, a target group is associated with certain delight features. New parents may typically be delighted by an audio-recording feature, which allows them, for instance, to record the first words their child speaks.

In the next section, we will explain how these target groups and their associated delight features, together with the layered evaluation structure, constitute the foundation for our user-decision and product-navigation support functionalities.

3. USER INTERACTION OVERVIEW

In a complex eCommerce decision-making environment, individuals are, due to limited cognitive resources, often unable to evaluate extensively all possible alternatives before making a final decision. According to consumer decision-making theory complexity is reduced with a two-stage process where the depth of information processing varies by stage (Payne et al., 1988). First, the consumer screens the set of products for the most promising candidates. Then, the resulting "consideration set" is evaluated in more depth.

To create an electronic decision-making environment and to focus on the learning aspects in the process, we propose that this staged model be refined into seven phases, which emphasize three main aspects (see Figure 3) of the interaction:

- Preference discovery: First the consumer needs to formalize her potential uses of a product, maybe discover additional uses, and learn how features relate to these uses.
- Preference optimization: Having available a set of preferences based on features, the consumer can further understand and optimize evaluation criteria.
- Preference debugging: Finally, the consumer has to verify the completeness and correctness of the evaluation structure in order to gain confidence in the final choice.

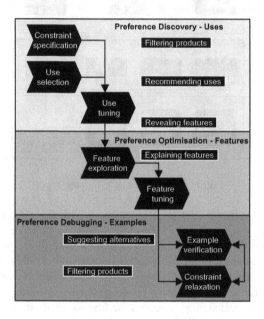

Figure 3. *Phases of user interaction.*

Figure 3 also shows (as black boxes) the various means of navigation and decision support that are necessary for our approach, e.g. the functionality to filter products or to recommend uses (see below).

4. PREFERENCE DISCOVERY

During preference discovery the system aids consumers in discovering their buying preferences by providing support for specifying needs (technical constraints and expected uses), learning about additional uses, and understanding the relation of product features to uses.

4.1 Constraint specification

Our assumption is that initially, before even entering a shop, every consumer will have one or more constraints for the product in mind. Typically this is a maximum price or price range, but it could also be a mandatory feature or a condition such as "no products from company X".

In our approach such hard criteria are defined as constraints on product attribute values, which constitute the input for a filtering process. The filtering process rules out unsuitable candidates from the search space that fail to fulfill these constraints (e.g. because they are too expensive). This is the first element of a screening stage in the general decision-making process mentioned above.

At the beginning of the conversation, these constraints have to be thoroughly respected by the virtual salesperson, whereas at a later stage in the conversation these constraints may be violated—either because the consumer learned more about the product space or because the system tries to verify the consumer's evaluation structure.

In our approach, constraint specification is not mandatory. A consumer can always decide to use no initial constraints and proceed to the next phase, use selection.

4.2 Use selection

After the optional specification of constraints, the consumer has to select the potential uses for the desired product. In this phase we present to the consumer the most important uses for the product as represented in the higher layer of the general user model. The consumer can then select as many possible uses as desired. Examples of uses in our scenario are "for taking pictures at night" or "for traveling".

Having an initial use profile available, the system can determine the consumer's degree of membership to one of the predefined target groups. The use profile available for this group, including importance ratings for the various uses, can then be presented to the consumer. This profile might contain additional uses that were not initially presented to the consumer for selection (e.g. "for recording sound"). It is up to the consumer to ignore these proposals.

4.3 Use tuning

In this phase, the user can select or deselect uses and modify importance ratings for uses. Unselected uses are removed from the scoring tree. Depending on the active selection (the current use profile), one highly recommended product is determined by the system and presented as an example to the consumer (see the prototype scenario in Section 6).

This highly recommended product achieves the highest score (use factor) on the basis of the consumer's current use profile (taking into account the defined constraints). The consumer can modify her use profile as often as desired and monitor the corresponding changes in the recommendation.

Furthermore, the consumer has the option to inspect the highly recommended product with regard to its specific appropriacy (score) for certain uses. This explanation functionality fosters learning in that the consumer can inspect how use criteria relate to feature criteria in the evaluation structure and thereby derive knowledge such as "this camera is highly recommended for taking baby pictures because it has very good usability and the casing is very sturdy". This explanation capability increases the credibility of the system by allowing the user to understand the way the system evaluates products and arrives at recommendations.

If the user feels satisfied about the state of her use profile or is curious to learn more about the product candidates, the conversation can proceed from the use level to the feature level in order to optimize the evaluation structure.

5. PREFERENCE OPTIMIZATION AND DEBUGGING

In this section we briefly outline the interaction phases and support functionalities for optimizing and debugging the consumer's preferences.

5.1 Feature exploration and tuning

After the preference discovery process, all attributes and attribute values of the current highly recommended product are exposed to the consumer together with the feature criteria assessing these attributes. In order to focus on features only, the higher layer of uses is removed from the presentation. To remove the higher level, the importance ratings of the current use profile are propagated to the feature evaluation level by multiplying feature weights with their associated use weights. Now the consumer can optimize her feature profile by adjusting feature weights or even modifying attribute utility functions.

At any time the consumer can go back to the use selection phase and assess how changes on the feature level affect the overall use factor of the recommended product. Thereby the consumer can further investigate how features relate to uses and may iteratively define a detailed and customized preference structure.

5.2 Example verification / constraint relaxation

After this multistep preference elicitation activity, some level of familiarity of the consumer with the dimensions of the product space can be assumed. We can also expect that the current highly recommended product is the best one according the preferences of the consumer. Hence it is now advisable for the system to focus on closing the deal.

In general, our approach for preference debugging aims to increase the consumer's confidence in the buying decision by showing more examples/alternatives. The reason for this is that we want the consumer to make the decision, and not the system. Consumers will perceive a recommendation as more credible if they see alternatives and can judge for themselves whether they are inferior or superior with regard to the current recommendation. The problem is now for the system to use the collected consumer-preference data to pick the appropriate examples to support customers in their view that they have found the best offer.

Previous work in the area of navigation by examples (Shimazu, 2001) indicates that it is advisable to show three products to the consumer. In our approach, we follow this recommendation, but we use different methods for selecting the examples. The starting point in our approach is the highly recommended product, which is always one of the three presented alternatives. For picking the other two alternatives from the product space we suggest the following two techniques.

Since target groups are defined with most-preferred uses and delight features (see Section 2), it is now possible to search for a product that is superior to the current recommendation by either offering a delight feature or being especially suitable for another use that this specific consumer did not explicitly consider (upgrading). This additional use is identified through the associated target group's use profile.

To derive a lesser alternative (downgrading), we can seek products that either have a comparable overall use factor but violate one of the initial constraints (see Section 4.1) or that are slightly cheaper with a minimal loss of overall use factor.

Facing these lesser and superior choices, and still given the ability to explore the features of all presented alternatives, the consumer can now verify by examples whether

- the preference profile chosen is consistent and complete,
- the constraints defined for the product space are still suitable.

By displaying an upgrading option, the consumer may learn, for instance, about appealing features that she has never thought about, but that are only available for products above the originally specified price range.

If the consumer decides to rank one of the alternatives as the current best, again the algorithms for downgrading and upgrading can be applied to determine two similar alternatives. The preference optimization phase terminates when

a) the consumer is confident to buy,
b) all suitable alternatives have been evaluated,
c) the consumer exits the conversation

6. PROTOTYPE SCENARIO

To gain more practical experience with this approach we have designed a system prototype that allows us to validate our ideas. The showcase in our prototype is an online shop for digital cameras. The screens provided below are mock-up screens illustrating a usage scenario created for the prototype design.

In our scenario Jack, an expectant father, is searching for a digital camera to document the first years of the baby. Jack is interested in technical specifications and has been thinking about buying a digital camera for quite a while. In the past, he had no compelling reason to justify the expenditure to his wife, Janet. Now, with the new baby arriving, the time seems right.

Jack decides to do some research about which camera to buy. He locates an online shop where he is presented a questionnaire that lets him state how he intends to use the digital camera. Jack fills out the form as shown in Figure 4. Apart from specifying four of his intended uses (e.g. to take baby pictures), Jack also indicates that he wants his camera to have at least a 3X optical zoom for portrait shots. After completing the form he pushes the "Show Example Recommendation ..." button and a new web page is presented (see Figure 5).

Figure 4. *Web page supporting constraint and use specification.*

Figure 5. *Web page supporting constraint and uses tuning.*

Upon inspecting the page, Jack realizes that for each of the uses he indicated, the system has created a line under the label "Selected uses", his indication of the preferred camera type is repeated, as is his requirement regarding the 3X zoom. In addition, the system has displayed two "Related uses", both of which appear to be of interest if you want to document the development of a baby ("Record sounds" and "Record video sequence"). Jack also notices that the currently recommended camera does not provide support for recording sound and only limited support for recording video sequences. He therefore decides to increase the importance of these two uses and request a new recommendation. Just before hitting the "New Recommendation" button he realizes that he would be interested in knowing why the current camera is highly rated for taking baby pictures. He therefore follows the link of the "++" evaluation of the Canon S45 example recommendation. As a result he is presented a pop-up window that explains how the system generated this particular evaluation (see Figure 6).

Jack inspects the explanation and is satisfied with the system's definition of what makes a camera good for taking baby pictures. He therefore closes the window and selects the button "New Recommendation", which leads to the web page shown in Figure 7.

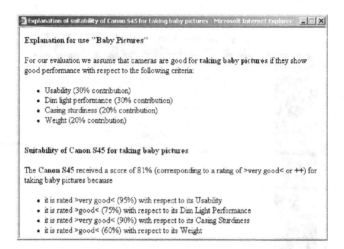

Figure 6. *Suitability rating. Explanation for camera use "Baby Pictures"*.

Jack realizes that the two uses previously listed as "Related uses" have now moved to the list of "Selected uses". A new related use (Large-size prints), for which the current camera does not provide optimal performance, is listed. Jack also notices that an additional technical requirement (Weight) was suggested by the system. Being prompted like this, Jack realizes that he would prefer to use the new camera as a replacement for his current SLR camera, which requires the production of larger-size prints from digital pictures. He therefore increases the importance of the "Large-size prints" use. Finally, the currently suggested camera does not provide optimal support for flash and is not very good for making medium-sized prints from digital pictures. These two functionalities seem very important to Jack, however, so he increases the corresponding importance ratings. The system had also suggested an additional technical requirement regarding the weight of the camera, but since Jack already owns quite a heavy camera and its weight never bothered him, he reduces the importance of this requirement to the lowest possible value. Satisfied with his current preference representation, Jack requests another update to the recommendation, which leads to the output displayed in Figure 8.

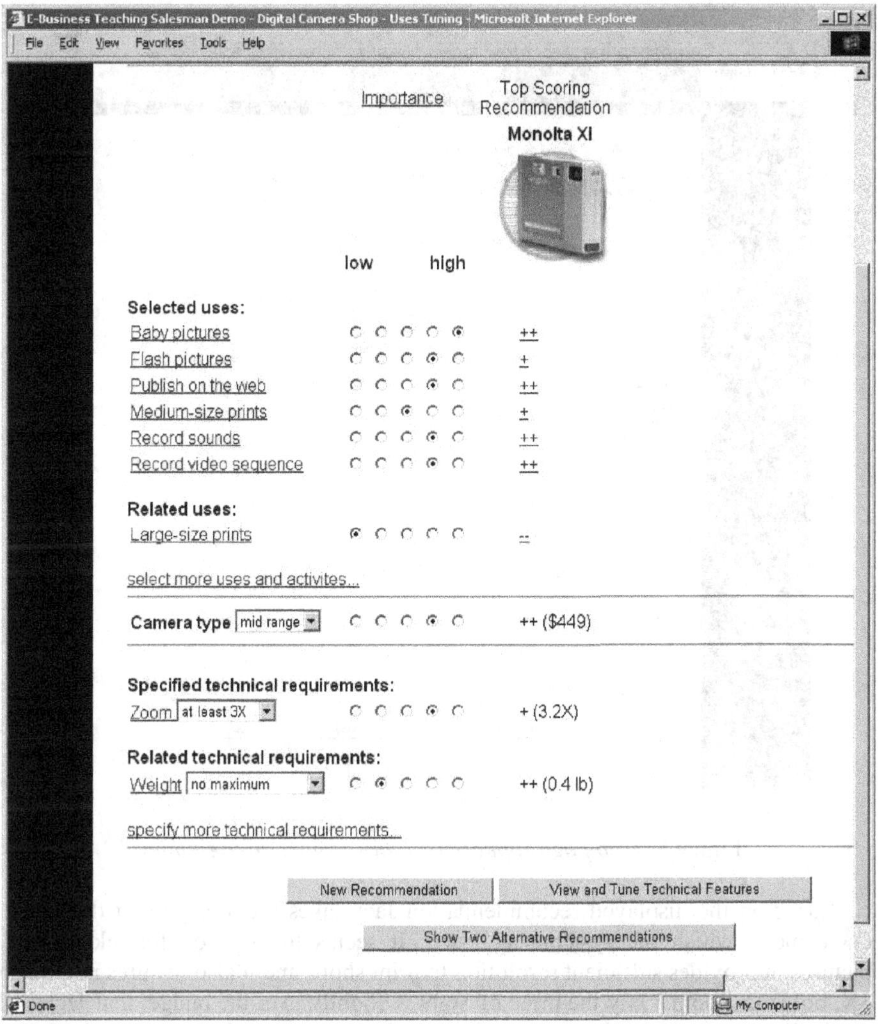

Figure 7. *Web page supporting a second round of use tuning.*

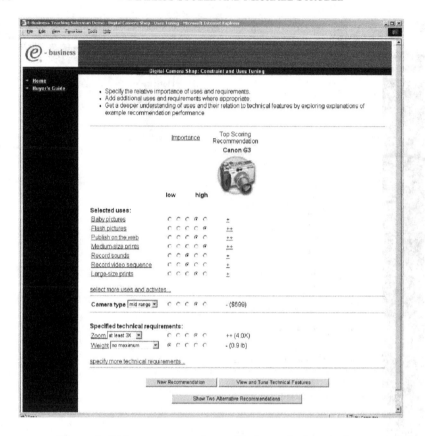

Figure 8. *Web page supporting a third round of use tuning.*

Based on the displayed recommendation Jack takes a closer look at the Canon G3 camera, which the system suggested. It seems to be good for taking baby pictures, it provides sufficient resolution to print shots, and it also features not only a 3X, but a 4X zoom. Only the price of $699 is slightly over the budget that Jack had originally allocated for the camera. Jack feels the need to know more about this particular camera and hits the button "View and Tune Technical Features". As a result he is taken to the web page displayed in Figure 9.

Jack spends quite a while on this page inspecting some of the "Maximal" values in more detail to see, for example, a list of products that outperform the Canon G3 with respect to the optical zoom range. Jack also makes sure that the areas in which "his" Canon G3 only shows average performance are areas that are less important to him. For this he inspects the definition of features by selecting the link associated with the feature, which causes an explanation to be presented in a pop-up window. After this investigation, Jack is quite certain that the G3 is probably the camera to buy. To enhance his confidence, Jack selects the option "Show Two Alternatives", which was also available in the previous pages.

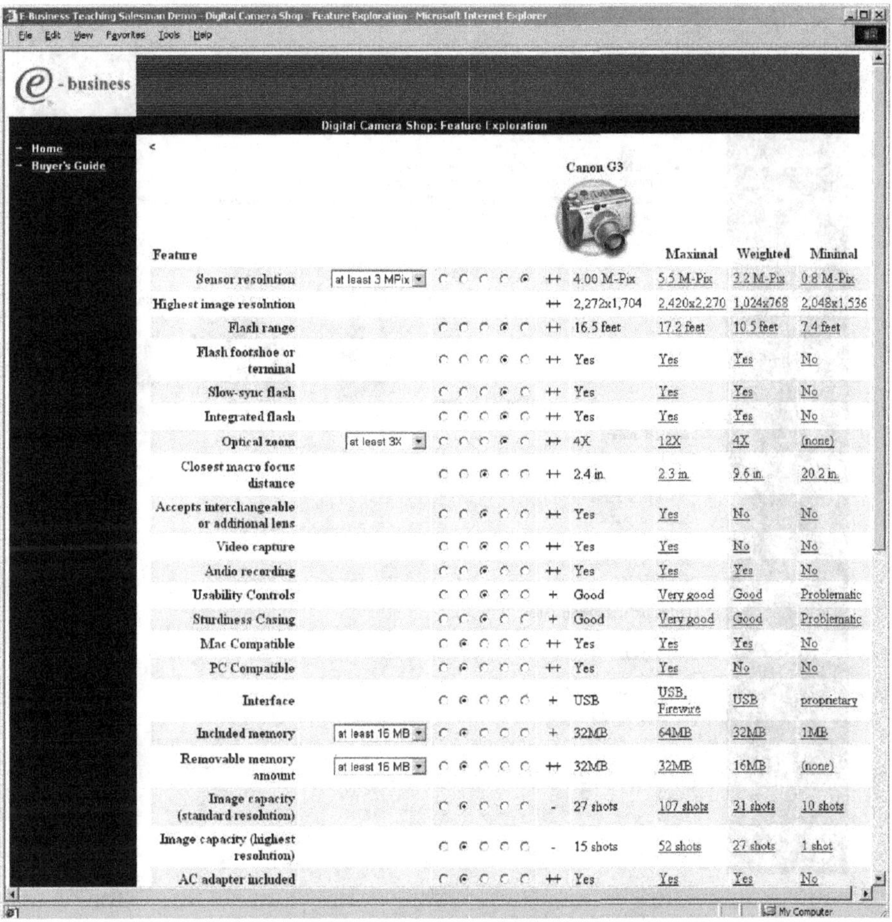

Figure 9. *Web page supporting feature exploration.*

Feature	Selector			Canon G3	Maximal	Weighted	Minimal
Sensor resolution	at least 3 MPix	○ ○ ○ ◉ ○	++	4.00 M-Pix	5.5 M-Pix	3.2 M-Pix	0.8 M-Pix
Highest image resolution			++	2,272x1,704	2,420x2,270	1,024x768	2,048x1,536
Flash range		○ ○ ○ ◉ ○	++	16.5 feet	17.2 feet	10.5 feet	7.4 feet
Flash footshoe or terminal		○ ○ ○ ○ ○	++	Yes	Yes	Yes	No
Slow-sync flash		○ ○ ○ ◉ ○	++	Yes	Yes	Yes	No
Integrated flash		○ ○ ○ ◉ ○	++	Yes	Yes	Yes	No
Optical zoom	at least 3X	○ ○ ○ ◉ ○	++	4X	12X	4X	(none)
Closest macro focus distance		○ ○ ◉ ○ ○	++	2.4 in.	2.3 in.	9.6 in.	20.2 in.
Accepts interchangeable or additional lens		○ ○ ◉ ○ ○	++	Yes	Yes	No	No
Video capture		○ ○ ◉ ○ ○	++	Yes	Yes	No	No
Audio recording		○ ○ ◉ ○ ○	++	Yes	Yes	Yes	No
Usability Controls		○ ○ ◉ ○ ○	+	Good	Very good	Good	Problematic
Sturdiness Casing		○ ○ ◉ ○ ○	+	Good	Very good	Good	Problematic
Mac Compatible		○ ◉ ○ ○ ○	++	Yes	Yes	Yes	No
PC Compatible		○ ◉ ○ ○ ○	++	Yes	Yes	No	No
Interface		○ ◉ ○ ○ ○	+	USB	USB, Firewire	USB	proprietary
Included memory	at least 16 MB	○ ◉ ○ ○ ○	+	32MB	64MB	32MB	1MB
Removable memory amount	at least 16 MB	○ ◉ ○ ○ ○	++	32MB	32MB	16MB	(none)
Image capacity (standard resolution)		○ ◉ ○ ○ ○	-	27 shots	107 shots	31 shots	10 shots
Image capacity (highest resolution)		○ ◉ ○ ○ ○	-	15 shots	52 shots	27 shots	1 shot
AC adapter included		○ ◉ ○ ○ ○	++	Yes	Yes	Yes	No

The resulting page (shown in Figure 10), supporting the "preference debugging" phase, is similar in layout and content to those pages supporting use tuning. However, instead of showing only the top-scoring recommendation, two other cameras (labeled "upgrade" and "downgrade") are shown. Jack inspects the descriptions of both alternative suggestions and concludes that the better performance offered by the Minolta camera is not sufficient for him to spend an additional $200. He also concludes that the Nikon camera, while being similar to the G3 in many respects and even outperforming it in resolution and manual controllability, is probably too complex for easy handling. Assessing all the generated recommendation information, his developed knowledge regarding the relationship of uses and features as well as his exploration of potential alternatives, Jack is finally convinced that, based on his requirements, the G3 is the best camera to buy.

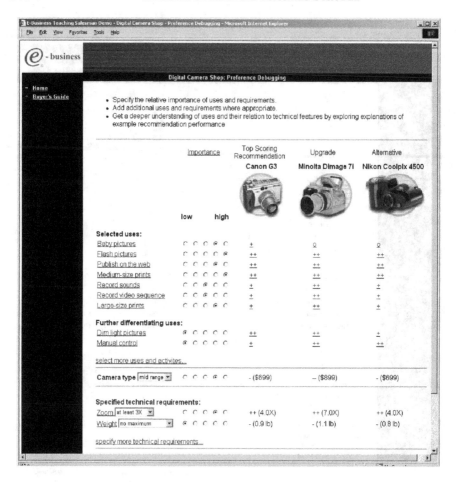

Figure 10. *Web page supporting preference debugging.*

7. DISCUSSION

In summary, the work presented in this paper is based on the following three main observations:

- Initially most consumers feel more comfortable talking with a salesperson about their needs and potential uses than about the features of the desired product.
- However, in a later stage of the conversation, they want to know more about the features of a product in order to feel confident in making a sound and objective decision.
- To gain confidence in their decision, consumers have to be taught enough about potential uses and associated product features.

To reflect these observations, we propose a B2C eCommerce system that supports the required learning process. The system elicits the needs and constraints of a consumer, then proposes additional uses and an initial evaluation structure for a product, and thereby reveals how uses relate to product features. Finally the system tries to close deal by recommending alternatives (upgrades and downgrades), which allows the consumer to check the developed evaluation structure for consistency and completeness.

Throughout this iterative conversation, our approach provides consumers with many opportunities to control the interaction. This allows users of an information system to test and update hypotheses based on their inner mental model. In our case, consumers certainly have an implicit mental model of their preferences, which they can compare repeatedly with the results (recommendation of suitable candidates) achieved with the explicit preference representation (evaluation structure) in the eCommerce system. This interactivity enables a better match between consumer judgments and underlying utilities (Ariel, 2000, p. 245). Hence, we believe that consumers, through the assistance of our recommender system, can be confident

- that they know what they want to use the desired product for.
- that they know how the identified uses relate to more specific criteria in the evaluation structure that evaluate particular product features.
- that the current evaluation structure is complete and consistent with their intuitive view of what they want and need.
- that they were objectively supported in finding the best product in this shop.

Needs-based product recommendation in itself is not a new concept. Jameson et al. (1995) proposed the concept of evaluation-oriented information provisioning systems (EOPS) to characterize a class of systems that interactively model user preferences and use the constructed model to evaluate items, thereby supporting users in their decision making. The system presented here falls into this general class of systems. However, our differs from prior work in that area in that we do not assume that users approach the system with a pre-exiting and fixed set of preferences that the system has to approximate. Instead, we agree with Häubl et al. (this volume) that the use of recommender systems influences users' preference structure. In our system we therefore aim to support users' learning process and their active discovery and construction of preferences. We drive this process by matching the selected uses with the target group profiles and employ the information about related uses and delight features to make users aware of potentially interesting product properties. To further support the contextualized learning of users we present one or more example recommendations in each interaction step.

Other recommender systems also rely on example presentation as a means to drive the interaction (for example Shimazu, 2001). Unlike these proposed techniques, we primarily show examples not to elicit or further narrow down the preferences of consumers (preference discovery), but to enhance their confidence in the buying decision (preference debugging). As a result, we do not select extreme examples, for instance to explore the boundaries of the product space (Shimazu,

2001). Instead, we use upgrading and downgrading to pick products that allow the consumer to verify her evaluation structure for completeness and correctness.

Among the systems reviewed by Jameson et al. (1995) the EOPS with the most similarities to our system is a recommender system described by Popp and Lödel (1996) for computer equipment. The system uses stereotype profiles to deduce and suggest computer needs (such as "records management" and "mobility") based on the user's profession. Users can then review the suggested needs, remove unnecessary needs and add a list of possible needs. In a second step the list of needs is translated (using production rules) into a weighted combination of feature-oriented evaluation functions. The function is used to rank items in the product catalog. If necessary users can inspect and adapt the inferred feature weights to fine-tune the overall evaluation function. The main goal of the system is to provide users with automated expert advice, present a list of computers ordered by their suitability, and to then present detailed product information in a personalized way. The goal of our system, in contrast, is to educate users so that they are able to make informed decisions. For this we use a multi-level evaluation function that contains a high-level evaluation function for each use specified by the user. The advantage of this approach is that users can request an automatically generated explanation of the needs-oriented evaluation function and thereby learn how the system evaluates the suitability of products for specific needs.

The use of hierarchical evaluation functions for modeling user preferences is not new. Other EOPS also use multi-level evaluation functions (Jameson et al., 1995). However, similar to AHP (Saaty, 1980) these approaches rely on a strictly hierarchical organization of criteria, with higher-level nodes typically representing abstractions or summarizations of lower-level criteria. Our "hierarchy", in contrast, is actually a network structure in which base feature criteria contribute to multiple use criteria (needs). These use criteria are not abstractions of the underlying feature evaluations, but represent those activity-oriented product evaluation criteria that were selected by the user.

We recently performed a first round of exploratory tests with eight users recruited among employees of the IBM Zurich Research Laboratory. The testers were presented with a fully functional prototype system matching closely the design described in the previous section. The preliminary test showed that most users were interested in exploring the explanations and understanding how the system evaluated the suitability of cameras for their selected uses. We also found that the explanations, combined with the option to adapt the evaluation function, provide users with a feeling of control. The system thereby satisfies the important requirement for adaptive eCommerce systems identified by Alpert et al. (2003).

Ricci and Del Missier (this volume) discuss a system supporting the planning of trips involving multiple components. Individual components (such as accommodation) are selected in a feature-oriented way. Adding use-oriented criteria to such a system would require that the suitability of trips for high-level criteria (e.g. a honey moon) could be represented in terms of low-level criteria (e.g. style = romantic). This would require a richer information structure than is currently available. Although this information would be more expensive to elicit and maintain, it would frequently relieve users of having to study the individual pictures and textual descriptions of travel components to determine their suitability for the intended purpose. Whether the added benefit for users justifies the required upfront investment and increased maintenance costs has to be decided on a case-by-case basis. The advantage of the approach suggested here is that, contrary to others (Ardissono & Goy, 2000), the use-oriented evaluations of catalog items are deduced automatically from base product features using the general evaluation criteria. This also means that changes in the evaluation criteria (reflecting changes in expert opinion about expected performance levels) do not require an expensive manual update of product information. Still, maintaining a rapidly changing set of (technical) product specifications will represent a considerable investment. In some product areas, such as home electronics, independent companies have started to make a business out of collecting this information and providing it to interested parties as a service. Sellers that use such services can thereby escape the "small catalogue" problem. If the eCommerce system does not feature all potential offerings in the product domain (e.g. all available cameras from all major manufacturers), the consumer will always distrust the recommendation, even if the underlying criteria are made transparent, because a globally predominant solution might only be found outside the system's local context.

A typical fact in the practice of selling is that the strategy for picking example products might also be driven to some extent by the preference of the salesperson, and not only by the preferences of the consumer. The salesperson may have excess inventory or outdated products that she wishes to sell. This strategy could be incorporated in the example verification step through the addition of a salesperson utility function and measures of relative importance for the consumer and seller utility (see for example Stolze & Ströbel, 2001b). The disadvantage of the introduction of seller preferences is that the consumer has reason to distrust the resulting recommendations because they are no longer based solely on her preferences. To ensure transparency in the system's operations and to avoid compromising the credibility of the system, the seller-driven recommendation will have to be marked comparably to sponsored links in the result lists of search engines.

The pressure to sell on the seller's side can also create the opportunity for special deals and discounts or, more generally, may lead to negotiation situations. As a detailed account of the preferences of the other party is very favorable for achieving integrative, win-win solutions in negotiations (Pruitt & Lewis, 1975), we could extend our approach with an additional bargaining phase. Because multi-criteria preferences as well as the dimensions of possible concessions and potential upgrades are already part of the world knowledge in our proposed system, the negotiations in this bargaining phase could transcend the typical one-dimensional price haggling and natively include configuration aspects for multiple attributes of the product (see for example Bichler, 1999).

Finally, it would be very unfortunate, from the consumer's as well as the salesperson's perspective, to throw away the detailed evaluation structure of a consumer obtained in the electronic shopping process. For example, the consumer, in the case of an unsuccessful outcome in one shop, would presumably certainly be happy to use the already optimized and debugged evaluation structure again in another shop, or might wish to make it available to a friend with similar needs. To support functionalities such as the reuse of buying preferences, we have suggested the shopping gate (Stolze & Ströbel, 2001a)—a site on the Internet where consumers can create, maintain, and share shopping roles, which include, for instance, demographic data and buying preferences. Obviously, the preference discovery, optimization, and debugging approach presented in this paper can be used to support consumers in developing and refining their evaluation structure for a certain shopping role.

8. REFERENCES

Ardissono, L. and A. Goy (2000). Tailoring the Interaction with Users in Web Stores. User Modeling and User-Adapted Interaction 10(4): 251-303.

Ariely, D. (2000) Controlling the Information Flow: Effects on Consumers' Decision Making and Preferences. Journal of Consumer Research, Vol. 27, pp. 233-248.

Bichler, M. (1999) Decision Analysis—A Critical Enabler for Multi-attribute Auctions. In: Proceedings 12th International Bled Electronic Commerce Conference, Bled, Slovenia.

Fogg, B. J. (2002). Persuasive Technology: Using Computers to Change What We Think and Do, Morgan Kaufmann, San Francisco, CA.

Felix, D., Niederberger, C., Steiger, P., Stolze, M. (2001) Feature-oriented vs. Needs-oriented Product Access for Non-Expert Online Shoppers. In: Proceedings 1st IFIP Conference on e-commerce, e-business and e-government, Zurich, Switzerland, pp. 399-406.

Fink, J., Kobsa, A. (2000). A Review and Analysis of Commercial User Modelling Servers for Personalization on the World Wide Web. User Modeling and User-Adapted Interaction, Vol. 10, Nos. 3-4, pp. 209-249.

Grenci, R. T., Todd, P. A. (2002) Solutions-Driven Marketing. Communications of the ACM, Vol. 45, No. 3, pp. 65-71.

Herlocker, J. L., Konstan, J. A., Riedl, J. (2000). Explaining Collaborative Filtering Recommendations. In: Proceedings of the ACM 2000 Conference on Computer Supported Cooperative Work, December 2000, pp. 241-250.

Jameson, A., Schäfer, R., Simons, J., and Weis, T. (1995). Adaptive provision of evaluation-oriented information: Tasks and techniques. In Proceedings of the Fourteenth International Joint Conference on Artificial Intelligence (IJCAI), 1886--1893.

Karat, C.-M., C. Brodie, Karat, J., Vergo, J., & Alpert, S. (2003). Personalizing the User Experience on ibm.com. IBM Systems Journal 42(4): 686-701.

Keeney, R., Raiffa, H. (1976) Decisions with Multiple Objectives. Wiley, New York.

Kobsa, A., Koenemann, J., Pohl, W. (2001) Personalized Hypermedia Presentation Techniques for Improving Online Customer Relationships. The Knowledge Engineering Review, Vol. 16, No. 2, pp. 111-155.

Payne, J., Bettman, J., Johnson, E. (1988) Adaptive Strategy Selection in Decision-Making. Journal of Experimental Psychology, Vol. 14, pp. 534-552.

Popp, H. and D. Lödel (1996). Fuzzy Techniques and User Modeling in Sales Assistants. User Modeling and User-Adapted Interaction 5(3-4): 349-370.

Pruitt, D., Lewis, S. (1975) Development of Integrative Solutions in Bilateral Negotiations. In: Journal of Personality and Social Psychology, Vol. 31, No. 4, pp. 621-633.

Saaty, T. (1980) The Analytic Hierarchy Process. McGraw Hill, New York, reprinted by RWS Publications, Pittsburgh PA, 1996.

Schafer, J. B., Konstan, J. A., Riedl, E. (2001) E-Commerce Recommendation Applications. Data Mining and Knowledge Discovery, Vol. 5, Nos. 1/2, pp. 115-153.

Sinha, R., Swearingen, K. (2002). The Role of Transparency in Recommender Systems. In: Proceedings of ACM CHI 02 Conference on Human Factors in Computing Systems, Conference Companion, pp. 830-831.

Shimazu, H. (2001) ExpertClerk: Navigating Shopper's Buying Process with the Combination of Asking and Proposing. In: Proceedings International Joint Conference on Artificial Intelligence 2001, pp. 1443-1450.

Spiekermann, S., Parachiv, C. (2002) Motivating Human-Agent Interaction: Transferring Insights from Behavioral Marketing to Interface Design. Electronic Commerce Research, Vol. 2, No. 3, pp. 255-285.

Stolze, M. (2000) Soft Navigation in Electronic Product Catalogs. Journal on Digital Libraries, Vol. 3, No. 1, pp. 60-66.

Stolze, M., Ströbel, M. (2001a) The Shopping Gate—Enabling Role- and Preference-Specific e-Commerce Shopping Experiences. In: Web Intelligence: Research and Development, edited by N. Zhong et al., Lecture Notes in Artificial Intelligence, Vol. 2198, Springer, Berlin Heidelberg, pp. 549-561.

Stolze, M., Ströbel, M. (2001b) Utility-based Decision Tree Optimization: A Framework for Adaptive Interviewing. In: User Modelling 2001, edited by M. Bauer et al., Lecture Notes in Artificial Intelligence, Vol. 2109, Springer, Berlin Heidelberg, pp. 105-116.

Zimmerman, J., Kurapati, K. (2002). Exposing Profiles to Build Trust in a Recommender. In: Proceedings of ACM CHI 02 Conference on Human Factors in Computing Systems, Conference Companion, pp. 608-609.

MAXIMILIAN TELTZROW AND ALFRED KOBSA

IMPACTS OF USER PRIVACY PREFERENCES ON PERSONALIZED SYSTEMS

A Comparative Study [1]

1. INTRODUCTION

Personalized (or "user-adaptive") systems have gained substantial momentum with the rise of the World Wide Web. The market research firm Jupiter (Foster, 2000) defines personalization as predictive analysis of consumer data used to adapt targeted media, advertising and merchandising to consumer needs. According to Jupiter, personalization can be viewed as a cycle of recurring processes consisting of 'data collection', 'profiling' and 'matching': from collected data, user profiles can be created that are the basis for adapting user interfaces to individuals or groups of individuals. A more web-oriented definition was proposed by Kobsa et al. (2001) who regard a personalized hypermedia application as a hypermedia system that adapts the content, structure and/or presentation of the networked hypermedia objects to each individual user's characteristics, usage behavior and/or usage environment. In contrast to user-adaptable systems where the user is in control of the initiation, proposal, selection and production of the adaptation, user-adaptive systems perform all steps autonomously.

The advantages of personalization can be manifold. Website visitors see the major benefits in sites being able to offer more relevant content and to recall user preferences and interests (Cyber Dialogue, 2000). The personalization of hypermedia is beneficial for several other purposes as well, most notably for improving the learning progress in educational software (Brusilovsky *et al.*, 1998; Specht, 1998). Given the increasing amount of information offered on the Internet, the development of advanced personalized services seems to become inevitable.

Personalization systems need to acquire a certain amount of data about users' interests, behavior, demographics and actions before they can start adapting to them.

[1] This research has been supported by the National Science Foundation under Grant No. 0308277, the Deutsche Forschungsgemeinschaft Berlin-Brandenburg Graduate School in Distributed Information Systems (DFG grant no. GRK 316/2), and the Humboldt Foundation (TransCoop Program). We would like to thank Stefan Wrobel for his help in the analysis of survey results.

315

Clare-Marie Karat et al. (eds.), Designing Personalized User Experiences in eCommerce, 315—332.

Thus, they are often useful in domains only where users engage in extended (and most often repeated) system use. They may not be appropriate for infrequent users with typically short sessions. The extensive and repeated collection of detailed user data, however, may provoke consumer privacy concerns, which have been identified as a primary impediment to users' willingness to buy online (Pavlou, 2003). Consumer surveys show that the number of consumers refusing to shop online because of privacy concerns is as high as 64% (Culnan and Milne, 2001). Finding the right balance between privacy protection and personalization remains a challenging task. Therefore, our chapter discusses the impacts of consumers' privacy concerns on personalization systems. Furthermore, we will provide suggestions on how to increase consumer trust in such systems.

Section 2 categorizes personalization systems according to the input data they require. Section 3 summarizes privacy concerns from more than 30 consumer surveys and relates their effects on personalization systems to the categories of Section 2. Differences between consumers' privacy views and their actual behaviors, and between consumer and industry opinions on privacy, are also presented. Section 4 discusses the impact of the privacy concerns that were summarized in Section 2 on the personalization systems described in previous chapters of this book. Finally, Section 5 summarizes possible approaches to better address the tension between privacy and personalization.

2. INPUT DATA FOR PERSONALIZATION

Kobsa (2001) divides the data that are relevant for personalization purposes into 'user data', 'usage data', and 'environment data'. 'User data' denote information about personal characteristics of a user, while 'usage data' relate to a user's (interactive) behavior. A special kind of 'usage data' is 'usage regularities', which describe frequently re-occurring interactions of users. 'Environment data' refer to the user's software and hardware, and the characteristics of the user's current locale.

Table 1 lists the most frequently occurring subtypes of these data. The taxonomy allows one to refer to specific kinds of personalization systems more easily, and facilitates our analysis of privacy concerns and their impacts on certain system types.

3. RESULTS FROM PRIVACY SURVEYS

3.1 Impacts on user-adaptive systems

We categorized 30 recent consumer surveys on Internet privacy (or summaries of such surveys), and analyzed their potential impacts on the different types of personalization systems listed in Table 1. Questions from different surveys addressing the same privacy aspects were grouped together, to convey a more complete picture of user concerns. Eleven documents included all questions, six provided an extensive discussion of survey results, and ten contained factual executive summaries. For three studies, only press releases were available.

Table 1. *Types of personalization-relevant data and examined systems (summary of the taxonomy in Kobsa et al., 2001).*

Input Data	Examples of User-Adaptive Systems
A) User data:	
Demographic data	Personalized web sites based on user profiles; software providers: Broadvision, Personify, NetPerceptions etc.
User knowledge	Expertise-dependent personalization; product and technical descriptions: Sales Assistant (Popp and Lödel, 1996), SETA (Ardissono and Goy, 2000); learning systems: KN-AHS (Kobsa *et al.*, 1994), Brusilovsky, 2001
User skills and capabilities	Help Systems: Unix Consultant (Chin, 1989), Küpper and Kobsa, 1999; disabilities: AVANTI (Fink *et al.*, 1998)
User interests and preferences	Recommender systems (Resnick and Varian, 1997); used car domain: Jameson *et al.*, 1995; domain of telephony devices: Ardissono and Goy, 1999
User goals and plans	Personalized support for users with targeted browsing behavior, plan recognition: (Lesh *et al.*, 1999), PUSH (Höök *et al.*, 1996), HYPERFLEX (Kaplan *et al.*, 1993)
B) Usage data:	
Selective actions	Adaptation based on link-selection: WebWatcher (Joachims *et al.*, 1997), Letizia (Lieberman, 1995); image-selection: Adaptive Graphics Analyser (Holynski, 1988)
Temporal viewing behavior	Adaptation based on viewing time; streaming objects: Joerding, 1999; temporal navigation behavior: Chittaro and Ronan, 2000; micro-interaction: Sakagami *et al.*, 1998
Ratings	Adaptation based on object ratings; product suggestions: Firefly (Shardanand and Maes, 1995), GroupLens (Konstan *et al.*, 1997); web pages: Pazzani and Billsus, 1997
Purchases and purchase-related actions	Suggestions of similar goods after product selection: Amazon.com; other purchase-related actions: registering, transferring products into virtual shopping cart, quizzes
Other (dis-) con-firmatory actions	Adaptation based on other user actions, e.g. saving, printing documents, bookmarking a web page: Konstan *et al.*, 1997
C) Usage regularities:	
Usage frequency	Adaptation based on usage frequency; icon toolbar: Debevc *et al.*, 1996, Flexcel (Krogsæter *et al.*, 1994); web page visits: AVANTI (Fink *et al.*, 1998)
Situation-action correlations	Interface agents; routing mails: Mitchell *et al.*, 1994, Maes, 1994, meeting requests: Kozierok and Maes, 1993
Action Sequences	Recommendations based on frequently used action sequences, e.g. past actions, action sequences of other users
D) Environment data:	
Software environment	Adaptation based on users' browser versions and platforms, availability of plug-ins, Java and JavaScript versions
Hardware environment	Adaptation based on users' bandwidth, processor speed, display devices (e.g. resolution), input devices
Locale	Adaptation based on users' current location (e.g. country code),

| characteristics of usage locale

We distinguished several categories of privacy aspects. The category 'privacy of user data in general' has a direct impact on any personalization systems that requires personal data (such as the user's name, address, income etc.). The category 'privacy in a commercial context' primarily affects personalized systems in e-commerce. 'Tracking of user sessions' and 'use of cookies' influence user-adaptive systems requiring usage data. A few studies focus on 'e-mail privacy'. This category might have an impact on user-adaptive systems that generate targeted e-mails. Two studies directly address the topic of privacy and personalization (Mabley, 2000; Personalization Consortium, 2000). They are highly interesting because they directly affect most personalization systems.

Results regarding user data in general

1. Internet Users who are concerned about the security of personal information: 83% (Cyber Dialogue, 2001), 70% (Behrens, 2001), 72% (UMR, 2001), 84% (Fox *et al.*, 2000)
2. People who have refused to give (personal) information to a web site: 82% (Culnan and Milne, 2001)
3. Internet users who would never provide personal information to a web site: 27% (Fox *et al.*, 2000)
4. Internet users who supplied false or fictitious information to a web site when asked to register: 34% (Culnan and Milne, 2001), 24% (Fox *et al.*, 2000)
5. Online users who think that sites who share personal information with other sites invade privacy: 49% (Cyber Dialogue, 2001)

A significant concern about the use of personal information can be seen in these results, which is a problem for those personalization systems in Table 1 that require 'user data' (such as demographic data', data about 'user knowledge', etc.). Systems that record 'purchases and purchase-related actions' may also be affected. More than a quarter of the respondents even indicated that they would never consider providing personal information to a web site. Quite a few users indicated having supplied false or fictitious information to a web site when asked to register, which makes user linking across sessions and thereby accurate recommendations based on 'user interests and preferences' very difficult.

Results regarding user data in a commercial context

1. People wanting businesses to seek permission before using their personal information for marketing: 90% (Roy Morgan Research, 2001)
2. Non-online shoppers who did not purchase online because of privacy concerns: 66% (Ipsos Reid, 2001), 68% (Interactive Policy, 2002), 64% (Culnan and Milne, 2001)
3. Online shoppers who would buy more if they were not worried about privacy/security issues: 37% (Forrester, 2001), 20% (Department for Trade and Industry, 2001)

4. Shoppers who abandoned online shopping carts because of privacy reasons: 27% (Cyber Dialogue, 2001)
5. People who are concerned if a business shares their data for a different than the original purpose: 91% (UMR, 2001), 90% (Roy Morgan Research, 2001)

These results suggest that in a commercial context, privacy concerns may play an even more important role than for general personalized systems. Most people want to be asked before their personal information is used, and many regard privacy as a must for Internet shopping. Thus, commercial personalization systems need to include privacy features. In particular, those systems in Table 1 that require 'demographic data', 'user knowledge', 'user interests and preferences', 'user goals and plans' and 'purchase-related actions' are affected.

Furthermore, more than 90% of respondents are concerned if a business shares their information for a different than the original purpose. This has a severe impact on central user modeling servers that collect data from, and share them with, different user-adaptive applications, unless sharing can be controlled by the user (Kobsa, 2001; Schreck and Kobsa, 2003).

Results regarding user tracking and cookies

1. People who are concerned about being tracked on the Internet: 60% (Cyber Dialogue, 2001), 54% (Fox et al., 2000), 63% (Harris, 2000)
2. People who are concerned that someone might know what web sites they visited: 31% (Fox et al., 2000)
3. Internet users who generally accept cookies: 62% (Personalization Consortium, 2000)
4. Internet users who set their computers to reject cookies: 25% (Culnan and Milne, 2001), 3% (Cyber Dialogue, 2001), 31% in warning modus (Cyber Dialogue, 2001), 10% (Fox et al., 2000)
5. Internet users who delete cookies periodically: 52% (Personalization Consortium, 2000)
6. User who feel uncomfortable being tracked across multiple web sites: 91% (Harris, 2000)

Users' privacy concerns about tracking and cookies that became manifest in the first result affect the acceptance of personalization systems based on 'usage data' and 'usage regularities' (see Table 1). In particular, systems using 'selective actions', 'temporal viewing behavior' and 'action sequences' conflict with users' privacy preferences. Results 2 – 5 directly affect machine-learning methods that operate on user log data since without cookies, sessions of the same user cannot be linked any more. Result 6 affects personalization systems that combine information from several sources, in particular those systems that use data from 'action sequences', 'demographics', 'purchase-related actions' and the user's 'locale'.

Most users do not consider current forms of tracking as helpful methods to collect data for personalization. Users' participation in deciding when and what usage information should be tracked might decrease such privacy concerns and will be discussed in Section 4 of this chapter.

Results regarding e-mail privacy

1. People who have asked for removal from e-mail lists: 78% (Cyber Dialogue, 2001), 80% (Culnan and Milne, 2001)
2. People who complain about irrelevant e-mail: 62% (Ipsos Reid, 2001)
3. People who have received unsolicited e-mail: 95% (Cyber Dialogue, 2001)
4. People who have received offensive e-mail: 28% (Fox *et al.*, 2000)

Results 2 and 3 constitute a problem for the acceptance of personalized e-mail. The problem affects primarily those systems in Table 1 that use 'situation-action correlation'. The findings indicate that many deployed e-mail personalization systems, such as software for the management of targeted marketing campaigns, are not yet able to address user needs specifically enough to evoke positive reactions among the recipients.

Results regarding privacy and personalization

1. Online users who see personalization as a good thing: 59% (Harris, 2000)
2. Online users who do not see personalization as a good thing: 37% (Harris, 2000)
3. Types of information users are willing to provide in return for personalized content: name: 88%, education: 88%, age: 86%, hobbies: 83%, salary 59%, credit card number: 13% (Cyber Dialogue, 2001)
4. Internet users who think tracking allows the site to provide information tailored to specific users: 27% (Fox *et al.*, 2000)
5. Online users who think that sites who share information with other sites try to better interact: 28% (Cyber Dialogue, 2001)
6. Online users who find it useful if site remembers basic information (name, address): 73% (Personalization Consortium, 2000)
7. Online users who find it useful if a site remembers information (preferred colors, delivery options etc.): 50% (Personalization Consortium, 2000)
8. People who are bothered if a web site asks for information one has already provided (e.g., mailing address): 62% (Personalization Consortium, 2000)
9. People who are willing to give information to receive a personalized online experience: 51% (Personalization Consortium, 2000), 40% (Roy Morgan Research, 2001), 51% (Privacy & American Business, 1999)

The results of the last category directly reflect users' attitudes towards personalization, and their willingness to share personal information in return for personalized content. Results 1 and 2 affect all systems in Table 1: a significant portion of the respondents does not seem to see enough value in personalization that they would be willing to give out personal data. If any possible, personalization should therefore be designed as an option that can be switched off. Results 3 and 9 affect all systems that rely on 'user data', and results 6 - 7 additionally those that rely on 'purchases and purchase-related actions'. Result 4 applies to all systems that utilize 'usage data' and information about the 'locale' of the user. Result 5, finally, applies to all personalized systems that share information via a central user modeling server (Kobsa, 2001).

3.2 Differences in consumer statements and actual privacy practices

This meta-analysis demonstrates that consumers are highly concerned about the privacy implications of various data collection methods, but many would share some data in return for personalization.[2] Users however do not seem to always have a good understanding of their privacy needs in a personalization context. Stated privacy preferences and actual behavior often diverge:

- User tracking evokes significant privacy concerns, but only 10% (27%) of American Internet users have set their browsers to reject cookies (Fox et al., 2000; Roy Morgan Research, 2001).
- 76% of survey respondents claimed that privacy policies on web sites were very important to them (Behrens, 2001), but in fact users barely view such pages when visiting web sites.[3]
- In an experiment, Berendt et al. (2004) found that users often do not live up to their self-reported privacy preferences: subjects claimed to be highly concerned about their privacy, but shared very personal and sensitive information with a personalized web site.

3.3 Differences in the privacy views of consumers and industry

Besides differences in consumers' self-perception and actual behavior, our analysis of survey results also uncovered a few major discrepancies in the privacy views of consumers and industry. Consumer expectations and actual industry practices should however be in line with each other, so that consumers can build trust which is the basis for the acceptance of personalization. For instance, 54% do not believe that most businesses handle the personal information they collect in a proper and confidential way (Responsys.com, 2000; Harris Interactive, 2003). In contrast, 90% of industry respondents believe that this is the case for their own business, and 46% that this is the case for industry in general.[4]

---

[2] Users' willingness to share information with a web site may also depend on other factors that are not considered here such as the usability of a site, users' general level of trust towards a site, and the company or industry to which the site belongs (Princeton Survey Research Associates 2002). For example, good company reputation makes 74% of the surveyed Internet users more comfortable disclosing personal information (Ipsos Reid 2001).

[3] Web site operators report a fairly low attention to privacy policies. For example, on the day after the company Excite@home was featured in a 60 Minutes segment about Internet privacy, only 100 out of 20 million unique visitors accessed that company's privacy pages (Wham 2001).

[4] However, only 40% of businesses say steps have been taken to secure personal information held by a site (Internet Privacy Survey 2001), and 55% do not store personal data in encrypted form. 15% share user data with third parties without having obtained users' permission (Deloitte 2001).

Consumer demands and current practice in companies also diverge significantly on the issue of data control. Most Internet users (86%) believe that they should be allowed control over what information is stored by a business (Fox *et al.*, 2000), but only 17% of businesses allow users to delete at least some personal information (Andersen, 2001). Furthermore, 40% of businesses do not provide access to personal data for verification, correction and updates (Deloitte, 2001).

Industry and consumers also disagree significantly on the value of privacy laws. Nine of ten marketers claim that the current regime of self-regulation works for their companies, and 64% think that government involvement will ultimately hurt the growth of e-commerce (Responsys.com, 2002). In contrast, two-thirds of e-mail users think that the federal government should pass more laws to ensure citizens' privacy online (Gallup Organization, 2001), while only 15% supported self-regulation (Harris, 2000). However, Harris (2001a) found that trust in the effectiveness of privacy legislation has meanwhile decreased among consumers.

Although both governments and private organizations have made serious efforts to ease users' privacy concerns, much remains to be done to build and maintain customer confidence, which is a prerequisite for successful personalization.

3.4 Discussion of the methodology

The cited studies were mostly conducted by well-known research institutions and market research firms between 2000 and 2003. The number of respondents in the studies varied between 500 and 4500, with an average of about 2000. The answers were collected by telephone interviews and online questionnaires. From the 30 surveys analyzed, 21 were conducted in the U.S., three in Canada, two in Australia and New Zealand, two in Britain and one in the European Union. One survey was based on an international respondent sample.

Though this meta-analysis provides a more comprehensive and objective over-view of privacy concerns and their impacts on personalization than can be expected from a single study, some caution should be exercised. A general problem is the lack of comparability of the studies: small differences in the wording of the questions, their context in the questionnaires, the recruitment method and the sample population make user statements difficult to compare. Harper and Singleton (2001) criticized the use of manipulative questions in many privacy studies, a lack of trade-offs between privacy and other desires, and imprecise terminology (e.g. the term "privacy" is often understood as a synonym for security, or a panacea against identity fraud and spam). Finally, as mentioned above, disparities seem to exist between people's responses to general, context-less privacy questions, and their behavior when working with concrete websites having specific goals in mind.

4. PRIVACY IMPACTS IN PERSONALIZATION DOMAINS ADDRESSED BY OTHER CHAPTERS OF THIS BOOK

The previous sections discussed impacts of users' privacy concerns on different types of personalization systems. To round out our analysis, we looked at the personalization approaches described in other chapters of this book and analyzed three privacy-related aspects: (1) which input data from Table 1 is required by these personalization systems, (2) which user privacy concerns might therefore affect these systems following the results of Section 3.1 and additional findings from privacy surveys, and (3) how users' privacy concerns could be addressed to increase trust in these systems (this third aspect will be discussed in more detail in Section 5). Most chapters focus on personalization in e-commerce, and a few on e-finance, e-travel and e-government. We will group the chapters of this book accordingly.

4.1 E-Commerce, retail

In Brodie *et al.*'s chapter on "How Personalization of an E-Commerce Website Affects Consumer Trust", the authors address the issue of user trust in personalized e-commerce applications. The chapter explores how a company's choice of personalization policies and features might affect visitors' willingness to share personal information. The authors' findings and recommendations are relevant for most types of personalization systems listed in Table 1.

Their study with a large B2B website identified several requirements for personalization. Most importantly, they found that users should be given more control of their data, since users were more willing to share personal information with the company when they were allowed to view, edit and delete their data. Brodie *et al.* suggest letting users specify when they think data collection could be useful. Their findings confirm results from several consumer surveys: in one study, 69% of consumers found it important to have control of their data (Harris, 2003). Consumers also react more positively to organizations if they have a higher perceived level control (Hine and Eve, 1998). Giving users control of when to collect data might also increase the acceptance of online user tracking, which is often considered as a privacy threat (Harris, 2000).

Second, Brodie *et al.* investigated whether asking for only the information that is needed to provide an immediate service would increase the willingness of website users to share data. One survey had already revealed that most users would be willing to provide personal information in return for personalization (Personalization Consortium, 2000). The results of Brodie *et al.* enhance our understanding of this willingness in that indeed only information needed to provide an immediate service should be requested, and not all information for all personalized services that the website can potentially provide at some point.

Third, the authors suggest letting users select among different identities when interacting with a site. Users should be able to specify different interaction roles for personalization, e.g. as an employee at work or a private individual at home. Giving users more control over the persona they disclose could increase their trust in a company's ability to provide useful personalization.

Similar methods to ease privacy concerns could be applied in the system described by Hoelscher and Dietrich in their chapter "E-Commerce Personalization and Real-Time Site Monitoring". Their 7d system is based on 'demographic data', 'usage data' and 'usage regularities', aggregating the entirety of a user's interactions with a site and attempting to draw useful conclusions based thereon.

This combination of data sources may raise severe privacy concerns however: more than half of all Internet users are concerned about being tracked on the Internet (Cyber Dialogue, 2001). Thus, user concerns about merging different data need to be addressed adequately to increase acceptance and usage of such personalization systems. Asking users for explicit consent – as described by Brodie et al. – might be a reasonable way to lessen consumer concerns. Furthermore, giving users more control over the persona they disclose could be a protection against privacy threats. Personal information could be saved under pseudonyms and not users' real names. Communicating such a policy could significantly ease users' privacy concerns. Furthermore, privacy legislation needs to be considered. According to the EU Directive on Privacy and Electronic Communications (EU, 2002), purchase data must be deleted if they are not needed any more for the original purpose, unless the user explicitly permitted a longer retention or their use for secondary purposes.

In their chapter "Recommending as Personalized Teaching", Stolze and Ströbel focus on needs-based recommendation systems for web sites. The authors developed a recommender prototype that enhances customers' understanding of the mapping between stated needs and personalized product recommendations.

The described system requires data from the categories 'user interests and preferences' and 'user goals and plans' (see Table 1). Privacy concerns about personal information may hinder the acceptance and use of such systems, however. Only about 50% of Internet users indicate to be willing to divulge personal information to receive a personalized online experience (Personalization Consortium, 2000; Roy Morgan Research, 2001; Privacy & American Business, 1999). The authors suggest explaining the underlying personalization algorithms to users, who thereby may feel they can better evaluate the appropriateness and credibility of such a system. This approach is useful from a privacy perspective, as users may develop more trust in personalization systems if they better understand their potential benefits, and specifically, how the personalization relates to their own needs (Hine and Eve, 1998).

Häubl et al.'s work on personalization systems deals with certain 'user data' and 'usage data'. Specifically, it employs information about 'user interests and preferences', 'selective actions' and 'ratings' to create recommendations for users. The chapter describes the benefits that personalized electronic shopping environments may provide. For example, one user experiment showed that product recommendations might allow consumers to reduce search costs and improve decision quality. This finding confirms results from user surveys: most people would welcome personalization services that simplify their browsing experience (Personalization Consortium, 2000; Harris, 2000). Besides the various personalization benefits described in this chapter, privacy concerns need to be considered as well. 82% of users have refused to give personal information to a web site due to privacy concerns (Culnan and Milne, 2001), and 27% would never share personal information with a web site (Fox *et al.* 2000). Thus, for a decision aid to be effective, users must be convinced to trust it. The approaches suggested in the chapters by Brodie *et al.* and Stolze and Ströbel to increase users' confidence and trust in personalization systems may apply here as well.

Degemmis *et al.*'s chapter on "Improving Collaborative Recommender Systems by Means of User Profiles" presents a hybrid approach combining collaborative and feature-based filtering to construct individual user models. Their system exploits 'usage data' and may raise similar privacy concerns as the one by Hoelscher and Dietrich. Additionally, people using recommender systems may not want their habits or views to be widely known (Resnick, 1997). Actions need to be taken to decrease user concerns about merging different data sources, which is disliked by most people (Harris, 2000). Thus, the described system needs privacy preservation mechanisms such as explicit user consent and data access control, to reduce consumer concerns and to comply with international privacy regulations.

4.2 Travel

In their chapter "Supporting Travel Decision Making Through Personalized Recommendation", Ricci and Del Missier propose a combination of collaborative and content-based recommendation to personalize a travel site. Users can provide both content features (characteristics of their planned travel) and collaborative features (characteristics of themselves, particularly their travel preferences). The system first uses content features to retrieve travel options, where the user may relax or tighten the result set. Then the collaborative component searches for similar past travel plans of other people, to produce a ranked list of recommendations.

The system collects a variety of personal information related to a user's travel plan. Personal information is stored in a recommendation session and includes travel preferences, travel products chosen and – as soon as the user registers – also personally identifiable information (PII) such as age, address, nationality and gender. According to the terminology in Table 1, the system requires the data types 'user interests and preferences', 'user goals and plans' and 'demographic data'.

From a privacy point of view, the proposed collaborative filtering may raise few concerns as long as users can remain anonymous. The content-based filtering technique tends to be more privacy-critical since it is based on explicit user needs, which may entail that users become uniquely identified if considerable information is available about them (cf. Sweeney, 2001). The privacy criticality increases when users must register with the travel recommender system, since then travel preferences can be linked with PII, which evokes severe privacy concerns and may also conflict with existing laws (Harris, 2000; EU, 2002). Thus, privacy approaches as discussed before and in section 5 of this chapter are necessary to balance privacy concerns and personalization benefits.

4.3 E-Government

One of the main issues in the chapter by Halstead-Nussloch is the relationship between personalization, privacy and trust in e-government. It draws comparisons between e-government and e-commerce to identify characteristics of personalized user experiences. A central argument is that e-government is different from e-commerce because e-government has a wider range of requirements for accountability and openness. For example, governments issue basic identity records such as birth certificates, driver's licenses and passports, which are often shared with public and private organizations. In the future, biometrics and other privacy-sensitive information may be added to such records. On the one hand, personalization in e-government could decrease paperwork and increase the efficiency of the administration. On the other hand, however, privacy concerns may limit the acceptance of personalization in e-government: 60% believe that the government possesses too much personal information about individuals (First Amendment Center, 2002). Thus, clear privacy commitments are necessary to increase trust in the government's fair use of personal information to provide a basis for accepted personalization in e-government.

Halstead-Nussloch discusses several approaches to achieve these goals: Legislation – as promoted in the EU – is seen as one solution. Numerous privacy regulations have been enacted in the US as well (cf. section 5.1 in Halstead-Nussloch's chapter). The author recommends to further evaluate regulation with respect to usability, to keep personalization intuitive and natural. Furthermore, opt-in processes should be used to obtain users' explicit consent. Most Internet users prefer this solution: 86% are in favor of "opt-in" privacy policies that require companies to ask people for permission to use their personal information (Fox et al., 2000). Halstead-Nussloch also suggests the use of group identities, which entail fewer privacy risks than individual e-identities. Aggregation methods as suggested in the privacy and security community (e.g. Agrawal, 2002) could be a helpful addendum to this endeavor. Finally, the author argues for awareness-raising about privacy and personalization, and for reducing the mismatch between user concerns and actual privacy impacts (cf. section 3.1 of this chapter).

4.4 Banking and insurance

Hiltunen et al.'s chapter on "Personalized Electronic Banking Services: Case Nordea" deals with personalization in Internet banking. Banks dispose of a wealth of customer data. Multi-channel banks have the potential to combine data from numerous sources, including physical branches, call centers and Internet sites. The chapter introduces the business case of the Nordea bank, where a variety of data is collected including demographics, market research data, usage patterns, customization choices, customer behavior in traditional businesses, attitudes, interests and life events, customer programs, and customer feedback. The authors' personalization approach includes virtually all data types in the taxonomy in Table 1. Screen size adaptation, browser optimization, personal greetings and individual product recommendations are just a few examples of how this data can be used for personalization.

Since data collection is so extensive, virtually all privacy concerns apply that were discussed in Section 3.1. Consumers may however harbor additional privacy concerns specifically about e-banking. The market research firm Jupiter found that security and privacy fears prevent more than 40% of online banking customers in Europe from managing their finances online (Jones *et al.*, 1999). Since most countries do not permit anonymous bank accounts, anonymous access cannot be used to alleviate users' privacy concerns. The trade-off between privacy threats and personalization benefits can therefore only be addressed by laws, user participation and control. From a regulatory point of view, most countries do not have specific provisions for financial service institutions beyond their national privacy laws. In the US, the "Gramm-Leach-Bliley Act" of 1999 regulates how financial institutions may handle personal information. The Act requires financial institutions to give consumers an opportunity to "opt out" before PII is shared with nonaffiliated third parties. Furthermore, a privacy policy must be adopted describing the categories of data collected and recipients of the information.

Communicating the bank's compliance with privacy laws and corporate privacy policies at its website may decrease privacy concerns. Giving users the choice to "opt-in" – as discussed in Halstead-Nussloch's chapter – might be an additional means to lessen privacy concerns. Finally, giving users access to their data and allowing them to specify whether or not they desire personalization services also seems recommendable to increase the acceptance of personalization in e-banking.

The chapter "Personalization and Trust: a Reciprocal Relationship?" by Briggs *et al.*, finally, discusses four fictitious online insurance websites that differed in the factors "personalized vs. non-personalized" and "established vs. new". In the categorization of Table 1, the required input was 'user data'. The authors found no significant differences in the four conditions regarding subjects' willingness to disclose personal data, nor in their trust in the quality of the advice.

Since insurance companies are similar to banks in many ways, the same privacy considerations as spelled out for the chapter of Hiltunen *et al.* seem to apply.

5. FUTURE RESEARCH DIRECTIONS FOR PRIVACY-PRESERVING PERSONALIZATION

Our meta-analysis of consumer surveys demonstrated that users' privacy concerns are major and have a direct impact on personalization systems. Two different directions can be pursued to alleviate these concerns. In one approach, users receive commitments that their personal data will be used for specific purposes only, including personalization. Such commitments can be given in, e.g., individual negotiations or publicly displayed privacy promises ("privacy policies"), or they can be mandated in privacy laws. It is necessary though that these privacy commitments be guaranteed. Ideally, they ought to be enforced through technical means (Agrawal *et al.*, 2002; Karjoth *et al.*, 2003; Fischer-Hübner, 2001), or otherwise through audits and legal recourse. Since individual privacy preferences may considerably vary between users, Kobsa (2003) proposes a meta-architecture for personalized systems that allows them to cater to individual privacy preferences and to the privacy laws that apply to the current usage situation. The personalized system would then exhibit the maximum degree of personalization that is permissible under these constraints.

From the analysis of personalization systems in previous chapters, additional privacy requirements can be inferred. First, users of personalized systems should be given ample control of their data (Karat *et al.*, 2003; Harris, 2000; Fox *et al.*, 2000). The chapters by Brodie *et al.* and Stolze and Ströbel elaborate on ways to do this. Second, personalization systems should better communicate potential privacy impacts. The AT&T Privacy Bird[5], IE6 and Stolze and Ströbel's approach to explain recommendation algorithms are first steps towards helping users better understand personalization and the potential privacy impact of their interactions. The negotiation and contextualized explanation of privacy and personalization needs to be further researched (Teltzrow and Kobsa, 2004).

The other approach is to allow users to remain anonymous with regard to the personalized system and the whole network infrastructure, whilst enabling the system to still recognize the same user in different sessions so that it can cater to her individually (Kobsa and Schreck, 2003). Karat *et al.* (2003) also address this requirement through different levels of identity. Anonymous interaction seems to be desired by users (however, only a single user poll addressed this question explicitly so far (GVU, 1998)). One can expect that anonymity will encourage users to be more open when interacting with a personalized system, thus facilitating and improving the adaptation to the respective user. The fact that privacy laws do not apply any more when the interaction is anonymous also relieves the providers of personalized systems from restrictions and duties imposed by such laws (they may however choose to observe these laws nevertheless, or to provide other privacy guarantees on top of anonymous access). Finally, anonymous interaction is even legally mandated in some countries if it can be realized with reasonable efforts (TSDPL, 2001).

It is currently unclear which of these two directions should be preferably pursued. Each alternative has several advantages and disadvantages. Neither is a full substitute for the other, and neither is guaranteed to alleviate users' privacy concerns, which ultimately result from a lack of trust. For the time being, both directions need to be pursued.

6. REFERENCES

Agrawal, R., Kiernan, J., Srikant, R., and Xu, Y. (2002) *Hippocratic Databases. 28th International Conference on Very Large Databases*, Hong Kong, China.

Andersen Legal, Internet Privacy Survey (2001) *A Re-Survey of the Privacy Practices of Australia's Most Popular Websites*. Sydney: Andersen Legal, 12 April 2001.

Ardissono, L. and Goy, A. (2000) *Tailoring the interaction with users in web stores*. User Modeling and User-Adapted Interaction 10(4) 251–303.

---

[5] http://www.privacybird.com

Behrens, L. (2001) *Privacy and Security: The Hidden Growth Strategy.* In Gartner G2, 31 May 2001.

Berendt, B., Günther, O., and Spiekermann, S. (to appear). *Privacy in E-Commerce: Stated preferences vs. actual behavior.* Communications of the ACM, 2004.

Brusilovsky, P., Kobsa, A. and Vassileva, J. (Eds), 1998, *Adaptive Hypertext and Hypermedia.* Dordrecht, Netherlands: Kluwer Academic Publishers.

Brusilovsky, P. (2001) *Adaptive hypermedia.* User Modeling and User-Adapted Interaction, 11(1–2), 87–110.

Center for Democracy Technology (2001) *Online Banking Privacy: A Slow, Confusing Start to Giving Customers Control Over Their Information.* Washington DC: CDT.

Chin, D.N. (1989) *KNOME: modeling what the user knows in UC.* In Kobsa, A. and Wahlster, W. (Eds.) *User Models in Dialog Systems* Springer Verlag 74–107.

Chittaro, L. and Ranon, R. (2000) *Adding adaptive features to virtual reality interfaces for e-commerce.* In Brusilivsky, P., Stock O. and Strappavara, C. (Eds.) *Adaptive Hypermedia and Adaptive Web-Based Systems.* Springer, 86–91.

Culnan, M J. and Milne, G. R. (2001) *The Culnan-Milne Survey on Consumers & Online Privacy Notices: Summary of Responses.* In Interagency Public Workshop (Ed.) *Get Noticed: Effective Financial Privacy Notices*, Washington, D.C.

Cyber Dialogue (2001) *UCO Software To Address Retailers $6.2 Billion Privacy Problem*, Press Release, http://www.cyberdialogue.com/news/releases/2001/11-07-uco-retail.pdf

Debevc, M., Meyer, B., Donlagic, D., and Svecko, R (1996) *Design and evaluation of an adaptive icon toolbar.* User Modeling and User-Adapted Interaction 6(1) 1–21.

Deloitte Touche Tohmatsu and Dimension Data (2001) *Survey Reveals Major Corporations are Getting Ready for New Privacy Law.* Canberra: Deloitte, September 17, 2001.

Department for Trade and Industry (2001) Informing Consumers about E-Commerce conducted by MORI, London: DTI, http://www.mori.com/polls/2001/pdf/dti-e-commerce.pdf

EU (2002) *Directive 2002/58/EC of the European Parliament and of the Council Concerning the Processing of Personal Data and the Protection of Privacy in the Electronic Communications Sector.* http://europa.eu.int/eur-lex/pri/en/oj/dat/2002/l_201/l_20120020731en00370047.pdf

Fink, J., Kobsa, A. and Nill, A. (1998) *Adaptable and adaptive information provision for all users, including disabled and elderly people.* The New Review of Hypermedia and Multimedia 4 163–188.

First Amendment Center (2001) *Freedom of Information in the Digital Age.* Project of the ASNE Freedom of Information Committee and The First Amendment Center. http://www.freedomforum.org/publications/first/foi/foiinthedigitalage.pdf

Fischer-Hübner, S. (2001) *IT-Security and Privacy: Design and Use of Privacy-Enhancing Security Mechanisms.* LNCS 1958, Heidelberg, Germany: Springer.

Forrester Research (2001) *Privacy Issues Inhibit Online Spending* (survey summary). Cambridge, MA. http://www.nua.com/surveys/?f=VS&art_id=905357259&rel=true

Foster, C. (2000) *The Personalization Chain.* In Jupiter Communications, *Site Operations*, Vol. 3, 2000.

Fox, S., Rainie, L. (2000) *Trust and Privacy Online: Why Americans Want to Rewrite the Rules.* Pew Internet & American Life Project, Washington DC. http://www.pewinternet.org/reports/toc.asp?Report=19

Gallup Organization (2001) *Majority of E-mail Users Express Concern about Internet Privacy.* Washington DC: The Gallup Organization, June 28, 2001. http://www.gallup.com/subscription/?m=f&c_id=10732

GVU (1998) *GVU's 10th WWW User Survey.* Graphics, Visualization and Usability Lab, Georgia Tech.

Harper, J., Singleton, S. (2001) *With a grain of salt, What Consumer Privacy Survey don't tell us.* Competitive Enterprise Institute. http://www.cei.org/PDFs/with_a_grain_of_salt.pdf

Harris Interactive (2000) *A Survey of Consumer Privacy Attitudes and Behaviors.* Rochester, NY.

Harris Interactive (2001) *Privacy Notices Research, Final Results.* Privacy Leadership Initiative, Rochester, NY.

Harris Interactive (2003) *Most People Are Privacy Pragmatists.* Rochester NY. March 19, 2003.

Hine, C, Eve, J. (1998) *Privacy in the Marketplace.* Information Society 14 (4), 253-262.

Holynski, M. (1988) *User-adaptive computer graphics.* International Journal of Man-Machine Studies **29,** 539–548.

Höök, K., Karlgren, J., Waern, A., Dahlbäck, N., Jansson, C., Karlgren, K. and Lemaire, B. (1996) *A glass box approach to adaptive hypermedia.* User Modeling and User-Adapted Interaction **6**(2–3), 157–184.

Interactive Policy Making (2002) *Views on Data Protection, Questionnaire on the Implementation of the Data Protection Directive (95/46/EC).* Results of Online Consultation 20 June - 15 September 2002, Brussels.

Ipsos-Reid and Columbus Group, 2001, Privacy Policies Critical to Online Consumer Trust, Canadian Inter@ctive Reid Report.

Jameson, A., Schäfer, R., Simons, J. and Weis, T. (1995) *Adaptive provision of evaluation-oriented information: tasks and techniques.* Proceedings of the Fourteenth International Joint Conference on Artificial Intelligence, Montreal, Canada, Morgan Kaufmann, 1886–1893.

Joachims, T., Freitag, D., and Mitchell, T., (1997) *Webwatcher: a tour guide for the World Wide Web.* In Proceedings of the Fifteenth International Joint Conference on Artificial Intelligence. Nagoya, Japan, Morgan Kaufmann Publishers, 770-777.

Joerding, T. (1999) *A temporary user modeling approach for adaptive shopping on the web.* Proceedings of the 2nd Workshop on Adaptive Systems and User Modeling on the WWW, WWW-8, Toronto, Canada and UM99, Banff, Canada.

Jones, N., Neufeld, E., Waagstein, L., Stemmer, A. (1999) *Online Financial Services - Integrated Service Is Key To Online Money Management.* Jupiter Communications, Strategic Planning Services, (10), 1-19.

Kaplan, C., Fenwick, J., and Chen, J. (1993) *Adaptive hypertext navigation based on user goals and context.* User Modeling and User-Adapted Interaction 3(3) 193–220.

Karat, C., Brodie, C., Karat, J., Vergo, J., and Alpert, S. (2003) *Personalizing the User Experience on ibm.com.* In Vredenburg, K. (Ed.), *IBM Systems Journal,* 42, 2, 686-701.

Karjoth, G., Schunter, M., and Waidner, M. (2003) *Platform for Enterprise Privacy Practices: Privacy-enabled Management of Customer Data*. In 2nd *Workshop on Privacy Enhancing Technologies*, LNCS, Volume 2482 / 2003, Berlin: Springer-Verlag, 69 – 84.

Kobsa, A., Müller, D., and Nill, A. (1994) *KN-AHS: an adaptive hypertext client of the user modeling system BGP-MS*. In *Proceedings of the Fourth International Conference on User Modeling*, Cape Cod, MA, 99–105. Reprinted in M. Marbury and W. Wahlster (eds), 1998, *Intelligent User Interfaces* Morgan Kaufman, 372–378.

Kobsa, A. and Schreck, J. (2003) *Privacy through Pseudonymity in User-Adaptive Systems*. ACM Transactions on Internet Technology 3 (2), 149-183

Kobsa, A. (2001) *Generic User Modeling Systems*. User Modeling and User-Adapted Interaction, *11*. 49-63.

Kobsa, A. (2003) *A Component Architecture for Dynamically Managing Privacy Constraints in Personalized Web-Based Systems*. In Dingledine, R. (Ed.) Privacy Enhancing Technologies: Third International Workshop, PET 2003, Dresden, Germany, Springer-Verlag, LNCS 2760, 177-188.

Kobsa, A., Koenemann, J., Pohl, W. (2001) *Personalised hypermedia presentation techniques for improving online customer relationships. The Knowledge Engineering Review*, Vol. 16(2), 111–155. Cambridge University Press

Kobsa, A. (2001) *Tailoring Privacy to Users' Needs*. Invited Keynote, *8th International Conference on User Modeling*, Sonthofen, Germany, Springer Verlag, 303-313.

Konstan, J.A., Miller, B.N., Maltz, D., Herlocker, J.L., Gordon, L.R. and Riedl, J. (1997) *GroupLens: applying collaborative filtering to Usenet news*. Communications of the ACM **40**(3) 77–87.

Kozierok, R. and Maes, P. (1993) *A learning interface agent for scheduling meetings*. In Gray, W.D., Hefley, W.E. and Murray, D. (Eds.) *Proceedings of the International Workshop on Intelligent User Interfaces*. ACM Press, 81–88.

Krogsæter, M., Oppermann, R. and Thomas, C.G. (1994) *A user interface integrating adaptability and adaptivity*. In R Oppermann (Ed.) *Adaptive User Support: Ergonomic Design of Manually and Automatically Adaptable Software*. Lawrence Erlbaum, 97-125.

Küpper, D. and Kobsa, A. (1999) *User-tailored plan generation*. In Kay, J. (Ed.) *UM99 User Modeling: Proceedings of the Seventh International Conference*, Banff, Canada, Springer-Verlag 45–54.

Lesh, N., Rich, C. and Sidner, C.L. (1999) *Using plan recognition in human-computer collaboration*. In Kay, J. (Ed.) *UM99 User Modeling: Proceedings of the Seventh International Conference*, Banff, Canada, Springer-Verlag, 23–32.

Lieberman, H. (1995) *Letizia: An agent that assists web browsing*. In *Proceedings of the International Joint Conference on Artificial Intelligence*, Montreal, Canada Morgan Kaufmann, 924-929.

Mabley, K. (2000) *Privacy vs. personalization, part three: a delicate balance*. New York, NY: Cyber Dialogue Inc. http://www.cyberdialogue.com/library/pdfs/wp-cd-2000-privacy.pdf

Maes, P. (1994) *Agents that reduce work and information overload*. Communications of the ACM **37**(7) 31–40.

McAteer, S., Graves, L., Gluck, M., May, M., Allard, K. (1999) *Proactive personalization – learning to swim, not drown in consumer data*. Jupiter Study, New York City, 4-12.

Mitchell, T., Caruana, R., Freitag, D., McDermott, J. and Zabowski, D. (1994) *Experience with a learning personal assistant.* Communications of the ACM **37**(7) 81-91.

Pavlou, P. A. (2003) *Consumer Acceptance of Electronic Commerce – Integrating Trust and Risk with the Technology Acceptance Model.* International Journal of Electronic Commerce **7**(3) 69-103.

Pazzani, M. and Billsus, D. (1997) *Learning and revising user profiles: the identification of interesting web sites.* Machine Learning **27** 313–331.

Personalization Consortium (2000) *Personalization & Privacy Survey.* Edgewater Place, MA. http://www.personalization.org/SurveyResults.pdf

Popp, H. and Lödel, D. (1996) *Fuzzy techniques and user modeling in sales assistants.* User Modeling and User-Adapted Interaction **5**(3–4) 349–370.

Privacy & American Business (1999) *Personalized Marketing and Privacy on The Net: What Consumers Want,* November 1999. http://www.pandab.org/doubleclicksummary.html

Resnick, P. and Varian, H.R. (1997) *Recommender systems.* Communications of the ACM, **40**(3) 56–58.

Responsys.com (2000) *Online Marketers Have Little Confidence in Self-Regulation of Internet Privacy.* Sponsored by Millard Brown IntelliQuest. Palo Alto, CA, September 26, 2000.

Roy Morgan Research (2001) *Privacy and the Community.* Prepared for the Office of the Federal Privacy Commissioner, Sydney, July 31, 2001. http://privacy.gov.au/publications/rcommunity.html

Sakagami, H., Kamba, T., Sugiura, A. and Koseki, Y. (1998) *Effective personalization of push-type systems: visualizing information freshness.* In *Proceedings of the 7th World Wide Web Conference, Brisbane, Australia.*

Shardanand, U. and Maes, P. (1995) *Social information filtering: algorithms for automating word of mouth.* In *Proceedings of the Human Factors in Computing Systems Conference (CHI-95), Denver, CO.* ACM Press 210–217.

Specht, M. (1998) *Empirical evaluation of adaptive annotation in hypermedia.* In *Proceedings of the ED-MEDIA98,* Freiburg, Germany, p.1327–1332.

Sweeney, L. (2001) *Computational Disclosure Control: A Primer on Data Privacy Protection,* Ph.D. Thesis, MIT, Cambridge, MA.

Teltzrow, M. and Kobsa, A. (2004) *Communication of Privacy and Personalization in E-Business.* In: Proceedings of the Workshop WHOLES: A Multiple View of Individual Privacy in a Networked World, Stockholm, Sweden.

TSDPL (2001) *Teleservices Data Protection Law (Article 3 of the Law on the Legal Requirements for Electronic Business Dealings of 14 Dec. 2001).* German Federal Law Gazette 1, 3721.

UMR (2001) *Privacy Concerns Loom Large.* Conducted for the Privacy Commissioner of New Zealand. Survey summary, Auckland: PC of New Zealand. http://www.privacy.org.nz/privword/42pr.html

Wham, T. (2001) *Workshop on the Information Marketplace: Merging and Exchanging Consumer Data.* Interview Transcript, Federal Trade Commission. http://www.ftc.gov/bcp/workshops/infomktplace/transcript.htm

JAN O. BLOM

CHALLENGES FOR USER-CENTRIC PERSONALIZATION RESEARCH

1. INTRODUCTION

Personalized hypermedia applications have increased in importance in conjunction with the 'third stage of web evolution', where the contents of the web pages are dynamically created (Luedi, 1997), and may be adapted as a function of each individual user[1]. Adaptive hypermedia systems provide an alternative to the "one-size-fits-all" approach: they build a model of the goals, preferences and knowledge of each individual user, in order to adapt to the needs of that user (Brusilovsky, 2001). Many authors (cf., Berghel, 1995; Hysell, 1998; Luedi, 1997; Manber et al., 2000) highlight the importance of the use of these technologies. Personalization, it is believed, has the potential to increase the loyalty and satisfaction of online customers (Schafer et al, 1999). The dynamic content enables engaging dialogue to take place between the customer and the service provider and furthermore, merchants are allowed to track and mine data on customer behaviour in order to predict needs better than with static web pages (Peppers and Rogers, 1997).

The term personalization refers to a variety of processes, ranging from adaptive changes produced by the system to adaptability, where the user produces the change (Oppermann and Simm, 1994). To provide just a few examples of applications equipped with personalization features, Fink et al (1998) report about a system that automatically inserts shortcut links for web pages that are frequently visited by a given user. My Yahoo displays weather forecasts as a function of the post code of the customer (Manber et al., 2000), and News Dude (Billsus and Pazzani, 1999) presents news stories to the user, who then rates the articles according to whether they are interesting or not. To predict whether its user will be interested in a new

---

[1] The first stage of the web evolution, according to Luedi, implied the use of static, preconstructed web sites. The second stage followed when it was possible to create dynamic web sites, wherein pages were constructed on fly. These presented the same content to everyone, which is not necessarily the case in the third stage of the evolution, in which the content may be adapted at the level of an individual.

Clare-Marie Karat et al. (eds.), Designing Personalized User Experiences in eCommerce, 333—348.

story, News Dude forms a content-based profile, where similarity to other articles is based on co-occurrence of words appearing in the stories. These are all cases of adaptivity, the system being responsible for producing the changes. As an instance of adaptability, Blom and Monk (2003) describe personalization of appearance, a commonly observed behavioural trend among PC and mobile phone users.

Blom (2000) defined personalization as a process that changes the functionality, interface, information content, or distinctiveness of a system. He also pointed out that whether personalization is system- or user-initiated should be viewed as a dimension rather than as a dichotomy as often both the system and the user participate in the process. For instance, the system may recognise that some aspects of the user's interaction with the software could be optimised but the change does not take place until the user has authorised it.

Current academic interest toward personalization focuses either on classifying various personalization methods (cf., Kobsa et al, 2001) or on describing the underlying marketing principles (Peppers and Rogers, 1997). The former could be described as a system-centred approach, and the latter as a business-oriented perspective (Blom, 2002a). The third end of the triangle is missing to a large extent. There are not many records in the personalization literature of explicitly user-centred accounts to understanding this process. Despite this, there is an increasing trend in the use of personalization technologies. This is a rather surprising situation: it is analogous to speeding up a train of whose direction is unknown. For instance, the extent to which personalization contributes to establishing a one-to-one relationship, the main assumption of the "personalization imperative", has not been extensively studied. The user effects of personalization have not been systematically specified and further, we do not know how exactly the content should be adapted to lead to particular, desired user effects.

In summary, user-centric personalization research is at an early stage. Consequently one of the most topical issues here is associated with establishing a common ground for the research community. Reflecting on work that has already been performed in this area could be beneficial from the point of view of guiding the development of the research movement. This chapter is based on discussing user-centric personalization research in the light of lessons learned when conducting doctoral research on this area (Blom, 2002b). The PhD was concerned with user effects of personalization. A range of methods was utilised and a variety of personalization features was covered. It comes as no surprise, therefore, that issues emerged that may have a formative value when trying to identify a course for future research in this area. The next section provides an overview of the thesis. The subsequent sections are concerned with discussing issues that I personally foresee as the biggest challenges in this area. Individuals interested in pursuing user-centric personalization research may consult these, particularly from the point of view of formulating and scoping the research questions.

2. PSYCHOLOGICAL IMPLICATIONS OF PERSONALIZED USER INTERFACES: THESIS DESCRIPTION

The PhD (Blom, 2002b) was divided between three parts. Part 1 investigated the interaction between personalization and personification, i.e., the degree to which the interface reflects human-like attributes. In two controlled experiments utilising between subjects design, the participants were asked to interact with a fictional online bank. Their tasks on the site included, e.g., paying bills and purchasing travel insurance. The dependent variables included engagement, workload, impressionistic trust, and a range of other emotional attributes.

Personalization was manipulated by incorporating nine different personalization features in each of the two experiments. In Experiment 1, three of these features were user-initiated. The user was asked to personalise the appearance of the main page, by e.g., selecting a color scheme, a logo and a slogan to be displayed on top of the page. The participants also selected the types of news and advertisements they would like the service to provide them with. The six system-initiated personalization features were as follows. First, the details of the bill-paying form were pre-filled. Second, information on the types of shares other customers had bought was provided to the users. Third, the participants were provided with a personalized travel insurance, tailored as a function of the answers submitted in a short online questionnaire. Fourth, a travel agency was recommended to the participants on the basis of them being university students. Fifth, upon using the service for the second time, the participants were reminded about the commercial information they had selected in session 1. Sixth, the first name of each participant was used throughout the two sessions.

Some of the features used in Experiment 1 were replaced with more intelligent ones in Experiment 2. The participants were provided with book recommendations using a simple content-based algorithm. The main page also provided feedback on the transactions any given user had completed on the site.

The results acquired in Experiment 1 led to the conclusion that at least under some circumstances, the effects of personalization on a user's subjective experience of interacting with a web site can depend on the degree of personification (Blom and Monk, 2001). More particularly, personalization had a positive impact on engagement and workload when it was coupled with a personified interface.

The findings of Experiment 1 were not entirely replicated in Experiment 2, however, which could be at least partially attributed to the difference in the range of personalization features between the experiments. It was assumed that looking at individual personalization features in isolation would be a somewhat safer approach. Thus in Part 2 of the thesis, collaborative filtering and personalization of appearance were selected for further scrutiny. Due to a lack of theory on the user implications of personalization, qualitative methods were adopted. Grounded theory techniques (Strauss and Corbin, 1990) were used to analyse discussion group data arising from users reflecting on their perceptions toward interacting with the two particular personalization features. The analysis process led to the emergence of user-centric theories of personalization for the respective features. First, Theory of Personalized

Recommendations [henceforth TPR] (Blom, 2002a) lists factors that affect an individual's disposition of using the recommendations provided by the system. This theory will be further discussed in Section 6 of this paper. Second, the Theory of Personalization of Appearance [henceforth TPA] describes the factors that affect an individual's disposition to personalize the product. It also lists the effects of the process. The latter theory was further refined with the help of two follow-up studies that were concerned with personalization of mobile phones and desktops of home computers (Blom and Monk, 2003). As a result, the theory became more general and applicable to a wider range of contexts.

In Part 3, a questionnaire and an experiment were performed to validate the structure of the TPA. Both of the validation studies suggested that the TPA provides an accurate description of the phenomenon it aims to describe.

2.1   Personalization as a process of change

The way personalisation was treated in the thesis deviates from how it is generally approached in the eCommerce domain. As discussed in the first section of the paper, instead of considering adaptive, system-initiated instances only, personalization was also taken to refer to processes achieved explicitly by the user. To use Jameson's (2002) terminology, personalization implied both user-adaptive systems and adaptable systems. In the former area, the changes are produced by the system on the basis of user model acquisition and application that involve some sort of learning, inference, or decision-making. The latter technology, on the other hand, is about the user explicitly tailoring the system to her preferences. The two theories that emerged in the course of the thesis exemplify this difference. The TPR is associated with recommender systems, a stereotypical case of eCommerce-related personalization. The TPA, on the other hand, expands the notion of personalization by focusing on a process not associated with any artificial intelligence and by viewing this process in a non-commercial context.

There was a valid reason for adopting a wider focus, however. The essence of personalization is that a specific part of the system, be it functionality, interface, appearance or information content, is changed to better reflect the interests or characteristics of the user. Change is at the heart of personalization, while also acting as the common denominator of adaptivity and adaptability. Thus when attempting to define personalization, particularly from a user-centric position, it does not necessarily make sense to limit one's scope to adaptivity: in some instances, the process may be initiated or produced by the system, whereas in other cases, the user herself acts as the agent of change.

A great deal of the thesis research was directed at a commercial context and many of the methodological issues are equally applicable to all areas of personalization. Consequently, four challenges arose that have implications on the theme of the present book and that will be elaborated on in this paper. First, the lack of a unified user-centric personalization framework is an issue that adds friction to the user-centric research. Second, the question of what exactly are the positive effects of personalization is an interesting one, and deserves further discussion. Third, ecological validity often limits the value of experimental personalization research. Ways to alleviate this problem will be discussed. Fourth, the importance of interaction design is highlighted, as a complementing alternative to research focusing on the personalization algorithm.

3. IDENTIFICATION OF A COMMON FRAME OF REFERENCE

According to Orwant (1996), any system with novice/expert modes incorporates a rudimentary, one-bit user model. On the other side of the scale is an ideal user model, possessing intimate and thorough knowledge of its user, one that knows more about the user than the user knows about herself. Although the complex end of the dimension is likely to remain science fiction rather than become reality, Orwant's notion of increasing complexity is useful in that it helps explain the wide range of approaches used to study personalization. Personalization features reported in the literature represent different levels of complexity and hence the user models on which the personalized changes are based are rarely the same. For instance, recommender systems may derive their predictions using collaborative filtering (Guttman et al, 1998) or content-based filtering (Billsus and Pazzani, 1999). The ways in which the information required to produce the personalized information differ between these two examples. The former technology may require the user to rate items, whereas the latter could be based on the types of links the user has previously visited. From the point of view of the user, these two technologies may well be associated with deviating effects, as they differ in terms of interaction required from the user.

In addition to variation with regard to user models, personalization is being incorporated in a variety of application areas, such as collaborative filtering, information filtering, augmentation systems, persuasive technology, affective computing, and messaging systems (Saari and Turpeinen, Chapter N). Moreover, some studies operate with one specific personalization feature only, whereas others investigate the effects of a number of features. Empirical evaluation of a recommender system algorithm (cf., Huang et al, 2002) is a prototypical example of looking at the effects of just one feature. Blom and Monk (2001), on the other hand, were interested in the combined effects of nine different features, ranging from user-initiated personalization of appearance to the system making recommendations on a travel insurance.

Summarising the above paragraphs, personalization technologies represent a wide range of application areas, algorithms and user interactions. As a consequence, the degree to which one can reliably generalise the findings with regard to a particular personalization technology to cover a wider range may remain limited. There is a need to scope the focus and be precise about what exactly is being investigated. The fact that there is confusion regarding the way in which personalization is defined in the first place complicates the challenge of scoping one's focus. For instance, a personalization practitioner working for an eCommerce company may conceptualise personalization in terms of adaptive features incorporated on a web site (cf. Schafer et al, 1999). Mobile phone industry, on the other hand, often focuses on the user-initiated aspects of personalization, such as on the customization of screen graphics and ringing tones (Kiljander and Järnström, 2003).

Without a mutually accepted frame of reference it is difficult to define the area of one's interest and manage to communicate the findings to the community of practitioners and academics in a clear and unambiguous way. The first and foremost challenge for the research community thus lies in reaching a consensus over a taxonomy of personalization that differentiates between different forms of personalization. Kobsa et al (2001) provide a comprehensive classification of the ways in which data is acquired when producing adaptive changes. To be able to initiate or produce the personalization process, the system has to either take into account the user's characteristics or base the changes on observing the user's actions. Environmental information can also be used, such as the type of software and hardware, or the locale of the client. Kobsa et al's (2001) acquisition data framework captures the system-initiated instances of personalization in an elegant manner. It does not take into account the user implications of this process, however, which would be beneficial for individuals approaching personalization from the user's point of view.

Blom's (2000) taxonomy, while providing a system-centric definition of personalization, sets out the motivational forces that influence a user's decision to interact with a personalized application. A distinction is made between work-related and socially-related goals that underlie an individual's interaction with the personalized system. Blom (2000) mentions facilitating access to information content as an example of a work-related goal. This would be relevant when receiving predictions from a recommender system. An instance of an emotional goal, on the other hand, would be to elicit an emotional response with the help of the personalized product. For instance, an individual might choose a particular ringing tone to a mobile phone because it might be associated with emotions, such as pleasure or excitement.

The motivations listed by this taxonomy serve as a useful way to distinguish between personalization one would associate with eCommerce and that incorporated beyond the commercial context, such as personalization of appearance of a mobile phone or desktop of a computer. The former is more readily associated with work-related goals, whereas in the latter area, emotional goals are often at play. The taxonomy is limited, however, as it does not take into account the interests of the service provider. This would be relevant in the eCommerce domain, in which the policies and practices embraced by the site owners have an impact on the user's interaction with the system. Another limitation of the taxonomy is that it is not based on empirical research. An empirically justified framework would thus be needed, one that would be able to both categorize the possible instances of personalization, and emphasize the user implications of this process. What, then, are the user implications worth focusing on? The next section explores the issue of user benefits in the context of personalized user interfaces.

4. BENEFITS OF PERSONALIZATION

The section above makes the case of reaching a consensus over a user-centric definition of personalization. From a theoretical point of view, one of the key challenges in the user-centric research front is to investigate the benefits of incorporating personalization. Empirical evaluation of personalization systems has, to a great extent, taken this route. For instance, agreement and recall ability as regard to the personalized information could be taken as indicators of the success of a personalization feature (cf., Huang et al, 2002). Empirical evaluation is associated with the development of individual features, however, while not answering the question: "What are the general benefits of personalization?". One useful starting point in trying to tackle this question would be to concentrate on the assumptions placed by the marketing perspective. Is it really the case that personalization increases loyalty, and furthermore, does personalization facilitate the creation of a relationship between customers and the service provider?

When investigating the positive user effects of personalization, the point made in the previous section about the danger of over-generalising the results acquired with regard to a particular personalization feature becomes valid. There is nothing that guarantees that the implications associated with personalization feature A will also be observed in feature B. The situation becomes more complicated, when looking at the combined effects of a number of features. To illustrate this, the table below quotes Schafer et al's (2002) list of the various personalization features incorporated on Amazon.com™, CDNOW™, and Moviefinder.com.

Table 1. *Examples of the combinations of personalization features provided by various eCommerce services (Schafer et al, 2002).*

Service	Personalization features incorporated
Amazon.com™ (www.amazon.com)	**Customers who bought**: recommending books frequently purchased by customers who purchased the selected book.
	Eyes: customers are notified by email of new items added to the Amazon catalogue.
	Book Matcher: customers rate books and may request recommendations for ones they liked.
	Customer comments: receiving text recommendations based on the opinions of other customers.
CDNOW™ (www.cdnow.com)	**Album Advisor**: allows, e.g., customers to locate the information page for a given album.
	My CDNOW: enables customers to set up their own music store, based on albums and artists they like.
Moviefinder.com (www.moviefinder.com)	**Match Maker**: allows customers to locate movies with a similar "mood, theme, genre, or cast" to a given movie.
	We Predict: recommends movies to customers based on their previously indicated interests.

The combinations of personalization features incorporated by the three services described above are all different. User interaction associated with these features takes place at various stages of the purchase process, and further, each feature is presented to the user in a unique way.

In the light of the vast number of personalization features, and combinations of these, the prospect of a universal positive effect becomes interesting. It may well be, that there are benefits that may be observed when incorporating a number of well-selected features in an appropriate way. Systematic studies testing the effects of different features and combinations would yield interesting data on this question. The approach used by Brodie et al (Chapter N) stands as a good illustration of what could be done here. Brodie et al (Chapter N) performed heuristic analysis of a number of online services, discussed their own company's involvement in personalization research and interviewed stakeholders to produce a set of personalization features that were valuable in the context of the tasks the participants were attempting to complete. This kind of a selection process could conceivably be used across different types of eCommerce services to test whether a carefully selected combination of personalization features results in similar kinds of user reactions across the domains.

When it comes to incorporating an entire set of personalisation features in a service, it is logical to assume that a number of well-selected personalization features across the various stages of the purchase process have a stronger impact on the user than just one feature incorporated at one point of the interaction. The big questions associated with this approach are of course: "Which features have the most pronounced effects?" and "What exactly is the added value associated with personalization?".

5. ECOLOGICAL VALIDITY

There are many examples of user studies that have been conducted on fictional personalization features. For instance, Blom and Monk (2001) asked the participants to interact with a fictional online banking service incorporating personalization and Briggs et al (Chapter N) tested the impacts of personalization with the help of a fictional travel company.

It is characteristic to this paradigm, perhaps best characterised as experimental personalization simulation, that the interaction with the personalization feature is induced. That is, the interaction does not take place spontaneously, but rather, at the request of the experimenter, reducing the ecological validity of the paradigm. There is also a danger that the personalization feature is presented to the user in isolation of other features typically appearing on an eCommerce web site. This is arguably problematic an issue from the point of view of eCommerce applications, in which aspects such as brand and aesthetics of the site may well interact with the effects of the personalization feature. An issue that is likely to further reduce the ecological validity of the experimental personalization simulation paradigm is that the studies are often lab-based.

Although the difference between induced lab-based and spontaneous behaviour taking place in naturalistic environment is not unique to personalization research (in fact the contrast represents one of the most prominent differences between experimental and field research), I nevertheless regard it as one of the biggest challenges associated with the user-centric personalization perspective. Despite the reduced ecological validity, experimental personalization simulation is worth considering because dynamic web sites, in addition to improving the experimenter's control over manipulation of the personalization feature, provide a high degree of control over manipulating the levels of the independent variables.

The goal here lies in managing to make the induced, experimental form of personalization feel like it is spontaneous and part of natural interaction with an eCommerce service. The table below lists factors may promote this effect. Each alleviating factor is coupled with an example from the literature, in which this issue has been resolved successfully.

Table 2. *Factors that may increase the ecological validity of the personalization study.*

Alleviating factor	Example from the literature
Provide access to the recommended objects.	As a reward for using a recommender system associated with digital cameras, Spiekermann (2001) offered a 10% chance on a sizeable reduction on the price of the camera to the user population.
Provide a meaningful use scenario for the participant.	Briggs et al (Chapter N) selected the participants for the experiment on the basis of a real need associated with the theme of the fictional service. The system tested was an online insurance agent recommending a travel insurance, and the sample consisted of individuals having been planning a journey in the near future.
Ensure that the design of the web site is professional.	Briggs et al (Chapter N) hired a professional web site designer to construct the service to be tested.
Allow the participant to interact with the application at a place and time of her choice.	Blom and Monk (2001) did not invite the participants to the lab, but instead they were allowed to log on to the service from any computer equipped with an Internet connection at any time of day.

The two first factors in Table 2 are concerned with the personalization feature studied. Rewarding the users with objects they are recommended with, be it books, cameras, CDs, etc., is a clever way of making the use of the system feel realistic. This method is conceivably resource-demanding; the clever bit about the Spiekermann (2001) study is that only a small proportion of the sample actually received the reward. While the chances of being rewarded with the discount were slim, the prospect was probably enough, however, to make some participants take the recommendations seriously.

Recruiting individuals to the experiment possessing a genuine need as regard to the objects of recommendations, the second factor in Table 2, demands fewer resources than providing access to the objects. It is conceivable that an individual having been thinking of buying a given product will pay attention to recommendations associated with this particular product area, despite receiving the information in a lab-based setting or through a fictional service. Managing to recruit people perceiving the area of personalization as meaningful is easier said than done, however, while also raising the issue of assessing the degree to which this succeeded by using a set of control questions tapping into this.

Moving beyond personalization, ensuring that the look and feel of the service is professional is likely to promote the perception of the service being real rather than fictional. Allowing the participants to interact with the experimental service in a place and at a time chosen by each participant may decrease the extent to which the interaction is perceived as induced. The downside to such liberated interaction is that lack of control over the conditions in which the participant accomplishes the tasks is likely to introduce noise to the findings.

The issues listed in Table 2 represent by no means a complete list of issues that play a role in influencing the ecological validity of personalization research. One should also note that they do not necessarily apply to all cases. For instance, providing access to the products recommended by the system is only viable when investigating recommender systems. In general, one could conclude, however, that experimental personalization simulation may sometimes suffer from a lack of ecological validity, and that attempts should be made to alleviate this problem. It is important to address and alleviate this problem rather than accept it.

6. DESIGN DRIVERS FOR PERSONALIZATION

A commonality between all forms of personalization is that the changes are expected to result in the system becoming more relevant to the needs and desires of the user, in becoming personally relevant to the individual (Blom, 2000). Let us concentrate on a subset of personalization to further explore this assumption. recommender systems produce personalized predictions to the user regarding the object of interest, be it films, news, books, or clothing. In collaborative filtering (Guttman et al, 1998) the user indicates her interests by rating items. The system then identifies a set of individuals whose profiles correlate to those of the user. The preferences of these like-minded consumers are used to produce the predictions. Content-based filtering, such as the News Dude example cited in the introduction, is another common method of powering a recommender system. Regardless of the algorithm used to derive the personalized information it could be taken as given, however, that the designers of the recommender systems aim to create algorithms that manage to produce accurate and relevant predictions regarding the end user.

In the light of the desire to produce relevant changes, it is not surprising that academic focus on recommender systems is mostly based on attempts to produce efficient personalization algorithms (Blom, 2002a; Cosley et al., 2003). For instance, Smyth (2000) reported about a hybrid recommender system for TV programs, one that uses both collaborative and content-based filtering so as to overcome the problematic aspects of using only one of the technologies. The degree of the user population agreeing with the predictions was used as the evaluation criterion for the system.

One of the most valuable theoretical insights of my PhD research (Blom, 2002b) was that in addition to concentrating on the algorithmic aspects of personalization, the way in which the algorithm is wrapped up, i.e., the presentation of the personalized content, may also play a role in the acceptance of the predictions. In an attempt to explore individuals' attitudes toward interacting with a recommender system, Blom (2002) conducted a two-stage study on the use of Moviecritic, a collaborative filtering service providing personalized film recommendations. The aim of the study was to explore qualitatively individuals' opinions toward using the service. Of particular interest was how the users would perceive the personalization features incorporated by the service. Stage 1 of the study required altogether 35 participants to attend individual instruction sessions in which they were asked to become members with the service, rate a number of films, and receive film recommendations. In Part 2 of the study, the participants were allocated to one of seven groups, in which they discussed their opinions on using the recommender system. The transcripts of the sessions were analysed using grounded theory (GT) techniques, which imply a "general methodology of analysis linked with data collection that uses systematically applied set of methods to create an inductive theory" (Glaser 1992, p.16).

The analysis resulted in a theory of personalization, which identifies a set of factors influencing individual's decision to use predictions provided by a recommender system. To illustrate the dynamics of the theory, two categories will be elaborated on, Knowledge of Algorithm and Anthropomorphism. When it comes to the former, many users expressed a desire to understand the logic of the algorithm of the software that generated the recommendations. Understanding the logic behind a computer-based algorithm was perceived to be different from understanding the logic other people use:

> "I'm human, I know how they think [other humans], whereas a computer I have absolutely no way of telling how they've come to that decision."

Second, some individuals tended not to trust the recommendations, as they attributed human-like abilities to the system. The most common form of anthropomorphism was to regard the system as categorizing the user:

> "It's not nice when humans categorize you. Let alone when something that doesn't even see you, doesn't have feelings, decides that it knows what you like."

Several participants thought that the fact that the recommendations were based on regularities in others' film preferences made them more acceptable:

> "I'm aware on both sites [Excite.com and Moviecritic.com] that no matter how much they try, it's just electrical program, very inhuman. But that's where Moviecritic has got this advantage: all these people voting, that's the human bit of it. So I'm more likely to trust that than the computer-programming bit."

An obvious design implication of the above is that it could be important to associate information provided by a recommender system with a human image. In addition to basing the recommendations on preferences of human beings, the human aspect could be also emphasized by coupling the recommendations with access to other customers' comments regarding the objects of the recommendations and through using linguistic and graphic metaphors eliciting a human image.

The screen capture below illustrates FilmFreax.com, a fictional service providing movie recommendations. The two categories are facilitated so as to increase the user acceptance of the system.

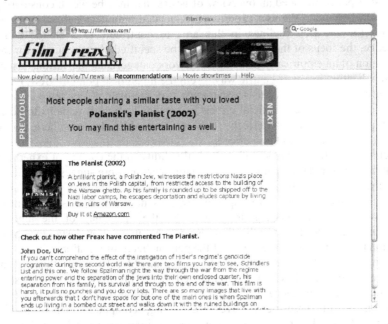

Figure 1. *A fictional recommender system utilizing Blom's (2002) Theory of Personalised Recommendations.*

The screen capture aims to illustrate how the findings of user-centric research may inform the interaction design of the recommender system. Revealing the way in which the recommendation in this particular case was derived facilitates the category Knowledge of Algorithm. Human image is supported through incorporating a logo and name for the service that both elicit the notion of interacting with other people[2]. The service provides access to other customers' comments and finally, the algorithm is based on finding regularities among a number of individuals.

---

[2] It could also be viable to use a social agent to elicit a human image. This option was disregarded, however, as it has been claimed that social agents elicit wrong kinds of mental models regarding the functionality of the system and may thus lead to disappointments (Dehn and van Mulken, 2000).

7. DISCUSSION AND CONCLUSIONS

The present paper provided an overview of issues that may be worth considering in the course of studying the user experience associated with personalized systems. In order for the research findings in this area to contribute to a shared body of knowledge, the focus of the research needs to be specified. A prerequisite for this is the adoption of an empirically justified framework categorising the various instances of personalization in a user-centric way. From the theoretical point of view, research focusing on the personalized user experience may facilitate eCommerce systems in terms of identifying the beneficial effects of personalization. It remains to be seen, whether general positive user effects, such as increased loyalty, exist here, and what kind of a feature set yields these effects.

Section 5 discusses the lack of ecological validity in the context of experimental personalization simulation paradigm. Alleviating factors were suggested, which may be of value when planning studies exploring the user implications of personalization. Finally, Section 6 provides an example of how presentational aspects may contribute to the success of the system, in addition to the efficiency of the algorithm. Combining user-centric personalization research and interaction design may provide a solution to shaping the presentation of the personalized information.

ECommerce technologies and trends evolve quickly. To tackle this, a general challenge arises that has not been touched upon in this paper. Orchestrating personalized user experiences that adapt to the evolution of the market requires the integration of all three perspectives: marketing, computer science, and user experience. As an illustration, let us consider the increasing uptake of the mobile platform as a channel for commercial transactions. Mobile users are reluctant to spend time browsing and reading broadcast messages because of limited information display area for navigation, limited client data storage, and tedious text-entry techniques (Ho and Kwok, 2002). Technological developments are needed to answer these problems. The business models developed for mobile commerce are at least partially dependent on the technological advances made. User research, in turn, through contextually based understanding of the end-user, could identify the needs that are relevant in the mobile arena. Communication between these three perspectives is not a trivial thing, and requires a co-ordinated effort from behalf of all stakeholders.

8. ACKNOWLEDGEMENTS

I am in great debt to my PhD supervisor Andrew Monk and to NRC, which supported my thesis research. I wish to acknowledge Younghee Jung and Panu Korhonen from Nokia Research Center for their support in the course of writing this chapter. Finally, Rafael Grignani from Nokia Research Center has produced the screen capture illustrated in Figure 1.

9. REFERENCES

Berghel, H. (1995). Cyber-surfing: the state-of-the-art in client server browsing and navigation, pp. 1-4, *Proceedings of the 1995 ACM symposium on applied computing,* Nashville, Tennessee.

Billsus, D., & Pazzani, M.(1999). A hybrid user model for news story classification. *Proceedings of the 7th international conference on user modelling,* Wienna, Austria.

Blom, J. (2000). Personalization - a taxonomy, pp. 313-314, E*xtended Abstracts of the CHI 2000 conference on human factors in computing systems,* the Hague, Netherlands.

Blom, J. (2001). 1-to-1 E-Commerce: who's the one? pp. 341-342, *Extended Abstracts of the CHI 2001 conference on human factors in computing systems,* Seattle.

Blom, J. (2002a). Theory of personalized recommendations, pp. 540-541, *Proceedings of the CHI 2002 conference on human factors in computing systems,* Minneapolis.

Blom, J. (2002b). *Psychological implications of personalised UIs.* DPhil Thesis, University of York, York, UK.

Blom, J., & Monk, A. (2003). Theory of personalisation of appearance: why people personalise their mobile phones and PCs. *Human-Computer Interaction, 18*(3), 193-228.

Brusilovsky, P. (2001). Adaptive hypermedia. *User Modeling and User Adapted Interaction, 11* (1-2), 87-110.

Cosley, D., Lam, S., Albert, I., Konstan, & Riedl, J. (2003). Is seeing believing? How recommender system interfaces affect users' opinions, pp. 341-342, *Proceedings of the CHI 2003 conference on human factors in computing systems,* Ft Lauderdale.

Dehn, D.M., & van Mulken, S. (2000). The impact of animated interface agents: A review of empirical research. *International Journal of Human-Computer Studies, 52,* 1-22.

Fink, J., Kobsa, A., & Nill, A. (1998). Adaptable and adaptive information provision for all users, including disabled and elderly people. *The New Review of Hypermedia and Multimedia, 4,* 163-188.

Glaser, B. (1992). *Basics of grounded theory analysis.* Mill Valley, CA: Sociology Press.

Guttman, R., Moukas, A., & Maes, P. (1998). Agent-mediated e-commerce: a survey. *Knowledge Engineering Review, 13*(2), 147-159.

Ho, S., & Kwok, S. (2002). The attraction of personalized service for users in mobile commerce: an empirical study. *ACM SIGecom Exchanges, 3* (4), 10-18.

Huang, Z., Chung, W., Ong, T., & Chen, H. (2002). Studying users: a graph-based recommender system for digital library, pp. 65-73, *Proceedings of the second ACM/IEEE-CS joint conference on digital libraries,* Portland, Oregon.

Hysell, D. (1998). Meeting the needs of a diverse WWW audience, pp. 164 – 172, *Proceedings of the 16th annual international conference on computer documentation.* Quebec, Canada.

Jameson, A. (2002). Adaptive interfaces and agents. In J. Jacko & A. Sears (Eds.), *Handbook of human-computer interaction.* New York: Lawrence Erlbaum Associates.

Kiljander, K., & Järnström, J., (2003). User interface styles. In C. Lindholm, T. Keinonen & H. Kiljander (Eds.), *Mobile usability: how Nokia changed the face of the mobile phone.* New York: McGraw-Hill Companies.

Kobsa, A., Koenemann, J., & Pohl, W., (2001). Personalized hypermedia presentation techniques for improving online customer relationships, *The Knowledge Engineering Review* 16(2), 111-155. http://www.ics.uci.edu/~kobsa/papers/2001-KER-kobsa.pdf

Luedi, F. (1997). Personalize or perish. *Electronic Markets, 7*(3), 22-25.

Manber, U., Patel, A., & Robison, J. (2000). Experience with personalization on Yahoo. *Communications of the ACM, 43*(8), 35-39.

Oppermann, R., & Simm, H. (1994). Adaptability: user-inititiated individualization. In R. Oppermann (Ed.), *Adaptive user support. Ergonomic design of manually and automatically adaptable software.* New Jersey: Lawrence Erlbaum and Associates.

Orwant, J. (19996). For Want of a Bit the User Was Lost: Cheap User Modeling. *IBM Systems Journal, 35* (3), 398-416.

Peppers, D., & Rogers, M. (1997). Enterprise one to one: tools for competing in the interactive age. New York: Currency Doubleday.

Schafer, J., Konstan, J., & Riedl, J. (1999). Recommender systems in e-commerce. *Proceedings of E-COMMERCE 1999,* Denver, Cl. 158-166.

Smyth, B. (2000). A personalized television listing service. *Communications of the ACM, 43*(8), 107-111.

Spiekermann, S. (2001). *Online information search with Electronic agents: drivers, impediments, and privacy issues*. PhD Thesis, Humbold Universität zu Berlin, Berlin, Germany.
Strauss, A., & Corbin, J. (1990). *Basics of qualitative research*. London: Sage.